Introducing
Microsoft®
Windows® 98

Beta Edition

Russell Borland

Introducing Microsoft Windows 98

Published by Microsoft Press
A Division of Microsoft Corporation
One Microsoft Way
Redmond, Washington 98052-6399

Library of Congress Cataloging-in-Publication Data pending.

Printed and bound in the United States of America.

1 2 3 4 5 6 7 8 9   QMQM   2 1 0 9 8 7

Distributed to the book trade in Canada by Macmillan of Canada, a division of Canada Publishing
Corporation.

A CIP catalogue record for this book is available from the British Library.

Microsoft Press books are available through booksellers and distributors worldwide. For further information about international editions, contact your local Microsoft Corporation office. Or contact Microsoft Press
International directly at fax (425) 936-7329. Visit our Web site at mspress.microsoft.com.

Acquisitions Editor: Kim Fryer
Project Editor: Sally Stickney
Technical Editors: Jean Ross, Marc Young

Contents

Acknowledgments   ix

Limitations   x

Introduction   xi

PART I   Installation and Setup

1   Instructions for Installing Windows 98   3

System Requirements   3   • Installing Windows 98   4   • Helpful Setup Features in Windows 98   5   • The Setup Process   9   • Uninstall   10   • Online Registration Wizard   11

2   Overview of New Features in Windows 98   15

Platform for Innovation   15   • More Power   16   • Improved Reliability and Manageability   21   • Internet Integration (Microsoft Internet Explorer 4.0)   22

PART II   Windows 98 Faces on the Internet

3   The Faces of Windows 98   27

Revised Desktop Tools Plus Internet Integration   27   • The Start Button   28   • The Taskbar   35   • Single Explorer   41   • Active Desktop   42   • Desktop Power for Experienced Users   46

4   Introducing Internet Explorer 4.0   61

New Features in Internet Explorer 4.0   63   • Dynamic HTML   73   • ActiveX Support   76   • Communicating and Collaborating with Internet Explorer 4.0   78   • Webcasting   82   • Beyond Basic Webcasting: Addressing

Webcrawling Issues 94 • True Web Integration 100 • Administration Tools in Internet Explorer 4.0 102 • Security Features of Internet Explorer 4.0 106 • Internet Connection Wizard 115

5 **Internet Conferencing and Application Sharing with NetMeeting 2.0** 117

Conferencing Options of NetMeeting 2.0 118 • User Interface Enhancements in NetMeeting 2.0 119 • NetMeeting 2.0 in Action 120 • Multipoint Data Conferencing 122 • Microsoft Chat 126 • Video Conferencing and Videophone 129 • Internet Phone and Audio Conferencing 131 • Intelligent Audio and Video Stream Control 131 • Using NetMeeting to Call Someone 131 • System Policies 135 • NetMeeting 2.0: A Standards-Based Platform 136 • Microsoft NetMeeting 2.0 Resource Kit 140

6 **Broadcasting on Your Desktop with NetShow 2.0** 141

Features and Benefits of NetShow 2.0 142 • NetShow Features New to Version 2.0 145 • Key Technologies of NetShow 147 • Components of NetShow Architecture 153 • Putting NetShow to Work 155

7 **Windows Messaging** 157

The Windows Messaging Subsystem 158 • Outlook Express 161 • The Microsoft Mail Post Office 170 • Microsoft Fax 170

8 **Authoring and Publishing** 179

Creating Your Own Web Pages with FrontPad 179 • Customizing Your Start Page with Personal Home Page Wizard 182 • Publishing with Personal Web Server 184 • Posting a Web Site with the Web Publishing Wizard 187 • Other Tools for Authors and Developers 188

PART III **Extending Your Reach with Windows 98**

9 **Networking in Windows 98** 193

Networking Features of Windows 98 194 • Easy Networking with Windows 98 194 • Network Architecture in Windows 98 200 • Network Provider Interface: Concurrent Support for Multiple Network Servers 202 • Installable File System: Support for Multiple Network Redirectors 204 • NDIS 4.1: Multiple Protocol Support 205 • Novell NetWare Integration 206 • Microsoft Network Integration 212 • Network Compatibility 214 • Protocol

Support 214 • Network Interprocess Communications Interfaces 225 • Windows Scripting Host 226 • Long Filename Support 226 • Network Printing 226 • Distributed Component Object Model 227 • Network Security 227 • Remote Access Server 230

10 Printing 233

Thc 32-Bit Print Subsystem 234 • Support for MS-DOS–Based Applications 236 • Deferred Printing Support 236 • Image Color Matching Support 236 • Installing and Configuring a Printer 238 • Managing Print Jobs 240 • Network Printing 241 • Plug and Play Support 241

11 Communications 243

Benefits to the Windows 98 User 243 • The Communications Architecture 244 • The Telephony API 248 • Centralized Modem Setup and Configuration 250 • Device/Hardware Support 252 • HyperTerminal 254 • Phone Dialer 254

12 Mobile Computing Services 257

Three Observations About Mobile Computer Users 257 • Three User Challenges 258

13 Multimedia Services 279

Making Multimedia Easier 280 • An Ideal Platform for Home Entertainment 283 • Multimedia Support 285 • A Powerful Development Environment 287 • Professional Quality 289

14 Accessibility 291

Accessibility Features in Microsoft Windows 98 292 • Features for Users with Limited Vision 295 • Windows 98 Features for Easier Keyboard and Mouse Input 296 • Features for Users Who Are Hearing Impaired 298 • Support for Alternative Input Devices 298 • Features for Software Developers 299

15 Applications and Utilities in Windows 98 301

The Quick Viewers 301 • WordPad 304 • Paint 304 • Hyper-Terminal 305 • The MS-DOS Editor 306 • Disk Utilities 307

PART IV   Hardware and Software Support

16   Base System Architecture   315

Important Base Architecture Components of Windows 98   316   • A Fully
Integrated Operating System   316   • 32-Bit vs. 16-Bit Components   318   •
The System Architecture Layout in Windows 98   325   • Support for
Win16-Based Applications   325   • Support for Running MS-DOS–Based
Applications   328   • Support for Win32-Based Applications   336   • 32-Bit File
System Architecture   339   • DriveSpace Disk Compression   353   • Memory
Management   356   • The Registry: A Centralized Configuration Store   357   •
Font Support   360

17   Plug and Play   361

What Is Plug and Play?   362   • Configuration Process in a Plug and Play
System   363   • Plug and Play Support in Windows 98   364   • Plug and Play
Architecture in Windows 98   366   • Plug and Play Hardware Design   368   •
For More Information   369

18   Display Support   371

Display Settings   372   • Energy Star Monitor Support   374   • Multiple Display
Support   374   • Display Driver Support in Windows 98   376

19   Device Support   379

Device Driver Philosophy   379   • Power Management Improvements   380   •
Disk Device Support   382   • Mouse and Pointing Device Support   387

20   International Language Support   391

Major Features Supporting International Use of Windows 98   391   • The Localization of Windows 98   393   • International Language Issues   394   • Multilingual Content Support   396   • The Win32 National Language Support APIs   399

21   Robustness   401

Features Supporting Robustness in Windows 98   402   • Robustness
for MS-DOS–Based Applications   404   • Robustness for Win16-Based
Applications   405   • Robustness for Win32-Based Applications   406

22   **Systems Management** 409

The Registry 411 • User Management 415

23   **TV Viewer** 421

Using the TV Toolbar 421 • Getting Help 422 • Signing On 423 • Using
the Program Guide 424 • Controlling TV Viewer 430 • Searching for a
Program 432 • Choosing Favorite Channels 434 • Setting Reminders 435 •
Supervising TV Viewing 436 • Troubleshooting 440

Index 441

Acknowledgments

Thanks are due the Microsoft Press Editorial and Production staff, who put in extraordinary effort to bring this book to you in a timely manner: Kim Fryer, acquisitions editor; Sally Stickney, project and manuscript editor; Kathleen Atkins and Victoria Thulman, manuscript editors; Jean Ross and Marc Young, technical editors; Sandra Haynes, principal compositor; Travis Beaven, illustrations; Bill Teel, screen shots; and Shawn Peck, supervising proofreader.

Dedicated to the vision of a computing appliance
on every desktop and in every home,
that puts information everywhere at your fingertips,
toward which Windows 98 is yet another step.

Limitations

This document is provided for informational purposes only. The information contained in this document represents the current view of Microsoft Corporation on the issues discussed as of the date of publication. Because Microsoft must respond to changes in market conditions, it should not be interpreted to be a commitment on the part of Microsoft, and Microsoft cannot guarantee the accuracy of any information presented after the date of publication.

Information provided in this document is provided "as is" without warranty of any kind, either express or implied, including but not limited to the implied warranties of merchantability, fitness for a particular purpose, and freedom from infringement. The user assumes the entire risk as to the accuracy and use of this document. This document may be copied and distributed subject to the following conditions: (1) all text must be copied without modification and all pages must be included; (2) all copies must contain Microsoft's copyright notice and any other notices provided therein; and (3) this document may not be distributed for profit.

Introduction

This book describes Microsoft Windows 98, the successor to Microsoft Windows 95, which revolutionized the look and feel of Microsoft Windows. Building on the strong foundation of Windows 95, Windows 98 expands on the innovations it inherited.

With Windows 98, you can take full advantage of powerful new technologies and entertainment platforms, bringing the larger world of the Internet and intranets to your desktop via Microsoft Internet Explorer 4.0. As you'll see later in this Introduction, the new features of Windows 98 benefit all kinds of users. Whether you're a home user, a corporate user, or a mobile user, a developer or a system administrator, you'll find that Windows 98 makes your PC more reliable, faster, more tightly Web integrated, more manageable, and more fun. And besides providing exciting new capabilities, Windows 98 continues to support older Windows-based applications and technologies, allowing corporations to leverage their existing investments.

To provide you with as complete a view of Windows 98 as possible in a short space, this book includes some topics that have undergone little or no change since Windows 95. For readers who are familiar with Windows 95, the more interesting parts of this book will probably be the descriptions of the new features and benefits of Windows 98.

As a first step in setting the stage for describing the ways in which Windows 98 improves on Windows 95, the next section provides a brief history of Windows 95.

Window 95—A Brief History

Since its introduction in August 1995, Windows 95 has become established as a solid desktop operating system. The ease of use, supportability, and compatibility of this 32-bit operating system have allowed all customers to increase productivity, save time, and have more fun. Here are some facts to provide you with some perspective:

- Windows 95 has surpassed 50 million units sold. International Data Corporation (IDC) expects the installed base of Windows 95 to grow to 132 million in 1997.

- Customers can choose from 348 hardware vendors, 267 software vendors, and 273 PC manufacturers that have earned the Designed for Windows 95 logo.
- The latest versions of best-selling consumer, VAR (value added reseller), and business applications are written for 32-bit Windows.
- Ninety-five percent of the leading education software publishers are developing Windows 95–based applications.

The reason for the acceptance of Windows 95 is Microsoft's continued focus on customers' needs. In particular, users choose Windows 95 because of the following reasons:

- It's easy to use.
- It includes technologies that enhance supportability.
- It works with the hardware and software customers have.
- It provides complete network connectivity to all major systems.
- Windows is the platform for Internet technology development.

In the next section, you'll find a brief overview of the improvements offered by Windows 98.

The New, Improved Version—Windows 98

Windows 98 is designed to help you in some of the following ways.

Take advantage of hardware and software innovations

In the last few years, major advances in computer hardware and software have achieved industry support. Innovations such as Universal Serial Bus, IEEE 1394, FAT32, and DVD promise new levels of PC usability. Windows 98 provides built-in support for these hardware and software advancements so that you can take full advantage of them.

Work in an easier, faster, and more productive environment

Microsoft always works to make computing easier and to provide information at your fingertips. The new features and technologies in Windows 98 can help you find and format the information you want faster than ever, increase the speed of your applications and network connections, and automate connecting to a network drive and creating shortcuts.

Work in a more reliable and more manageable environment

One of Microsoft's goals is to reduce the costs of owning PCs while increasing the value of using them. Windows 98 includes features and functionality to configure systems, troubleshoot problems, and keep PCs up-to-date. Windows 98 can automatically install new drivers, patches, and other updated components.

Take advantage of the Internet with complete Internet integration

By incorporating version 4.0 of the Internet Explorer Web browser, Windows 98 contains everything you need to take full advantage of the Internet and your company intranet. Advanced browsing capabilities, Internet communication tools, and technologies for automating Internet and intranet information delivery provide a new level of Internet integration in Windows 98.

Have more fun

Support for multimedia will allow you to receive high-quality movies and audio—even DIRECTV—directly on your desktop.

Further Resources

If you want to keep track of all the late-breaking news about Windows 98, you can consult Microsoft's World Wide Web site at:

http://www.microsoft.com/regwiz/personalinfo.asp

At this site, you can subscribe to Microsoft's *Exploring Windows*. You can also subscribe to *Windows Technology News* for the latest technical information pertinent to those who are building, buying, or supporting a Windows 98 or Microsoft Windows NT system. For those with a corporate focus, subscribe to *BackOffice News* for crisp, informative highlights about Microsoft BackOffice and third-party related products for business computing. If you have a modem or access to the Internet, you can always get up-to-the-minute information, new white papers, press releases, and other pertinent documentation on Windows 98 directly from Microsoft.

You can also subscribe to Microsoft's *Exploring Windows* electronic newsletter by sending e-mail to:

microsoft-request@microsoft.nwnet.com

Just type *subscribe explore* on a single line in the body of the message.

For a more pointed view about the changes in Windows 98 as it nears completion, take a look at this book's updates page on Microsoft Press's Web site at:

http://mspress.microsoft.com/mspress/products/1428

Installation
and Setup

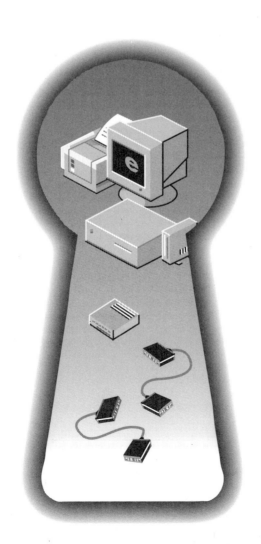

1

Instructions for Installing Windows 98

THE FIRST CONTACT MANY USERS WILL have with Microsoft Windows 98 is when they are initially installing it on their computers. To ensure that the installation process goes smoothly, the Setup program for Windows 98 has been completely rewritten to offer greater flexibility and better customization than Microsoft Windows 95 had. Novice and intermediate users won't be confronted with a series of configuration-related questions they don't know how to answer, and advanced users won't have their patience tested. The new Setup program makes installing Windows 98 a simple process for all levels of users.

> **NOTE**
>
> After Microsoft Windows 98 is released, users will be able to purchase new PCs with Windows 98 already installed and will most likely never need to run the Setup program.

System Requirements

To run Windows 98, you'll need either a PC running Windows 95 or a PC with a freshly formatted hard disk. You can't upgrade a Microsoft Windows 3.x machine with this release. At a minimum, your system should be a 386 with 4 megabytes (MB) of RAM. You can expect better performance from a 486 or more powerful PC equipped with at least 8 MB of RAM.

Installing Windows 98

To install Windows 98, run the Setup program on your Windows 98 CD. You can run this program from within an existing Windows 95 installation or on a freshly formatted hard disk.

Installing Windows 98 from Within Windows 95

To install Windows 98 from within Windows 95, follow these steps:

1. Insert your Windows 98 CD into your CD-ROM drive. The Setup program will start automatically.
2. Follow the instructions on the screen.

Installing Windows 98 on a Freshly Formatted Hard Disk

To install Windows 98 on a freshly formatted hard disk, follow the steps listed below the Note.

> **NOTE**
> The following steps involve the use of FDISK.EXE. If you're not familiar with this program, refer to your MS-DOS or Windows 95 documentation.

1. Create a Windows 95 Boot Floppy. To create this disk, do the following:
   - Click the Start button.
   - On the Start menu, click Settings, and then click Control Panel on the cascading menu.
   - In the Control Panel window, double-click Add/Remove Programs.
   - In the Add/Remove Programs Properties dialog box, click the Startup Disk tab, and then click Create Disk.
   - Follow the instructions that appear on your screen.

> **IMPORTANT**
> Make sure that the Windows 95 Boot Floppy contains FDISK.EXE and FORMAT.COM.

2. Insert the Windows 95 Boot Floppy in your first floppy disk drive, and then restart your computer.

3. After your computer starts, you'll see the MS-DOS prompt C:\>. Type *A:* at the prompt to switch to your A drive. Type *FDISK*, and then press Enter.

NOTE

Running FDISK will delete *all* information on your hard disk.

---

4. Delete any and all partitions from your hard disk.
5. Create a Primary DOS partition and make sure that it is set to ACTIVE.
6. Exit FDISK.
7. Once your computer has restarted, type *FORMAT C: /S*, and then press Enter.
8. Once the format is complete, remove the Windows 95 Boot Floppy.
9. Press Ctrl+Alt+Delete to restart your computer.
10. You now need to reenable your CD-ROM drive. To do this, install your real-mode, MS-DOS–based IDE or SCSI CD-ROM drivers.
11. Restart your computer.
12. Insert the Windows 98 CD in your CD-ROM drive.
13. Run SETUP.EXE from the MS-DOS prompt.
14. Follow the instructions on the screen.

Helpful Setup Features in Windows 98

The Windows 98 Setup program has several features that make it easier and faster to use than Setup programs in the past.

A GUI-Based Setup Program

Setup in Windows 98 features a GUI-based setup process. Using a GUI-based setup simplifies the interaction with the user by providing better visual feedback and greater flexibility for navigating through the setup process. To support a GUI-based setup, Windows 98 features a Setup program that runs entirely from within the Windows environment. Users who already have Windows 95 on their PCs can run Windows 98 Setup the same way that they would run an installation program for any Windows-based application. For new installations, Windows 98 Setup includes the necessary components to install a minimal version of Windows to support the GUI-based setup process.

The GUI-based Windows 98 Setup provides better visual feedback to users throughout the installation process. Users are constantly shown where they are in the setup process and are given a number of visual cues that indicate what task the system is engaged in during the setup process.

Hardware Detection

During the setup process, Windows 98 detects the hardware devices and components configured on the computer and uses this information to install drivers and set the appropriate entries in the Registry. Windows 98 provides hardware detection and configuration mechanisms and detection support for a wide range of devices.

Windows 98 offers straightforward detection support for the base computer components, such as communication ports and processor type, but provides robust detection of system devices, including video display adapters, pointing devices, hard disk controllers, floppy disk controllers, and network interface cards.

Hardware resources—such as IRQs, I/O addresses, or the DMA address—that are in use by more than one device can cause havoc when you're installing an operating system and could prevent the system from starting properly. Windows 98 Setup helps detect any hardware resource conflicts during the configuration process.

Windows 98 detects hardware components and devices in one of two ways:

- It employs Plug and Play detection to identify Plug and Play devices and peripherals.
- It uses a manual query detection mechanism for legacy devices and peripheral devices.

After Setup detects a device, Windows 98 installs the appropriate device drivers and configures the system.

Better Control over Installed Components

Users now have greater control over components and various parts of Windows 98 that are installed during the setup process. Because of the modular architecture of Windows 98, users will be able to select the options that Windows 98 will install for the given functionality they desire.

Setup's Smart Recovery Mechanism

Windows 98 provides a recovery mechanism in the case of Setup failure. During the setup process, Windows 98 creates and maintains a log as the setup operations are performed and the hardware devices are detected. If Setup fails—for example, because of a hang during hardware detection—the last entry in the Setup log identifies where the process was interrupted. To recover and resume, users simply rerun

Setup. The Setup program recognizes that it was run before and begins from where it left off. In the case of a hang during a hardware detection procedure, the system bypasses the detection module where the hang occurred and allows users to manually select the correct device installed on or connected to the system.

Built-In Verification of System Files

During the setup and configuration process (and during subsequent maintenance of the Windows 98 system), Windows 98 creates and maintains a log of the installed components. This information is used as part of Setup's smart recovery support and also to verify the integrity of installed components.

If users run Setup after Windows 98 is already installed, Setup asks them whether they want to reinstall Windows 98 or simply to verify installed components. If they want to verify installed components, Setup examines the setup log and runs through the setup process *without* installing all system components. Instead, it verifies the integrity of the files that were installed against the files provided on the Windows 98 installation disc. If the integrity check fails because of either a missing or corrupted file on the Windows 98 computer, Setup automatically reinstalls the missing or corrupted file.

This capability in Windows 98 greatly simplifies the process of resolving missing files or corrupted configurations. As a result, less time and money are required to support desktop configurations.

Network Setup

Microsoft Windows 98 can be installed on a network to upgrade existing Windows 95 users. Windows 98 offers the same capabilities for running Windows from a network as Windows 95 does but also provides additional functionality to better meet the needs of MIS organizations.

In addition to basic support for stand-alone computers, Windows 98 includes Setup provisions for better supporting the following configurations:

- Installing and running Windows 98 from a local computer on a network
- Installing and running Windows 98 from a network server instead of installing it on the local computer
- Installing Windows 98 on a network server and supporting diskless computers that RIPL boot from the network server
- Installing Windows 98 on a network server and supporting computers with a single floppy drive that run Windows 98 from the network server

You'll find more information about network support in Windows 98 in Chapter 9, "Networking."

Network Installation Location Remembered

When users modify the configuration of their PCs in a networked environment, the Windows 98 Setup program makes the installation of new drivers easy by remembering the location on the network from which Windows 98 was installed. Whether the server is a NetWare server or a Microsoft Windows NT server, when users add a device or require additional driver support files to properly run Windows 98, Setup automatically attempts to get the files from the network server. Setup stores a UNC pathname in the Registry, eliminating the need to maintain a permanent network connection on the PC.

Batch Installation Support

Windows 98 features a batch installation option that permits the use of an installation script to automate the installation process. MIS organizations or VARs can simplify the installation procedure for users by specifying answers to questions that Setup asks as well as defaults for installing and configuring devices such as printers.

System administrators can use the NetSetup tool provided with Windows 98 to create a batch script that specifies all of the options that Setup needs, thereby providing support for hands-free installation.

Windows 95 Configuration Preserved

During the upgrade process, Windows 98 uses existing configuration information to set installation defaults and examines the contents of specific INI files and Registry values to further determine the appropriate Setup options.

Windows 98 preserves configuration information and maps user interface–related features or functionality from Windows 95 to that of the interface used by Windows 98.

Other Setup Enhancements

The Windows 98 Setup program has been enhanced in several ways to decrease setup time while increasing setup reliability:

- When upgrading from Windows 95, Windows 98 uses the same settings as the current installation, so it is able to proceed through the setup process more quickly, with less user interaction.
- Legacy hardware detection now takes place during the first boot of Windows 98—after all Plug and Play devices have been set up—enabling detection to run more quickly and reliably.
- Setup gives you the option of backing up system files on the hard disk so that you can uninstall Windows 98 and use Windows 95 again.

- The Emergency Boot Disk (EBD) now contains a generic real mode ATAPI CD-ROM driver, allowing compatible CD-ROM devices to be available when running from the EBD. This driver might not work with all CD-ROM devices but is offered as a possible replacement if the real-mode drivers that came with your machine are unavailable.

The Setup Process

Setup in Windows 98 provides options to support the following four common scenarios:

- **Typical** Most users will select this option to perform a typical installation of Windows 98.
- **Portable** This option installs the components of Windows 98 that are useful for portable or mobile computer users.
- **Compact** This option performs a compact installation of Windows 98, installing the minimum files needed for proper operation.
- **Custom** This option provides full customization of the Windows 98 setup process, allowing users to install all or only selected components.

The setup process in Windows 98 is divided into the following four logical phases:

- Copying component files for Windows 98
- Detecting hardware
- Asking configuration questions
- Configuring the final system

The following sections describe what happens in each of these phases.

The Copying Files Phase

This phase of the setup is the most straightforward. After users start Setup, Setup begins copying files from the Windows 98 installation disc (or from a network server, if specified). When the necessary files have been copied to the PC, Setup prompts users to remove any disks in floppy drives and then reboot the system to proceed with configuration.

The Hardware Detection Phase

During the hardware detection phase, Setup analyzes installed system components and detects installed hardware devices and connected peripherals. During this phase of the setup process, Windows 98 analyzes the system to identify the hardware resources that are available (for example, IRQs, I/O addresses, and DMA addresses), identifies the configuration of installed hardware components (for example, IRQs in use), and builds the hardware tree in the Registry.

Windows 98 uses a number of mechanisms to detect installed hardware devices during setup. For legacy PCs, Windows 98 maintains a database of known hardware devices and performs a manual detection to check I/O ports and specific memory addresses to attempt to identify whether they are being used by recognized devices. Windows 98 also checks for Plug and Play peripherals connected to legacy PCs, which return their own device identification codes. For PCs that contain a Plug and Play BIOS, Windows 98 queries the PC for installed components and the configuration used by these components. (Windows 98 also checks for Plug and Play peripherals connected to Plug and Play PCs.)

During the hardware detection phase, Windows 98 tries to identify hardware conflicts and provides a mechanism to resolve conflicts early in the installation process to overcome hardware configuration issues.

The Configuration Questions Phase

Windows 98 uses information found in the hardware detection phase to determine which system components it should install. Users can review the components Windows 98 will install and remove or add any components.

The Final System Configuration Phase

During the final system configuration phase, Setup upgrades the existing configuration of Windows. After files are updated and the system is configured, Setup guides users through a process to configure peripheral devices, such as modems or printers, that are connected to the system. When this configuration is complete, Windows 98 is ready to use.

Uninstall

Windows 98 includes an uninstall capability. You'll see a Wizard page during Setup that asks if you want to back up your system files for a subsequent uninstall. Telling Setup that you want to back up your system files will instruct Setup to store your existing system files on your hard disk for a possible future uninstall.

To uninstall Windows 98 and return to Windows 95, users need only go to the Add/Remove Programs icon on the Control Panel and choose the appropriate option on the Install/Uninstall property page.

Online Registration Wizard

When users buy software products, they typically fill out and send in a registration card to notify the software company that they are now licensees of the software and thereby eligible for special benefits, such as notification of updated versions. Windows 98 contains a traditional paper registration card but also includes an electronic version of the paper registration card, known as the Registration Wizard, shown in Figure 1-1.

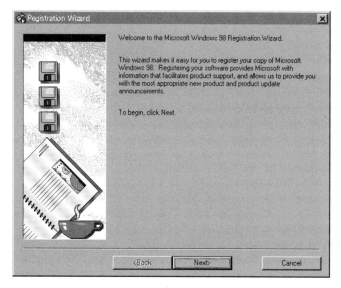

Figure 1-1   *The Registration Wizard makes registering your software product easy and convenient.*

Why Is Microsoft Offering Users an Electronic Registration Card?

Many users today don't bother to register their software simply because they find it inconvenient to fill out and mail a paper registration card. Others struggle to fill out the information correctly, unsure of such details as the type of hardware system they have or the product's version number. At Microsoft's end, paper registration cards must be hand transcribed into the customer database in a computer-readable form, a time-consuming and error-prone process.

With Windows 98, Microsoft offers users the option of registering via an easy-to-use Registration Wizard, shown in Figure 1-2 on the following page. The Registration Wizard guides users step by step through the process of registering and fills in many of the blanks for users. And because the information is submitted to Microsoft electronically, it can be processed faster and more accurately.

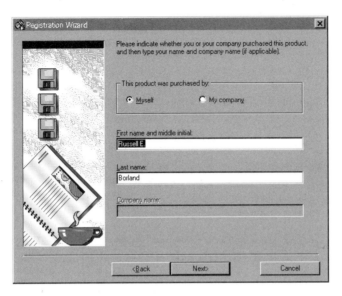

Figure 1-2 *The Registration Wizard prompts for the same type of information as the paper-based registration card does.*

What Happens When Users Register?

Keep in mind that registration is completely optional. If users do choose to register, using either the paper card or the Registration Wizard, they are added to a database of registered customers. These users are among the first to receive notification about updated versions (usually including information on special upgrade pricing), new products, and other benefits. Registration enables Microsoft to send information about its programs tailored to users' needs and interests. Registration information stays at Microsoft and is never provided to other parties. Occasionally, third parties ask to send information they think might be valuable to registered users, but users can specify during registration that they don't want to receive such materials.

How Does the Registration Wizard Work?

The Registration Wizard helps users provide the same type of information they would supply on the paper registration form. For example, the user is first asked for name, company name, address, and phone number. The user is then given the option of sending information about the computer system's configuration and hardware peripherals (such as modem or CD-ROM drive). The Registration Wizard makes it easy for users to provide information about their system configuration because it automatically queries the system Registry of the computer and displays a list of the computer's configuration information. The Wizard also asks users if they want to send information about the applications on their systems. Sending information about hardware and software configuration is not required for registration and is not sent unless users explicitly choose to send it to Microsoft.

Why would users want to send additional information on configuration? The information helps Microsoft build better products and helps provide users with better product support and better programs. For example, information about users' systems, such as memory and hard disk space and the presence of a CD-ROM drive, helps Microsoft understand customers' configurations and therefore design products that meet the majority of users' needs.

The Registration Wizard sends *no* information without users' explicit permission. Information cannot be sent accidentally from the hard drive or from memory. There is no way for the Registration Wizard to upload information that users did not see on the screen. (See Figure 1-3.)

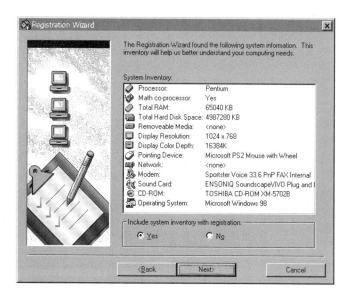

Figure 1-3 *Users must confirm prompt to include system inventory with registration before the wizard will proceed.*

If users want to see the exact information gathered during online registration, they can view the REGINFO.TXT file found in the C:\WINDOWS directory of the computer.

2

Overview of New
Features in Windows 98

THE MATERIAL IN THIS CHAPTER DESCRIBES the new features in Microsoft Windows 98. These features can be divided roughly into the following categories:

- Platform for innovation
- Easier, faster, and more powerful
- Improved reliability and manageability
- Internet integration (Microsoft Internet Explorer 4.0)

Platform for Innovation

These features support hardware and software advancements in Windows 98.

Win32 Driver Model

The Win32 Driver Model (WDM) is an all new, unified driver model for Windows 98 and Microsoft Windows NT 5.0. WDM will enable new devices to have a single driver for both operating systems. WDM has been implemented by adding selected NT Kernel services into Windows 98 via a special virtual device driver (NTKERN.VXD). This driver allows Windows 98 to maintain full legacy device driver support while adding support for new WDM drivers.

FAT32

FAT32 is an improved version of the FAT file system. FAT32 allows disks over 2 gigabytes to be formatted as a single drive. It also uses smaller clusters than FAT drives do, which results in a more efficient use of space on large disks.

FAT32 Conversion Utility

For added flexibility, Windows 98 includes a graphical FAT32 conversion utility, which can quickly and safely convert a hard drive from the original version of FAT to FAT32.

Power Management Improvements

Windows 98 includes built-in support for Advanced Configuration and Power Interface (ACPI). ACPI is an open industry specification proposed by Intel, Microsoft, and Toshiba that defines hardware interfaces that allow for standard power management functionality throughout a PC system. In addition to ACPI support, Windows 98 includes support for the Advanced Power Management (APM) 1.2 extensions, including disk spindown, PCMCIA, modem power down, and resume on ring.

Multiple Display Support

Multiple display support allows you to use multiple monitors and/or multiple graphics adapters on a single PC. The ability to display your work environment on multiple monitors can be extremely beneficial in many environments, including desktop publishing, Web development, video editing, and gaming.

Support for a New Generation of Hardware

One of the major goals of Windows 98 is to provide complete support for users who want to take advantage of the array of innovations that have emerged in computer hardware over the last few years. Some of the key hardware standards supported by Windows 98 include Universal Serial Bus (USB), IEEE 1394, Accelerated Graphics Port (AGP), ACPI, and Digital Video (or Versatile) Disc (DVD).

More Power

These features are part of the new interface for Windows 98 and provide easier, faster, and more powerful ways to work with Windows 98, application programs, and special hardware settings.

Integrated Internet Shell

With the integrated Internet shell included with Windows 98, Internet access becomes a seamless part of the user interface. You'll no longer have to learn multiple applications—one to look at your local information, perhaps another to look at your network, and unquestionably another to use the Internet or an intranet. The integrated Internet shell in Windows 98 unifies this assortment of applications into one utility to universally view local, network, intranet, and Internet data so that you can get to the information you need faster and easier.

Windows Scripting Host

Windows 98 supports direct script execution from the user interface or the command line. (A script is simply a series of commands that can be executed automatically.) This support is provided via the Windows Scripting Host (WSH) and allows administrators and users to save time by automating many user interface actions, such as creating a shortcut, connecting to a network server, disconnecting from a network server, and so forth. The WSH is extremely flexible, with built-in support for Microsoft Visual Basic scripts, Java scripts, and a language-independent architecture that will allow other software companies to build Microsoft ActiveX scripting engines for languages such as Perl, TCL, REXX, and Python.

Display Setting Enhancements

Display setting enhancements provide support for dynamically changing screen resolution and color depth. You can also set the adapter refresh rate with most newer display driver chipsets. Windows 98 also includes the display enhancements previously available in Microsoft Plus! (Microsoft Plus! is an add-on pack for Microsoft Windows 95 that provides several minor operating system enhancements.) Other display setting enhancements with Windows 98 include full window drag, wallpaper stretching, large icons, and high-color icons.

Setup Enhancements

Several enhancements have been made to the Windows 98 Setup program in an effort to decrease setup time while increasing setup reliability. These setup enhancements are described more fully in Chapter 1.

Start Menu Organizer Wizard

The new Start Menu Organizer Wizard simplifies the process of adding to, removing from, configuring, and maintaining the Start menu.

Internet Connection Wizard

The Internet Connection Wizard (ICW) provides Windows users with all the functionality necessary to connect their desktops to the Internet quickly and easily. With
ICW installed, you can easily configure your machine for Internet communication,
sign up for an account with any participating Internet Service Provider (ISP), and set
up any custom software required by that provider.

Built-In Support for Microsoft Intellimouse

The new Microsoft Intellimouse "wheel" allows users to concentrate on the document or spreadsheet rather than on moving the mouse to icons or scroll bars to navigate the program.

Dial-Up Networking Improvements (Including Multilink
Channel Aggregation)

The Dial-Up Networking included with Windows 98 has been updated to support
Dial-Up Scripting, which can automate the process of connecting to bulletin boards
and online services. Dial-Up Networking also offers user interface enhancements to
simplify setting up and using dial-up connections and supports Multilink Channel
Aggregation, which enables users to combine all available dial-up lines to achieve
higher transfer speeds. For example, you can combine two or more ISDN lines to
achieve speeds of up to 128 Kbps, or you can combine two or more standard modem lines. This can provide dramatic performance improvements when you're dialing into the Internet or a corporate network.

Disk Defragmenter Optimization Wizard

The new Disk Defragmenter Optimization Wizard uses the process of disk defragmentation to increase the running speed of your most frequently used applications.
To accomplish this, the wizard creates a log file that identifies the programs you use
most often. Once this log file has been created, the disk defragmenter can use it to
store the files associated with your most frequently run programs. (The files will be
stored contiguously on your hard disk.) Placing all the files associated with a given
application in the same location on your hard disk will optimize the speed with which
your application runs.

Windows Tune Up Wizard

The Windows Tune Up Wizard allows you to schedule a day and a time each week
for your computer to clean itself up. The wizard also allows you to schedule a day
and a time for the ScanDisk utility to run. And you can use the Tune Up Wizard to
schedule days and times for your system to clean up unnecessary files and to perform
disk defragmentation on your most often used applications to make them run faster.

Built-In Support for Infrared Data Association 3.0

Windows 98 includes support for the Infrared Data Association (IrDA) standard for wireless connectivity. IrDA support enables Windows 98 users to connect easily to peripheral devices or other PCs without using connecting cables. This driver set provides infrared-equipped laptop or desktop computers with the capability of networking, transferring files, and printing wirelessly with other IrDA-compatible infrared devices.

Online Services Folder

The Windows 98 desktop contains an Online Services Folder with links to America Online (AOL), AT&T WorldNet, CompuServe 3.0, Prodigy, and Microsoft Network (MSN) clients. When you click the link to the client, a setup program starts that automatically registers you with that Internet Service Provider.

Client Support for Point-to-Point Tunneling Protocol

The Point-to-Point Tunneling Protocol (PPTP) provides a way to use public data networks, such as the Internet, to create virtual private networks connecting client PCs with servers. PPTP offers protocol encapsulation to support multiple protocols via TCP/IP connections and data encryption for privacy, making it safer to send information over nonsecure networks. This technology extends the Dial-Up Networking capability by enabling remote access and by securely extending private networks across the Internet without the need to change client software.

Remote Access Server

Windows 98 includes all the components necessary to enable your desktop to act as a dial-up server. Dial-up clients will be able to connect remotely to a Windows 98 machine for local resource access or to either an IPX/SPX or a NetBEUI network (or both).

PCMCIA Enhancements

Windows 98 has several PCMCIA technology enhancements:

- **Support for PC Card32 (CardBus)** CardBus brings 32-bit performance to the small PC Card form factor. It enables notebooks to implement high-bandwidth applications such as video capture and 100 Mbaud networking.
- **Support for PC Cards that operate at 3.3 volts** This enables hardware manufacturers to lower the power consumption of their devices by using 3.3 volts rather than 5 volts.

- **Support for Multifunction PC Cards** This allows two or more functions (such as LAN and modem, or SCSI and sound) on a single physical PC Card. Supporting multifunction cards helps decrease the cost-per-function of PC Cards and more efficiently uses the limited number of slots on most PCs, permitting more functions per PC.

ActiveMovie

ActiveMovie is a new media-streaming architecture for Windows that delivers high-quality video playback while exposing an extensible set of interfaces on which you can build multimedia applications and tools. ActiveMovie enables playback of popular media types, including MPEG audio, WAV audio, MPEG video, AVI video, and Apple QuickTime video.

Support for Intel MMX Processors

Third parties building software that exploits the Intel Pentium Multimedia Extensions (MMX) for fast audio and video support on the next generation of Intel Pentium processor have support in Windows 98.

Distributed Component Object Model

The Component Object Model (COM) allows software developers to create component applications. Now Distributed COM (DCOM) in Windows 98 (and Windows NT 4.0) provides the infrastructure that allows DCOM applications (the technology formally known as Network OLE) to communicate across networks without needing to be redeveloped.

Client Support for NetWare Directory Services

Windows 98 includes Client Services for NetWare that support Novell NetWare Directory Services (NDS). These services enable Windows 98 users to log onto Novell NetWare 4.x servers running NDS to access files and print resources. This service provides the key features that Novell users need: NDS authentication, ability to browse NDS resources, ability to print to NDS print queues, and full support for processing NetWare login scripts, NDS property pages, and NDS passwords.

32-Bit Data Link Control

The Data Link Control (DLC) protocol is used primarily to access IBM mainframe and IBM AS/400 computers. The 32-bit DLC protocol software built into Windows 98 enables a network administrator to add support for 32-bit and 16-bit DLC programs.

Improved Reliability and Manageability

These features are new or improved utilities that make Windows and the operation of your computer both more reliable and more manageable.

Internet System Update

Internet System Update helps you ensure that you're using the latest drivers and file systems available. It is a new Web-based service (ActiveX control) that scans your system to determine what hardware and software you have installed and then compares that information to a back-end database to determine whether newer drivers or system files are available. If newer drivers or system files are available, the service can automatically install them. This process is completely configurable. You can choose which updated drivers and system files to download or you can simply have the drivers downloaded with no user interaction. There's even a "rollback" feature that can remove a driver that has been automatically installed via Internet System Update.

System File Checker Utility

System File Checker is a new utility that provides an easy way to verify that the Windows 98 system files (such as *.dll, *.com, *.vxd, *.drv, *.ocx, *.inf, and *.hlp) have not been modified or corrupted. The utility also provides an easy mechanism for restoring the original versions of system files that have changed. System File Checker will be extremely valuable in helping users and support personnel to track changes (file corruption, application installation, application removal, accidental deleting of files, and so on) made to Windows 98 systems and to restore original files in the event a change causes a conflict.

Microsoft System Information Utility

Microsoft System Information utility collects information about the software and hardware state of a given machine. The information collected can range from hardware to software, device drivers, or resources currently in use. This information can be invaluable in identifying, troubleshooting, and solving hardware, software, and configuration problems.

New Dr. Watson Utility

Windows 98 includes an enhanced version of the Dr. Watson utility. With Dr. Watson enabled, when a software fault occurs (general protection fault, hang, or other stoppage), Dr. Watson intercepts it and indicates what software faulted and why. In addition, Dr. Watson collects detailed information about the state of your system at the time the fault occurred. It logs this information to disk and can display it on screen to assist administrative and product support personnel in determining the cause of the fault.

New Backup Utility

A new backup utility supports SCSI tape devices and makes backing up your data easier and faster.

Automatic ScanDisk After Improper Shutdown

Windows 98 has been enhanced to run ScanDisk automatically in the event that the operating system is shut down improperly or your hard disk suffers a hard error. This addition will go a long way in helping users ensure that their hard drives are in proper working order and free of lost clusters, cross-linked files, and other faults.

Internet Integration (Microsoft Internet Explorer 4.0)

Microsoft Internet Explorer 4.0 also has some intriguing new features in Windows 98.

Advanced Internet Browsing Functionality

The inclusion of Microsoft Internet Explorer 4.0 in Windows 98 provides you with the easiest, fastest, and most entertaining way to browse the Web. Your browsing is made possible by several advanced capabilities of Microsoft Internet Explorer 4.0, including these:

- Advanced browsing tools, such as AutoComplete; enhanced Web searching; improved favorites; navigation history on the Forward and Back buttons; and improved printing
- Support for all major Internet standards, including HTML; Java; ActiveX; JavaScript; Visual Basic, Scripting Edition (VBScript); and major security standards
- Improved performance with Dynamic HTML, a just-in-time Java compiler, and basic code "tuning"

Suite of Tools for Internet Communication

Windows 98 also contains rich tools for online communication:

- Microsoft Outlook Express, a full-featured e-mail and news reading client
- Microsoft NetMeeting, a complete Internet conferencing solution that offers standards-based audio, data, and video conferencing functionality

- Microsoft NetShow, which enables you to watch and listen to live or recorded broadcasts without waiting for downloads or slowing down network performance
- Microsoft FrontPad, a WYSIWYG HTML editor based on the full-featured version of Microsoft FrontPage 97 that provides easy-to-use HTML editing capabilities, allowing even novice users to create Web pages easily.
- Personal Web Server (and the Web Publishing Wizard), which provides an easy way to publish Web pages on intranets or the Internet.

Personalized Internet Information Delivery

Users say that their number one problem with the World Wide Web is getting the information they need. Windows 98 addresses this problem by providing a mechanism that can automatically select and schedule downloads of the information you care about. This enables you to see what has changed on a Web site without physically visiting the site and lets you view the site even when you're not connected to the Web.

Windows 98 Faces on the Internet

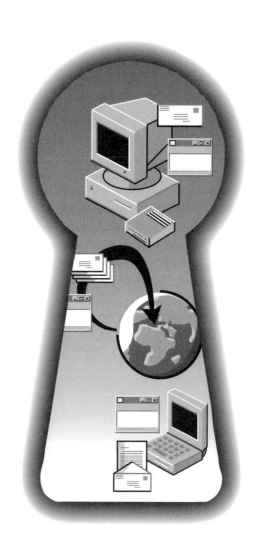

3

The Faces of Windows 98

WHEN YOU FIRST START MICROSOFT WINDOWS 98, you'll see a familiar "face"—the Microsoft Windows desktop. With two mouse clicks, you can change the look of Windows 98 to the new Active Desktop. Through the "eyes" of the Active Desktop on Windows 98, you'll be introduced to a whole new view—your computer is now part of the larger world of networks, intranets, and the Internet. (Windows 98 might well be set up to start in the new Active Desktop. In that case, two mouse clicks can switch the face of Windows 98 back to the familiar standard desktop.) This chapter introduces the many faces of Windows 98.

Revised Desktop Tools Plus Internet Integration

Regardless of which desktop you work from—the standard Windows desktop or the Active Desktop—Windows 98 contains revised versions of the desktop tools that were in Microsoft Windows 95; namely, the taskbar and the Start menu.

Windows 95 introduced the taskbar with its Start button. The taskbar's mission was to make 95 percent of what a typical user wants to do with Windows easy to accomplish at all times. The taskbar started out specifically as a program launcher and task switcher for novices. Because of its simplicity and power, however, the taskbar also became popular with experienced users, who took advantage of its many advanced capabilities. This reorganization of the desktop was a big change from the look and feel of Windows 3.x and so required users to spend time learning a completely new interface.

A main goal of Windows 98 is to add Internet awareness to Windows 95 without requiring user retraining. To accomplish this, My Computer, Network Neighborhood, the Start menu, and other parts of the user interface have become Web-savvy. Rather than layering additional functionality on top of the operating system and changing the user interface, Windows 98 provides you with a single easy way to access information—whether it resides on the local machine, the local area network (LAN), or the Internet. You can also create your own customized workspace, whether you access information from local, network, intranet, or Internet sites.

Enhanced Start Menu and Taskbar

Windows 98 adds Web awareness by enhancements to the Start menu and the taskbar. The enhancements to the Start button menu make it easier to use—you can now easily customize the Start menu as well as define shortcuts to tools you use regularly. The enhancements to the taskbar make its role more extensive than when it served as an anchor in Windows 95.

Here are the key features of the revised Start menu and taskbar:

- **Start menu does Web tasks** New commands for Favorites and a new Find command named On The Internet appear on the Start menu, making it easy to get to sites you visit frequently.

- **Start menu customization** You can now customize the Favorites menu, the entire Programs menu, and even the top of the Start menu by dragging and dropping.

- **Windows taskbar extensibility** The taskbar has become open and extensible, with a default address bar for entering Web addresses. You can also create custom toolbars simply by dragging a folder or Web site window onto the taskbar.

The Start Button

With Windows 95, the speed with which applications launch improved dramatically (3x–9x). This improvement is carried over to Windows 98 thanks to the Start button, which is shown in Figure 3-1.

The Start button in Windows 98 is much more than a program launcher, however. The following sections describe its basic capabilities (inherited from Windows 95) and its expanded capabilities in Windows 98.

Figure 3-1 *The Windows 98 Start button and its menu*

Programs

The Start button's Programs menu allows you to launch programs as quickly as ever. This menu is the same as it was in Windows 95, with one exception: now you can reorganize the order in which programs and groups are listed on the Programs menu.

Favorites

The Favorites menu, shown in Figure 3-2 on the following page, lists your Internet Favorites and any other folders or files you visit regularly. Click a listed favorite to connect to a favorite Web site or to open a folder or document. The Favorites submenu lists all the items stored in the Favorites folder on your hard disk.

- **Channels** Clicking the Channels folder gives you quick access to the channels on MSN, The Microsoft Network.

- **Links** Clicking the Links folder shows you a list of Web sites you can access simply by clicking on them, without having to first open Microsoft Internet Explorer.

Figure 3-2   *Windows 98 Favorites menu*

Documents

The Start button's Documents menu contains a list of the last 15 documents opened. This menu provides quick access to the information you worked with most recently and helps prevent time-consuming and frustrating browsing. It also helps you think of your work in terms of documents rather than applications.

Settings

The Start button's Settings menu now displays the new Settings Wizards command as well as the Control Panel and Printers commands you saw in Windows 95. The Taskbar command that was on the Settings menu is now the Taskbar & Start Menu command. You use the Settings Wizards to change system settings quickly and easily. The Settings Wizard has no new features, but you now have faster access to them. The settings you can change with the Settings Wizard appear in Figure 3-3.

The settings you can change are all within the Control Panel window. In Windows 95, you had to open Control Panel to set the options for all the items in the list above the Open Control Panel option. The following list briefly explains each choice in the Settings Wizard:

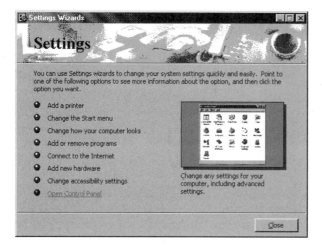

Figure 3-3   *The Windows 98 Settings Wizards*

- Add A Printer starts the Add Printer Wizard.
- Change The Start Menu opens the Taskbar Properties dialog box (Start Menu Programs tab).
- Change How Your Computer Looks opens the Display Properties dialog box.
- Add Or Remove Programs opens the Add/Remove Programs Properties dialog box (Install/Uninstall tab).
- Connect To The Internet starts the Internet Connection Wizard.
- Add New Hardware starts the Add New Hardware Wizard.
- Change Accessibility Settings opens the Accessibility Properties dialog box.
- Open Control Panel opens the Control Panel. This choice works the same as clicking Control Panel on the Settings menu. (See "The Control Panel" section later in the chapter for more details.)

Find

A powerful Find utility is built into Windows 98. As you can see in Figure 3-4 on the following page, the Find command on the Windows 98 Start menu adds a couple of new items to its list.

The Files Or Folders and Computer items are the same as they were in Windows 95. The On The Internet and People items are new.

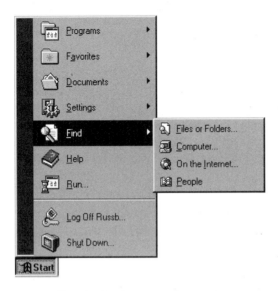

Figure 3-4 *New stuff on the Find command menu*

Finding files or folders

The Files Or Folders command on the Find menu displays the dialog box shown in Figure 3-5.

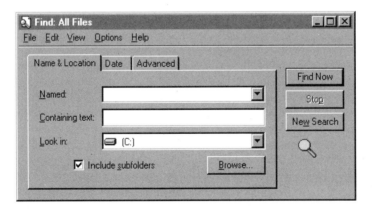

Figure 3-5 *Finding files or folders in Windows 98*

The Find dialog box for folders and files provides the following search capabilities:

- **Partial name searches** Type *rep* in the Named text box, and all files and folders with *rep* somewhere in their names are found.

- **Searches on last modification date** Because files can be searched on their last modification dates, you can specify on the Date tab to perform searches such as *Find all Word documents modified in the last 3 days.*

- **Full-text searches** You can search for documents containing specified text by typing the text you're looking for in the Containing Text text box.

- **Saving search results** You can save the results of complex or useful searches.

- **File management from the search results pane** You can perform operations such as renaming files or viewing file properties within the results pane in the same way as you can in Microsoft Windows Explorer.

Finding on the Internet

The Find On The Internet command makes it easy to get to sites you visit frequently. Full LDAP (Lightweight Directory Access Protocol) directory service support gives you access to virtual Internet White Pages and makes it easy to find anyone on corporate LDAP servers or to use the built-in support for Four11, InfoSpace, Bigfoot, or WhoWhere to locate anyone on the Internet.

Finding people

Depending on your installation of Windows 95, you might see a Using Microsoft Outlook command. The People command on the Find menu is an alternative to such application-specific commands. For the People command, Windows 98 uses your address books to locate information about a person whose name is stored in an address book, whether it's a Microsoft Outlook, Microsoft Exchange, or other e-mail or contact information address book.

Help

Help has been overhauled in Windows 98 and is easily accessible from the Start button. The user interface has changed from the standard Help format to look more like a Web interface. This new format includes links to Help available through the Internet. (For more information on Help, see the "More Help" section later in the chapter.)

Run

The Start button's Run item provides enhanced command-line type functionality.

Log Off Name

For a quick change between users, click the new Log Off command on the Start button. This option replaces the Close All Programs And Log On As A Different User option that was listed in the Shutdown dialog box in Windows 95. This option isn't available from the Shutdown dialog box in Windows 98.

> **TIP**
>
> Because the Log Off command identifies the name of the user who is logged in, it's now easier to identify who is using the computer.

Shutting Down

The Shut Down item provides easily accessible and safe Shut Down, Restart, and Restart In MS-DOS Mode commands.

Other Start Menu Commands

If you're running Windows 98 on a laptop—especially on a laptop that you use both in and out of a docking station—your Start menu shows two other commands: Eject and Suspend. (You might also see the Suspend command on some desktop computers.) The Eject command uses software control to release the laptop from docking stations that use a motor drive to secure and eject the laptop. The Suspend command powers down the computer to save power. The monitor and hard disk drive are the major power consumers in a PC. Suspend puts them to "sleep." With the OnNow feature, as described in Chapter 19, "Device Support," the computer is ready to "wake up" when you want to work or when an incoming call reaches the computer. With this command, you can reduce power consumption yet have your computer ready to work in an instant or to receive an incoming fax message or other call (such as a networking request when your hard disk is set up to share folders or to act as a server).

Start Menu Organizer Wizard

The Start menu is designed to assist in starting programs, utilities, and other files that you use regularly. The new Start Menu Organizer Wizard simplifies the process of adding to, removing from, configuring, and maintaining the Start menu. The benefit of this wizard is that you can keep the Start menu organized and up-to-date.

Over time, as files and programs are added and removed, the Start menu can contain "broken" shortcuts. This happens, for example, when an application is installed and later removed but the shortcut is left on the Start menu or when a program places a shortcut to Readme files and Help files in the program folder. The Start Menu Organizer Wizard analyzes the shortcuts on the Start menu and takes the following actions:

- Deletes shortcuts that point to removed applications
- Removes shortcuts that point to empty folders
- Deletes or moves shortcuts that haven't been used within a specified amount of time
- Removes shortcuts that point to unnecessary Readme and Help files
- Lets you add or remove components

No matter what level of computer experience you have, this wizard can help you keep your Start menu up-to-date, customized, and free of unwanted and unnecessary shortcuts.

Other Start Menu Enhancements

In addition to the changes listed in the preceding sections, the Start menu has two other enhancements:

- **Click and drag** To remove an item from the Start menu, drag it off the Start menu.
- **Shortcut menus** To display a shortcut menu, right-click any Start menu program item.

The Taskbar

The objective of the taskbar is to make switching among multiple applications as simple as changing channels on a television set. Every open window has a button on the taskbar. You can see all the active tasks simply by looking at the taskbar. Switching applications is a simple matter of clicking the desired "channel" on the taskbar. When a task is minimized into the taskbar or restored from the taskbar, animation helps new users understand "where" the task goes.

In Windows 98, in addition to the task buttons for running applications and open folders, the taskbar can now contain several toolbars.

Task Buttons and Taskbar Configuration

Task buttons resize themselves automatically depending on the number of active tasks. If the buttons get too small to be useful, you can customize the taskbar. In fact, a host of taskbar configuration options allow you to customize it in other ways, including the following:

- **Reposition** You can drag the taskbar to any perimeter position on the screen.
- **Resize** You can raise the height of the taskbar by dragging its top edge (or inside edge if you position the taskbar to the side or top of the screen).
- **Auto hide** You can hide the taskbar, having it appear on the screen only when the mouse hits the screen edge, by right-clicking the taskbar and then selecting Properties from the shortcut menu.
- **Toolbars** The Windows 98 taskbar can contain several toolbars in addition to the icons for running applications. (For details on these toolbars, see the "Toolbars on the Taskbar" section below.)

In addition to making task switching dramatically easier and more accessible from the taskbar, Windows 98 includes the updated version of the Alt+Tab "cool switch" introduced in Windows 95. It displays an iconic road map of all active tasks to prevent users from getting lost in an infinite Alt+Tab loop.

Desktop Button

The Quick Launch toolbar contains a Desktop button, shown here:

When you click it, the Desktop button minimizes all windows open on your desktop. When you click it again, this button restores the windows of all running programs to the Desktop. This button is faster than choosing Minimize All Windows from the taskbar shortcut menu.

When you press the Desktop button to minimize, the button stays pressed until you either press it again (to return all open windows to their preminimized size) or click an icon on the taskbar (to return a single window to its preminimized size).

Toolbars on the Taskbar

As you can see in Figure 3-6, the taskbar shortcut menu has several new options. For each toolbar, you can display or hide the name of the toolbar (Show Title) and display or hide the names of the icons on the toolbars (Show Text). The toolbar requires less space when you turn off the toolbar titles and text.

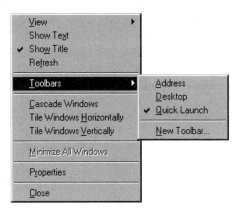

Figure 3-6 *The Toolbars submenu on the taskbar shortcut menu*

The Toolbars submenu

Using the Toolbars submenu shown in Figure 3-6, you can place Web addresses, links, desktop icons, and complete folders on the taskbar. The submenu also contains the Quick Launch option, which you can place on the taskbar to start Internet Explorer quickly.

Address

As you can see in Figure 3-7, the address toolbar contains the same address slot as Internet Explorer does. Web addresses you have visited appear in a drop-down list.

Figure 3-7 *Address toolbar on the taskbar*

Links

Clicking the Links option on the Toolbars submenu displays a toolbar that contains the same links available on Internet Explorer's Links toolbar: Best Of The Web, Microsoft, Product News, Today's Links, and Web Gallery. The Links toolbar, which is shown in Figure 3-8 on the following page, works the same way as the Address toolbar described in the preceding section.

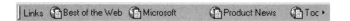

Figure 3-8   *The Links toolbar*

Desktop

The Desktop option displays all the icons on your desktop on the taskbar, as shown in Figure 3-9.

Figure 3-9   *Desktop toolbar on taskbar with labels shown*

Clicking the right mouse button on the label Desktop displays a shortcut menu that also contains a Show Text command. When you turn off this command (remove the check mark), Windows 98 hides the text that was next to the icons, as shown in Figure 3-10.

Figure 3-10   *Desktop toolbar on taskbar with labels hidden*

Even with Show Text turned off, you can still see the name of an icon by positioning the mouse pointer over the icon to display a ToolTip that specifies the icon's name.

Quick launching

Clicking the Quick Launch option on the Toolbars submenu places the Internet Explorer toolbar on the taskbar, as shown in Figure 3-11.

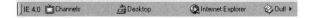

Figure 3-11   *The Internet Explorer toolbar on the taskbar*

Simply click the Internet Explorer button to launch Internet Explorer. Click the Channels button to launch Internet Explorer set up to view MSN channels.

Manipulating taskbar toolbars

Windows 98 provides a number of options for working with toolbars on the taskbar. You can change the number of toolbars you can see as well as the way in which you view them.

Creating a new toolbar

The New Toolbar command helps you select a folder to display on the taskbar. Clicking New Toolbar on the Toolbars submenu displays the Browse For Folder dialog box shown in Figure 3-12.

Figure 3-12   *The Browse For Folder dialog box, in which you select a folder you want to place on the taskbar*

With this dialog box, you can put any folder on your taskbar—your Internet Favorites, Control Panel, My Documents, and even the Recycle Bin and MS-DOS folders. Figure 3-13 shows the taskbar with My Computer added as a new toolbar.

Figure 3-13   *My Computer toolbar added to the taskbar*

Adjusting your view of toolbar buttons

A taskbar toolbar might contain more buttons than can fit within its taskbar space. This is especially true if you display more than one toolbar. When a toolbar contains more buttons than fit within its allotted width, the toolbar uses directional arrowheads to show you that the toolbar contains more buttons. When you click the directional arrowhead, the buttons slide in the direction opposite the arrowhead's point to reveal more buttons. As long as the toolbar contains buttons outside the current view of the toolbar, you see the arrowheads: with an arrowhead on the right end, you can scroll to the buttons that are out of view to the right; with one on the left end, you can scroll to the buttons that are out of view to the left.

Resizing taskbar toolbars

The toolbars on the taskbar can appear in several sizes. You can collapse a toolbar so that you see only the knurled bars at the left end of the toolbar. The toolbar can also be an intermediate size, which you determine by splitting the available width of the taskbar among two or more toolbars. Or the toolbar can be its maximum width, which is the remaining width of the taskbar when all the other toolbars are collapsed.

To change the width of a toolbar, position the mouse pointer along the toolbar's left end. The mouse pointer changes to a two-headed arrow. Now simply drag the left end to the right to collapse its width (and widen the toolbar to its left). Or drag the left end to the left to widen the toolbar's width (and collapse the toolbars to its left).

You can also change the size of toolbars through the shortcut menu. Under the View option, you can select Large Icons or Small Icons.

Positioning taskbar toolbars

You can drag the toolbar label along the taskbar or onto your desktop. Dragging onto your desktop sets up a floating toolbar, as shown in Figure 3-14.

Figure 3-14   *Floating My Computer toolbar*

TIP

Float a toolbar when you want to clear up space on your taskbar.

You can also drag a taskbar toolbar to the side or the top of the screen to park it there. The toolbar then works the same as the taskbar does.

When you float a taskbar toolbar, you can resize it in the same way that you resize any window: simply drag a border or a corner. You'll want to do this when the floating taskbar is larger than the space needed to display the icons on the toolbar.

Piling on taskbar toolbars

You can drag a taskbar toolbar to add it to a floating toolbar. Figure 3-15 shows four floating toolbars combined as one floating panel.

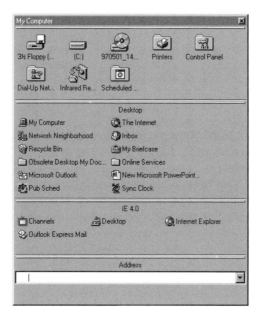

Figure 3-15 *Four toolbars added together in one floating toolbar window*

Single Explorer

With the single Microsoft Explorer, the process of finding information is unified in one place so that you can view local, network, intranet, and Internet data with the same tool. The single Explorer has several key features:

- **Consistent navigation** You can now browse your local hard drives or the network the same way as you browse the Web.

- **Context-sensitive toolbars and menus** Windows 98 detects the type of information visible in the current view—whether it's in HTML, local files, or folders—and automatically adjusts the toolbars and menus accordingly.

- **Browser-enabled everywhere** The single Explorer provides the ability to view multiple types of content in any folder, whether files and folders or HTML.

- **Global Favorites** With new global Favorites, you can keep track of your favorite folders, files, servers, and Web sites—you'll have seamless navigation from local to Web content.

- **Web View** Web View extends the original views in Windows 95 (Large Icons, Small Icons, List, and Details) with a fifth unique view, As Web Page, which can represent folders as Web pages. In Web View, you can browse a local or network folder as if you were browsing the Web.

- **Customize This Folder Wizard** To create a custom Web view of a folder, Windows 98 comes with a step-by-step wizard that walks you through the process of setting up a custom view of a folder on your PC. You can access it from the View menu in any Windows folder view.

Active Desktop

Active Desktop brings your favorite Internet Web pages to your desktop background. Since your Windows 98 desktop is now active, the page is "live." You can scroll the page, click Web links, view animation, listen to sound, and do anything else you do with a Web page from Internet Explorer.

To configure Active Desktop, right-click the Desktop and then click Properties on the shortcut menu. When the Display Properties dialog box appears, click the Web tab. An example of the tab, with two items added to the Active Desktop, appears in Figure 3-16.

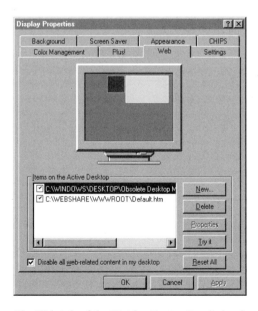

Figure 3-16   *The Web tab of the Display Properties dialog box*

The Items On The Active Desktop pane displays the objects (files, folders, or Web pages) added to the Active Desktop. If you set up Web pages that automatically update periodically, you see the updates on your desktop automatically.

The Disable All Web-Related Content In My Desktop option hides the Active Desktop items without removing them from the list. This option acts the same as turning off the Active Desktop command on the desktop shortcut menu (as described in the next section). Turning off this option displays the standard Windows 95 desktop but with the changes described earlier in this chapter that are part of Windows 98.

Switching Quickly Between Standard and Active Desktop

After you set up your Active Desktop, you might want to return to the standard desktop for a time or permanently. To switch quickly from Active Desktop to standard desktop, right-click on the desktop and then click Active Desktop on the shortcut menu. Click View As Web Page to clear the check mark. To rapidly reactivate the Active Desktop you had set up, right-click on the standard desktop and then click Active Desktop. Click View As Web Page to set the check mark.

If you want to change the Active Desktop, you need to click the Properties command on the shortcut menu, as described in the preceding section.

Adding Items to the Active Desktop

You can add Web site addresses, HTML documents, and pictures to your Active Desktop. To add an item to the Active Desktop, click the New button on the Web tab of the Display Properties dialog box. You first see a message that asks if you want to connect to the Active Desktop Gallery on the Microsoft Web site. If you have an active connection to the Web, you can click Yes. If you don't have an active Web connection or you don't want to visit the gallery, click No. If you click Yes or No, you see the first panel of the New Active Desktop Item Wizard, shown in Figure 3-17 on the following page.

You can type either a URL or a file pathname. To look for a file, click Browse, and then locate the file you want to add to the Active Desktop. In the Files Of Type box in the Browse dialog box, you can select Internet Shortcut (the default), Channel Description File (for adding MSN channels to the Active Desktop), HTML Document (one that's stored on a disk connected to your computer), or Picture (bitmap, GIF, or JPEG). When the Location box in the New Active Desktop Item wizard is filled in, click OK. Windows adds the new item to the list.

TIP

If you're adding a Web site to your Active Desktop, you should know the Web address before you start to add it. If necessary, search the Web for the URL before you take these steps.

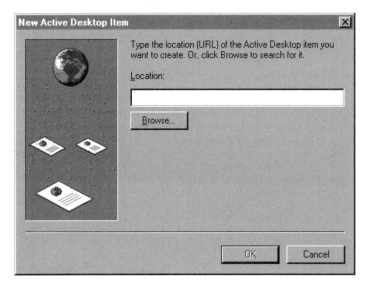

Figure 3-17 *The first panel of the New Active Desktop Item wizard, for adding Web pictures or Web sites to your Active Desktop*

If you add a Web site, you see the Subscribe dialog box, as shown in Figure 3-18.

Figure 3-18 *Subscribe dialog box*

You can change the schedule of updating a page, set the type of notification you receive about updated pages, and set up the login name and password for protected Web sites. Clicking the Customize button starts the Website Subscription Wizard for performing these changes and setups. The Login button opens the Login dialog box, in case you need to change only the login setup.

An Active Desktop with an HTML document and an animated GIF appears in Figure 3-19. Notice that Active Desktop items appear in the background, even behind the desktop icons.

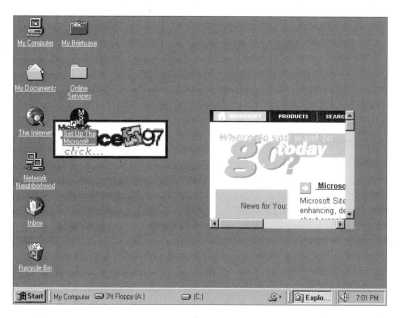

Figure 3-19   *Windows 98 Active Desktop with an HTML document and animated GIF as the background*

Deactivating or removing items from the Active Desktop

On the Web tab of the Display Properties dialog box, you can deactivate an item or remove it entirely. To deactivate an item, clear the check box beside its name in the list. To remove it, select the object and then click the Delete button.

With or Without Desktop Icons

When you first turn on Active Desktop, Windows 98 still shows the desktop icons you saw in Windows 95. You can hide these icons. To do so, right-click the Active Desktop and then click Show Icons on the shortcut menu to clear the check mark. To turn icons back on in the Active Desktop, right-click the Active Desktop and then click Show Icons on the shortcut menu.

Hiding the desktop icons doesn't make them inaccessible. The taskbar now provides a Desktop toolbar, which displays your desktop icons. (For more information about taskbar toolbars, see the "Toolbars on the Taskbar" section earlier in the chapter.)

Desktop Power for Experienced Users

Experienced users gain many of the same benefits from the taskbar and the Start button—quickly launching a new program, rapidly switching to another task, and so on—as novices do. However, experienced users need more:

- They need a powerful way to browse and manage file hierarchies, whether or not they are local.
- They need to be able to customize the user interface to suit their needs and tastes.
- They need to be able to take shortcuts to get tasks done more quickly and efficiently.
- They need to be able to *do* more.

The new user interface in Windows 98 enables experienced users to do more, as the following sections describe.

Shortcuts: For Accessing Objects

Shortcuts are an extremely powerful tool for increasing efficiency, and they work much the same way in Windows 98 as they do in Windows 95. They are especially useful in a networked environment. You can create a shortcut to any object, such as a file, program, network folder, Control Panel tool, disk drive, or Web page and place it anywhere in the user interface or in an application. Opening the shortcut opens the object that the shortcut is "pointing" to. For example, if you create a shortcut to My Network Folder on a network server and drop the shortcut on the local desktop, opening the shortcut actually opens My Network Folder. Icons that have a small "jump" arrow in the lower-left corner, as shown here, represent shortcuts:

You create shortcuts by selecting an object in Windows Explorer and choosing Create Shortcut from the File menu or by right-clicking the object and choosing Create Shortcut. After you create shortcuts, you can rename them. If the shortcut is for an object that was created after installation of Windows 98 and the object is renamed, Windows 98 changes the shortcut definition to reflect the new name. For example, if you create a shortcut on the local desktop to \\Server\Share\Public Folder and the folder is subsequently renamed, the shortcut will still work. You can delete a shortcut without affecting the object to which it points.

Uses for shortcuts are virtually limitless, but the following are some common powerful uses for them:

- **Shortcuts in the Programs folder** In Windows 98, the icons that appear on the Start button's Programs menu, which you can customize by choosing Settings and then Taskbar & Start Menu from the Start menu, also appear as shortcuts in the Programs folder. When a shortcut is added to or deleted from the Programs folder, it is also added to or deleted from the Programs menu. As a result, you can keep shortcuts to all your favorite programs in one central place, regardless of where the programs are stored.

- **Shortcuts on the desktop** You can create shortcuts to commonly accessed files, programs, drives, folders, and utilities right on your desktop. This capability is especially powerful with network resources because it allows you to avoid complicated browsing or drive mapping to access network folders.

- **Embedded shortcuts in applications** You can drag a shortcut to a file stored on the network to an e-mail message. When the message recipient double-clicks the shortcut, the network file opens. This process is much more efficient than embedding the file in an e-mail message because the message is smaller; embedding shortcuts also cuts down on file version proliferation.

Properties: For Customizing All Objects

Property sheets are found throughout Windows 98. All objects in the user interface carry context-sensitive properties that you can access and customize by choosing Properties from the File menu or by right-clicking the object and choosing Properties.

Right-Clicking: For Performing Actions on Objects

Right-clicking, like properties, is a pervasive, context-sensitive feature of Windows 98. Usability tests have shown that right-clicking as a shortcut way of performing common actions on an object is a very popular power-user feature. In general, however, right-clicking is not a feature that novices discover or remember, so most functions that can be performed by right-clicking can also be performed by choosing the corresponding menu commands.

Focus on Documents: Working the Way Users Work

OLE introduced the concept of "document-centricity" by incorporating in-place editing of objects. In a document-centric environment, the application window changes and the document stays the same, so that software works the way people work, rather than vice versa.

The user interface in Windows 98 uses the concept of document-centricity in the following subtle but powerful ways:

- **Windows as views of objects** When you open an object from anywhere in the user interface, a new window opens. Logically, the title of the new window is the same as that of the object's icon. For example, when the icon of a Microsoft Word document named My Document is double-clicked from anywhere in the user interface, a new window entitled My Document - Microsoft Word opens.

- **Document creation from within folders and in the Windows Explorer** From within any folder in Windows 98, you can create new files in place by choosing New from the File menu and then selecting a file type. On the desktop, you can right-click to display the shortcut menu, which contains these same commands. An icon like the one shown here (for a Microsoft PowerPoint document) is then created to represent the new file:

This flexibility makes it very convenient to manage files based on projects, rather than at the whim of an application.

Long Filenames

Windows 98 allows filenames of up to 255 characters. An example is shown here:

To ensure backward compatibility with existing MS-DOS–based and Win16-based applications, file extensions have not been eliminated entirely; they are simply hidden from view by default.

You can rename files in place in Windows 98 by selecting the file, clicking the filename, and typing the new name. Hidden file extensions are not affected when files are renamed. You can also rename files from within the common dialog boxes, such as the Open and Save As dialog boxes.

ToolTips for Window Controls

In Windows 98, positioning the mouse pointer over the System menu, the Minimize button, the Restore button, the Maximize button, and the Close button displays a ToolTip with the name of the button.

Scrolling Menus

In Windows 95, if a Start menu submenu contained more commands than could fit on one panel, Windows 95 displayed a second (or even third) panel to continue the list. Windows 98 uses instead a scrolling menu, the same as you find in Microsoft Office 97 applications. A scrolling menu has only one panel. If the number of commands exceeds the length of the panel, you see a scroll arrow at the bottom of the list. Position the mouse pointer on the scroll arrow to scroll the menu. After you scroll the menu, a scroll arrow appears at the top of the list so that you can scroll to the top of the list again.

Windows Explorer

Windows Explorer, shown in Figure 3-20, is powerful, flexible, efficient, and extensible. For many power users of Windows 98, Windows Explorer will be the primary interface for navigating through information.

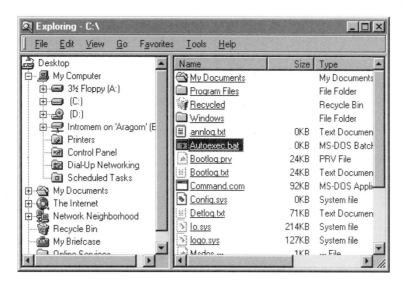

Figure 3-20 *Windows Explorer*

Here is an overview of the major features of Windows Explorer:

- **Single view of a world of information**   Windows Explorer is the eyes of any PC running Windows 98. With it, you can view the entire namespace (all resources, local or connected) from the equivalent of 10,000 feet, or you can zoom down to the equivalent of 10 inches. You can quickly and easily browse and manage My Computer and the Network Neighborhood through Windows Explorer.

- **Flexible and customizable**   From the Windows Explorer toolbar and the View menu, you can choose to view folder contents in several ways, including Large Icon, Small Icon, List, and Details views. In Details view, you can easily sort folder contents by name, size, type, and modification date by clicking the column title. (Clicking a column title a second time reverses the sorting order.)

- **Rich information about objects in Details view**   Details view provides a wealth of context-sensitive information about folder contents:
  - Files retain their identifying icons.
  - Drive sizes and free space (even mapped network drives) are reported in My Computer.
  - Descriptions of Control Panel tools are provided.
  - Jobs in the print queue are listed in the Printers folder.
  - Comments on other computers in the Network Neighborhood can be viewed.

All the powerful right-click and properties features described earlier in this chapter are available in Windows Explorer.

My Computer

The Windows design team made the following discoveries about basic file management and browsing:

- Exposed hierarchies are intimidating and unintuitive.
- Dual-pane views—hierarchy on the left and contents on the right—are also intimidating and unintuitive. Novices have difficulty understanding the connection between the logical tree hierarchy pane and the contents pane.

- An object-oriented user interface works well for basic tasks but not for complex ones. The general belief is that the more object oriented a user interface is, the easier it is to use. However, this is not the case. Although the direct manipulation of screen objects to achieve logical results is important for basic tasks (such as dragging a file from a folder to the desktop), direct manipulation to carry out more advanced tasks (such as dragging a file to a printer icon) is not intuitive. On the other hand, selecting an object with the mouse and then browsing menus or buttons for actions to perform on that object is intuitive.

- Large icon views are much more comfortable than list views.

- Whether novice users can find what they're looking for and whether they feel comfortable and "grounded" along the way are the defining characteristics of a good browsing experience. Efficiency and speed are less important.

The My Computer default browsing model in Windows 98 is based on these findings.

In Windows 95, you open a folder or drive by double-clicking it or by selecting it and choosing Open from the File menu. In Windows 98, the default window setup requires only a single click, just as following a hyperlink on a Web page does. This setup is called Web View because you "surf" your computer's disks, network drives, and Web sites in the same way in every window. New windows open in large icon view, as shown in Figure 3-21, which also shows several new features of windows in Windows 98.

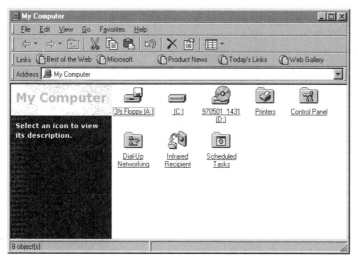

Figure 3-21   *"Surfing" My Computer*

The view of the My Computer window in Figure 3-21 on the preceding page shows the three toolbars that you can add to a window: Standard Buttons, Address Bar, and Links. The Standard Buttons are the familiar buttons of Internet Explorer with two additional buttons: Up, the same as the Up One Level button in Windows 95; and Views, a button that puts the View menu commands on a button.

Notice that in Web view the icons named in the window show underlines. These underlines indicate that these icons are hyperlinks that open the disk drives. In windows that show folders, the hyperlinks open the folder or a file. In this view, to select an icon, you simply point to it; you don't have to click it, as you did in Windows 95. (You can turn off the single-click feature and revert to the Windows 95 method. To do so, choose Options from the View menu, and then select Classic Style on the General tab.)

TIP

To select more than one item in a folder, point to the first item, and then hold down either the Shift key (to select a number of files in succession) or the Ctrl key (to select individual files not in succession), and then point to the last file you want to select (Shift key method) or point to the other files you want to select (Ctrl key method). You must pause over an icon to select it.

Along the left side, the panel displays helpful information. If you point to a disk drive, the panel displays drive information—size and free space. If you point to a folder or file, the panel displays a description of the folder. When you open a folder, this panel disappears.

Explorer bars

Along the left side of the window, you can display one of four Explorer bars: Search, Favorites, History, and Channels. The Explorer Bar submenu on the View menu also contains a None command for turning off an Explorer Bar.

- **Search** The Search Explorer Bar sets up searching on the Internet so that you can locate Web pages that contain the information you're looking for.

- **Favorites** The Favorites Explorer Bar displays items stored in your Favorites folder. This way you can conveniently jump to any favorite Web site, disk, network connection, document, or folder.

- **History** The History Explorer Bar displays two categories: Week Of (the week before today) and Today. Each list displays Web connections you've made so that you can easily and quickly reconnect to a Web site you visited today or in the preceding week.

- **Channels** The Channels Explorer Bar displays the MSN channels you've set up in your Channels folder. Using this bar, you can quickly turn on an MSN channel.

The Network Neighborhood

The network client in Windows 98 makes browsing networks not only possible but also easy, regardless of the network provider (Microsoft Windows NT Server, Novell NetWare, Windows 95, and Windows 98). (For more details about the networking capabilities of Windows 98, see Chapter 9, "Networking.")

Network browsing is accomplished by means of the Network Neighborhood, which sits on the desktop and logically represents the resources not available in My Computer. (The Find/Network Computer command on the Start menu is an alternative to the Network Neighborhood icon.) Its icon is shown here:

Browsing the network with the Network Neighborhood is as easy as browsing a local hard disk and supplies the following benefits:

- **Top-level configuration** The network administrator can configure the Network Neighborhood to display only those PCs, servers, and printers that are in the user's immediate workgroup. Top-level configuration insulates the user from the vastness of large corporate networks. The user can still browse the larger network by opening Entire Network from within the Network Neighborhood. (Until Windows 95, browsing the larger network wasn't possible.) When you browse a server, network connections are made without drive mapping (the assigning of new drive letters to a specific network resource).

- **Systemwide support for UNC pathnames** This technology makes obsolete the process of mapping drives and allows natural network browsing through the Network Neighborhood. UNC pathname support allows a whole host of usability improvements, of which network browsing is just one.

- **The Network Control Panel tool** This tool consolidates all networking configuration in one location, thereby eliminating the difficulty of configuring networking.

- **Easy drive mapping** A Map Network Drive option on the Windows Explorer Tools menu makes drive mapping available in Windows 98. (Power users can also right-click My Computer.) Mapped drives appear as connections in My Computer.

- **Networking and mobility** The user interface in Windows 98 was designed with networking and remote access in mind. For example, when a file is copied over a slow-link (a modem connection), the Copy dialog box includes an "Estimated time to completion" status message.

- **Networking integration with new common dialog boxes** The common dialog boxes, which are standardized in applications that make use of them, provide a consistent way to open and save files on network resources as well as on local drives. In addition, you can browse the Network Neighborhood directly from the common dialog boxes, and you can perform the majority of basic file management tasks from them.

The Recycle Bin

The Recycle Bin is an easily recognizable metaphor for being able to "throw away" files and then recover them simply by removing them from the bin. Files deleted in Windows 98, or deleted from the common dialog boxes in applications that support them, are moved to the Recycle Bin. You can remove an item from the Recycle Bin and drag or cut/copy/paste it to another location, or you can restore it to its original location by selecting the file in Windows Explorer and choosing Undo Delete from the Edit menu.

The Recycle Bin graphically indicates whether it is empty or contains items. Information about "deleted" items is available in the Recycle Bin's Details view, as shown in Figure 3-22.

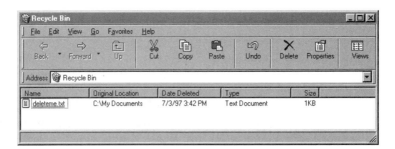

Figure 3-22 *The Recycle Bin in Details view showing deleted items and additional information*

Undoing File Operations

When working with files on your system, how many times have you said to yourself, "I didn't mean to do that!" after accidentally deleting, renaming, moving, or copying a file that you didn't intend to? Windows 98 has a simple answer for putting things back the way they were: it provides a multilevel undo feature that allows you to undo one or more of your preceding actions. You can undo file deletions, renames, moves, or copies simply by choosing Undo from the Edit menu of any user interface window, as shown in Figure 3-23.

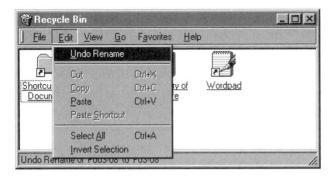

Figure 3-23   *The Undo command on the Edit menu, which you can use to undo file operations*

Wizards

Originally developed in Microsoft's Applications Group and used in Microsoft applications such as Word and Excel, wizards are a proven tool that make it easy for all levels of users to take advantage of powerful but complex functionality. Windows 98 uses wizards throughout the operating system to perform the following operations:

- Display Setup options during the installation process
- Add a new device, such as a printer or a modem, to the system
- Set up remote access in the Network Neighborhood
- Create a shortcut for an application
- Install a new application
- Create a Briefcase for synchronizing files between two PCs
- Create a workgroup post office for use with the Microsoft Messaging e-mail client
- Organize the Start menu
- Tune up Windows
- Customize folders

More Help

Online Help in Windows 98 has some new faces. Now Windows Help files can be written as HTML pages, with all the attributes of ActiveX controls, animation, and links. (The Help system introduced in Windows 95 is still included and used for many applications and elements of Windows 98.) Figure 3-24 on the following page shows a Help file done up in HTML.

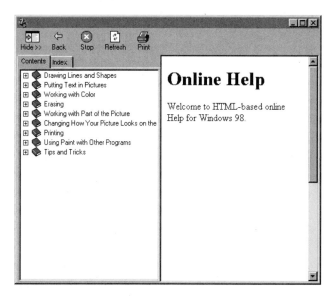

Figure 3-24 *A page from an HTML Help file*

Following are brief descriptions of the major features of the Help system in Windows 98:

- **Web interface** HTML Help files in Windows 98 behave like windows on disk drives and on the Web.

- **The Contents tab** Organized like a book's table of contents, the Contents tab displays top-level "chapters" (iconically represented as books), which you can expand to display topics (iconically represented as pages). Many chapters also have Tips and Tricks sections.

TIP

Right-click on the Contents tab to display a shortcut menu with Open All and Close All commands. To expand all books to show their pages, click Open All. After you open some books, click Close All to close all the open books.

- **The Index tab** You can type or select a topic that suits your information needs, and then click the Display button to display either the information (when only a single chunk of information is available) or a dialog box in which you can select a more specific topic to display.

- **The Hide and Show buttons** If you don't want to see the Contents and Index tabs as you view Help information, you can click the Hide button. This gives you more screen space to do your work while consulting Help. To view the Contents and Index tabs again, click Show.

- **Highly visible Print button** Now when you want to print a Help topic, the print button is in full sight—simply click it.

TIP

To copy Help text, select what you want to copy, right-click on the selected text, and then click Copy on the shortcut menu. If you want to select an entire Help topic, right-click in the Help information, and then click Select All.

- **Shortcut buttons** Shortcut buttons make using Help easy in Windows 98. Some Help topics contain shortcut buttons that take you to the referenced area in Windows 98. The Help window remains visible so that you can work on the task and consult Help at the same time.
- **What's This? button** Many dialog boxes in Windows 98 have a ? button at the right end of their title bars. When you click this button, the pointer changes to a question mark. Clicking any object in the dialog box with this pointer brings up a short description of the object.

Windows 98 HelpDesk

Launching the Windows 98 HelpDesk is the first step in resolving a technical support issue. Links direct you to local and Internet resources, including Online Help, Troubleshooting Wizards, the Microsoft Knowledge Base, the MTS Windows Support Home Page, Windows Update Manager, and the Windows 98 Web-based Bug Reporting Tool. When you have a My Computer window or Control Panel open, you see along the left side a panel that contains two hyperlinks to Microsoft. The Microsoft Home link takes you to the home Web page at Microsoft. The Technical Support link takes you to the MTS Windows Support Home Page. (Of course, you must have an active Internet connection to use these links.)

The Control Panel

The Control Panel consolidates all command, control, and configuration functions in one location. As shown in Figure 3-25 on the next page, in Windows 98, distinct graphics make all important functions instantly recognizable, and previews are offered where appropriate. Also note the two hyperlinks in the left-side panel. You can click these links to jump to the Microsoft Web site and to technical support help.

The individual functions available through the Control Panel tool are discussed in the relevant chapters of this book—for example, the Network tool is discussed in Chapter 9, "Networking." However, one Control Panel tool, Display, controls the configuration of the user interface in Windows 98 and allows users to customize the user interface itself. (See Figure 3-26 on the next page.)

Figure 3-25   *The large icon Web view of the Control Panel*

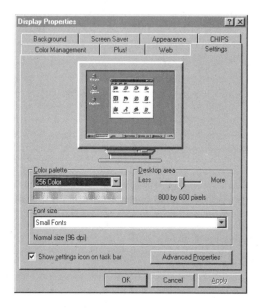

Figure 3-26   *The Display Properties Settings tab*

As shown in Figure 3-26, the Display Properties property sheet has the following six tabs:

- **Background** Allows pattern and wallpaper configuration and preview.
- **Screen Saver** Allows screen saver configuration and preview. One new type of screen saver has been added to the list—Channel Subscription Preview. This screen saver uses the MSN channel you select as your screen saver. (Of course, you must have an MSN account.)
- **Appearance** Allows configuration and preview of all the user interface metrics (fonts, sizes, colors, and so on).
- **Settings** Allows configuration of monitor resolution and color palette size.
- **Web** Allows setting up the Active Desktop.
- **Plus!** Allows setting special features, such as font smoothing, full window drag, and changing the icons for the standard shortcuts on the Desktop (My Computer, Network Neighborhood, Recycle Bin—full, and Recycle Bin—empty). The Plus! tab is available only as an add-on package in Windows 95, but it's standard in Windows 98.

Depending on your hardware configuration, you might also see either or both of the following tabs:

- **Color Management** Allows you to select the default color profile for your monitor.
- **CHIPS** Allows you to set hardware options such as refresh rate and display options (CRT, LCD, or both).

The Printers Folder

The Printers folder, shown in Figure 3-27, offers one-stop shopping for printer management and configuration.

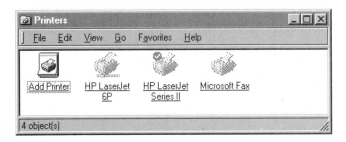

Figure 3-27 *The Printers folder in Windows 98*

The Printers folder is discussed in more detail in Chapter 10, "Printing."

Font Settings

The Fonts folder in the Windows directory represents a single namespace in which all fonts used in the system can be installed or manipulated. (If any fonts are identified in the WIN.INI file, Windows 98 moves them to the Fonts folder on startup, so all fonts in the system reside in a single location.) Different views of the Fonts folder present additional information about the fonts installed in the system. Figure 3-28 shows the large icon view.

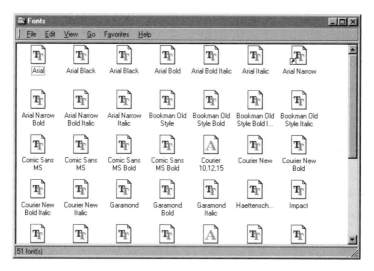

Figure 3-28 *The large icon view of the Fonts folder*

Operations can be performed on fonts in the same way they are performed on other file system objects. For example, you can remove a font from the Fonts folder by dragging it to another location, delete a font from the system by deleting it from the Fonts folder, and add a font to the system by dragging it from another location into the Fonts folder.

4

Introducing Internet Explorer 4.0

MICROSOFT INTERNET EXPLORER 4.0 IS AN open, integrated suite of Internet software that includes the industry's premier Internet client and basic collaboration solution for users, IT managers, and developers. Internet Explorer 4.0 expands on the innovation introduced in Internet Explorer 3.0 to achieve Microsoft's vision: complete integration of the Internet and the PC. The result is a dramatically easier and more personalized way for you to get the most out of the Internet.

Microsoft listened closely to users while designing Internet Explorer 4.0. Users had complaints in five major areas that they clearly wanted addressed:

- Finding useful information on the Internet is difficult.
- Internet bandwidth limits the productivity and enjoyment of browsing the Web.
- Web content rarely lives up to expectations.
- Communication capabilities are sorely lacking.
- The tools and methods for browsing the Web and using PCs are inconsistent.

Internet Explorer 4.0 addresses each of these areas by introducing innovations that fall into four basic categories:

- **Best browser** Internet Explorer 4.0 builds user-focused improvements onto Internet Explorer 3.0's strengths. Internet Explorer 4.0 introduces Dynamic HTML, which offers significant benefits to users and provides next-generation development capabilities that Web site authors can use to maximize the impact of their content while minimizing round-trips to the server.

- **Complete communication and collaboration** Internet Explorer 4.0 delivers a complete and integrated set of tools for every type of user—from basic services such as e-mail to more advanced capabilities such as conferencing, broadcasting, and Web authoring.

- **Webcasting of sites and channels** The Web can now be brought to the desktop. You can have the information you care about delivered directly to your desktop when you want it, in the format you want it. Internet Explorer 4.0 also notifies you automatically when your favorite Web sites change and lets you read sites offline for greater convenience and less expense.

- **True Web integration** True Web integration means two things in Internet Explorer 4.0. First, the Internet and intranets become a seamless part of your desktop operating system, with the browser and browserlike exploration available in every Microsoft Windows view. Second, Internet Explorer 4.0 delivers tight integration across its suite of products. That means consistency— including a common toolbar—across all the applications and an easy way to switch among tools.

Just who is the new version of Internet Explorer for? The answer is "everyone," and here's why:

- For users, Internet Explorer 4.0 delivers a richer, more integrated and personalized browsing experience, providing an easy, complete way to browse the Internet, intranets, and their local PC. Users will be able to interact with Web sites, take advantage of full-featured communication capabilities, and find information on the Web more easily than ever.

- For international users, Internet Explorer 4.0 provides the best Unicode support available, support for multilingual display and input, and an easy resource format that facilitates localization. To support international developers, Microsoft delivers Internet Explorer 4.0 in 12 languages: English, Chinese (simplified), Chinese (traditional), French, German, Greek, Italian, Japanese, Korean, Portuguese (Brazilian), Polish, and Spanish.

- For corporate IS and IT managers, Internet Explorer 4.0's combining of the browser and the operating system reduces overall cost of ownership while at the same time allowing users to be more productive, extending existing functionality, and leveraging the existing investment in training, thereby reducing training costs. New and improved administration tools, including sophisticated security features, will ease migration to the intranet and make it easier for administrators to maintain and control internal Webs.

- Webmasters, Internet content providers, and developers can take advantage of Internet Explorer 4.0's platform for innovation, which supports the broadest range of Internet standards in the industry. Internet Explorer 4.0 also delivers powerful new capabilities through Dynamic HTML, which is introduced in this product, and ActiveX controls. Developers will be able to create fully interactive products with compelling content.

New Features in Internet Explorer 4.0

With the Internet Explorer 4.0 suite, you get the fastest, most personalized Web browser around. You also get the broadest set of communication and collaboration tools available, which you can use for everything from sending richly formatted e-mail to using your computer as an Internet phone, designing your own Web site, or holding a video conversation. The new features make Internet Explorer 4.0 easy to use, complete, and personal:

- **It's easier** Browsing the Internet is easier now that you can take advantage of improved searching, an AutoComplete feature that makes typing Internet addresses easier, and Smart Favorites, which lets let you know when your favorite Web sites have been updated. And if you choose the Integrated Shell option, you'll now have a single way to browse the Internet, an intranet, and your computer.

- **It's complete** Internet Explorer 4.0 comes with all you need to get the most out of the Internet. In addition to the best Internet browser available, you get full-featured tools for e-mail, newsgroups, video conferences, chat sessions, application-sharing, broadcasting, and authoring and publishing Web pages.

- **It's personal** You can have the Web *your* way with Internet Explorer 4.0. You can customize Quick Links and organize your favorite Web sites simply by dragging and dropping. You can create a personalized Internet Start page. Using the Integrated Shell option, you can turn your desktop into your own interactive, multimedia Web page in which the content you care about most updates automatically.

In the following sections, some of the key new features of Internet Explorer 4.0 are described.

Java Innovations

Internet Explorer 4.0 includes features that make it easier for developers to create richer, more full-featured Java applications for the Web. The performance improvements in Internet Explorer 4.0 make the applications run faster than ever. Internet Explorer 4.0 also introduces enhancements to security, ensuring that interacting with Java applications won't harm your computer or threaten your privacy.

- **Improved performance** Internet Explorer 4.0 maintains its performance leadership as the fastest way to run Java applications, delivering performance improvements in the virtual machine, Just-in-Time compiler, and class libraries.

- **Full integration with ActiveX** Developers can now access ActiveX controls as Java Beans (components), and Java Beans as ActiveX controls. This integration is seamless, automatic, and bidirectional. In addition, developers will now have a seamless operation for debugging between Microsoft Visual Basic, Scripting Edition (VBScript), JScript, and Java.

- **New Object Model** Internet Explorer 4.0's new Object Model is exposed through Java libraries, allowing Java developers to manipulate pages dynamically and tightly integrate Java applications with Web pages.

- **Improved Abstract Windowing Toolkit (AWT)** The new AWT reduces overhead and improves performance.

- **New Application Foundation Classes (AFC)** Support for Java includes Microsoft's recent introduction of AFC, a comprehensive set of cross-platform class libraries that help software developers quickly create commercial-quality applications, for Java. AFC delivers a rich suite of graphics as well as user interface and multimedia capabilities to authors using Java in their Web pages. Internet Explorer 4.0 is the first browser to support AFC.

- **Java Development Kit (JDK) 1.1 compatibility** Internet Explorer 4.0 is fully compatible with all the cross-platform features of JDK 1.1.

- **New multimedia class libraries** All the functionality of DirectX 5 media and the DirectX 5 foundation is provided as cross-platform Java class libraries, enabling developers to manipulate and animate a full set of media types.

- **Capabilities-based security model** Internet Explorer 4.0 expands the code-signing Authenticode feature to specify at a granular level which system capabilities—for example, the file system—a Java application can access through the use of digital signatures.

Search Bar

When you click the Search button on the toolbar, Internet Explorer 4.0 displays a Search bar, shown in Figure 4-1. The Search bar displays search results independent of the main browser area. This capability responds to one of the main difficulties Web users report: finding it cumbersome to return to their search results after visiting a site. The Search bar slightly reduces available content area and remains visible until you press the Search button again. Each time you open the Search bar, you'll see a drop-down list of search engines that you can choose from. The results of the search appear only in the Search bar. When you rest the pointer over a result, Internet Explorer 4.0 also displays a summary of the site in a ToolTip.

Figure 4-1   *The Search bar activated in the Internet Explorer 4.0 browser*

When you select a site from the Results list, the site appears in the main browser area, keeping the Search bar available for future searches. The results remain in the Search bar, so you can easily move from result to result without repeatedly using the Back button to return to the search results page. Internet Explorer 4.0 also preserves the state of the search, so if you click the Search button again during the same session, the results of the previous search are displayed.

The Search bar takes advantage of the component architecture of Internet Explorer 4.0—it's not simply a frame but a separate browser control.

Smart Toolbar

Internet Explorer 4.0 includes an "intelligent" toolbar that recognizes whether you're looking at an HTML page or files and folders. As shown in Figure 4-2, the Smart Toolbar automatically reconfigures itself, adding and subtracting tools based on the type of file being displayed.

Figure 4-2   *The Smart Toolbar changes between browsing a Web page (top bar) and browsing files and folders (bottom bar)*

For example, you don't need a Stop button if you're looking at a folder or a file. You're not actually downloading anything. By the same token, you don't need Cut and Paste buttons when you're viewing a Web page that you can't edit. The Smart Toolbar makes the proper adjustments but always gives you the options of moving Back and Forward.

> **NOTE**
> The Smart Address bar also knows the difference between your system directories and folders (\\) and an Internet or intranet address (//). Simply type where you want to go in the Address bar.

History Bar

The History bar lists the Web pages you've visited, making it easy to jump back to a site that you went to days or even weeks ago. The pages are grouped by time, site, and individual page.

Thumbnail View

You can preview multiple Web sites simultaneously without visiting the sites by selecting Thumbnail View. Because Thumbnail View is extensible, you can apply it to any folder to take a quick peek at its contents.

Thumbnail views of Web Favorites

Have you ever seen some cool site on the Web and added it to your list of Favorites but then can't remember which of your Favorites it is? Try this:

1. In Windows Explorer, go to your Favorites folder. For example, type *C:/Windows/Favorites* in the Address bar to move to your Favorites folder.
2. Click Thumbnails on the View menu.

Now just watch the thumbnail views of all your favorite sites appear in the right-hand frame.

You can accomplish the same thing by clicking Favorites on the toolbar in either Windows Explorer or Internet Explorer and then clicking Organize Favorites. When the Favorites frame appears, right-click on it, point to View, and click Thumbnails. Your Organize Favorites window will look something like Figure 4-3.

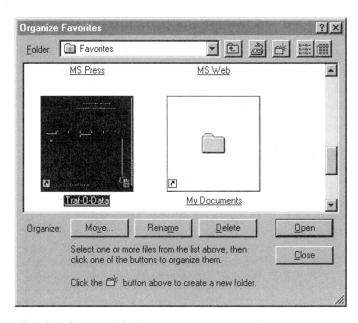

Figure 4-3   *Thumbnail View in the Organize Favorites window*

Refreshing a Web thumbnail

To see the current version of a Web page that changes regularly, right-click a thumbnail and select Refresh Thumbnail from the shortcut menu.

Thumbnail views of other folders

Thumbnail views also give you a bird's-eye view of your important folders. To see thumbnail views of folders other than Favorites, take the steps listed at the top of the following page.

1. In the Address bar, type the path to the folder you want to view and press Enter.

2. Right-click on the folder, and select Properties from the shortcut menu.

3. In the Properties dialog box, check Enable Thumbnail View and click OK. (See Figure 4-4.)

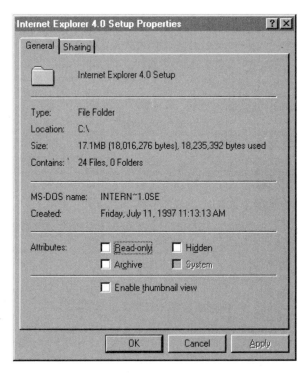

Figure 4-4   *Enabling Thumbnail View for a folder*

AutoComplete

AutoComplete makes it simple for you to type in URLs and reduces the opportunity for typographical mistakes. It does so by providing heuristics for completing URL addresses based on sites you've visited before. It also adds prefixes and suffixes to Internet addresses and corrects syntax errors. AutoComplete is similar to the AutoFill feature in Microsoft Excel.

AutoComplete uses your history to predict what you'll enter in the Address bar. The predicted text is displayed as a selected region of characters. You can easily override the suggestions, however, by typing over them.

AutoComplete includes the following features and shortcuts:

- Skip to break or separation characters (such as \\ \ . , ? +) in URLs by pressing and holding Ctrl and then pressing the left or right arrow key.
- Search your history file by typing the beginning of an address and then pressing the up or down arrow key to complete it.
- Press Ctrl+Enter to cause a quick completion to *http://www.<what you typed>.com*. You can customize this feature through a Registry key.
- Right-click the Address bar to display a context menu, which includes available completions for the current text.

The AutoComplete features in the Windows Run command (on the Start menu) are provided not only for Internet addresses but also for file paths.

Smart Favorites

Smart Favorites automatically checks your favorite Web pages for updates since the last time you visited. It notifies you of any updates by adding a red "gleam" next to the site on the Favorites menu, as shown in Figure 4-5, as well as displaying a ToolTip that lists both the last time you viewed the site and the last time the site was updated.

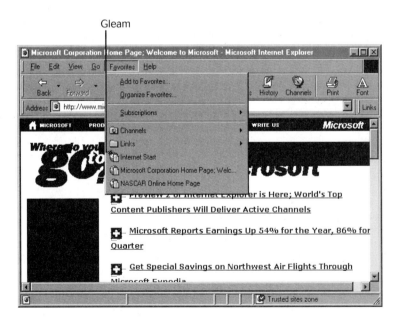

Figure 4-5 *Smart Favorites*

NOTE

Don't confuse Smart Favorites with Internet Explorer 4.0's Webcasting, which automatically downloads sites that have changed. Smart Favorites let you see which of your favorite sites have changed but without automatically downloading them all. Because many users have a slew of favorites, Smart Favorites can save you connection costs.

With Smart Favorites, Web site authors can include their own text in metatags, and their customized content will appear in a ToolTip when the user rests the pointer over the site name in the Favorites menu. The following metatags are an example of inserting author information into a Web site ToolTip:

```
<meta http-equiv="Bulletin-Text" content="Just Released:
Microsoft Internet Explorer 4.0. Download It Today.">
<meta http-equiv ="Content-Type" CONTENT="text/html; charset=iso-8859-1">
<meta name="Author" content="Microsoft Corporation">
<meta name="Description" content="Microsoft Corporate Information, Product
Support, and More">
```

TIP

Web site authors will want to include these tags in the headers of their Web pages for several reasons. When a company is releasing a new product, for example, users can get that information directly from their Favorites menu. If a site has new articles that will appeal to readers, authors can insert the information in the header tags and Internet Explorer 4.0 will display it prominently. Smart Favorites makes it easy for site authors to put information directly in front of users to motivate them to browse a particular site.

You can also direct Internet Explorer 4.0 to download a site to your computer, automatically dialing the connection and downloading the content to view offline. You can specify how often each site is checked and download only what has changed. You can also specify how many levels are downloaded from a site and how you're to be notified when a favorite site has been updated—either by a an icon on the Windows taskbar or by an e-mail message.

Drag and Drop Quick Links

It's even easier to get to your favorite sites with Internet Explorer 4.0. Now you can customize the Quick Links on the Links bar with a drag of your mouse. Find a link to a page that you'd like to have a Quick Link button for on your toolbar, and then simply drag the link to one of the buttons on the Links bar.

You can also create shortcuts to Web sites by dragging and dropping. From any Web site or folder, click the icon in the upper-left corner of the Internet Explorer window and drag anywhere to create a shortcut. With local or local area network (LAN) content, right-clicking and then dragging the icon enables you to move, copy, or create a shortcut to that location.

Back and Forward Buttons

You won't need to click the Back or Forward button repeatedly to return to a page. By right-clicking the Back and Forward buttons, you can view a list of the sites you've visited most recently on a drop-down menu. You can also access the drop-down menu by clicking the new down arrow on the right-hand side of the Back and Forward buttons. Then just click the listing you want, and you'll return to that page immediately.

Full-Screen Mode

Internet Explorer 4.0 provides Full-screen mode, which removes all toolbars, desk icons, and scrollbars from the screen to make more room for Web pages. This view reduces the need for you to scroll down to see the full contents of a page. Content providers can also employ Kiosk mode, in which the computer serves as a one-purpose tool such as a terminal emulator.

To clear the screen for Web content, select Full Screen from the View menu. The only element remaining on the screen in addition to the Web page is a floating palette with which you can turn off Full-screen mode at any time.

Improved Printing

Users have always found it frustrating to have to display every page they want to print. They've also been dissatisfied because the formatting of a Web page was different than the formatting of a printed document. Internet Explorer 4.0 is the first browser to begin implementing the new cascading style sheet extensions for printing, which are currently in a World Wide Web Consortium (W3C) proposal.

Internet Explorer 4.0 uses the standard cascading style sheet specification to define numerous page-formatting features, including background printing of documents; recursive printing of all links on a document; and intelligent frame printing options, such as printing only one frame or all the frames on a page. Your printed content will look as great as online content. Internet Explorer 4.0 also caches the hyperlinks on a page for printing, making it easy to print an entire Web site with one visit.

Ratings System

If you're concerned about the types of information your children or employees can access on the Internet, you'll be interested in the feature in Internet Explorer 4.0 that lets you block what people can see on your computer or network. Internet Explorer 4.0 provides this protection by supporting a ratings standard from the Platform for Internet Content Selection (PICS) committee. The ratings standard lets you control access to online material using any PICS-based Internet ratings system. The built-in ratings system, named RSACi, lets you block an entire type of content—such as language, nudity, sex, or violence—or set access to a degree that's acceptable to you. Figure 4-6 shows the Content Advisor dialog box, accessed from the Content tab on the Options dialog box, in which you set Ratings.

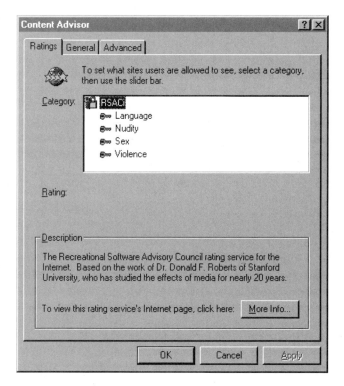

Figure 4-6   *Set system ratings for your computer in the Content Advisor dialog box*

How the ratings system works

Parents and supervisors can use Internet Explorer 4.0 to set passwords that are required to view any Web site. Access to unrated Web sites can also be blocked. And because the system is open, you can set up your own ratings system to select what types of content you deem inappropriate for viewing on your computer or network. To learn more about ratings systems you can use with Internet Explorer 4.0, see the PICS Web site at:

http://www.w3.orgPICS/

For more information on obtaining a rating for your own site, go to the Recreational Software Advisory Council site at:

http://www.rsac.org/

Dynamic HTML

Until now, Web authors have faced a tough trade-off: they've added cool new features to their Web pages, but more often than not, those features have brought surfing to a crawl for users. The feature usually took a long time to download or involved interactivity, which usually required that an entire page be reloaded whenever the user clicked an item offering something special. Internet Explorer 4.0 solves this dilemma with Microsoft's Dynamic HTML, a collection of features that extends the capabilities of traditional HTML, giving Web authors more flexibility, design options, and creative control over the appearance and behavior of Web pages as well as an easier and faster way to author interactive Web pages. Dynamic HTML, which was developed in collaboration with the W3C and is fully compatible with all existing W3C recommendations, allows Web authors to add a new dimension of interactivity without slowing performance in the process.

Dynamic HTML offers an entirely new way for Web authors to control the HTML tags they already know. Now every element on a Web page—whether it's an image, link, applet, heading, or the like—is an object to which Web authors can add functionality. Much of Dynamic HTML's functionality and flexibility comes from adding "intelligence" to the user's computer. When the user places the mouse over the object or clicks on it, the element can deliver additional information or options—without having to go back to a Web server to do so. In this way, authors can use Dynamic HTML to pack greater value into their Web sites.

Here are some of the key aspects of Dynamic HTML that will soon make traditional, static HTML pages a thing of the past:

- **Full HTML Object Model** Dynamic HTML's central Object Model is what gives authors access to every HTML tag on a page. You don't need to be an expert programmer to create a truly dynamic experience for the user—simply add a little JavaScript or VBScript to the standard tags already in use throughout the Web. You can also extend the capabilities of Dynamic HTML through Java applets or ActiveX controls.

- **2-D positioning** Now Web authors can position elements with precision to make sites look precisely as they want them to. They can also make objects overlap and become transparent. Combined with Dynamic HTML's other features, these new positioning capabilities allow authors to move elements around, thereby animating their pages. Users who aren't running Internet Explorer 4.0 won't catch all the new capabilities, but they'll always see a great-looking page because the model is based on HTML and style sheets.

- **Data binding** Once users receive data from a Web site that's enabled with Dynamic HTML, they can sort, filter, and modify the data repeatedly—without ever hitting the server again. By reducing the number of hits to the server, data binding speeds up operations for both the user and the Web site.

- **Dynamic HTML multimedia controls** Dynamic HTML's multimedia effects make Internet Explorer 4.0 the most exciting Web browser available, providing CD-ROM quality to multimedia pages and allowing them to download quickly. The multimedia controls shipped with Internet Explorer 4.0 make it easy for authors to create exciting pages that tap into the power of Dynamic HTML.

These aspects are described in more detail in the following sections.

Object Model of Dynamic HTML

What you see is only the start of what you get from a Web page when it's authored using Dynamic HTML's Full HTML Object Model, which is based on the Document Object Model proposed by Microsoft to the W3C. Consider an organizational chart, for example. The new Object Model allows a Web author to build the chart so that when a user moves the mouse over a person's name, a pop-up box tells the user more about that person and his or her group. For additional information, the user can simply click a link in the box. This way of presenting the information saves space on the page—and the user's valuable time—by "hiding" information and options until the user wants them.

Another example of how Web authors can use the Object Model is to build a table of contents that users can expand or contract to quickly see key information on a page. Such a table of contents is easy to generate in Dynamic HTML—even for sites that already exist—because the Object Model gives authors control over all the HTML tags on a page. In this case, the author simply adds a few lines of scripting to take the existing heading tags and arrange them into a linked table of contents on the user's command.

Here are some of the things Web authors can do with the Dynamic HTML Object Model simply by adding a little JavaScript or VBScript to standard HTML:

- Build in text that changes and images that move and hide, changing dynamically according to what the user does with the mouse.

- In a picture, have text display when the user moves the mouse over any button.

- Hide and show text as well as move objects around the page.

- Add several layers of information—plus a refreshing splash of color—to ordinary text. Set up a title to dynamically display main headings on a mouse click. Set up the headings to change font color as you point to them. Allow another click to display subheadings that link the user to pages within the Internet Explorer 4.0 site.

- With the Dynamic HTML Object Model mouse-over event capabilities, place the mouse over the words on the page to change the color of the text to signal emphasis and focus.

Dynamic HTML's 2-D Positioning

Web authors have at times felt like backseat drivers. Try as they might to make pages match an image in their mind—often manipulating large bitmaps or laboring with tables to do so—they've often come away feeling as if the steering wheel is in someone else's hands.

With Dynamic HTML's 2-D Positioning, authors now have complete control over the positioning of images and elements and can determine what happens where on every page they create. In addition to being able to specify the exact placement of text and images on a page, authors can now create multiple layers using standards-based cascading style sheets so that images overlap and appear transparent, creating new visual effects that animate pages. Authors can also build interactivity into their sites by combining 2-D Positioning with scripting.

Data Binding in Dynamic HTML

Until now, sending and receiving data over the Web has been difficult and inefficient. Whenever you wanted to look at the data a different way, you had to go back to the Web server and then wait for the entire page to reload. That's all changed with Internet Explorer 4.0. With Internet Explorer 4.0, Web authors can take advantage of Dynamic HTML's data awareness, or data binding, capabilities to create powerful and useful Web-based business applications.

Once you receive information from a site that takes advantage of Dynamic HTML and data binding, you can sort and filter the data repeatedly without initiating another round-trip to the server. For example, let's say you're shopping for a car and request a list of all cars between $15,000 and $20,000. After receiving the list, you decide to narrow the search to only sports cars within that price range. Your computer does all the subsequent processing, refreshing the page to reflect the result of the sort operation. The result: faster performance and less traffic on the Web server. Data binding delivers a painless way to create pages that display such information as lists of prices, product descriptions, airline flights, and company benefits.

Data binding requires little or no additional programming, instead allowing authors simply to insert data into a Web page as an applet or an object that can then be manipulated. HTML elements can be bound to the data using the HTML Data Binding extensions, which have been proposed to the W3C for incorporation into the HTML standard. Authors can choose from data source objects included in Internet Explorer 4.0 or in third-party data source objects, or they can easily build new ones. Once the object is dropped into an HTML page, Internet Explorer 4.0 will recognize it as a data provider. It's that simple.

For more examples of data source objects, check out the Data Source Object Gallery on the Site Builder's Network Web site at:

http://www.microsoft.com/sitebuilder/gallery/files/datasrc/

Data binding delivers all the Best of the Web content when you first download the site. Then, as you select various categories of information, data binding filters the information on your computer—without revisiting the server. That way the content you want to read displays instantly, no matter how many pages you view or the number of times you filter the information.

Data binding provides you with quick access to information and enables you to enter information, make selections, and manipulate data any way you want. Best of all, Data Binding allows you to view pages instantly—even while complex tables are being rendered.

ActiveX Support

Web sites come alive with ActiveX—the standard that Web developers worldwide are using to create dramatic multimedia effects, interactive objects, and sophisticated applications. ActiveX support in Internet Explorer 4.0 allows ActiveX controls to be faster, smaller, and more fun than ever before. In addition, Internet Explorer 4.0 makes it easy for you to quickly uninstall controls you no longer need.

ActiveX technology provides a means for creating innovative, Web-based software components using your existing knowledge and code base. Developers can write ActiveX controls in any language, including C++, Microsoft Visual Basic, and Java. Internet Explorer 4.0 comes installed with a set of new ActiveX multimedia controls that make it easy for developers to deliver dazzling yet low-bandwidth effects on their Web pages. Also, ActiveX controls have full access to the Object Model in Internet Explorer 4.0, which allows developers to manipulate pages dynamically.

For developers who want to create their own ActiveX controls, Internet Explorer 4.0 presents new opportunities to create faster, smaller, and more integrated controls than ever. Here are some of the highlights:

- **Windowless controls** Allow developers to create transparent and nonrectangular controls—a crucial feature for overlapping controls with Internet Explorer 4.0's 2-D layout feature
- **Apartment model controls** Increase performance by taking advantage of the fact that Internet Explorer 4.0 is a threaded container
- **Quick activation** Greatly simplifies the process of initializing controls
- **Support for downloading data asynchronously** Boosts performance for controls that need to download images or other complex data

ActiveX Scripting

Web authors can use ActiveX Scripting to make pages more interactive—capable of asking questions, responding to queries, checking user data, calculating expressions, and connecting to other controls. Expanded support for ActiveX Scripting in Internet Explorer 4.0 provides the fastest, most comprehensive, and language-independent script-handling capability available on the Internet today. Now you can view Web pages that use any popular scripting language—including VBScript and JScript.

ActiveX Scripting lets ActiveX controls "talk" to each other and to other Web applets. It allows ActiveX and Java controls to access the Object Model in Internet Explorer 4.0, which in turn allows developers to author pages that users can manipulate.

In addition to the scripting support in the Internet Explorer 4.0 browser, Microsoft provides the following powerful scripting options:

- The Windows Scripting Host (WSH) is a simple, powerful, and flexible scripting solution for the 32-bit Windows platform. WSH enables scripts—including those written in VBScript and JavaScript—to be run directly on the Windows desktop without being embedded in an HTML document. This low-memory scripting host is ideal for noninteractive scripting needs such as logon and administrative scripting. WSH can be run from either the Windows-based host (WSCRIPT.EXE) or the command shell–based host (CSCRIPT.EXE).
- Microsoft Internet Information Server now supports Active Server Pages, which enables scripts to be run on Web servers. In other words, it enables server-side scripting over the Internet or an intranet.

Communicating and Collaborating with Internet Explorer 4.0

Collaboration across the Internet and intranets is one of the most exciting, avidly discussed topics today. Microsoft is committed to a complete communication and collaboration suite of tools, and the Internet Explorer 4.0 suite provides a solution for whatever Internet-based or intranet-based communication needs users have. Using its modular installation program, you can set up only the pieces you need or take advantage of the extensibility and openness of Internet Explorer 4.0 by integrating it with your existing solutions.

Internet Explorer 4.0 contains the following components for communication and collaboration:

- NetMeeting for conferencing and application sharing—see Chapter 5, "NetMeeting"

- NetShow for broadcasting—see Chapter 6, "NetShow"

- Outlook Express for messaging—see Chapter 7, "Windows Messaging"

- FrontPad for Web authoring and Personal Web Server, Web Publishing Wizard, Site Builder Network, and Internet Client Software Development Kit for Web publishing—see Chapter 8, "Authoring and Publishing"

The Internet Explorer 4.0 suite allows seamless integration from one application to the next—all applications are tightly integrated and developed with a common menu and toolbar user interface. This arrangement simplifies training since a user who learns one application in the suite already has a head start on learning another one.

Internet Explorer 4.0 is built for extensibility; an organization that uses it doesn't need to discard its existing tools. For example, a corporation can use an existing messaging solution and still enjoy many integration features with the Internet Explorer suite. Figure 4-7 shows the Programs tab of the Options dialog box, in which you can set messaging options.

In addition, Internet Explorer 4.0 offers a scalable solution for users who need high-end applications. For example, for users who need a richer mail client, Microsoft Outlook can replace Microsoft Outlook Express mail. While Microsoft FrontPad is terrific for making Web pages, Microsoft FrontPage is the full Web site development platform for developers who want even more options. And for a true enterprise Web server, users should move from the Personal Web Server to Microsoft Internet Information Server, which has all the security, scalability, and robustness that a Web site needs with the scale of the Internet today.

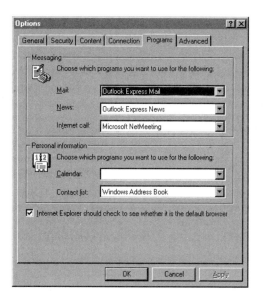

Figure 4-7   *Set your messaging and contacts options in the Options dialog box*

Multimedia: Sites Come Alive with Internet Explorer 4.0

The Web gets more exciting every day as Web pages incorporate new multimedia capabilities such as movies, sounds, animations, and 3-D worlds. Internet Explorer 4.0 supports all the latest multimedia standards—including the Virtual Reality Modeling Language (VRML) 2.0—and makes viewing multimedia over the Internet faster and more fun.

Web developers will find it's now easier than ever to use multimedia effects to create compelling and interactive Web pages. Internet Explorer 4.0's new Dynamic HTML multimedia technology makes it easy to add filters and transitions to pages, create effects that work on a timer, and alter the surface of a bitmap. In addition, Internet Explorer 4.0 adds the following capabilities to help Web authors build more multimedia content into their pages:

- **Dynamic HTML multimedia** A set of new controls that make it easy to add exciting multimedia effects to Web pages that download quickly
- **Interactive music control** A new control that can create music that responds to a user's actions—instantly
- **ActiveMovie control** A control that provides cross-platform video and audio technology
- **NetShow** A powerful technology that allows you to broadcast multimedia events over the Internet or a corporate intranet (See Chapter 6 for a detailed look at NetShow.)

Multimedia effects with Dynamic HTML

Multimedia on the Web is often lackluster or takes a frustratingly long amount of time to download. To deliver the quality of graphics and animation that users have come to expect from CD-ROM products and television, Internet Explorer 4.0 includes multimedia effects with Dynamic HTML. Web authors and developers can use Dynamic HTML multimedia effects to create complex, animated graphics that download quickly.

Although the mechanisms for these new controls make it easy to create dynamic behaviors, their capabilities go far beyond those offered by most multimedia tools. In addition, Dynamic HTML multimedia controls deliver rich animation without decreasing server performance and with minimal download time on desktop PCs. Quick downloads result from the fact the controls come in small files that are rendered on the user's computer.

Interactive Music control

Internet Explorer 4.0 introduces the new Interactive Music control—an ActiveX control that composes and plays music in response to a user's actions in real time. The Interactive Music control creates a soundtrack of the user's actions—such as in a computer game or a guided tour of a Web site—without using WAV or MIDI files that require time to download.

This lightweight, flexible music control adds life and excitement to Web pages and ensures consistent and configurable musical playback through any sound card. The Interactive Music control delivers the following benefits:

- Offers a variety of musical output, which engages users more than hearing the same sounds playing over and over
- Dynamically performs harmonically correct motifs in response to mouse movements and other user input
- Transitions from one type of music to another seamlessly
- Plays a definitive musical exit when the user leaves a page
- Plays transitional music as the user moves between Web pages

Special Bonus Pack available for Internet Explorer 4.0 users

The Interactive Music Bonus Pack is the quick and easy way to experience music on the Web. Specially created for Internet Explorer 4.0 users, this pack features five new styles: Heartland, Textures, Dark Chase, Smokin', and Lay Back. From Internet Explorer 4.0, download the pack for Microsoft Windows 98 from the Internet Explorer Suite Components option at:

http://www.microsoft.com/ie/ie40/download/

Then check out Microsoft's new Interactive Music site at:

http://www.microsoft.com/music/

To make pages sound even more dynamic, download the Microsoft Synthesizer from:

http://www.microsoft.com/music/MSSynth/Synth.htm

This add-on takes advantage of the musical output created by the Interactive Music control to add depth and definition to music that MIDI can't touch—regardless of what kind of sound card you have installed.

ActiveMovie

Microsoft ActiveMovie technology (part of DirectShow) is another reason why Internet Explorer 4.0 is the best browser for viewing multimedia sites. ActiveMovie supports all the popular Web-based audio and video formats, including Moving Pictures Experts Group (MPEG)—the format that allows TV-quality video and CD-quality audio. To reduce waiting time, ActiveMovie uses "progressive downloading," which lets you start playing an audio or video clip while it's still downloading in the background.

ActiveMovie provides the following benefits:

- Fast and easy playback of all types of media on the Internet, including MPEG Audio and Video, AVI, QuickTime, MIDI, AU, WAV, and AIFF
- Software-based MPEG playback, which delivers full-screen, television-quality video on mainstream systems
- A flexible, extensible architecture, which easily integrates new technologies

HTML Help: Standards-Based Help on the Web

HTML Help is the next generation of Microsoft WinHelp 4.0, really a superset of WinHelp 4.0, and delivers the best online documentation for the Internet. HTML Help blends rich visuals, HTML, and Web technologies such as ActiveX, Java, JavaScript, and VBScript to allow Web authors to offer an interactive Help experience. HTML Help combines this valuable tool set with quality desktop publication layout capabilities using cascading style sheets to create the ideal environment for authors creating online Help, multimedia titles, or Web sites.

HTML Help enhances the rich feature set of WinHelp, including tables of contents, a keyword index, and full-text search capabilities, and combines it with content written in HTML. In addition, HTML Help offers tools such as Dialog Box Help Editor, which makes it much easier to create context-sensitive Help without developer support. Because HTML Help is cross-platform and open, it supports whatever version of HTML you need to author your system.

HTML Help technology consists of the following components:

- **HTML Help ActiveX control** Lets you insert exploration controls such as tables of contents, indexes, pop-ups, related information, and shortcuts into an HTML file. You can also add other functionality, such as initial splash screens and version dialog boxes.

- **Compressed HTML** Allows you to combine all sources (HTML, ActiveX controls, ActiveX Scripting, Java applets, graphics, multimedia, full-text search indexes, keywords, and more) and compress them into a single file, greatly reducing the amount of disk space required for the HTML files.

- **Microsoft HTML Help Workshop** Enables you to edit your table of contents, index, and HTML files, taking much of the work out of creating and maintaining an HTML Help project.

- **HTML Help Authoring DLL** Allows you to view detailed information for entries in the table of contents—a useful feature when you're trying to locate an HTML document linked from an entry in your contents.

- **Layout engine** Lets you use any browser, such as Microsoft Internet Explorer 3.02, or application that supports ActiveX.

- **HTML Help window** Lets authors display their HTML files in a customized, resizeable window, independent of the user's browser.

- **Microsoft Flash** Allows you to convert existing bitmaps and metafiles to GIF and JPEG formats, to create USEMAP coordinates, to perform screen captures, and more.

Webcasting

Today's new "push" and "pull" technologies are what Webcasting is all about. With Internet Explorer 4.0, Microsoft provides an open, standards-based solution that allows Web authors to send information to users either on Web pages, by way of software components, in e-mail messages, or through broadcast content. Webcasting makes information easy to access, plus it automatically notifies users when their favorite Web sites have changed and lets them read the pages offline.

Internet Explorer 4.0 automatically enables Webcasting of any existing Web site without requiring modifications to the site. To Webcast content from a conventional Web site, Internet Explorer 4.0 performs a scheduled "Webcrawl" of the site content, checking for updated content and optionally downloading information for offline use. A user can initiate this process by "subscribing" to a Web site using the Favorites menu in Internet Explorer 4.0.

Users can take advantage of the following Webcasting methods offered via Internet Explorer 4.0: subscriptions and premium channels.

Subscriptions

An important part of efficient information delivery is providing a mechanism for selecting and scheduling downloads of information automatically. Users who frequently visit the same Web sites can subscribe to the site, which enables their computer to periodically download Web pages that have changed. This enables users to see what has changed on the Web site without actually visiting the site. Once subscribed, users are periodically notified of changes through a number of user-selected methods, ranging from e-mail notification to taskbar notification.

NOTE

When a user subscribes to a site, no payment is involved. The word *subscription* in this context denotes scheduled delivery of content.

Key features of subscriptions

- **Receiving new content** Each time you add a favorite, you can subscribe to the site or page; then, Internet Explorer 4.0 will download the page to the cache based on scheduling preference and notify you of changes. Once the subscribed site or page is received, you can disconnect from the Internet and still view and work with the data.

- **Scheduling site downloads** You can choose when you want the computer to retrieve the information you've subscribed to. You have numerous default choices (such as daily, weekly, or custom), or you can choose to manually request an update. (See the "Schedule" section later in the chapter for more details.)

- **Notification of new content** When subscribing, you have a number of options for how you're to be notified of the content changes on the site. (See the "Notification" section later in the chapter for more details.)

Benefits of subscriptions

Subscriptions let you stay in touch with current Web site information. For mobile users, staying in touch *and* being able to take the information on the road with them is a necessity. The following examples demonstrate these key benefits:

- **Improving the ability to stay current with Web site changes** Let's say you regularly view 10 key Web sites every day. To do so in the past, you had to open the browser, visit each site, and then scan numerous pages to see what had been updated. With Smart Favorites, Internet Explorer 4.0 polls the site in the background (by using a technology called WebCheck), looks at the tags, and then notifies you of the changes.

- **Take the Web on the road (mobile Web computing)** Let's say that every day you ride the train to work and you enjoy reading a newspaper during your trip. With Subscriptions, you can simply subscribe to an online newspaper, schedule it to update while you're getting ready for work, and then read the news on the train. This option is also extremely beneficial to users who travel a lot by airplane.

- **Optimizing connect time** Today, most users have something specific to do when they connect to the Internet. It's easy to get sidetracked, however, with the ever-present links to multiple sites. Using subscriptions in conjunction with the scheduling capabilities in Internet Explorer 4.0, you can select the sites you're interested in, connect to the Web, download the sites, and then disconnect from the Web and read all the information later. This saves valuable connect time and expense.

How subscriptions work

Any site that is in your Favorites list is grouped into the Smart Favorites category. Internet Explorer 4.0 will automatically look at those sites and alert you when they've been updated. The Add To Favorites dialog box, shown in Figure 4-8, has a new check box that enables you to subscribe to your favorite sites.

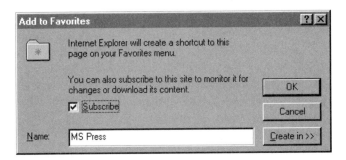

Figure 4-8   *Adding a subscription—just like adding a favorite*

You can also subscribe by selecting Subscribe from the Favorites menu. With either method, you'll see the Subscribe dialog box (shown in Figure 4-9), which presents the subscription information and allows you to confirm or customize the default subscription. If you choose to customize the subscription, a wizard walks you through the process of deciding various options. The most important choice you'll make is deciding between monitoring only for content changes vs. downloading updated content for offline use. (See "The underlying technology of subscribing to a Web site" section on page 87 for more details about this choice.) In addition, the Subscription Wizard allows you to customize the Webcrawl, choose the schedule for visiting the site, and pick the method of notification about site changes.

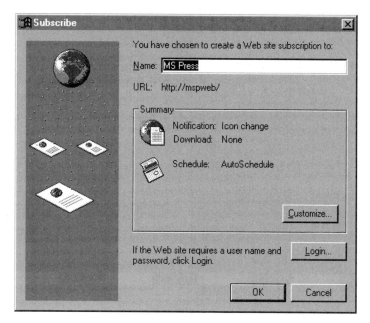

Figure 4-9   *Subscription summary information*

You can also control the amount of download time and disk space used by each subscription. All subscription information is kept in a new Subscriptions folder (shown in Figure 4-10) created by Internet Explorer 4.0, which makes it easy to find out when sites have been last checked or downloaded.

Gleam

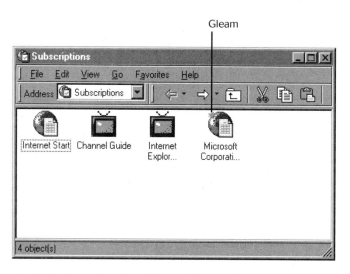

Figure 4-10   *A red gleam marks subscriptions with new content*

Schedule

As mentioned earlier, you can schedule when to have information downloaded to your computer—daily, weekly, or at some custom interval you choose. You can also manually request a download. You can set the schedule options on the Properties page of the Web page you're scheduling, as shown in Figure 4-11.

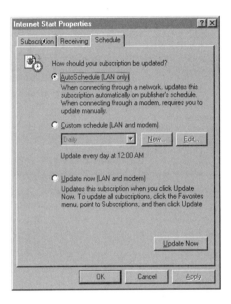

Figure 4-11   *Scheduling a subscription update*

Notification

You can be notified of changes on the site you subscribe to in the following ways:

- **Show notification icon on the taskbar** This option will enable a subscription task icon on the taskbar. When the site is updated, a red gleam appears over the icon. Sites that have been updated appear on the menu when you click the subscription task on the taskbar. You have the option of updating your subscriptions and setting global subscription properties from this menu.

- **Send notification through Outlook Express** This option results in an e-mail message notifying you when a subscribed site is updated. The message also includes a link to that site. With enhanced e-mail clients that support rich MIME HTML, Internet Explorer 4.0 sends the entire updated Web page as an e-mail message. The link takes you to the Internet, and you can receive this information directly inside your e-mail client. With Internet Explorer 4.0, you can subscribe to any site in the world and receive these rich e-mail messages; you're not limited to any specific set of vendors.

NOTE

E-mail notifications would use MHTML to send HTML-in-e-mail with any standard HTML-enabled POP3 or SMTP e-mail application. In the absence of HTML e-mail, this MHTML will display as a text message containing an HTML attachment.

- **Favorites notification** On the Favorites menu, a red gleam appears next to each subscribed site that has been updated, as shown in Figure 4-12. You can point to the site to see a brief description of the site changes.

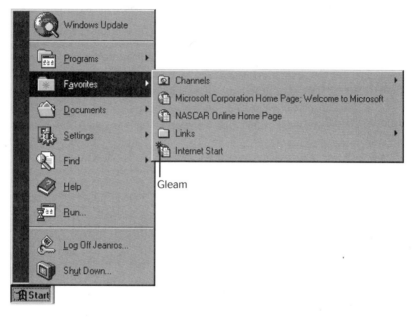

Figure 4-12   *List of Favorites with a gleam on an updated subscription*

The underlying technology of subscribing to a Web site

As mentioned earlier, you can choose between two flavors of Web site subscription, depending on whether you've chosen only to monitor for content changes or to download content for offline use.

If you customize a subscription only to check for updated content, Internet Explorer 4.0 periodically visits the site, checks the subscribed page to see if content has changed, and notifies you if new content is available. In this case, *no content is downloaded*. This process is illustrated in Figure 4-13 on the following page.

Figure 4-13 *Subscribing to a Web site (monitoring changes only)*

If you want to view subscribed content, Internet Explorer 4.0 follows the process illustrated in Figure 4-14. Internet Explorer 4.0 visits the site on a scheduled basis and crawls the pages (according to your preferences), downloads *only the modified pages,* and notifies you that new content is available for offline browsing.

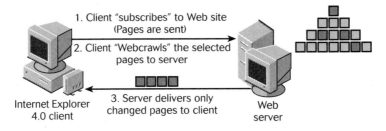

Figure 4-14 *Subscribing to a Web site for offline use (only new or updated content is downloaded)*

Internet Explorer 4.0 will automatically authenticate your ID when crawling sites that require a user name and password; Internet Explorer 4.0 uses a single cache that is shared between the Web browser and the Webcrawler, thus avoiding dual copies of the same HTML file.

NOTE

If you're offline and you click on a link to a page that isn't cached, a dialog box offers you the option of connecting to the Internet to view the unavailable page.

The Webcrawl mechanism of Webcasting is not a true "push" but is rather a "smart scheduled pull." Like almost all other push products on the market, Internet Explorer 4.0's ability to notify users of new content makes the "smart pull" feel like push content. Internet Explorer 4.0 depends on such smart pull for Webcasting existing sites on HTTP servers, but the Webcasting architecture can also scale up to provide for rich, multicast "true push."

The site author

Absolutely no reauthoring work of an existing Web site is necessary to enable users to subscribe to the site. However, an author who expects site subscriptions can do two things to improve the users' Webcasting experience:

- On certain sites, a two- to three-level–deep Webcrawl might prove useless, either because not enough interesting content is available or because too much undesired content will be downloaded. On such sites, an author can rearrange the site structure to be more suitable for Webcrawling.

> **NOTE**
> This limitation is inherent in Webcrawl-based Webcasting. To alleviate this problem, Internet Explorer 4.0 provides the Webcrawl option of downloading HTML-only (without images) for offline use. This option requires less bandwidth and less disk space, making it possible to crawl deeper to reach useful content.

- To further optimize the Webcasting experience, an author can convert his or her Web site into a channel by adding a single Channel Definition Format (CDF) file to the site, as described in the following sections.

Premium Channels

A formidable challenge for the Web today is providing a forum to deliver appealing content that takes advantage of the latest Web technology. Internet Explorer 4.0 gives content providers an opportunity to truly innovate, turning a portion of their Web site into a channel that resides directly on the user's desktop. Microsoft is working closely with leading content providers to advance the viewer experience through premium channels.

Premium channels offer the following benefits:

- **Premium content** You're just a click away from the top content providers in the world.
- **Active platform support** Inside the channels, you'll see the most interesting, interactive content available; premium channels are designed specifically for Internet Explorer 4.0, with support for Dynamic HTML, ActiveX, and Java.
- **Customization** You can choose the content you're most interested in and have it delivered directly to your desktop. Just use the Channel bar to select your favorite topics. Internet Explorer 4.0 will retrieve the topics, and you can read them at your leisure, even offline. You'll spend less time surfing the Web because you'll get only the content you need.
- **Exciting viewing experience** Before Internet Explorer 4.0, developers had no reason to spend time enabling their Web pages to take advantage of the newer, advanced technologies of the Internet. They typically developed for

the lowest common denominator. With the Internet Explorer 4.0 channel se-lector directly on the desktop, however, developers can make their content both informative and engaging.

- **Efficiency** With the current limitations of HTML, developers found it diffi-cult and time-consuming to create truly engaging content that users could download and view quickly. With Dynamic HTML opening the door to more interactive Web sites and multimedia extensions, content providers can create fantastic sites that don't require users to make time-consuming trips to the Web server.

How premium channels work

On the desktop, an Internet Explorer 4.0 user has a Channel bar that contains a set of buttons. Each button is stored as an Internet shortcut file in the Channels folder on the user's hard disk. When the user clicks a button, Internet Explorer 4.0 opens (if it isn't already open) and displays the channel page that's linked to the shortcut. The channel page can support anything an Internet Explorer 4.0 HTML page can support, such as Java, ActiveX, or Dynamic HTML.

Every channel is a subscribed site, so the pages displayed are the ones most recently cached on the user's hard disk. Performance is fast because the page is displayed from the hard disk. The channel creator provides a list of URLs—a Web collection file—that describes what content (HTML, images, class, and so on) is to be down-loaded to the user's hard disk, as well as the schedule for downloading it, if the creator wants to control the download schedule. If the channel creator doesn't include those parameters, users can control when Internet Explorer 4.0 downloads the content. The Channel delivery architecture for premium channels (as well as ticker pages and screensaver pages) is shown in Figure 4-15.

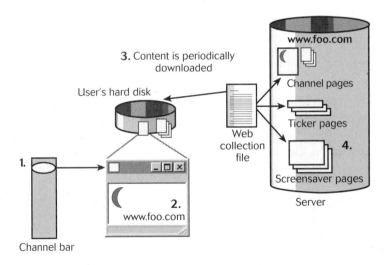

Figure 4-15 *Channel delivery architecture*

In the Web collection, the content provider can specify pages that are to be displayed in the default screensaver or perhaps a desktop ticker. Again, these are ordinary HTML pages displayed in a window more specialized than an ordinary browser.

NOTE

The desktop components in both channels and the Active Desktop must still provide information when users are away from their offices and when they don't have a permanent connection to the Internet. Therefore, the Active Desktop is enabled to work offline. Because most dial-up users don't have a constant connection to the Internet, a desktop component should display some reasonable content in the absence of a connection. This feature is key since the desktop is visible as soon as the user starts the operating system, even before initiating a dial-up.

For this reason, any data files that the component requires should be cached on the local machine. Fortunately, the Internet Explorer 4.0 subscription feature can easily be configured to cache any object linked to a desktop component. In the typical case, in which a component is built from an HTML document inside a floating frame, Internet Explorer 4.0 subscriptions can be set to download automatically any inline images, objects, or applets and to download any number of HTML links *N* levels deep. The component can also specify individual subscriptions for any data files or objects it might reference.

Subscribing to a channel

You can subscribe to a site's channel in one of two ways: either by choosing the Subscribe action from the Favorites menu or by clicking on a hyperlink to a CDF file (explained below) or a button advertised on the Web site. Both actions walk you through the process for subscribing to a channel—presenting the subscription summary, as shown in Figure 4-16 on the following page, and allowing you to change through the Channel Subscription Wizard. For the average user, subscribing to a channel is just like subscribing to any Web site. (The difference is that the channel is a Web site that includes a CDF file.) Again, the most important choice in the Channel Subscription Wizard is the choice between only monitoring for channel changes vs. downloading updated channel content for offline use. In addition to this choice, the Channel Subscription Wizard allows you to customize delivery of the Channel by choosing the update schedule and other preferences. If you want, Internet Explorer 4.0 can send you e-mail containing the top-level HTML page each time the channel content changes.

After subscribing to the Web site channel, Internet Explorer 4.0 automatically adds the subscribed channel logo to the Channel pane in the browser and to the Channel bar on the Active Desktop. (See Figure 4-17 on the following page.)

The Channel bar provides easy access to all subscribed channels. The Channel pane notifies you when content has been updated and allows you to browse the hierarchical structure of a channel (the information contained in the CDF file).

Figure 4-16   *Channel Subscriptions dialog box*

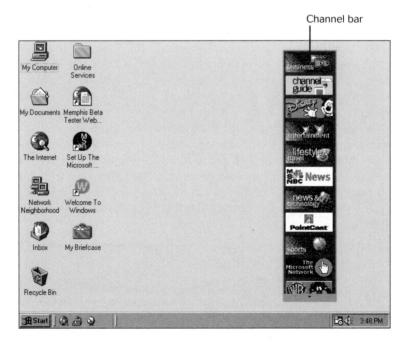

Figure 4-17   *The Channel bar on the Active Desktop*

The underlying technology of channel subscription

Behind the scenes, any Web site that provides a CDF file can be subscribed to as a channel. Any HTML page on the site can point to this CDF file, using either the <A> (anchor) tag or the <LINK> tag in HTML. As with subscriptions in general, channel subscription comes in two flavors, depending on whether you choose only to monitor for content changes or to view content offline.

If you customize a subscription only to check for updated content, Internet Explorer 4.0 periodically visits the site, *downloads only the CDF file*, and updates the channel hierarchy displayed inside the Channel pane (illustrated in Figure 4-18).

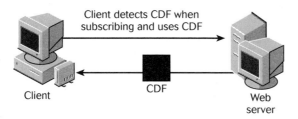

Figure 4-18 *Client downloads CDF on a scheduled basis to show new channel headlines and hierarchy*

NOTE

The CDF provides rich information about new content, including headlines displayed in the Channel pane. The CDF also provides categorized links to channel topics. Keep in mind, however, that clicking on any of these topics will require additional HTML pages to be downloaded because they haven't yet been delivered for offline use.

If a dial-up user subscribes to a channel for offline use, Internet Explorer 4.0 periodically visits the site, *downloads the CDF and all associated channel content referenced in the CDF,* and updates the channel hierarchy displayed inside the Channel pane (illustrated in Figure 4-19 on the following page). The CDF file provides information about newly updated content, including headlines displayed in the Channel pane. Furthermore, all the pages pointed to by links in the Channel pane and all the channel content is available for offline use.

NOTE

After downloading the channel's CDF file, Internet Explorer 4.0 will not download any channel content other than specified pages that haven't been downloaded before (including content that has been updated). Keep in mind that *any* content format can accompany a CDF file when updating a channel, independent of whether it is an HTML page or a more complex Java or ActiveX application.

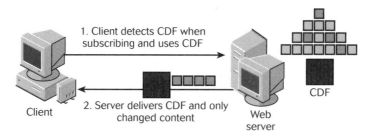

Figure 4-19 *Client downloads CDF and all accompanying pages from the Web site on a scheduled basis*

Beyond Basic Webcasting: Addressing Webcrawling Issues

Internet Explorer 4.0 Webcasting is divided into three scalable tiers:

- Basic Webcasting explains Webcasting of existing Web sites and how users can have any conventional Web site "pushed" to them without any work by the site author.

- Managed Webcasting explains how a Web site author can extend Webcasting through channels and CDF.

- "True" Webcasting discusses Webcasting using multicast or "true-push" delivery, addressing scalability within a large corporation with bandwidth limitations.

Basic Webcasting

Basic Webcasting has some key advantages, but the technology it employs, the Webcrawler, has some fundamental drawbacks:

- **Webcrawling is hard for users** While it appears fairly easy to set up any Web site to be Webcrawled, the user has to choose numerous options ranging from scheduling, content delivery, types of content, and more.

- **Too much information is downloaded to the client** A Webcrawler starts from the top level in the Web tree. If the user wants a specific piece of information from the Web site and that piece is a couple of levels down from the top of the tree, the Webcrawler will automatically download all the information down to the level that the user requested.

- **Need for personalization and logical grouping of Web content** With the Webcrawler, the user can't specify types of information but rather just has to use the Webcrawler to grab all the information and then sift through it to determine what's useful. The Web site author has no way of offering the user logical groups of information.

- **Need for smart scheduling and site control** With the Webcrawler, the user sets the retrieval schedule for information. This schedule might conflict with the actual scheduled update to the Web site. For example, if updates are published to a Web site every day at 9:00 a.m. and 3:00 p.m. but the user has the Webcrawler set to update at 2:00 p.m., the user will clearly miss key updates to the Web site. Scheduling conflicts like this could be avoided if the Web site could instruct the user's PC to schedule the update.

- **Some Web sites can and do disable Webcrawling** Webcrawling can cause a heavy load to the Web server since the site will be entirely crawled by any user who has subscribed to it. Therefore, many Web sites simply do not allow their site to be crawled.

To address these key limitations of Webcrawling, Microsoft has introduced the next level of Webcasting, Managed Webcasting.

Managed Webcasting Using the CDF

The Channel Definition Format (CDF), introduced earlier in the chapter, allows an author to optimize, personalize, and fully control how a site is Webcast. Authoring a CDF file is the only step required to convert any existing Web site into a channel.

While delivering a basic solution for Webcasting, a simple Webcrawl doesn't provide adequate functionality to create a useful "push" experience for many of today's Web sites. Some common customer and site concerns include these:

- **Unknown site structure** A Webcrawl uses the page-link tree structure of a Web site to determine what content to push (smart-pull) because sites provide no additional information about the structured organization of content.

- **Hit-or-miss content usefulness** The HTML in today's Web sites provides no cues to help a Webcrawl decide which links point to useful content and which point to useless content. Because no such cues exist, most crawlers set a maximum number of levels and a disk-space limit and hope that the content crawled proves useful.

- **Webcrawl schedules don't match content-update schedules** Because existing Web sites don't advertise content-update schedules, a scheduled Webcrawl might check for updates too often or not often enough.

To address these issues, Microsoft worked with various industry leaders in creating and proposing the CDF to the W3C. This file format is based on the broadly supported Extensible Markup Language (XML) standard. CDF is an open and easily authored format for publishing a channel, allowing Web publishers to personalize and streamline the delivery of information. Internet Explorer 4.0, which will automatically enable any Web site to be a Web broadcaster, implements CDF, optimizing the delivery of push content to Internet Explorer 4.0 users.

CDF offers immediate benefits to users and to developers, including the following:

- **Optimization** CDF allows for optimization of scheduling and efficiency of content delivery. A site author can specify which content is automatically Webcast, solving the hit-or-miss problem with Webcrawling. CDF also allows a Web site to provide a content-update schedule, thus allowing for server-side load balancing and ensuring that no bandwidth is wasted on polling stale information. CDF gives content authors the power to decide how a Web site should be Webcast—that is, what content should be Webcast and how often it should be updated.

- **Structure** CDF provides structured content-indexing independent of content format. CDF provides an index or map of a Web site that describes the type of information contained on the site. Specifically, CDF describes logical groupings of information (for example, sports news vs. financial information), providing hierarchical structure and category information about a site, as shown in Figure 4-20. Because this information is completely independent of content format, a CDF-based channel can include any kind of Web content or applications built on HTML, JavaScript, Java, and ActiveX technology.

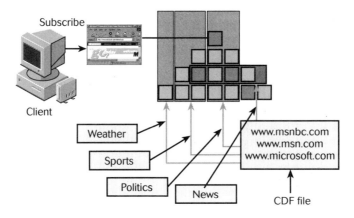

Figure 4-20   *CDF can separate content from structure*

- **Personalization** The HTTP cookie standard provides a powerful mechanism for personalizing Web content for each Web site user. Sites that employ CDF with Internet Explorer 4.0's Webcasting gain valuable functionality from this standard. A Web site can use standard HTTP cookies to deliver personalized information to users by dynamically generating a custom CDF based on user preferences. CDF thus uses the existing cookie standard for HTML personal-ization on the Web and takes it a step further with personalized channels.

- **Open format** Any company can author content to take advantage of CDF, any server can run Web sites that are enhanced by CDF, and any broadcast-enabled client software can access channels available on Web sites using CDF.

- **Proven technology** Microsoft's leadership in Internet client/server solutions and extensive work with leading Web content and technology developers will ensure that CDF will meet demanding market requirements.

- **Low cost** The CDF specification will save content development costs by allowing Web content developers easy access to a market of millions of compatible clients, using readily available software.

- **Use of compelling Internet technologies** CDF is extensible, enabling sites to publish channels using any or all of simple HTML, Dynamic HTML, ActiveX technologies, and other specialized broadcast technologies.

So what exactly is a CDF file? A bare-bones CDF file, such as the one shown in Figure 4-21, contains nothing but a list of URLs pointing to content. This file is easy to create and requires no changes to existing HTML pages. A more advanced CDF file includes URLs pointing to content but can also include a schedule for content updates, a hierarchical organization of the URLs describing the Web site structure, and Title and Abstract information describing individual content items.

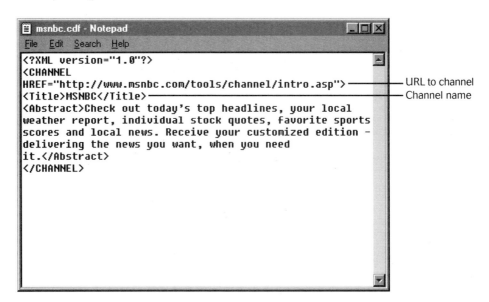

Figure 4-21 *A sample CDF file*

The CDF mechanism makes creating a channel a simple two-step process that doesn't require authoring of new content, reauthoring of existing content, or any programming on either the client or the server:

1. Write a CDF file with a list of URLs to existing content.
2. Link to this CDF file to make it discoverable.

True Webcasting: Scaling Up by Providing Extensible Architecture via Multicast

While traditional HTTP publishing is sufficient for most content delivery needs, in some scenarios a different delivery mechanism is required. Microsoft provides an open, extensible information delivery architecture that makes it possible to integrate the market's existing push products with the Internet Explorer 4.0 Webcasting client. Today users face potential conflicts and added learning time with multiple push software products on their PCs. Internet Explorer 4.0 can help reduce scheduling conflicts and user interface confusion by providing a standard method for users to schedule information delivery.

The Webcasting architecture in the Internet Explorer 4.0 client provides architectural hooks that allow third parties to provide value-added benefits to enrich the Webcasting experience. Specifically, the Webcasting architecture in Internet Explorer 4.0 allows for plugging in third-party client software that defines new URL transport protocols or provides an alternative delivery mechanism for channels.

Microsoft uses this extensible architecture to support multicast, or "true push," in Internet Explorer 4.0. By taking advantage of special network hardware, multicast protocols provide bandwidth-efficient broadcasting of content throughout a corporate network. Because of Microsoft's extensible Webcasting architecture, the NetShow networked multimedia software component in Internet Explorer 4.0 can receive channel content broadcast through such a protocol, as illustrated in Figure 4-22. Furthermore, in a recently announced relationship, NetShow will integrate with StarBurst Communications' reliable one-to-many Multicast File Transfer Protocol (MFTP) technology. With this technology available in Internet Explorer 4.0, organizations can now take advantage of the bandwidth efficiencies of IP multicast to reliably deliver content to their intranet- and Internet-based users.

To provide similar bandwidth savings to home users, Microsoft's recently announced Broadcast Architecture for Windows initiative will allow PC users to receive CDF-authored channel content over existing and future broadcast networks, including high-bandwidth direct broadcast satellites and analog and cable TV channels. This means that without dialing up or otherwise using a two-way connection to the Internet, channel content will be kept constantly fresh on users' PCs. In addition, Microsoft's relationship with AirMedia promises to make channel content available to home users everywhere over airwaves.

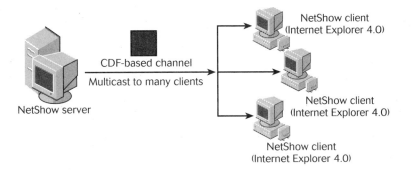

Figure 4-22 *Multicast protocols allow corporations to save bandwidth using Internet Explorer 4.0 Webcasting and CDF*

Third-Party Support for CDF: Clients, Servers, Tools, and Content

Most of today's leading push software vendors, including PointCast, BackWeb, AirMedia, FirstFloor, Torso, UserLand Software, DataChannel, Lanacom (now a part of BackWeb), NETdelivery, NCompass, Diffusion, Wayfarer, and many others, are embracing CDF. In a close relationship with Microsoft, PointCast has adopted CDF as the standard format for channel content, making it possible for authors to create channels that all Internet Explorer 4.0 users as well as PointCast's network of "push" clients can view. In addition to PointCast, BackWeb, AirMedia, and FirstFloor will be using Internet Explorer 4.0 as their strategic platform for information delivery and are working with Microsoft to provide integrated solutions for customers. Numerous server-side tool vendors such as DataChannel, UserLand Software, and Torso are making it easy to author channel content based on CDF. Finally, the Netscape Netcaster client software can support CDF files within the limitations of Netscape's simple Webcrawl technology.

For a complete list of vendors supporting CDF, see the following Web site:

http://www.microsoft.com/corpinfo/press/1997/Mar97/Cdfrpr.htm

Microsoft Software

In addition to the strong third-party support for CDF, numerous Microsoft server products and authoring tools will make it easier to push channel content to Internet Explorer 4.0 clients. For example, the next version of Microsoft FrontPage Web authoring and management software will provide direct support for authoring CDF channels within the product. The Active Server Pages architecture in Internet Information Server 3.0 makes it possible to dynamically generate CDF files using server-side scripts. The newly announced SiteServer 2.0 allows rich personalization of custom CDF channel content integrated with other Web site services. As mentioned earlier, NetShow and the new Broadcast Architecture for Windows initiative will enable multicast and broadcast of CDF-based channels. Finally, the Microsoft Proxy Server, which already reduces network traffic with its active intelligent caching and makes Internet access more manageable and secure, will be enhanced in its next release to support highly scalable and distributed cached networks optimized around Internet Explorer 4.0 Channels and CDF.

NOTE

By configuring Internet Explorer 4.0 clients to work with a shared caching proxy server, corporate administrators can mitigate the effects of channel load on network resources. This solution is not only for Internet-based content but also for large corporate intranets. Microsoft anticipates that some users of Proxy Server 2.0 should be able to realize reductions in network load for HTTP traffic by as much as 50 percent.

True Web Integration

For many people, the Internet has become the fastest way to get the information they need to perform daily tasks successfully. With the current technology, however, there is a distinct division between two different worlds: one containing local and network information and the other containing intranet and Internet data. Internet Explorer 4.0 with Shell Extensions eliminates that division. It integrates the Internet into every aspect of the PC—the desktop, file folders, the network, even the Start menu. Through rich integration with the operating system, Internet Explorer 4.0 delivers true Web integration.

True Web integration consists of several components:

- Single Explorer (described in the next section)
- Start menu and taskbar Web savviness—see Chapter 3, "The Faces of Windows 98"
- Active Desktop—see Chapter 3, "The Faces of Windows 98"

Single Explorer

Today users encounter more information than ever before. Not only do they contend with the thousands of documents that already exist in various formats on their hard drive or their company network, but they must also deal with the world of Web sites opened up via the Internet and the applications that contain the information they need. To access this information, users have had to learn multiple applications: one to look at their local information, another to look at their network, and unquestionably another to use the Internet or an intranet. With a single Explorer, Internet Explorer 4.0 works with the Windows operating system to unify this process into one utility to universally view local, network, Internet, and intranet data.

Integrating the best of the browser with the operating system's user interface produces several benefits:

- **Reduced training and support costs** Users need to learn only one application or one navigation method for accessing information anywhere, regardless of location or format. Also, by adding simple Web page exploration buttons (Back, Forward) with intelligent toolbars and favorites that go beyond Web pages, Internet Explorer 4.0 makes the operating system as easy to use as a Web browser.

- **Increased efficiency** A single Explorer makes Internet and intranet use more efficient for users and makes the PC more efficient for all applications. Because the Internet is always accessible from any window, users become more efficient since they don't need to start another application just to look at a Web site. The PC becomes more efficient as well—the total memory overhead of running the single Explorer is less than the overhead of running a separate Web browser application along with the operating system. With a single Explorer, more memory is available for other applications and overall system performance is enhanced.

- **Unifies an intranet and file-sharing network** Today user access to shared files is entirely different from access to intranet pages. Shared files don't allow hypertext views and can't be linked to related content. With Internet Explorer 4.0 and a customizable Web View of folders, users can add HTML pages to shared files and unify their file service with an intranet. Adding HTTP servers might be unnecessary; since Internet Explorer 4.0 users who visit a shared file the way they did before will now see an HTML view, complete with links to an intranet or the Internet if appropriate. Also, in today's migration to intranets, many organizations are spending large amounts of time and money trying to move all of their existing files from their file servers to new HTTP Web servers. Web View enables companies to migrate their existing directories to Web pages instantly, with no Web server required. By using Web View, organizations can leave files on their existing file servers yet take advantage of all the functionality the intranet offers.

- **Easy, fast customization** Currently, a well-written front-end application requires knowledge of high-level programming languages such as C or C++. With Internet Explorer 4.0, developers can easily generate front ends for anything from file server folders to floppy disks or CD-ROM titles since they can create Web pages using any technology—HTML, ActiveX, scripting, or Java. These pages can provide much richer information to users than current online text files.

How the single Explorer works

Internet Explorer 3.0 was developed with a component-based architecture. It included a browser OLE control, which developers could use to create their own Internet-enabled applications. This control was extremely powerful because it exposed all the functionality of Internet Explorer to the developer. It had the ability to display any HTML content, Java, Active Documents, or any other ActiveX control.

With the single Explorer, the Internet Explorer 4.0 developers performed two key tasks. First, they inserted the browser object into the operating system interface, extending it to enable any folder to display any of the content mentioned above. Next, they created an ActiveX control that displays the contents of a folder with the same look and feel as Windows Explorer but enhanced to behave like a Web page, with features such as single-click navigation and Back and Forward commands. Now, just like browsing the Web, a single click will take you to the "next page," whether it is opening a folder, a document, or an application.

Web PC

Internet Explorer 4.0 integrates the PC and the Internet into Microsoft's overall concept known as the Web PC. Web PC embraces the importance of integrating Web tasks into a proven and popular user interface that leverages current investments in training and solves key customer issues. Web PC is the next step in Microsoft's vision of Information at Your Fingertips—finding information should be easy and painless, regardless of where it is stored.

Administration Tools in Internet Explorer 4.0

As companies today are focusing more on reducing the total cost of owning and managing their distributed PC environments, it is critical for any software package to provide ways to automate common management tasks. Internet Explorer 4.0 includes several features to assist companies in software deployment, configuration, and desktop management.

The Internet Explorer 4.0 complete set of administration tools includes these:

- Active Setup
- Internet Explorer Administration Kit
- ActiveX Control Viewer
- Automatic Proxy Configuration

Active Setup

The Active Setup engine is a way for administrators to both ease the burden of installation and assist in the management of software once it is installed on their users' computers. Active Setup has the following features:

- **Efficient, modular setup engine** Active Setup optimizes network connection time by downloading only the initial install engine and identifying any potential problems (such as insufficient disk space) before downloading any application components. Administrators can create a single Internet Explorer 4.0 installation disk that contains only the install engine, which will then download application components from a network server.

- **Hands-free setup** Administrators can deliver scripted installations that don't require user input, automatically installing preselected application components and configuration settings.

- **Automatic migration of existing configurations** During setup, Internet Explorer 4.0 will import proxy settings, favorites and bookmarks, and cookies from a previous Internet Explorer or Netscape Navigator installation.

- **Enhanced logging features** Active Setup records a transaction log during the installation process, allowing users and administrators to troubleshoot any installation problems that might occur.

- **Multiple download site switching** During installation, if a problem on the server side of the process arises, Active Setup enables the client to switch to a new server automatically, continuing the installation seamlessly.

How Active Setup works

Active Setup has an efficient, modular setup engine. Internet Explorer 4.0 installation occurs as follows. First, the user chooses between minimal, standard, or full installations. At that point, the base Active Setup engine (approximately 200 KB) is downloaded. Active Setup then checks the available disk space for the appropriate installation option and downloads and installs *only* Internet Explorer 4.0 from the download site. Finally, Active Setup downloads and installs additional components from the download site.

During the setup process, Active Setup creates a number of log files that can pinpoint any issues that occur. The following log files are created in the Windows folder:

- **Active Setup Log.txt** Logs all actions during the Active Setup wizard or component install phases of setup. This log is useful if selected Internet Explorer 4.0 components don't get installed properly.

- **RunOnceEx Log.txt** Logs all actions during the dynamic-link library (DLL) registration phase. This log is useful if a message stating that a specific DLL didn't register properly occurs or if any unexpected dialog box appears during the final setup phase.

Most Web sites force users to select the site from which they download products or components. In this model, the user runs a risk of download failure if his or her connection to that specific server fails. Active Setup automatically selects the download server and manages which components come from which sites. This architecture allows installations to be split into multiple packages for easier download and smart recovery if setup fails.

Internet Explorer Administration Kit

The Microsoft Internet Explorer Administration Kit (IEAK) enables organizations to create and distribute a Web browser that reflects the specific needs of their organizations and users. With the IEAK, corporate administrators can create a hands-free customized installation of Internet Explorer 4.0 that is convenient to deploy and maintain.

A simple wizard guides corporate administrators, Internet content providers (ICPs), and Internet service providers (ISPs) through the process of creating customized self-installing versions of Internet Explorer 4.0 and any add-in products. They can then deploy the package royalty-free under the terms of Microsoft licensing and distribution agreements. Centralized administration and maintenance of the package is easy with the help of the INS Editor included with the IEAK. The INS Editor makes centralized administration a snap.

ActiveX Control Viewer

Introduced in Internet Explorer 3.0, ActiveX controls enable developers to use tools such as Microsoft Visual Basic, Microsoft Visual C++, or Borland Delphi to create small, fast software components that can be displayed inside Web pages. These tools allow developers to create Web-based applications much faster. Developers can simply reuse the code that they've already written, perhaps for internal custom applications, and insert it onto the Web page. It used to be difficult to manage these controls once they were installed on a client's PC. The ActiveX Control Viewer displays all the controls installed and even cleans them up when necessary.

Here are the key features of the ActiveX Control Viewer:

- **Integration with Windows user interface** The ActiveX Control Viewer exists as a simple directory inside the Windows folder, displaying all the installed ActiveX controls.

- **Delete controls** The ActiveX Control Viewer makes it easy to find all of the installed ActiveX controls and even delete them.

The ActiveX Control Viewer is a folder on your hard disk, named Downloaded ActiveX Controls. (See Figure 4-23.)

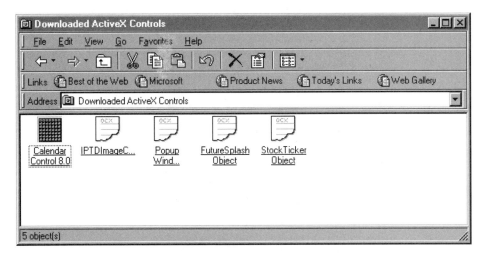

Figure 4-23 *Downloaded ActiveX Controls folder*

The ActiveX Control Viewer offers the following benefits:

- **Easy user control** With the ActiveX Control Viewer, you can easily see the controls installed on your PC and delete those you haven't used in a long time, maximizing your available disk space.

- **Find files faster** For a stricter corporate environment, ActiveX Control Viewer makes it much easier to locate unnecessary software that might not adhere to company standards.

Automatic Proxy Configuration

Internet Explorer 4.0 eases the administrative burden by allowing administrators to automatically configure proxy settings such as server addresses and bypass lists. Administrators can use the IEAK to configure proxy settings or to create a settings file using JScript.

Internet Explorer 4.0 can be configured to automatically retrieve proxy settings for each Internet protocol (HTTP, FTP, Secure, Gopher, SOCKS) from an INS file created with the IEAK or from an HTML file that contains JScript that executes whenever a network request is made. Multiple proxies can be configured for each protocol type, and Internet Explorer 4.0 can automatically cycle through the different proxy servers to avoid overloading any particular server. Proxy settings are set through the Internet Properties dialog box on the Connection tab, shown in Figure 4-24 on the following page.

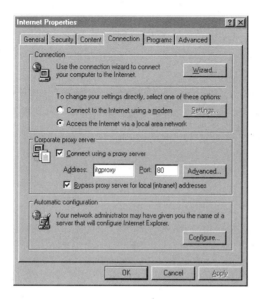

Figure 4-24   *Setting proxies in the Internet Properties dialog box*

Automatic Proxy offers the following benefits:

- **Centralized management and compatibility** Automatic Proxy Configuration makes it easy to administer a distributed network of PCs running Internet Explorer 4.0 by allowing administrators to set proxy configurations in a central location for all users. Any changes are propagated to all users as they run their browsers, without disrupting the work process.

- **Most compatible management solution** With Internet Explorer 4.0, support for both IEAK settings and JScript configurations ensure maximum compatibility with existing installations. Therefore, if companies are migrating their management solution from JScript to IEAK INS files (or vice versa), they can do so gradually because both solutions work seamlessly.

Security Features of Internet Explorer 4.0

The Internet provides a convenient and effective way to communicate and share information with others worldwide. However, many users are increasingly relying on the Web to use new applications such as online banking and shopping. Along with this increased reliance comes a greater need for security on the Internet. With its strong support of standard Internet security protocols, Internet Explorer 4.0 provides users with the following benefits:

- **Communicate privately** Internet Explorer 4.0 ensures that what users send over the Internet, whether it's a password or a credit card number, can't be read if intercepted.

- **Protect your identity on the Internet** Users who subscribe to a service or have personal information stored on a Web server can get a unique personal certificate that makes it virtually impossible for others to impersonate them when accessing a Web site.

- **Know whom you're talking to** Internet Explorer 4.0 can make sure users don't pass private information to the wrong people by enabling users to make sure that the server truly belongs to whom it appears to belong to.

- **Protect yourself and others from inappropriate content** By setting ratings using the Content Advisor, you can control what sites can be viewed on your computer. (For more information, see the "Ratings System" section earlier in the chapter.)

- **Prevent others from tracking your activities** Internet Explorer 4.0 lets users prevent Web sites from storing personal information on their computers.

- **Provide information on the source and reliability of online software** Using Microsoft Authenticode technology, Internet Explorer 4.0 tells users who published signed software and whether it has been tampered with, to help them decide whether to download software to their computer. Corporate administrators can now preinstall certificates so that users don't have to make decisions about downloading code on a case-by-case basis.

- **Securely store and control private information on the Internet** With Microsoft Protected Store, users can store credit card numbers and electronic cash securely, eliminating the need to memorize passwords and reenter numbers. For Webmasters, it provides a ready-made solution for user payment, reducing the cost of developing a Web site.

- **Provides an interface to third-party cryptographic service providers (CSPs)** This eliminates the need for software developers to create their own cryptography. The modular design of the CryptoAPI allows developers to work with a full range of CSPs that provide either software- or hardware-based cryptography, such as software algorithms or smart cards.

Microsoft actively participates in the Internet Engineering Task Force (IETF), the W3C, and other groups to develop Internet security standards. Recent Microsoft security initiatives include the code-signing proposal submitted to the W3C and the Transport Layer Security (TLS) efforts through the IETF, aimed at creating a single, secure, channel standard.

The following Internet Explorer 4.0 security features make it easier for you to protect your computer and your privacy while using the Internet:

- **Security zones** Now you can divide the Web into zones and have Internet Explorer 4.0 provide different levels of security depending on which zone you've assigned to a Web site.

- **Authenticode technology** As mentioned earlier, Authenticode certificates identify who published a piece of software—and verify that it hasn't been tampered with—to help you decide whether to download the software.

- **Certificate management** Now network administrators can control which Java applets, ActiveX controls, and other software can be run on their intranets, based on who published the software.

- **Capabilities-based Java security (sandboxing)** Internet Explorer 4.0's new security model for Java makes it easy for you to control how Java applets can interact with your computer system. Whether you're a user or a network administrator, you can now decide in advance what capabilities and levels of access to your computer or network you want to give to Java applets within security zones. For example, you can give broad access to Java applets from sources you trust but restrict applets from unknown sources to safe "sandboxes" where they can't harm files.

- **Privacy protection** Internet Explorer 4.0 supports all standard Internet security protocols to ensure your privacy when you communicate over the Web. A new feature prompts you before your user name or password are sent to a Web site that you haven't designated as trusted. For sites that you do trust, you can choose not to be prompted before your personal information is transmitted. Outlook Express—the Internet mail and news component of Internet Explorer 4.0—lets you encrypt your messages and ensure that no one can falsely assume your identity on the Internet.

These security features are described in more detail in the following sections.

NOTE

Internet Explorer 4.0 also includes all of the security fixes in Internet Explorer 3.02.

Security Zones

Security on the Internet is a complicated topic, but two simple facts sum up the situation:

- Users want to use powerful applications on Web sites they trust without being interrupted repeatedly by security warnings.

- When users visit Web sites that they don't trust, they want to make sure their computers and privacy aren't exposed to danger.

Internet Explorer 4.0 introduces a new security system that addresses both these facts and, in the process, makes it easier for users to make security decisions and for administrators to manage security for their corporations. With Internet Explorer 4.0's new security zones, you can now divide the Web into sites that you do and don't trust, deciding in advance what level of security to assign to each zone.

Security zones deliver power and protection

You can liken Internet Explorer 4.0's security zones to visas that some countries issue to travelers. If the country trusts you, they stamp your passport so that you can travel anywhere you like during your visit. If for some reason the country doesn't completely trust you, it strictly limits where you can go and what you can do during your stay.

Security zones work the same way, except that *you* are in the role of the country deciding how much access to allow to visitors to your computer. Web sites that you trust—such as those on your company's intranet or from established companies in whom you have confidence—can be designated as trusted, and they are allowed to run as much powerful, active content on your computer as you choose. Sites that you're not so sure about go into another "bucket," from which you can strictly limit their access to your computer. You set these zones through the Security tab on the Internet Properties dialog box, shown in Figure 4-25.

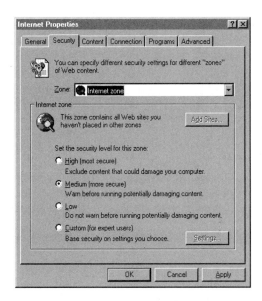

Figure 4-25   *Set security zones in the Internet Properties dialog box*

The beauty of security zones is that they provide advanced protection for your computer and your privacy without interrupting you with repeated warnings while you're visiting Web sites that you've already decided you can trust. Features for corporate administrators streamline the process even further, allowing companies to set automatic boundaries.

How security zones work

Internet Explorer 4.0 comes with three predefined zones: Internet, My Intranet, and Trusted Web Sites. Using the Internet Properties dialog box, you can set the security options you want for each zone and then add or remove sites from the zones depending on your level of trust in the site. Advanced users and administrators can also create new zones. In corporate environments, administrators can set up zones for users and even add or remove the authentication certificates of software publishers that they do or don't trust in advance so that users don't have to make security decisions while they're using the Internet.

For each security zone, you can choose a High, Medium, Low, or Custom security setting. While Microsoft recommends the High setting for sites in a zone of uncertain trustworthiness, you can safely use Medium in a trusted zone. The Custom option gives advanced users and administrators more control over all security options, including these:

- Access to files, ActiveX controls, and scripts
- The level of capabilities given to Java applets
- Whether sites must be identified with SSL authentication
- Password protection over NTLM (NT LanMan) (Depending on which zone a server is in, Internet Explorer 4.0 can send password information automatically, prompt the user for user and password information, or simply deny any login request.)

Microsoft Authenticode Technology

Software on the Internet is not labeled or shrink-wrapped as software in retail stores is. As a result, users might not know who published a piece of software, what the software will do on their computers, or if the software code has been tampered with.

Microsoft developed Authenticode technology to help address these concerns. When users download signed code to their computers, Authenticode verifies both the publisher and the integrity (that it hasn't been tampered with since the author published it) of the code. No software can be guaranteed to be 100 percent safe under all circumstances, but Authenticode gives you the opportunity to make an informed decision about whom to trust and to selectively block execution of certain code. Authenticode technology works with all common types of downloadable code, including Java applets, ActiveX controls, and plug-ins.

How Authenticode works

Microsoft provides Authenticode in conjunction with VeriSign, a leading certificate authority, and other certificate authorities that issue the digital identification that software publishers use to sign their code. If a piece of software has been digitally signed, Internet Explorer 4.0 can verify that the software originated from the named software publisher and that it hasn't been tampered with. Internet Explorer 4.0 will display a verification certificate if the software "passes the test."

Authenticode's new time-stamping feature establishes that a piece of software was properly signed during the valid lifetime of a publisher's certificate. (The reason certificates have a limited lifetime is to prevent giving counterfeiters enough time to eventually crack the code associated with the certificate.)

With Internet Explorer 4.0, Authenticode 2.0 delivers another new feature to protect Web surfers. Before downloading any potentially hazardous code, Internet Explorer 4.0 can automatically check to make sure a publisher's certificate has not been revoked. Publishers can have their certificates revoked if they abuse their code-signing agreement by, for example, creating malicious code that harms users' computers.

Developers can find tools for signing their code through the ActiveX SDK. For information on obtaining a personal certificate, see the "Obtaining and using personal certificates" section later in the chapter.

Certificate Management

Authentication certificates are a key tool in providing Internet security. Certificate management eases the administration of network security. The certificates, which are assigned to software publishers who meet defined levels of integrity and security in their code, give users a sure way to identify the origin of a piece of software on the Internet. This identification mechanism forms the basis of Authenticode.

Internet Explorer 4.0 makes further use of authentication certificates by introducing certificate management, a new capability that lets network administrators control which Java applets and ActiveX controls are allowed to run on their networks, based on who published the applets or controls. For example, an administrator can allow users to open and run all internally created controls but can keep all controls that originate from outside the corporate firewall from loading and running on company computers.

How certificate management works

Through the IEAK, administrators can preinstall certificates on a user's computer and can block users from downloading other certificates. Such preinstallation provides two main benefits.

- Administrators have greater control over which controls and software can be downloaded onto a user's computer.
- Users are presented with fewer warnings and choices for downloading software.

After the initial Internet Explorer 4.0 installation, administrators can remotely manage all allowed publisher (and site) certificates by adding new certificates to or even removing them from the allowed list.

Obtaining and using personal certificates

Personal certificates verify your identity on the Web. Through a special offer from VeriSign, Internet Explorer 3.0 and 4.0 users can obtain a "free Class 1 Digital ID" for their own personal use. For more information on personal certificates and instructions on getting your free certificate, visit:

http://www.microsoft.com/intdev/security/csa/capage-f.htm

Viewing site certificates

Site certificates verify that you're really connecting to the Web sites that you believe you're connecting to. Viewing information almost never presents a security risk, but sending information, such as your credit card number, often does. Before you send such information, security certificates are sent from the secure Web sites to Internet Explorer 4.0. The certificate provides certain information about security for that site. Certificates are issued to a particular organization for a specific period of time. Internet Explorer 4.0 verifies the Internet address stored in the certificate and that the current date precedes the expiration date.

To see the site certificates stored in Internet Explorer 4.0, click the View menu and then click Options. Click the Content tab, and then click the Sites button. Next time you connect to one of the listed Web services, you'll know you're connecting to the real thing.

Java Security (Sandboxing)

Support for sandboxing, the Java security model, was built into Internet Explorer 3.0 and has been enriched in Internet Explorer 4.0. Running a Java applet in a sandbox prevents it from accessing a computer or network resources but also greatly restricts what it can do. Authenticode provides additional protection for users in that they can verify the publisher and integrity of software components such as Java applets or ActiveX controls. Internet Explorer 4.0 users can review this information and make an informed decision about whether running such applets is in their best interest.

Internet Explorer 4.0 provides an enhanced capabilities-based sandbox security model that allows a finer degree of control over access of applets to users' computer resources, such as their hard disks, network connections, and so on. It presents users with a range of security options, such as allowing a Java applet to access a specific amount of hard disk space on a client computer.

Privacy Protection

The following sections describe the kinds of privacy protection built into Internet Explorer 4.0.

Secure channel services

Support for Secure Sockets Layer 2.0/3.0 (SSL) and Personal Communications Technology 1.0 (PCT) ensures that personal or business communications using the Internet or intranet are private. The SSL and PCT protocols create a secure channel so that no one can eavesdrop on communications. With secure communications guaranteed, users can buy consumer goods, reserve airplane tickets, or conduct personal banking on the Internet.

Transport Layer Security

Microsoft will soon add support for Transport Layer Security (TLS), a new secure channel protocol under development by the Internet Engineering Task Force. TLS builds on existing protocols to create an improved Internet secure channel protocol.

Personal Information Exchange

The Personal Information Exchange (PFX) is a set of public key–based security technologies that is part of the Microsoft Internet security framework. PFX supports Internet standards such as X.509 and PKCS#7 certificate formats. Microsoft has submitted PFX for consideration as a new PKCS standard.

Cookie privacy

Some Web sites use cookie technology to store information on a client computer. These cookies are usually used to provide Web site personalization features. With Internet Explorer 4.0, you can choose whether or not to store a cookie.

SOCKS firewall support

Many corporations provide their employees with access to the Internet through firewalls that protect the corporation from unwanted access. SOCKS is a standard protocol for traversing firewalls in a secure and controlled manner. Internet Explorer 4.0 is compatible with firewalls that use the SOCKS protocol. Hummingbird Communications, a leading provider of firewalls, provided this support.

Windows NT Server challenge/response

Corporations can take advantage of the Microsoft Windows NT Server challenge/response (NTLM) authentication that might already be in use on their Windows NT Server network. This enables users to have increased password protection and security while remaining interoperable with their existing Internet information servers.

CryptoAPI 2.0

CryptoAPI provides the underlying security services for secure channels and code signing. Through CryptoAPI, developers can easily integrate strong cryptography into their applications. Cryptographic Service Provider (CSP) modules interface with CryptoAPI and perform functions including key generation and exchange, data encryption and decryption, hashing, digital signatures, and signature verification. CryptoAPI is included as a core component of the latest versions of Windows. Internet Explorer 4.0 will automatically provide this support for earlier versions of Windows.

Microsoft Wallet

Microsoft Wallet supports securely storing important and private information, such as credit cards, electronic driver's licenses, ATM cards, and electronic cash. No application or person can view this information without a user's permission. In addition, a user decides where to store the information (on a computer, smart card, or floppy disk). Users have to enter password or account information only once and don't have to remember many different passwords. Users have complete control over who can see or use this information. Wallet allows information to be securely transferred to any computer and used with any application through the use of PFX technology. Designed for the future, Wallet supports additional payment methods (such as Internet cash) as well as other credentials and confidential information. This information can be set on the Content tab of the Options dialog box, shown in Figure 4-26.

PICS standards for Internet content

Parents want assurances that children can be blocked from visiting sites that display inappropriate information. Corporations have similar concerns, wanting to block the use of sites that offer no business value to their employees. Microsoft has been working closely with the PICS committee to help define standards for rating Internet content. (See the "Ratings System" section earlier in the chapter for more information about rating standards and setting a rating system with Internet Explorer 4.0.)

Forget your password?

And you have only two minutes to check the scores on your favorite sports Web site? With Internet Explorer 4.0, you don't have to type your user name and password every time you want to access a subscription Web service. Instead, Internet Explorer 4.0 functions as your virtual wallet, flashing your personal certificate to Web servers that want to verify your identity. It works the other way, too. You can also

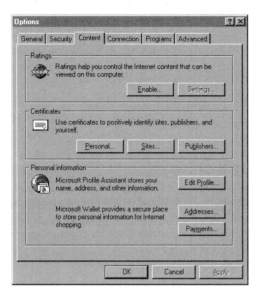

Figure 4-26   *Set your personal account information on the Content tab of the Options dialog box*

store site certificates of Web servers in Internet Explorer 4.0. This means you can verify the identity of any Web merchant or other Web server before you purchase goods or communicate with them.

Internet Connection Wizard

The Internet Connection Wizard for Internet Explorer 4.0 simplifies the process of signing up with an ISP and connecting to the Internet.

How Internet Connection Wizard Works

If you're new to the Internet, the wizard can help you find an ISP to guide you in setting up an Internet account. If you already have an ISP account, you can run the wizard to tell Internet Explorer 4.0 your account information.

Account information is stored on your hard disk in a connection file, so you can connect to the Internet without typing any additional information. Changing the information is as easy as clicking an icon.

To set up a connection or to change your account information, click the Start button, point to Programs, point to Internet Explorer (or Internet Explorer Suite), and then click Connection Wizard.

5

Internet Conferencing and Application Sharing with NetMeeting 2.0

MICROSOFT NETMEETING 2.0 DELIVERS a powerful conferencing solution in a complete, integrated package for the Internet. Many types of users—at home or school, in small businesses or large organizations—can now take full advantage of the global reach of the Internet or corporate intranets to communicate and collaborate more effectively in real-time. Figure 5-1 on the following page shows the opening screen of NetMeeting 2.0.

The video, audio, and data conferencing functions of NetMeeting 2.0 are all based on industry standards, so you can communicate with people who use compatible products from companies other than Microsoft. You'll have a wide selection of hardware and software vendors to choose from for products that build on this revolutionary way of communicating and collaborating.

NetMeeting 2.0 is fully compatible with earlier versions of NetMeeting; with the Microsoft User Location Server (ULS), which lets you find and connect with other people on the Internet; and with applications and solutions built using the Microsoft NetMeeting Software Development Kit.

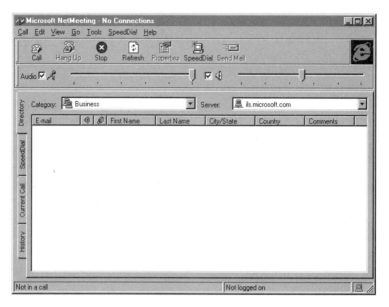

Figure 5-1   *NetMeeting 2.0 ready to be used in a business solution*

Conferencing Options of NetMeeting 2.0

With NetMeeting 2.0, you'll be able to take advantage of the following conferencing options:

- **Audio conferencing** NetMeeting serves as an "Internet phone," letting you talk with others in real-time over the Internet or an intranet and enjoy high-quality audio as you do so. All you need are a sound card, a microphone, and speakers. While you're conversing, you can bring in the data or video conferencing capabilities in NetMeeting to enhance your communication.

- **Video conferencing** When you add a video capture card and camera to your PC, you can hold a face-to-face conversation with another person over the Internet or an intranet with high-quality video. (You don't need a video camera on your PC to receive video.) You can even take a snapshot of a person or an object with your video camera and place it on the whiteboard for discussion or markup.

- **Multipoint conferencing** NetMeeting's comprehensive suite of data conferencing tools lets you collaborate and exchange information with two or more people in real-time. You can share information from one or more applications on your computer, exchange graphics or draw diagrams on a shared electronic whiteboard, send messages or take notes with the text-based chat program, and send files to other meeting members using the binary file transfer capability.

The conferencing functionality in NetMeeting 2.0 is based on international communication and conferencing standards, including the International Telecommunication Union (ITU) H.323 standard for audio and video conferencing and the ITU T.120 standard for multipoint data conferencing. The H.323 standard specifies the use of T.120 for data conferencing functionality, enabling audio, data, and video to be used together. H.323 gateway services are being developed that will allow NetMeeting users to access the Internet and call any telephone in the world through the public switched telephone network (PSTN). (For more detailed information on the ITU T.120 and H.323 standards, see the "International Communications and Conferencing Standards" section near the end of this chapter.)

Support for these standards ensures that you can call, connect, and communicate with other users who are using compatible conferencing products. You can also take advantage of conferencing services that support these standards. (For more information about this functionality, see the "Multipoint Data Conferencing" section later in this chapter.)

User Interface Enhancements in NetMeeting 2.0

NetMeeting 2.0 enhances the user interface of earlier versions of NetMeeting. Functions are now easier to locate, view, and use:

- Tabbed call windows within the NetMeeting main window make it easy to connect to other users and participate in the current call. Four windows let you choose among a variety of information: the directory of all users currently logged onto the directory server and their audio/video capabilities, SpeedDial entries and their status, the users participating in the current call, and a history log of all received calls.

- You can filter the directory entries to find and connect with other users. For example, you can filter the entries to identify only those currently participating in a call or only those with audio and video capabilities. Also, you can choose one of three user categories—personal, business, or adults-only—as an additional filter to show only those who have selected the same user category.

- To integrate more fully with Microsoft Internet Explorer, NetMeeting now includes a Go menu for accessing Web-based directory information, as well as Internet Mail and News. You can connect to other users from a Web-based directory view by entering the user's e-mail address, specifying the user's IP address, or typing the user's machine name.

- Refined NetMeeting Options tabs and wizards make it easier to set up and configure the NetMeeting environment. A new Calling tab lets you choose directory and SpeedDial options. An H.323 gateway calling option lets you connect to a person by using a telephone number.

- A graphical interface similar to the one in Microsoft Internet Explorer 3.0, including a common toolbar, makes it simple to move among applications that are part of the Internet Explorer suite. The toolbar is context-sensitive, displaying the most appropriate options based on the active window.

- The host computer lets the call originator hang up on one or more participants, so you can quickly remove unwanted participants from a group call.

- E-mail messaging gives you the option of sending e-mail to people who are not available for conferencing. NetMeeting uses MAPI to start a mail client of choice, automatically adds the subject information, and then includes a SpeedDial shortcut so that the person can easily call you back later.

NetMeeting 2.0 in Action

Using NetMeeting 2.0, your organization can increase productivity and save time and money. You can use the audio, video, and data conferencing features of NetMeeting 2.0 to improve many business processes and to solve problems. Here are some of the innovative ways in which you can use NetMeeting on the Internet and on corporate intranets:

- Virtual meetings
- Document collaboration
- Customer service
- Telecommuting
- Distance learning
- Technical support
- Home use

The following sections describe these scenarios.

Virtual Meetings

Now you can hold meetings and communicate with groups of people all over the world simultaneously using standard network connections, including the Internet. NetMeeting lets you connect with others at different locations and share information as if everyone were in the same room. Using the application sharing capability in NetMeeting, you can share MS-DOS text and virtually any Microsoft Windows–based application—from presentation graphics, word processing, and spreadsheet software to games and drawing programs—to enhance the meeting presentation. All meeting participants can see the same information in real-time. You can further enhance your NetMeeting experience by using audio and video capabilities to see other people and share conversations.

Document Collaboration

NetMeeting document collaboration lets you work together with many users on documents or information in real-time. You can share an application running on your computer with other people in the meeting. Everyone can view the information shared by the application, and any participant can take control of the shared application to edit or paste information in real-time.

Customer Service

Customer service lets you communicate directly with a customer service representative from a Web site and share information as part of a telephone call. From a Web site, you can use NetMeeting to connect to a customer service representative with a single telephone call and then use the audio and data conferencing features (or even video) to communicate about a product or service.

Telecommuting

For those who need to or want to work from home or from another remote site, NetMeeting makes telecommuting simple. NetMeeting users can extend their reach beyond file sharing or e-mail and take advantage of data conferencing capabilities on the road or in remote locations. You can stay in touch with co-workers much more effectively by collaborating in real-time or participating in a presentation while at a remote location.

Distance Learning

NetMeeting enables organizations to distribute educational presentations or information to many people in different locations in real-time over the Internet or corporate intranets. You can use NetMeeting to share presentation slides and other applications to train people in different locations. Companies can use NetMeeting to conduct product briefings and demonstrations over the Internet, opening up new avenues for marketing and reaching customers.

Technical Support

With NetMeeting, support organizations not only can see the scenario or problem situation on a remote user's computer but also can correct a problem during a support call without having to physically go to a remote location. With the application sharing feature in NetMeeting, you can share an application window with a help desk technician, who can walk you through the problem and possibly resolve the problem remotely. You can even remotely share your Control Panel so that the help desk technician can verify the computer configuration.

Home Users

Have you ever wanted to show your favorite Web site to a friend or share your favorite picture with a family member? NetMeeting 2.0 lets you communicate with family and friends over the Internet. With a sound card, speakers, and a microphone, you can talk to other people around the world using the NetMeeting Internet phone feature. Add on a Video for Windows–compatible video capture card and a camera, and you can both see and hear the person you're talking with.

Multipoint Data Conferencing

Multipoint data conferencing allows two or more people to work together as a group in real-time over the Internet or a corporate intranet. Users can share applications, exchange information between shared applications through a shared clipboard, transfer files, collaborate on a shared whiteboard, and communicate with a text-based chat feature. Support for the T.120 data conferencing standard enables interoperability with other T.120-based products and services. The features of multipoint data conferencing are described here:

- **Application sharing** Participants in the conference can share a program running on one computer. They can review the same data or information and watch the actions of others as they work on the program (for example, editing content or scrolling through information). Participants can share Windows-based applications transparently, without any special knowledge of the application capabilities. The person sharing the application can choose to collaborate with other conference participants, and the participants can take turns editing or controlling the application. Only the person sharing the program needs to have the given application installed on his or her computer.

- **Shared clipboard** The shared clipboard enables you to exchange its contents with other participants in a conference using familiar cut, copy, and paste operations. For example, you can copy information from a local document and paste the contents into a shared application as part of group collaboration. This capability provides seamless exchange of information between shared and local applications.

- **File transfer** With the file transfer capability, you can send one or more files in the background to one or all of the conference participants. You can send files to a particular person by right-clicking on that person's name in the Current Call window or by dragging and dropping the file into the Microsoft NetMeeting window and having it sent automatically to all meeting participants, each of whom can then accept or decline receipt. Again, this file transfer occurs in the background, as everyone continues sharing an application, using the whiteboard, or chatting. This file transfer capability is fully compliant with the T.127 standard.

- **Shared whiteboard** The whiteboard program is a multipage, multiuser drawing application that enables conference participants to sketch diagrams, create organization charts, or display other graphic information. Whiteboard is object-oriented (versus pixel-oriented), allowing you to move and manipulate its contents by clicking and dragging with the mouse. In addition, you can use the Remote Pointer (described later in this chapter) to point out specific contents or sections of shared pages. This capability extends the application sharing feature of NetMeeting by supporting ad hoc collaboration on a common drawing surface. (See the "Whiteboard" section below for more on this tool's functionality.)

- **Chat** You can type text messages to share common ideas or topics with other conference participants or record meeting notes and action items as part of a collaborative process. Conference participants can also use Chat to communicate in the absence of audio support. A new "whisper" feature lets you have a separate, private conversation with another person during a group chat session. From the Chat window, simply click on the person's name in the Send To list, and type your private text message that only you and the selected person will see.

Data Conferencing Functionality: True Application Sharing

After connecting two or more machines together, you can perform any of the following actions:

- **Share an application with others in a conference** As mentioned earlier, NetMeeting lets you share virtually any Windows-based application with others in a conference, enabling them to see the same information you have open on your screen. This functionality enhances your ability to communicate. To set up a shared application, follow these steps: start a Windows-based application (such as Microsoft Word, Microsoft Excel, Microsoft PowerPoint, or Microsoft Internet Explorer) on one computer; select the Share Application option from the Tools menu (or left-click the NetMeeting shortcut icon in the status area of the taskbar); and then choose the available application window. The shared window will automatically appear on the screens of others in the conference. Try scrolling, editing, and manipulating the contents of the shared application; although others in the conference will be able to see the updates to the shared window information, they won't be able to take control of the shared application until you enable collaboration.

- **Collaborate in real-time with others in a conference** To let other users take control of the shared application, just enable the Collaborate feature. You initiate collaboration by selecting Start Collaborating from the Tools menu (or by left-clicking the NetMeeting shortcut icon in the status area of the taskbar). Another user can collaborate by enabling Collaborate also or by double-clicking the shared application window. Once collaboration is enabled, conference participants can take turns working with the shared application.

- **Cut and copy and paste to and from a shared application and a local application** Through the NetMeeting shared clipboard, you can cut and copy and paste to and from a local application to and from a shared application. For example, you can open a workbook in a local copy of Excel, select information from a worksheet, copy it to the local clipboard (by selecting Copy from the Edit menu), take control of the shared application, and then select Paste from the Edit menu in the application. You can also cut and copy from the shared application to a local application.

- **Share any folder or operating system window** The application sharing capability of NetMeeting is very flexible and lets you share folders as well as applications so that others can see the same information on screen. Try opening the Control Panel and sharing it during a conference, enabling collaboration, and then viewing or changing system setting information. This feature is helpful for offering remote PC support.

- **Take back control of a shared application** If, during a conference, you want to cancel collaboration and instantly regain control of an application you shared, press the Esc key, which will instantly give you back control.

Whiteboard

As introduced earlier, the whiteboard feature of NetMeeting 2.0 is a handy way of sharing visual information in a conference. Figure 5-2 shows the whiteboard program in use by two participants.

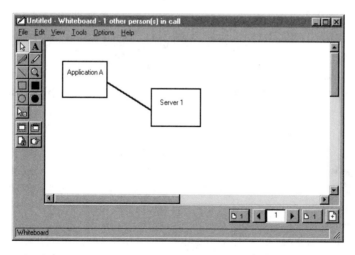

Figure 5-2 *Whiteboard with two participants*

Some characteristics of the whiteboard are described in the following sections.

Automatic launching

The whiteboard automatically launches when one person in the conference starts it. When the whiteboard is started on one computer in the conference, it is automatically launched on the other computers in the conference.

Real-time collaboration via graphics

The whiteboard lets you collaborate in real-time with others via graphic information. As you use the whiteboard features to create diagrams, others in the conference see the diagram components in real-time. As you draw circles, rectangles, and lines and type text, the information appears on the whiteboards of others in the conference, who can also be drawing to their whiteboards at the same time.

Desktop information

You can capture and paste window and desktop information into the whiteboard. Use the Select Window or Select Area tools to select screen-image information and paste it into the whiteboard. This feature allows you and others to mark up the image of the application window.

Drag and drop functionality

Drag and drop functionality makes it easy to include information on the whiteboard. Because you can drag and drop the contents of saved whiteboard information into the active whiteboard, you can use prearranged whiteboard information in a meeting. In addition, you can cut, copy, and paste information from any Windows-based application into the whiteboard.

The Remote Pointer

The Remote Pointer helps to highlight information on the whiteboard. You can use the Remote Pointer to point to a specific item or area on the whiteboard. Each conference participant has a different-colored pointer. When you select the Remote Pointer and move it around the screen to highlight different areas of the whiteboard space, other conference participants can see your actions. Figure 5-3 on the following page shows the Remote Pointer in action.

Multiple pages

NetMeeting allows you to use multiple pages in the whiteboard to facilitate communication. By disabling the Synchronize option from the Tools menu of the Whiteboard window, you can switch to another whiteboard page while others in the conference are viewing the previous page.

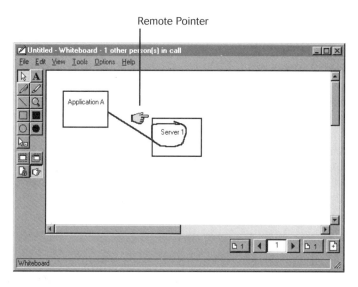

Remote Pointer

Figure 5-3 *Remote Pointer in NetMeeting whiteboard*

Saving for the future

After a conference, you can save whiteboard contents for future reference by clicking Save on the File menu. During a conference, you can load saved whiteboard pages (which means you can prepare information before a conference) and then drag and drop them into the whiteboard during the meeting.

Microsoft Chat

Using Microsoft Chat (formerly named Comic Chat), you can have real-time conversations with friends or business associates via the Internet or intranets in either text mode or comic mode. Figure 5-4 shows the Chat screen set up for two participants.

Text mode makes it easy to include lots of people in a chat. And when the pace of a conversation starts to pick up, text mode is the easiest and quickest way to view and add comments. In addition to providing customizable fonts, Chat's text mode allows you to deliver messages in a variety of ways: with a unique salutation, as a private (whisper) message to just one person, or with sound effects.

Comic mode lets you choose a cartoon character to represent you in a chat that unfolds as a comic strip. In the process, you can express a wide range of emotions using such methods as sending your thoughts, whispering to a selected recipient, shouting, or sending sound effects, to name just a few of the options you have. As the chat participants type text into Chat's comic mode, characters' utterances appear

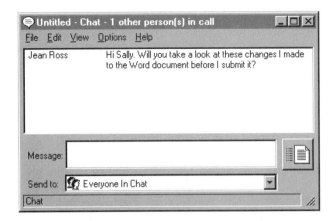

Figure 5-4   *An in-progress Chat session*

above them as word balloons. Because Chat automatically generates each panel on the fly, the presentation of the comic strip conversation is nearly instantaneous. Figure 5-5 shows an example of a Chat session in comic mode.

Figure 5-5   *Comic Chat characters*

Whether you choose to chat in text or comic mode, you can print your conversation and save it for offline viewing. You can also switch easily between text and comic modes with a single click, even during a chat.

Using Chat for personal reasons—such as gossiping with friends, holding a reunion with family members around the world, or meeting new people who share similar hobbies and interests—is fun. It's also easy to access and simple to use. Web authors can insert the Microsoft Chat control in their Web pages to instantly create a place where people can meet and converse. (See "The Chat Control" section on the next page for more information on how to insert this control in your Web pages.)

Chat is also an important tool for business communication. Chatting provides an easy means for employees to discuss ideas, resolve issues, and develop solutions in a group-like environment without having to be located in the same place. Businesses can add a Chat control to their intranet site to make it easy for their employees to keep in touch.

As mentioned in the preceding section, starting Chat on one computer in a conference automatically launches it on the other computers in the conference. Chat enables you to send messages to and receive messages from other meeting participants during a conference. Because each person in the conference can type text, Chat is a great way to keep meeting notes, track action items, or communicate during a business conference. Again, you can use Chat's whisper mode to send a private message to another meeting participant during a conference; a whisper message is always specified on the recipient's user interface as being a whisper message from the sender.

The Chat Control

The new Chat control is an ActiveX-based control that allows two or more users who are connected to a chat server to carry on a conversation—communicating with both text and data. The ActiveX control provides a default user interface that is completely customizable, but you can also design a custom user interface. The Chat control has an optional user interface that's very flexible, allowing you to include a Send button, Whisper button, Participant list box, History text box, and Send To text box.

You can also use Microsoft Visual Basic, Scripting Edition (VBScript) to insert the Chat control into a Web page. You can also use the Chat control in any ActiveX container application to create a chat client. Both implementations enable conversations between multiple users on client computers accessing a common chat server over the Internet.

If you've installed Internet Explorer, you can check out the Chat control at:

http://www.microsoft.com/ie/ie40/collab/chatsample.htm

This will download the Chat control if you don't have the control already.

To find out more about using the Microsoft Chat control, download the Microsoft Chat control SDK from:

http://www.microsoft.com/msdownload/ieadd.htm

Video Conferencing and Videophone

With NetMeeting 2.0, you can send and receive real-time visual images with another conference participant using any Video for Windows–compatible equipment. You can share ideas and information "face-to-face" and use the camera to instantly view items, such as hardware or devices, by displaying them in front of the lens. After connecting two people together with NetMeeting, you can use the video conferencing functionality simply by speaking into the microphone and looking into the video camera.

NetMeeting 2.0 video conferencing includes the following features:

- **Ability to receive images without video hardware** Even if you don't have a video capture card or a camera for sending video, you can still receive video images sent by other users.

- **High-quality video, even over low-bandwidth connections** NetMeeting 2.0 produces high-quality, real-time video images using a standard 28.8 Kbps modem Internet connection, IP over ISDN connection, or local area network (LAN) connection.

- **Compatibility with existing video capture hardware** NetMeeting 2.0 supports video capture cards and cameras that are compatible with Video for Windows drivers, which includes most commonly available video hardware.

- **Switchable audio and video** With NetMeeting 2.0, you can switch your audio and video connection from person to person. This feature makes it easy to communicate with different meeting participants. When in a multipoint call, you can switch video to another participant in the meeting. When three or more people are connected, choose the Switch Audio And Video option from the Tools menu and select the desired meeting participant (or right-click a participant in the conference whom you want to switch video to). NetMeeting switches the video to connect with that person.

- **Changeable video image size** You can change the size of the video you're sending to another user dynamically during a video conferencing session. After a NetMeeting call has been established, right-click a video window and choose the Properties option (or choose Options from the Tools menu). From the Video property page, choose the desired Send Image Size option. The size of your local video window will change, as will the video image the other meeting participants view. Also, you can choose whether or not to transmit video immediately when a call starts.

- **Remote change of video-quality level** When in a video conferencing session, you can remotely make the trade-off between faster video performance and better image quality. After a NetMeeting call has been established, right-click a video window and choose the Properties option (or choose Options from the Tools menu). From the Video property page, adjust the Video Quality slider bar to the desired setting. After you make the change, the image in the Remote Video window changes accordingly.

- **Windows clipboard accessibility** Copying video images into another application is simple. You can capture video image frames and place them on the clipboard for pasting into another Windows-based application you're using or into the NetMeeting whiteboard application. Right-click the appropriate video window, and choose Copy from the context menu. You can then paste the image frame into another application.

- **Detachable video window** NetMeeting gives you flexibility in managing the video windows during a NetMeeting call. You can keep the windows as part of the NetMeeting user interface to minimize the number of windows you need to manage, or you can drag one or both of the video windows from the NetMeeting application window and place it on the desktop. You can return the window to the NetMeeting user interface by dragging it back into the NetMeeting application window. Also, you can pause or resume sending video images by pressing a button on the video window.

- **Support for the ITU H.323 conference servers and gateways standard** NetMeeting 2.0 supports the H.323 standard for audio and video conferencing, which includes the H.263 video and G.723.1 and G.711 audio codecs. H.323 allows NetMeeting to interoperate with other compatible video phone clients, such as the Intel Internet Video Phone. NetMeeting 2.0 can also support multiuser audio and video meetings using a multipoint conferencing bridge service. Several leading industry vendors are currently developing H.323 conference servers and gateways that will enable NetMeeting users to participate in a meeting with multiple audio and video connections. The first of these products is expected to be available during the second half of 1997.

- **Support for Intel MMX Technology** If you have an Intel MMX-enabled computer, specialized NetMeeting codecs for MMX provide enhanced performance for video compression and decompression. You'll benefit from lower CPU utilization and improved video quality during calls.

- **Integration with system policy support** NetMeeting 2.0's video functions integrate with system policy support in Microsoft Windows 95, Microsoft Windows 98, and Microsoft Windows NT 4.0. This integration enables IS organizations to centrally control and manage video settings for their user communities.

Internet Phone and Audio Conferencing

As mentioned at the beginning of the chapter, you can make voice calls using Net-Meeting 2.0 and talk to people running NetMeeting and other compatible Internet phone products. Real-time, point-to-point audio conferencing over the Internet or a corporate intranet lets you make voice calls to associates and organizations around the world.

NetMeeting audio conferencing offers many features, including half-duplex and full-duplex audio support for real-time conversations; automatic microphone sensitivity-level setting to ensure that meeting participants hear each other clearly; and microphone muting, which lets you control the audio signal sent during a call. This audio conferencing supports network TCP/IP connections.

Intelligent Audio and Video Stream Control

NetMeeting features intelligent control of the audio and video stream, which auto-matically balances the load for network bandwidth, CPU use, and memory use. This intelligent stream control ensures that audio, video, and data are prioritized prop-erly so that NetMeeting maintains high-quality audio while transmitting and receiv-ing data and video during a call. Through system policy features, IS organizations can configure the stream control services to limit the bandwidth used for audio and video on a per-client basis during a meeting. For more information, see the "Microsoft NetMeeting 2.0 Resource Kit" section at the end of this chapter.

Using NetMeeting to Call Someone

After you have NetMeeting up and running, the next step is to call someone. Calling people over the Internet with NetMeeting is as easy as placing a phone call—maybe even easier. Whether the person you want to call is located in another city, state, or country, NetMeeting will help you connect with them.

Connecting Made Simple

NetMeeting provides flexible ways to connect to other users. You can connect two or more computers using one of several means:

- Typing in an IP address (as identified by running WINIPCFG.EXE under the Windows 98 operating system)
- Typing in the NetBIOS machine name for another computer (as configured on the Identification tab in the Network applet on the Control Panel in Win-dows 98)

- Typing in another user's e-mail address when used in conjunction with the Microsoft Internet Locator Server (ILS)
- Selecting the desired user from the directory on an ILS

The following sections describe some additional connection options of Net-Meeting 2.0.

SpeedDial

SpeedDial makes it easy to connect with frequent contacts. If you made a connection to another user through an ILS, the person's contact information is stored as a SpeedDial entry in NetMeeting. Through the NetMeeting SpeedDial tab, you can easily see whether the individual is online without having to search for his or her presence in the directory.

Multipoint data conferencing

Multipoint data conferencing allows multiple users to connect. NetMeeting lets you connect to two or more people for a conference. To establish a multipoint conference, call additional people or have them call you.

Directory filtering

Directory filtering makes it easy to find people to communicate with. You can filter the directory entries displayed on the Directory tab within the NetMeeting user interface. For example, you can view the information for people not currently in a call, people currently in a call, people with video cameras, or people in the same country. You can also sort the information in the directory window by clicking the desired column heading. For example, to view which users have audio capability, you can sort the audio column. From the Directory window, you can also adjust the position of the Directory information fields by clicking the heading for the desired column and then clicking and dragging to the desired position.

NetMeeting invitation

NetMeeting invitation makes it easy to invite users to call you. If a NetMeeting call is attempted but not completed when using an ILS to make the connection, NetMeeting gives you the option of sending the user an e-mail message inviting him or her to call you back. NetMeeting opens your preferred e-mail client and includes a SpeedDial shortcut to help the other user return your NetMeeting call.

The Do Not Disturb option

The Do Not Disturb option keeps others from interrupting you during a conference. When in a NetMeeting conference, you can enable the Do Not Disturb option to prevent others from interrupting your conference. When other users attempt to connect, they will be informed automatically that you did not accept their call and will be asked whether they want to send you a message. You can enable the Do Not Disturb option from the Call menu on the NetMeeting menu bar.

Web-based directory

A Web-based directory provides an alternate view of user directory entries in Net-Meeting. You can also place NetMeeting calls by selecting people from a Web-based directory. The ILS supports the display of a Web-based directory, providing another way to customize the appearance of the NetMeeting Directory and making it easy to place NetMeeting calls from a Web browser. From within the NetMeeting application, choose the Web Directory option from the Go menu. You can connect to another user by clicking the desired item.

Making NetMeeting Calls from Exchange and Outlook

NetMeeting includes a mail extension that works with Microsoft Exchange and Microsoft Outlook mail clients. You can place a call directly from the Exchange and Outlook menus based on NetMeeting entries in the mail address book. From your mail client's Tools menu, click Place A NetMeeting Call and choose a person to call from your mail address book. (Both of you must be logged onto the same directory server.) This feature gives you the flexibility of sending a mail message to a NetMeeting user or initiating a NetMeeting call directly from your mail address book.

Calling from Either Internet Explorer or Windows Explorer

You can place NetMeeting calls from either Microsoft Internet Explorer or Microsoft Windows Explorer. People can call you by clicking a NetMeeting link on your Web page. Using Internet Explorer, they can call you using the link on your Web page even if they don't have NetMeeting running. Type the following syntax to create a link on your Web page:

callto:<servername>/<e-mail address>

For example, if Carl Smith wanted to embed a link in his Web page so that other people could call him, he would add the following HTML:

Call me using NetMeeting at
callto:uls.microsoft.com/csmith@somedomain.com

It's also easy to call people from Windows Explorer if you know their e-mail address in the NetMeeting directory. Just follow these steps:

1. Click the Start button.
2. Click Run.

3. If you and the other person are logged onto the same server, type:

   callto:<e-mail address>

   For example, to call a person with the address *csmith@somedomain.com*, type:

   callto:csmith@somedomain.com

   If the person is logged into a different server than you, type:

   callto:<servername>/<e-mail address>

   For example, to call a person logged into *uls.microsoft.com* with an e-mail address of *csmith@somedomain.com*, type:

   callto:uls.microsoft.com/csmith@somedomain.com

   Then click OK.

Finding Other NetMeeting Users to Call (the Internet Locator Server)

The key to finding other people using NetMeeting on the Internet is the Microsoft Internet Locator Server (ILS), sometimes known as the ULS. Using the ILS, you can easily find other NetMeeting users who are currently running NetMeeting and awaiting your call. Click the Directory tab in NetMeeting, and you'll see the names of people currently using NetMeeting on a specific ILS. To see the list of users on another ILS, choose the ILS name from the drop-down list or type the desired server name in the Server text box on the Directory tab. You can also originate a call with NetMeeting directly from the Web page directory generated by the ILS.

The ILS directory represents people who are running NetMeeting at any given time. When a user starts NetMeeting, his or her name will appear in the ILS directory and he or she is ready to take a call. When that user exits NetMeeting, he or she is removed from the ILS directory; the directory is updated dynamically. Keep in mind that you have the option of not being listed in the ILS directory—you will still see the names of other people in the directory, but they cannot see your name. To change the status of your information in the directory, select Tools from the NetMeeting menu, choose the Options menu item, and click the Calling tab.

Multiple servers can exist on the Internet, allowing communities of users to be established. For example, Internet service providers can establish their own ILS sites and host communities of their users, making it easy for people to communicate using NetMeeting. In addition, different ILSs can be implemented in a corporate intranet environment, allowing different organizations, departments, or remote subsidiaries in a company to communicate with each other over an internal network.

How Do Users Find Me?

When you install NetMeeting for the first time, you are prompted to identify the name of the server on which you will "reside." The default ILS name that NetMeeting offers for most people is *ils.microsoft.com*, which is on the Internet. You might want to change the name of your server to speed up directory lookup for people you communicate with often or to establish your presence in another community.

Some other servers that are available on the Internet for finding NetMeeting users are listed in following table—you can choose to reside on any server you want. To view or change the name of your ILS, select Tools from the NetMeeting menu, choose the Options menu item, and click the Calling tab.

Internet Locator Servers

ILS Name	Description
ils.microsoft.com	Internet Locator Server operated by Microsoft
ils1.microsoft.com	Internet Locator Server operated by Microsoft
ils2.microsoft.com	Internet Locator Server operated by Microsoft
ils3.microsoft.com	Internet Locator Server operated by Microsoft
ils4.microsoft.com	Internet Locator Server operated by Microsoft
ils5.microsoft.com	Internet Locator Server operated by Microsoft
ils.four11.com	Internet Locator Server operated by Four11 Corporation
ils.family.four11.com	Internet Locator Server operated by Four11 Corporation
hawaii.acunet.net	Internet Locator Server operated by the POPULUS Web site

If you've set up your own ILS on the Internet, send mail to *msils@microsoft.com* so that you can be added to the list.

Setting up your own Internet Locator Server

If you are an Internet Webmaster or intranet system administrator, you can set up your own Internet Locator Server on the Internet or your corporate intranet. Connect to *http://www.backoffice.microsoft.com/* for more information.

System Policies

Administrators can implement NetMeeting system policies to control user and computer privileges. Using system policies, administrators can predefine settings and restrictions, such as preventing the use of audio features, and provide standard configurations for their user community. New system policies include the ability to limit the network bandwidth for audio and video streams. To learn more about setting system policies, see the *Microsoft NetMeeting 2.0 Resource Kit*, which is described in the last section of this chapter.

NetMeeting 2.0: A Standards-Based Platform

Standards are critical to achieving the vision of NetMeeting 2.0, which is to create and popularize the use of interoperable real-time communications and conferencing on the Internet. To achieve this vision, a real-time communications and conferencing product requires standards so users can connect with each other easily and reliably, as they can using a telephone. Consumers expect and demand that all products will operate error-free—that every connection will succeed, and that they can communicate with each other independent of the operating system or the product. Standards ensure this experience.

With standards, a product from one vendor can provide a guaranteed level of compatibility with products from other vendors. Vendors can continue to build compatible, add-on products that will successfully interoperate with different multimedia telephony products. Depending on the standards they support, users can potentially share applications and information, see each other with video, talk to one another, or perform all these functions simultaneously.

NetMeeting 2.0 continues to extend NetMeeting's leadership in two areas: as a standards-based product that lets users communicate and collaborate in real-time; and as a platform upon which developers can build and integrate conferencing solutions.

A number of major themes drive NetMeeting 2.0's feature set:

- **Continued integration of industry standards** Microsoft is firmly committed to building products and solutions based on industry standards. Supporting industry standards is the only way to ensure that products and services from different companies operate with each other no matter which platforms they were built for. NetMeeting 1.0 was the first product to introduce multipoint data conferencing based on the ITU T.120 standard. Implementing this protocol means that NetMeeting can interoperate with other T.120 clients and conferencing bridges. NetMeeting 2.0 extends this leadership by adding support for the ITU H.323 audio and video conferencing standard. By supporting this standard, NetMeeting 2.0 is the first real-time communications and conferencing client for the Internet to provide standards-based audio, video, and data conferencing capabilities. For more information about H.323, see "International Communications and Conferencing Standards." Also, NetMeeting 2.0 adds support for the Lightweight Directory Access Protocol (LDAP) standard, which helps NetMeeting users find other people on the Internet.

- **Communications and conferencing integrated with Web pages** The NetMeeting SDK gives Web site professionals the ability to integrate conferencing capabilities, letting NetMeeting users join meetings directly from Web pages. Added functions in NetMeeting 2.0 allow developers to integrate more conferencing capabilities. ActiveX scripting languages, including JavaScript-compatible scripting languages and VBScript, support these advanced functions.

- **Improved platform for building communication and conferencing products and services** The updated version of the NetMeeting SDK allows developers to take advantage of the new features and functions in NetMeeting 2.0. SDK developers can:
  - Integrate real-time multipoint data conferencing capabilities into existing conferencing solutions
  - Develop custom conferencing solutions to enhance service offerings
  - Extend the features of NetMeeting into their own client offerings
  - Provide more seamless integration with NetMeeting functions, as well as transparent integration of rich multimedia communications capabilities—such as audio, video, and data—with third-party products and solutions

- **Effective solutions for organizations** As the direct result of customer requests, NetMeeting 2.0 includes features that make it more effective in meeting organizations' communication and conferencing needs. The following customer-requested functions are included with NetMeeting 2.0:
  - Support for the Windows NT 4.0 operating system as well as for Windows 95 and Windows 98
  - Improved administration and manageability, with better control through system policies
  - More advanced setup and configuration tools that organizations can deploy
  - Support for system policies in Windows 95 and Windows NT 4.0, which enables IS organizations to centrally control and manage the features available to users on the corporate network

International Communications and Conferencing Standards

As mentioned earlier in the chapter, the two main standards supported by NetMeeting 2.0 are the International Telecommunication Union (ITU) T.120 and the H.323.

The T.120 standard

The ITU T.120 protocols enable developers to create compatible products and services for real-time, multipoint data connections and conferencing. T.120-based applications enable many users to participate in conferencing sessions over different types of networks and connections. Depending on the type of T.120 product, they can make connections, transmit and receive data, and collaborate using compatible data conferencing features, such as sharing applications, using a conferencing whiteboard, and transferring files. Microsoft and more than 100 other major companies support the T.120 standard.

The H.323 standard

H.323 is an ITU standard for terminals (PCs), equipment, and services for multimedia communication over LANs (such as the Internet) that don't provide a guaranteed quality of service. H.323 terminals and equipment can carry real-time video, audio, and data, or any combination of these elements. This standard is based on the IETF Real-time Transport Protocol (RTP) and Real-time Transport Control Protocol (RTCP), with additional protocols for call signaling, data sharing, and audiovisual communications.

Products that use H.323 for audio and video enable users to interconnect and communicate with other people over the Internet, just as people using different makes and models of telephones can communicate over PSTN lines. H.323 defines how audio and video information is formatted and packaged for transmission over the network. Standard audio and video codecs encode and decode input/output from audio and video sources for communicating between nodes.

Also, the H.323 specification identifies the use of T.120 services for data communications and conferencing within an H.323 session. This T.120 support means that data handling occurs in conjunction with H.323 audio and video rather than separately.

More than 120 leading companies have announced their intent to support and implement H.323 in their products and services. This broad support establishes H.323 as the leading solution for audio and video conferencing over the Internet.

The H.323 standard includes the following key features:

- **Standard support for audio (voice) conferencing** Provides standard mechanisms to encode and decode audio from a microphone for communicating between nodes. This allows users on different computing platforms to use products from different vendors to speak with each other over the network.

- **Standard support for video conferencing** Provides standard mechanisms to encode and decode images from a video source for communicating between nodes. This allows users on different computing platforms to use products from different vendors to communicate face-to-face over the network.

- **Integrates with T.120 for data communications** Services set forth by the T.120 specification handle the data portions of an H.323 session. The ITU T.120 standard specifies the method for handling multipoint data communications and specifies application-level protocols for sharing data.

The following standards are also part of the H.323 specification.

H.225.0

The H.225.0 standard defines a layer that does two things: formats the transmitted video, audio, data, and control streams for output to the network; and retrieves the received video, audio, data, and control streams from the network. H.225.0 utilizes the packet format specified by the Internet Engineering Task Force (IETF) RTP and RTCP specifications for sequence numbering and error detection as part of audio and video transmissions. Support for RTP and RTCP enables the receiving node to place the received packets in the proper order so that the user hears or sees the transmitted information correctly.

H.245

The H.245 standard provides the call control mechanism to enable H.323-compatible terminals to connect to each other.

G.723.1

The G.723.1 standard specifies the format and algorithm for the default audio codec used to send or receive voice over low-bandwidth network connections.

G.711

The G.711 standard specifies the format and algorithm for an alternative, higher bandwidth, audio codec used to send or receive voice over network connections.

H.263

The H.263 standard specifies the format and algorithm for the default video codec used to send or receive video over low-bandwidth network connections.

H.261

The H.261 standard specifies the format and algorithm for an alternative, higher bandwidth, video codec used to send or receive video images over network connections.

Setting industry standards

The following organizations are responsible for defining, approving, and communicating industry standards:

- **International Telecommunication Union (ITU)** Governments and the private sector coordinate global telecommunications networks and services through the ITU, which is headquartered in Geneva, Switzerland. This international organization coordinates, develops, regulates, and standardizes global telecommunications and organizes regional and world events. Visit *http://www.itu.ch/* for more information about ITU.

- **Internet Engineering Task Force (IETF)** The IETF is the protocol engineering and development arm of the Internet. This organization is a large, open, international community of network designers, operators, vendors, and researchers concerned with the evolution of the Internet architecture as well as with the smooth operation of the Internet. Visit *http://www.ietf.org/* for more information about IETF.

- **International Multimedia Teleconferencing Consortium (IMTC)** The IMTC is a nonprofit corporation founded to promote the creation and adoption of international standards for multipoint document and video teleconferencing. The IMTC and its members promote a "Standards First" initiative to guarantee interworking for all aspects of multimedia teleconferencing. Visit *http://www.imtc.org/* for more information about IMTC.

Microsoft NetMeeting 2.0 Resource Kit

The *Microsoft NetMeeting 2.0 Resource Kit* is your one-stop location for technical information. Written for system administrators, IS organizations, and solution providers, this resource kit provides useful information for deploying, supporting, and understanding NetMeeting 2.0. It includes chapters on the NetMeeting architecture, international conferencing standards supported by NetMeeting, and the interoperability of NetMeeting with other standards-based conferencing products and services. To download the *Microsoft NetMeeting 2.0 Resource Kit*, visit this site:

http://www.microsoft.com/netmeeting/reskit/

6

Broadcasting on Your Desktop with NetShow 2.0

THE INTERNET AND INTRANETS COME ALIVE with Microsoft NetShow 2.0, which lets you see and hear either live or recorded broadcasts on your PC without having to wait for time-consuming downloads or to experience sluggish network performance. And your network will be spared from the bandwidth degradation normally associated with rich-media broadcasting. NetShow 2.0 networked multimedia software and Microsoft Windows NT Server, with the help of Microsoft Internet Information Server (IIS) integration, combine to bring the vibrancy of multimedia to your desktop. NetShow, with its leading-edge multicast and on-demand media-streaming technology, is client/server software that also extends the power of broadcasting to Microsoft Internet Explorer 4.0.

NetShow accommodates many types of users—from Web surfers to Web professionals, from employees of small businesses and organizations to those who work in large corporations, from home users to Internet Service Providers—to create exciting multimedia experiences that you can access through Microsoft Internet Explorer, Netscape Navigator 3.0, and many other Web browsers.

NOTE

NetShow complements Microsoft NetMeeting (described in the preceding chapter), and the two make up Internet Explorer 4.0's main delivery systems for multimedia communication. NetShow efficiently delivers content from one source to many on the Internet or an intranet, and NetMeeting allows person-to-person and group interactive sessions.

Features and Benefits of NetShow 2.0

NetShow 2.0, with its tight integration with Internet Explorer 4.0, Windows NT, and Microsoft Internet Information Server and its support of open, industry standards, provides a wealth of features and benefits for developers, Web professionals, network managers, and other users.

NetShow 1.0 delivered basic audio and video services, enabled unicast and multicast delivery of live and on-demand content, and supplied the essential interfaces for codec vendors, tools vendors, and Webmasters to build value-added software for NetShow 1.0. NetShow 2.0 expands on the strengths of NetShow 1.0 to provide an open, standards-based system that can be used for producing audio and video broadcasts. In short, NetShow 2.0 brings broadcasting capabilities to your desktop. You'll experience interactive content including audio, illustrated audio (images synchronized with an audio track), and video on demand and live IP multicast audio, video, and file transfer. NetShow 2.0 includes both client and server components to add the functions of traditional broadcasting systems (audio and video) to HTTP. It also harnesses Internet technologies and the power of Windows NT Server to transform Web communications into a richer and more effective medium: the network show.

Key Features of NetShow 2.0

- **Client component designed for Internet Explorer 4.0** The NetShow client is an ActiveX control included in Internet Explorer 4.0 that receives multimedia content and allows you to play it back without waiting a long time for files to download. And because NetShow is an ActiveX control, you can use it to enhance applications with audio and video content with the same development tools you use to create HTML applications. A familiar HTML-based client makes it easy for you to learn operations quickly.

- **Internet Information Server (IIS) 3.0 integration** NetShow is administered through standard Windows NT Server and IIS administration utilities. IIS 3.0 integration makes it easier to use NetShow to build server-based Web applications and to create rich and dynamic content.

- **Broadcast TV metaphor for publishing and receiving content** NetShow allows publishers to deliver content organized into channels and shows, just as on television. On the client site, the Microsoft NetShow Program Guide provides an intuitive user interface to enable Web surfers to find channels and shows delivered on a specific site, just as an Electronic Program Guide does.

- **Live multicast audio** By allowing many users to tune into a single multicast transmission, network managers can dramatically reduce the load that would otherwise be placed on their networks when large numbers of users listen to live events.

- **Live multicast files** Multicast file transfer provides another way for network managers to save bandwidth when large quantities of data have to be distributed simultaneously to many users. You can use multicast file transfer to dynamically change files on Web sites to broadcast a variety of Web content.

- **Easy-to-use integrated tools** NetShow comes with simple starter tools that enable content developers to prepare many popular content formats for streaming as illustrated audio. You can use files in WAV, AVI, QuickTime, Microsoft PowerPoint, JPEG, GIF, PNG, and URL formats to generate illustrated audio. You can also leverage all the existing multimedia authoring tools to get your content ready to stream.

- **Streamed, synchronized illustrated audio** Unlike most audio-streaming or video-streaming products, NetShow enables content providers to generate sophisticated productions in which graphics, slides, photographs, and URLs can be synchronized with the audio stream.

- **Standards-based** NetShow is based on Internet standards, including IP multicast and RTP (Reliable Transport Protocol). As a result, NetShow users can distribute multicast audio to MBONE-compatible applications and can listen to MBONE multicasts (VAT compatible on client and server). NetShow also supports open client/server architecture as well as new standards-based codecs (MPEG 2 Layer–3 and MPEG 4) for enabling the delivery of higher quality audio and video content over dial-up to broadband speed.

- **Codec and network independence** Content providers can choose the best compression scheme (codec) for a particular type of application and content. NetShow ships with a variety of Windows ACM and VCM codecs. You have your choice of compression schemes, so you can choose the best one for your specific application and network bandwidth.

Some of these features are described in more detail or in various user contexts later in the chapter. For a list of new NetShow features that will be in Microsoft Windows 98, see the "NetShow Features New to Version 2.0" section later in this chapter.

Key Benefits of NetShow 2.0

- **Easy to get started** Client software automatically downloads from a Web page without user interaction, providing seamless installation. Sample Web pages that make it easy to get started are included with the client. Audio-only multicast server enables multicast evaluation without network management risks. In addition, live audio is delivered to all clients by using the same bandwidth normally used to send to one client.

- **Easy to use** Administering and operating NetShow is simple. The services are easy to configure, monitor, and manage using standard Windows NT server facilities. The NetShow server is tightly integrated with Microsoft's HTTP server technology included with Windows NT IIS 3.0. NetShow includes server components for Windows NT Server, client software for Microsoft Windows 95, Windows 98, and Windows NT, and simple authoring tools and administration utilities.

- **Industry support** NetShow's programming interfaces and ActiveX controls provide a platform for third-party development of applications, tools, and content. Leading network hardware and software companies now offer system components, tools, and services building on the NetShow platform. For more information on these companies and their press contacts, go to the following Web site:

    http://www.microsoft.com/netshow/

- **Free for unlimited number of users** Microsoft doesn't limit the number of NetShow users on the server at any given time through licensing.

- **Scalability** NetShow responds efficiently to stream requests and maintains high performance even in heavy-load scenarios. IP multicast allows data transmission to large numbers of users, scaling as transmission needs grow.

- **Multiple bit rate support** Content can be authored for any targeted bit rate, such as 14.4, 28.8, and so on.

- **Error mitigation and correction** NetShow uses error mitigation and correction to ensure high-quality audio, illustrated audio, and video delivery.

- **Reduced network traffic** NetShow uses IP multicast to distribute identical information to many users simultaneously. This contrasts with regular TCP/IP (IP unicast), in which the same information can be sent to many clients, but the sender must transmit an individual copy to each user. Microsoft, along with its NetShow partners, makes it possible to deploy this technology in a safe and controlled manner.

- **Faster receipt of multimedia content** When accessing networked multimedia content, you usually have to wait for the entire file to be transferred before you can use the information. Streaming allows you to see or hear the information as it arrives. NetShow is an open platform capable of high performance streaming under demanding network conditions.

NetShow Features New to Version 2.0

New features, which will be added incrementally to NetShow 2.0 over the course of subsequent beta releases before final product delivery, include delivery of live broadcast and improvements in the following areas: in distribution of the broadcast infrastructure, in broadcast management, in the quality of content, and in user interactions.

Delivery of Live Broadcast

NetShow 2.0 enables the delivery of live, real-time encoded audio, video, and illustrated audio content. This capability represents a major improvement over NetShow 1.0, which allowed live delivery of audio only over multicast-enabled networks, thus limiting the delivery of live events. NetShow 2.0 also allows the delivery of live content, as well as on-demand content, over any network, independent of the transmission techniques and network transports used. This means NetShow users can broadcast live and on-demand content using either unicast or multicast techniques, depending on their needs and the available network infrastructure. To further facilitate delivery, NetShow can automatically fail-over from multicast to unicast mode to accommodate networks not multicast-enabled or to adjust to other delivery needs.

Distribution of the Broadcast Infrastructure

Production deployments of audio and video broadcast on the Web need a server that can scale up to thousands of streams for enabling full-scale, one-to-many communication. NetShow 2.0 enables going beyond a single computer. Whereas NetShow 1.0 had all of the server components installed on a single Windows NT Server 4.0, NetShow 2.0 allows the system to be divided into several components that can be installed on separate Windows NT Server 4.0 computers. This feature improves the capability to deliver a higher number of streams and to optimize the server infrastructure needed for distributing content to clients. Using Windows NT Server DNS, it is possible to build a cluster of NetShow servers configured to deliver content to a greater number of clients. For example, if broadcasting a live event, the real-time encoding could be performed at the event site on a NetShow server optimized for encoding while the encoded content is transmitted simultaneously to a cluster of NetShow servers that could then deliver the content to their respective connected clients.

Improved Broadcasting Management

NetShow 2.0 administration is provided through an intuitive Web-based interface that enables both local and remote administration. Administrators can now manage server installations and make configuration changes without having to physically access each server. IT managers can set the maximum content throughput per file and per server to control network bandwidth utilization and to monitor the state of all key NetShow server services. Server performance and event monitoring are achieved through close integration with the Windows NT Server administration. In addition, NetShow 2.0 allows the configuring and scheduling of content streams for later delivery and supports the generation of basic announcements for notifying users of upcoming (or in-progress) sessions. This new functionality allows audio and video content to be organized into separate channels, each programmed with time-scheduled shows. This opens up vast opportunities for Web-based broadcasts similar to the delivery of content over current television and radio stations.

Improved Quality of Content

Networked multimedia wouldn't be possible without the dramatic progress of the past five years in compression algorithms and their implementation. Compression reduces the storage space and transmission bandwidth required for sounds, images, and video while improving playback quality. NetShow 2.0 delivers broadcast-quality audio, offering major improvements over NetShow 1.0. NetShow 2.0 includes an audio codec from Fraunhofer Institute for Integrated Circuits (Institut Integrierte Schaltungen) IIS that delivers mono and stereo audio at 28.8 Kbps and scales to near-CD quality audio over ISDN, ADSL (Asymmetric Digital Subscriber Line), cable modems, and local area networks (LANs). This provides a wide array of choices as network bandwidth increases. For video, NetShow 2.0 provides a premiere implementation of the forthcoming leading-edge MPEG-4 video standard. Microsoft, working closely with the MPEG-4 standards committee, is implementing in NetShow 2.0 one of the first codecs based on the emerging MPEG-4 video standard. At 28.8 Kbps, this codec produces market-leading video quality, which becomes ever more stunning as network bandwidth increases. The addition of these new audio and video codecs makes NetShow the most comprehensive platform for delivering high-quality content over a wide range of networks.

Improved User Interactions with Broadcasts on the Internet and on Corporate Intranets

NetShow enables Internet Explorer to receive a new class of innovative interactive content and to allow for one-to-many communication. Because the NetShow 2.0 client is an integral part of Internet Explorer 4.0, users can easily view NetShow-hosted broadcasts. This robust functionality allows Internet Explorer to provide complete solutions for communication and collaboration over the Internet and corporate intranets.

Key Technologies of NetShow

NetShow content is enabled by ActiveX controls. NetShow presentations are simple to create and deliver using HTML. You can easily add advanced interactivity to Web pages using Internet Explorer 4.0 and Dynamic HTML. With NetShow, you can combine video, images, TrueSpeech (a high-quality audio format), URL flipping, and any Microsoft Office documents (especially, for presentations, Microsoft PowerPoint slides) for entertaining, informative, and educational presentations.

Some of the key technical capabilities at the foundation of NetShow are described in the following sections.

Media Streaming

Streaming lets you see and hear information as it arrives. Unlike other streaming products, NetShow lets content providers generate compelling productions in which audio, graphics, video, URLs, and script commands can be synchronized based on a timeline. Most of the audio and video content currently hosted on intranets and Internet sites is downloadable. This means that the multimedia content must be copied to the user's local PC before it can be played. Streaming is a significant improvement over the download-and-play approach to multimedia file distribution because it allows content to be delivered to the client as a continuous flow of data with little waiting time before playback begins. The content arrives, is buffered briefly, plays, and is discarded. It is never actually stored on the user's computer. NetShow delivers media streaming of audio, video, and illustrated audio (which, as mentioned earlier, combines sound with the sequencing of images). NetShow users experience instant play, and they don't have to suffer through the frustration of waiting for content to download to determine whether it meets their needs or interests.

Unicast and Multicast

A stream of audio and video content can be delivered over a network using two techniques: unicast and multicast. With unicast delivery, a separate copy of the data is sent from the source to each client that requests it. With multicast delivery, a single copy of the data is sent to all clients that request it. Multicast allows a more targeted distribution than the one-to-all of broadcasting (in which everyone on a network is a recipient), while avoiding the increased traffic load of having to send the same message separately to each recipient as with unicasting. NetShow combines the best of these two delivery techniques, enabling network managers and others to choose which type of delivery is best suited for their applications and needs.

Tight Integration with Windows NT Server and IIS

NetShow and its streaming services are tightly integrated with Microsoft Windows NT Server to provide an efficient, reliable, scalable, and secure platform for delivering audio, illustrated audio, and video content over the Internet and corporate intranets. NetShow utilizes all key Windows NT Server manageability features, including a graphical administration console, performance monitoring, an integrated directory and security model, and the Event Log, which records program execution information. NetShow also fully supports Windows NT connectivity, including network environments such as IP, IPX, 14.4/28.8 POTS, ISDN, Ethernet, and others. Sharing the same user interface, APIs, services, and tools means that neither users nor computer professionals have to learn different interfaces or tools. An integrated server solution offers easier management, better connectivity, and lower support costs, and because NetShow and Microsoft Internet Information Server are designed to work together, they combine to deliver a complete, well-tested, and high-performance system for broadcasting multimedia.

Tight Integration with Internet Explorer

NetShow brings the power of broadcasting to Internet Explorer 4.0, enabling it to receive a new class of innovative interactive content. As noted earlier, the NetShow 2.0 client is now an integral part of Internet Explorer 4.0, extending its strength for one-to-many communications.

NetShow enables the synchronized streaming of audio and video with other Web page elements, such as URLs, to increase the impact of content delivery. The NetShow client can forward the received URL addresses to Internet Explorer 4.0, allowing a new Web page to be displayed in either the browser window or a frame contained within the page currently being viewed. Image and video hot spots can also be created. Although hyperlinks and image maps are a common concept in Web pages, they've been limited to text or regions of a static image. NetShow enhances hyperlinks and image maps by associating user interactivity with defined regions on dynamically changing images or even video. Additionally, Microsoft Visual Basic or Java scripts can be combined with NetShow content to enhance broadcasting with a multitude of Visual Basic and Java capabilities. The retrieval of live data will facilitate the development of specialized programs and generally enhance the user experience by providing a new class of interactive content.

Open, Standards-Based System

With audio and video poised to become an integral part of Internet applications, significant standards-setting activity has been taking place for aspects of video and audio delivery, such as transports and protocols for delivery of streaming media over IP networks.

NetShow supports a variety of network transport protocols, including UDP/IP, TCP/IP, HTTP, RTP, and IP multicast. Support for these standards facilitates integration with low-level network technologies, resulting in higher performance delivery of multimedia content. Also, clients behind firewalls can receive NetShow content without compromising network security. The client software automatically chooses appropriate settings on installation and then selects the proper protocol for the server to use, eliminating the need for system administrators to manually specify the mechanism to be used.

Robust and Efficient Server for Heavy-Duty Broadcast

NetShow Server 2.0 is designed for heavy-duty deployments. It has been designed from the ground up as a native Windows NT service to exploit the robust multi-threaded Windows NT architecture. NetShow server also operates with remarkable efficiency. For example, content transmitted to the client as a steady flow of small pieces of data is read by the server in large, contiguous pieces that are stored in a memory buffer to save processor and disk resources.

High Scalability

Because NetShow has been designed specifically for Windows NT Server, it is fully optimized to take advantage of Windows NT Server's high scalability and to provide both small-scale implementation and easy upgrading to higher performance systems. NetShow can adapt to an organization's growth patterns. NetShow scales to very high-performance, enterprise-class multiprocessor systems with many gigabytes of memory and terabytes of storage and exploits the ability of Windows NT Server to run on leading-edge microprocessors such as Intel's Pentium and Pentium Pro and DEC's Alpha.

Microsoft internal tests have shown that a NetShow server can handle over 1000 streams of data at 28.8 Kbps on an industry-standard Pentium Pro–based uniprocessor machine with 64 MB of RAM, with no impact on the quality of the content and services delivered to clients. In addition, NetShow scalability provides stunning performance at higher bit rates. For example, internal tests have shown NetShow to be able to handle over 100 streams of 1.5-Mbps content, enabling large-scale deployments over ADSL, cable modems, and corporate LANs.

Network Bandwidth Support

NetShow supports a wide range of network bandwidths. As bandwidth increases, NetShow can deliver content at higher bit rates, starting from audio optimized and compressed for 14.4-Kbps dial-up connections and going up to video optimized for 6-Mbps delivery. The ability to deliver illustrated audio content is also critical for optimizing content delivery and using network bandwidth efficiently. Illustrated audio allows ideas and information to be shared on narrow-band networks. Illustrated audio is similar in concept to an online slide show, in which audio is synchronized with specific images (such as PowerPoint slides) to create an interesting and effective interactive multimedia presentation. When working with video material, a content author can use illustrated audio to select key frames to illustrate and augment a sound track, while avoiding the problem of random frames often seen with slow-scan or reduced frame-rate systems. As more bandwidth becomes available, the content author can increase the frame rate, image size, and quality of the individual images. This trade-off between the bandwidth available on a given network and demands for quality and performance determines how content authors should develop their illustrated audio content.

Partitioning for Distribution

NetShow 2.0 enables the server to be partitioned into several components that can be installed on different Windows NT Server platforms. This feature allows the delivery of a higher number of streams to provide services to an otherwise unserviceable number of clients and also optimizes the server infrastructure used to distribute content to clients. This optimization enables the installation of a geographically distributed array of NetShow servers to optimize how content is distributed from the source to clients and also enables an array of less powerful and expensive computers to be deployed, rather than a smaller number of more powerful and costly platforms.

Web-Based Administration

NetShow administration is provided through an intuitive Web-based interface, which enables both local and remote administration. This lets administrators manage server installations and make configuration changes without having to physically access each server. Administrators can also set the maximum content throughput per file and per server in order to control network bandwidth utilization. NetShow administration runs on both Windows NT and Windows 95 operating systems.

NetShow has been designed to utilize Windows NT 4.0 server administration features such as the Event Log and Performance Monitor, which indicates the number of streams going out from the server, the percentage of CPU time being taken by the NetShow services running, and other performance-related data. An additional advantage arises from integration with tools that developers are already familiar with. In addition, tools are provided specifically to manage multimedia content.

Content can be stored on a hard drive, and whenever that data is published to a Web server and to clients, virtual directories can be created. This is especially helpful when content is being added and removed on a daily or even more frequent basis. And, as noted earlier, it is possible to place limits on the throughput of a server or limit the bandwidth available for streaming certain files, for example. These are functions corporate network managers will require before deploying a server on their intranets.

Opportunities for Content Delivery and Scheduling

NetShow 2.0 opens a new set of opportunities for Web-based broadcasts similar to the delivery of content for current TV broadcasts. NetShow 2.0 enables content to be configured and scheduled for later delivery and allows the generation of announcements to users of upcoming sessions and those in progress. The content-scheduling mechanism is based on a channel metaphor users are familiar with, and the system is designed to allow a server to have multiple channels. By way of analogy, a cable company manages multiple channels, carrying stations such as CNN, NBC, and others, which are organized in a numeric sequence to make television channel surfing easy. In this example, CNN might be channel 3, NBC channel 5, and so on. Each channel also has time-based shows, such as the 10:00 p.m. news, a movie at 11:00 p.m., and so forth. This organization allows users to find their favorite shows easily because they know when and where to find them. Following this same paradigm, NetShow 2.0 makes it possible to organize audio and video content into separate channels, each of which has time-scheduled shows programmed, in addition to supporting announcements to users of current or upcoming sessions.

Variety of Audio and Video Compression Tools

NetShow 2.0 provides a wide range of audio and video compression models to satisfy the needs of different forms of content at different network bandwidths and bit rates. The satisfaction of the viewer with the network experience depends greatly on compression technology. NetShow includes over 10 audio and video codecs to satisfy the needs of the great majority of content providers. In addition, any Audio Compression Module (ACM) or Video Compression Module (VCM) codec can be used with NetShow, providing even greater flexibility for content compression and authoring. A partial listing of the codecs supported in NetShow 2.0 follows.

H.263 video

H.263 is a video telephony standard developed by the International Telecommunication Union (ITU) that is designed to be suitable for low–bit-rate video (28.8 Kbps) network connections.

G.723.1 audio

G.723.1 is an audio standard developed by the ITU for audio telephony over POTS lines that runs at either 5.3 Kbps or 6.3 Kbps using an 8-KHz sample rate and produces audio similar to the TrueSpeech codec already included in NetShow 1.0. Its main features are low complexity, low latency, low bandwidth, and standards support.

Fraunhofer's MPEG Layer–3 audio

An ISO standard, MPEG Layer–3 codec, developed by Fraunhofer Institute for Integrated Circuits IIS, was designed for general-purpose use to deliver a broad range of functionality. This codec delivers the best audio quality of any included in NetShow 2.0.

MPEG-4 video

This codec is a limited implementation of the MPEG-4 video standard under development by the MPEG standards committee. This video codec delivers market-leading quality video at 28.8 Kbps and delivers stunning quality video as the network bandwidth increases.

Intelligent Network Fail-Over

The broad range of network transport protocols supported by NetShow allows content providers to choose the protocol most effective for delivery of their content, depending on the application scenario and network infrastructure available. NetShow allows content to be delivered using IP multicast, UDP/IP, TCP/IP, RTP, and HTTP, thus supporting a wide range of deployment scenarios. In addition, NetShow is optimized to reduce content delivery losses due to changes or obstacles in the network infrastructure. For example, NetShow exploits the benefits of IP multicast on multicast-enabled networks, automatically falls back to unicast UDP/IP traffic if necessary, then goes to unicast TCP/IP, and finally moves to HTTP traffic if unicast UDP/IP cannot be delivered by any means.

This powerful feature allows content providers to use NetShow to broadcast content using either unicast or multicast techniques without worrying about the nature of the available network infrastructure. NetShow will automatically fail-over from multicast to unicast mode and from UDP/IP to TCP/IP and HTTP transmission to ensure content delivery. This feature also allows content to be sent through firewalls, allowing corporate users to view NetShow content as easily as other users.

Firewall Support

NetShow supports a number of firewall products, including those available from Ascend Communications, Check Point Software Technologies, CYCON Technologies, LanOptics, Microsoft Proxy Server, Milkyway Networks, Technologic, and Trusted Information Systems. The number of firewalls supported will increase periodically as support for additional products and companies is added.

Client Cross-Platform Support

Support for cross-platform clients is a key customer requirement for NetShow. NetShow 2.0 provides client support for Windows 95 and Windows NT operating systems, and the client software has been enhanced to further facilitate cross-platform portability. The NetShow clients for Microsoft Windows 3.1, Macintosh, and UNIX platforms are scheduled to be available soon after the initial release of NetShow 2.0.

Rich-Client Programmability

The NetShow client ActiveX control provides an extraordinarily rich set of client APIs, which enable clients to harness the power of a comprehensive set of broadcast applications. Webmasters, systems integrators, and developers can quickly and easily use the NetShow ActiveX control functionality to create custom business solutions using a variety of visual programming tools.

Compelling Content

NetShow real-time functions are easy to set up and manage, making the delivery of real-time audio and video broadcast easy. NetShow also comes with complete documentation to ease the creation and delivery of the best broadcasting content on the Web.

Leading multimedia firms such as Macromedia, Vivo Software, VDOnet, Sonic Foundry, Xing Technology, and VXtreme are developing or shipping value-added products on NetShow, giving customers a wide variety of tools and encoders for content creation.

Components of NetShow Architecture

NetShow is a comprehensive, tightly integrated platform consisting of the NetShow server, client, and the production and authoring tools.

NetShow Server

The NetShow server consists of a set of services running on Windows NT Server 4.0 that unicast and multicast audio, video, and other files to client computers. The server itself is an engine that prepares data and transmits it over the network. The NetShow server can deliver both live and on-demand content. To deliver live, real-time content, the server works in concert with NetShow Real-Time Encoder, which compresses the audio and/or video feed in real time and passes it to the NetShow server for delivery to the network. Delivery of content on demand requires that it be stored on a server hard drive and passed to the network by the NetShow server.

The NetShow server is tightly integrated with Windows NT Server to provide an efficient, reliable, scalable, and secure platform for delivering audio, illustrated audio, and video content over the Internet and corporate intranets.

NetShow Client

The client player allows intranet and Internet surfers to play audio, illustrated audio, and full-motion video files. By simply activating a link to a file, the player launches automatically and begins playing the requested file. Within seconds, the content starts playing with no download required. The player enables the same functions as a regular VCR, allowing you to stop, pause, and start content, controlling the flow of content as appropriate to your needs.

The foundation of the NetShow client is an ActiveX control, which exposes an easy-to-use programming interface that allows management of the content playback. The integration of the NetShow OCX with Internet Explorer 4.0 makes content playback a much more powerful experience for the user.

NetShow Content Authoring and Production

A key component of the NetShow architecture is Active Streaming Format (ASF), an open, standards-based file format that prepares multimedia content for streaming. While not a replacement for data types such as WAV, AVI, QuickTime, MPEG, or other files, ASF adds error correction and other functions necessary for streaming. ASF also enables the synchronization of different data types on a common timeline so that JPEG images, bitmaps, or WAV files, for example, can be synchronized with each other to create illustrated audio.

ASF is an important component of the NetShow content authoring strategy, because content must be converted to ASF before delivery over a network. NetShow handles both real-time (live) and on-demand (stored) content.

- **Authoring of on-demand content** NetShow provides simple ASF authoring tools to convert AVI and QuickTime files to ASF or WAV files. Also provided is a simple user interface editor called WinASF, which connects WAV files and other objects. Work is also under way to allow third parties to support ASF features natively within their products.

- **Encoding live content** NetShow provides a set of tools to encode and author live multimedia streams. These tools allow content authors to encode live audio and video feeds and add them to dynamic mixtures of other media, such as audio, video, text, URLs, and script commands. Because these tools are used to indicate when and what media is to be injected into a live stream, the appropriate media components are synchronized, compressed, augmented with error-correction information, and transmitted over a network.

Putting NetShow to Work

Audio-enabled and video-enabled applications are the next wave of Internet-based technology. NetShow provides the complete platform for integrating video into applications such as online training, executive speeches to the desktop, customer support, video news services, Internet promotions, and sales support.

While the possibilities for using NetShow are endless, two areas stand out:

- Organizations can use NetShow to sell products or communicate ideas, using video and other multimedia elements to provide demonstrations and guided tours. NetShow can convey the look and feel of your products to prospective customers.
- NetShow is a great tool for training, allowing companies to bring video, images, and audio together in self-paced, freely accessible tutorials.

Entertainment and Information

Multimedia has always been used to entertain, and NetShow will help developers and content authors carry this function to the Internet. Web-based entertainment includes allowing users to tune into radio stations or video stations. Because audio and video enhances entertainment, many people go to sites rich in these. Companies that already provide entertainment on the Web can use NetShow to add visual content to their sites. Just the Web television and Web radio made possible with NetShow will provide third parties with tremendous opportunities.

NetShow makes Web sites come alive with interactive audio and video multimedia content, from musical events and similar entertainment to news and other broadcasts, over both the Internet and corporate intranets.

Training

Many organizations devote substantial resources to training. Using NetShow to extend the reach of professional instructors through corporate intranets lets organizations maximize the value of this investment. NetShow makes it easy for trainers to generate the content and for users to receive the training whenever and wherever they need it.

In conjunction with a speaker's slides, a recorded speech can form a NetShow broadcast. This presentation can also be transferred to a CD if desired. Training materials can thus be provided for all divisions and subsidiaries of a corporation, allowing traveling employees, for example, to see training materials they might otherwise have missed and with the full impact of the original presentation maintained. This capability can also reduce the travel costs and lost hours inherent in traveling to training seminars.

Computer vendors can have NetShow content appear when their products are started in order to train their customers in the use of the product, thereby lowering support costs. Updates can be provided through additional NetShow content broadcast over the Internet or other networks.

Advertising and Retailing

NetShow advertisements of products and services are much more compelling than static Web pages. Audio commentary can be used with images on a Web site to guide users through demonstrations of a product, a process, or the site itself. The synchronized sound and images of NetShow illustrated audio provide a rich environment for advertising, and they facilitate showing off a product or concept to best advantage, such as in a media catalog.

Firms with external Web sites can promote and sell products on the Web using NetShow. The business model for Web content and service providers is currently based on the number of hits that occur at a site, which NetShow can increase by making it easier to provide compelling content while conserving bandwidth and maximizing performance. All of this functionality maximizes the return on investment in Web advertising.

Corporate Communications

Everyone in an organization, regardless of geographic location, will be able to hear important organizational briefings, such as internal presentations or presentations for the press or analysts, live. These same presentations can also be captured to be played back later using the NetShow on-demand function. Employees and others will be able to view presentations at their convenience, and these recorded presentations can evolve into a library of on-demand information for reference and training.

Corporate communications often require an entire group to attend a specific event or meet at an inconvenient location. NetShow can reduce this burden by sending the content over a network to each employee's desktop or to a portable PC for those who are traveling. A product manager can use NetShow as a forum for regular presentations about the product, which employees can access from anywhere.

7

Windows Messaging

PERSONAL COMPUTERS TODAY ARE being used for an increasingly wide range of tasks beyond the simple creation and editing of documents. Electronic mail has become a primary communication vehicle, not only within many companies but also among individuals, families, and the public at large. Additionally, use of online information services has dramatically increased, due in large part to e-mail. Witness the astounding 15 percent *per month* growth rate seen by the Internet in addition to the rapid growth in online commercial services.

The growing use of messaging and communication services has resulted in a plethora of software tools. A very real problem users face today is that each of these different information sources and services comes with its own unique software and user interface. Users often have software for e-mail clients, groupware clients, online services clients, and perhaps some electronic fax software that came with their modems.

Microsoft Windows 98 addresses this growing complexity by including an integrated messaging and workgroup communications system that provides universal e-mail, fax, and information-sharing solutions. These different services are all presented in Windows 98 with a single user interface called Microsoft Outlook Express. Outlook Express includes the following features:

- Support for taking full advantage of MAPI-enabled applications, ranging from desktop productivity to workflow and document management
- The ability to move messages and documents between the file system and mail folders

- The ability to send and receive rich-text e-mail messages over virtually any e-mail system, including public networks such as the Internet

- A complete, built-in e-mail system to quickly get workgroups up and running, including the Microsoft Mail Post Office—the system can be easily upgraded to a full Microsoft Mail Server or Microsoft Exchange Server to connect multiple workgroups or the entire enterprise

- The ability to send faxes directly from the desktop and receive incoming faxes directly in Outlook Express's Universal Inbox

This chapter introduces Outlook Express and other components of the Windows Messaging subsystem, including Messaging Application Programming Interface (MAPI), the Microsoft Mail Post Office, and Microsoft Fax software.

The Windows Messaging Subsystem

Windows Messaging is built upon the open MAPI architecture, so it can work with many different e-mail systems and information services simultaneously and provide a Universal Inbox for communication between individuals and workgroups. Windows 98 includes a set of operating system–level components that provide built-in messaging services to any application that wishes to take advantage of them.

Windows 98 ships with a number of components that together make up the Windows Messaging subsystem. (The term *Windows Messaging subsystem* is sometimes used synonymously with MAPI because Windows 98 represents a complete implementation of the "extended" MAPI architecture.) These components include the following:

- **Microsoft Outlook Express** This is the built-in Universal Inbox in Windows 98, which is used to send, receive, and organize e-mail, faxes, and other information. It includes an OLE-compatible rich-text editor used for composing and reading messages as well as for powerful searching. Through the use of MAPI drivers (described later), Outlook Express can work directly with most public or private e-mail systems.

- **The Personal Address Book** The Personal Address Book contains not only e-mail addresses but also names, phone and fax numbers, mailing addresses, and other personal contact information. Through the open MAPI interfaces, the Personal Address Book is accessible from a wide variety of applications, and through the use of MAPI drivers, it is also the user interface for corporate e-mail and information services directories. The Personal Address Book can store addresses for multiple e-mail systems at the same time.

- **The Personal Information Store** This sophisticated local "database" file allows users to store e-mail messages, faxes, forms, documents, and other information in a common place. The Personal Information Store functions as the user's mailbox and includes a Universal Inbox and Outbox, as well as any other mail or document folders the user wishes to create. It supports long filenames, plus sorting on various fields of the stored objects.

- **The Messaging Application Programming Interface (MAPI)** The core system components of MAPI seamlessly connect Outlook Express and other mail-enabled and workgroup applications to various information services. MAPI also defines a Service Provider Interface (SPI) that allows MAPI drivers to be written for nearly any messaging or workgroup service.

- **The Microsoft Mail drivers** This set of MAPI drivers allows Outlook Express to be used with a Microsoft Mail Post Office—either the "workgroup edition" that's provided with Windows 98 or the "full" server edition that's available separately.

- **The Microsoft Fax driver** This MAPI driver allows Outlook Express to send and receive electronic faxes in the same way it sends and receives any other piece of e-mail. Documents can be exchanged as traditional "published" facsimiles or in their original "editable" format using Microsoft Fax's Binary File Transfer capability.

- **The Microsoft Internet Mail drivers** This set of MAPI drivers lets Outlook Express send and receive mail directly on the Internet using the built-in Transport Control Protocol/Internet Protocol (TCP/IP) and Point-to-Point Protocol (PPP) provided with Windows 98.

- **Optional third-party MAPI drivers** Drivers for other messaging systems are available separately from a large number of vendors. Examples of vendors working on MAPI drivers that integrate into Outlook Express include the following: America Online, Apple, AT&T, Banyan, CompuServe, DEC, Hewlett-Packard, Novell, Octel, RAM Mobile Data, and Skytel.

An Open Architecture for Open Connectivity

Outlook Express is designed to work with virtually any messaging or workgroup system, whether it is LAN-based, host-based, or an online service. Transparent access to these various messaging systems is available to *any* application, not just to Outlook Express. The key to this open architecture is MAPI, which is illustrated in Figure 7-1 on the following page.

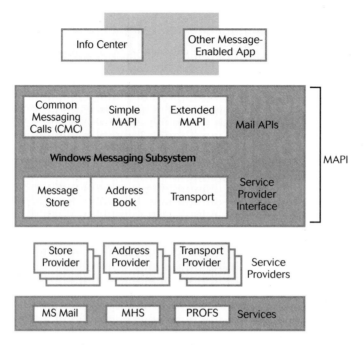

Figure 7-1   *The open MAPI architecture*

MAPI defines both an Application Programming Interface (API) and a Service Provider Interface (SPI). The API is used by end-user applications, including Outlook Express, whereas the SPI is used to write drivers (sometimes called *providers*). As Figure 7-1 shows, MAPI defines three different types of drivers:

- Store drivers, which let MAPI applications read and write to local or server-based message stores, mailboxes, and workgroup databases
- Address Book drivers, which allow seamless access to any directory service, mailing list, or other name database
- Transport drivers, which provide the ability to send and receive e-mail on any messaging system

As Figure 7-2 shows, you can install any combination of drivers so that your Outlook Express client can be used for multiple e-mail or workgroup systems at the same time.

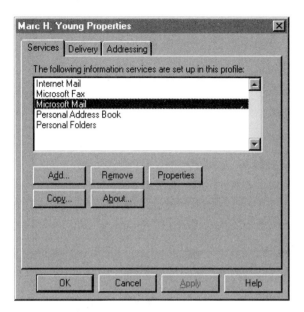

Figure 7-2   *Configuring Outlook Express for use with multiple services*

Outlook Express

E-mail has become the most popular Internet application in the world. Unfortunately, most e-mail is limited to text-only messages, perhaps with attachments. Microsoft Internet Explorer 4.0 allows an entirely new type of standards-based messaging, opening the door to a greater level of richness and detail. Outlook Express provides a host of new services that are tightly integrated with Internet Explorer, making it easy to communicate around the world.

Key Messaging Features and Benefits of Outlook Express

The new features of Outlook Express offer a number of significant benefits to users. Users can communicate more efficiently, richly, and securely, and developers can create client or server-based solutions using Multi-purpose Internet Mail Extensions (MIME) technology.

LDAP support

Because Internet Explorer 4.0 has full support for Lightweight Directory Access Protocol (LDAP) directory services, which provide access to virtual Internet white pages, finding e-mail addresses in Outlook Express is easy. You can locate anyone on corporate LDAP servers, and you can also use the built-in support for Four11, InfoSpace, Bigfoot, or WhoWhere? to locate an individual on the Internet. Internet Explorer's support for vCards enables the exchange of business card information.

Using the new LDAP-enabled address book, you can search popular Internet white pages directories using an individual's first name, last name, or e-mail name. You simply type the name on the To line in any message, and Outlook Express automatically searches the selected white pages directories to fill in the e-mail name.

Internet Explorer supports partial name checking against various LDAP servers. Outlook Express searches for partial names against whatever hierarchy you create. For example, by typing in a partial name, you can tell Outlook Express to search your local address book first, then your corporate LDAP servers, and finally, the Internet. Once the information is found, Outlook Express can store the address for later use.

The LDAP lookup engine implements a form of fuzzy logic to help you find others on the Internet. For example, if you entered *John Doe*, Outlook Express would look for successful matches according to the following:

- Exact match for John Doe
- First name exact match for John, last name match beginning with Doe
- First name beginning with John, last name exact match for Doe
- First name beginning with John, last name beginning with Doe
- The whole e-mail address beginning with John Doe

Messaging independence

Outlook Express ensures that you can read messages regardless of source, and it allows the interaction between protocols. Outlook Express supports all the different message protocols (POP3, IMAP, NNTP, SMTP, etc.) and then lets you mix and match them to suit your needs. So you could take a news message that you've received and place it in your mail folders. You can even leave it on an IMAP server, ignoring the fact that it came from an NNTP source. You can create e-mail messages for recipients who are either users or newsgroups, internal or external.

HTML support

Outlook Express now fully supports HTML. With support for MIME HTML, Internet Explorer 4.0 provides a new way to share Web content through e-mail. You can send full Web pages from the Internet or intranet to another user, even when you and the user are offline, by following these steps:

1. Open the page in Internet Explorer.
2. Click Mail on the toolbar, and then select the Send Current Document command, as shown in the following figure. Outlook Express drops the entire page into the mail message.

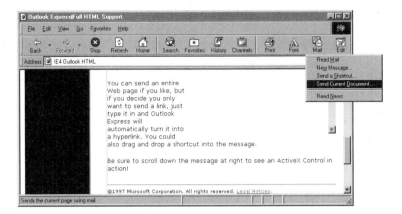

3. Fill in an e-mail address, or click the address card icon next to the To line. If you can't find the address you need, click the Find button in the Select Recipients dialog box.

4. When you have located the correct person, click OK, and then click the Send button to send the message.

Because not everyone with an e-mail address has a MIME HTML messaging client, Outlook Express makes sure that the appropriate message comes across regardless of the technology on the recipient's side. Here are some examples of how an e-mail message can be displayed to a recipient:

- If the recipient doesn't support MIME, the message will contain the text-based information first and then, after a separator, the raw HTML will follow.

- If the recipient supports MIME, the message will display the text-based information first and include the HTML as an attachment, which the user can view in her default browser.

- If the recipient supports MIME HTML, the full Web page in native format will be displayed inside the mail message.

If you decide that you would rather send a link to a Web page than send an entire Web page, type the link into the message and Outlook Express will automatically turn it into a hyperlink. You can also drag and drop a shortcut into the message.

S/MIME support and security

Outlook Express enables users to feel secure about both sending information across the Internet and receiving information from a valid source. This level of security is dependent upon public key encryption and certificates. Public key encryption uses two keys to transmit and receive secure messages: a user encrypts a message with one key, and only the accompanying key can decode the message. Users who want this extra level of security can make one of their keys available to the people they communicate with (public key) but keep the other key to themselves (private key).

Certificates are a way of wrapping up public keys, and they enable public keys to be shared. All security components in Internet Explorer and Outlook Express are based on standards-based public key algorithms. Users can obtain certificates from certifying authorities such as VeriSign; certifying authorities assure a user that a public key really belongs to the person the key identifies. A user can *digitally sign* (encrypt) a message with her private key, and anyone with her public key can read the message. The recipient of the message can verify who the message came from and that it has not been changed since it was sent by using the public key obtained from a verification service.

Conversely, a user can ensure that only the intended recipient of a message can read the message by encrypting the message using the recipient's public key. Because only the recipient's private key can decode the message, only the recipient will be able to read the message.

Integration with Internet Explorer

Outlook Express is tightly integrated with Microsoft Internet Explorer, making Internet Explorer's services appear to be just another part of the user's messaging system. Here are some examples of how this integration enhances messaging:

- E-mail folders and newsgroup servers are located in the same namespace, enabling you to move easily from e-mail to news.
- POP, IMAP, and NNTP server information is kept in the same hierarchy as Outlook Express.
- Outlook Express shares common menus and toolbars with other components.
- With one click from the browser, you can send a whole Web page to someone; the entire page—not just a link to a Web site—is embedded in the message.
- You can drag and drop an entire Web page or an Internet shortcut into the Inbox, and Outlook Express will send it out.
- You have quick access to Outlook Express from the other applications' toolbars.

Other messaging features

- **Offline reading and composing** This feature enables you to read and write e-mail or newsgroup messages without worrying about connection times.

- **Global address books** You can look up names and addresses from a local source, from other address books, or from any Internet white pages directory.

- **Find Message** This search feature can find messages—either news or mail—quickly and easily.

- **Open Suite** Internet Explorer 4.0 is open, so you can use any other e-mail client you prefer.

- **Auto-add** This feature builds the Personal Address Book on the fly so that all important e-mail addresses are saved easily.

- **Draft folder** This folder stores saved e-mail messages before they are sent, making it easy to keep track of messages in progress.

- **Multiple mailboxes** Support for multiple mailboxes makes retrieval of e-mail from several servers easy. Outlook Express can even dial multiple ISPs separately without user prompting.

- **Separate Send and Receive commands** The Send and Receive commands can be executed separately, so you can spend your online time efficiently. For example, if you are working on a slow link, you can choose only to send messages and not download large messages with attachments.

- **Enhanced Inbox Assistant** The Inbox Assistant rules have been enhanced so that you can forward, move, or copy messages automatically. Inbox Assistant rules make it easy to filter mail among family members who have separate accounts. When you have a slow connection, you can download small messages locally and keep everything else on your server. With the Delete Off Server feature, you can remove messages even before they're downloaded.

Rich-Text Mail Messages

E-mail is used six to eight times more often than word processors for tasks such as sending memos. People want to combine the power and immediacy of e-mail with the expressive capabilities of a word processor. Outlook Express includes a complete rich-text editor that is fully compatible with OLE, allowing you to both format text and embed objects in e-mail messages. The message in Figure 7-3 on the following page was composed in Outlook Express.

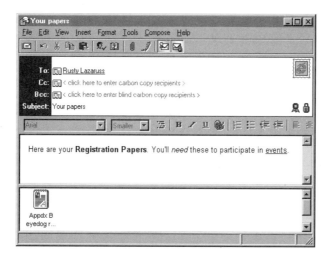

Figure 7-3   *A rich-text e-mail message with an embedded OLE object*

Because Outlook Express works as a universal e-mail client, it correctly transmits rich text and formatting over any mail system, even those that were not originally designed to handle rich text, such as the Internet. The rich-text information is automatically packaged as a separate compressed file attachment and is decompressed on the receiving end by another Windows 98 client. If the message is sent to someone who doesn't use Windows 98 or Windows 95—for example, over the Internet—the "plain text" equivalent of the message is received and any embedded objects are sent as binary attachments.

You can save for future reference messages received in the Inbox by dragging the messages into any of the other folders (message stores) in the mailbox. You can also drag a message to any directory on your local or network hard drives. In the latter case, the message becomes an EML file but maintains all of the messaging-specific fields, such as Sender and Recipient. At any time in the future, you can double-click the EML file to open it and then forward the file to other e-mail users.

The Personal Address Book

A universal e-mail client needs to work with a universal address book—one that can seamlessly handle e-mail addresses of different types. Windows 98 includes a Personal Address Book that is implemented as a MAPI service. As a result, in addition to the local address book that the user maintains, Outlook Express has transparent access to the address books and directory services of any other e-mail system that supports MAPI. For example, the same Personal Address Book could show a company's global address list or a corporate X.500 directory service.

For each new set of MAPI drivers installed, the Personal Address Book adds a new "template" to help you compose addresses of different types. For example, you type Internet e-mail addresses on a predefined Internet template; after you enter the names, you address e-mail to those people using just their names—you don't have to remember complex addressing conventions.

As shown in Figure 7-4, the Personal Address Book also allows users to keep vital personal information about people, such as their telephone numbers, postal addresses, and office locations. Any phone number in the address book can be auto-dialed using the built-in Windows 98 Telephony API (TAPI) services.

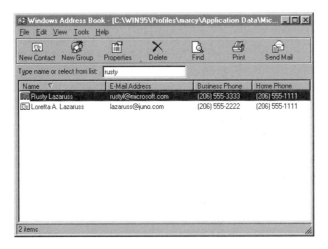

Figure 7-4   *The Outlook Express Personal Address Book*

The Information Stores

Messages are typically stored in your Personal Information Store. Although the Personal Information Store is a single file, you see this file as sets of folders containing messages or documents. Typically, you have a single information store containing an Inbox, an Outbox, and other mail folders. However, Outlook Express allows you to create as many "stores" as you want—for example, one store for current e-mail and another for backup or archive purposes. The built-in Personal Information Store is only one kind of information store. Any e-mail or workgroup system can expose its mailboxes or databases to users as information stores by creating an appropriate MAPI driver.

Information stores can be physically stored in local files, or they can represent a database on a network server. For example, when the Outlook Express client is connected to a Microsoft Exchange Server, you see sets of folders (information stores) that represent replicated databases or "groupware" applications on the server in addition to your standard mailbox folders.

In addition to storing mail messages, you can store files or documents in information stores by dragging the files or documents into these folders. (Additionally, any MAPI-compatible forms software can store its form data and form definitions in an information store.) You might want to store these items in an information store, rather than in the regular file system, for the following reasons:

- **MAPI Properties** MAPI associates additional fields, such as Sender, Subject, Received Time, Size, Importance, and Sensitivity, with items in information stores. These "properties" can be used for searching and sorting.

- **OLE Document Properties** Documents that are stored as OLE compound documents have many additional built-in properties, such as Title, Author, Keywords, Comments, Last Edited Time, and Number of Pages. When a document is placed in an information store, these built-in properties can be made available to the user through custom views.

Remote Mail

Windows 98 includes MAPI drivers for the Microsoft Mail e-mail system, so the Outlook Express client can send and receive mail as a member of a Microsoft Mail network—either a full, enterprise-wide mail system or a local workgroup mail system that uses the Windows 98 built-in Microsoft Mail Post Office. Outlook Express users can fully interoperate with existing Microsoft Mail users on other platforms, although rich-text messages are converted to plain-text messages when sent to an existing Microsoft Mail client.

In keeping with the Windows 98 focus on facilitating mobile and remote computing, Outlook Express is designed to provide the benefits of remote e-mail without requiring any additional client software or a special gateway to dial into. Mobile or remote users can easily send and receive e-mail by using the following features:

- **Remote Preview** Using the built-in Microsoft Mail drivers, you can dial into your network and preview the headers of your new messages—that is, you can see who sent the new mail, what the subject is, how large the message is, and the estimated time it will take to download the message.

- **Selective Download** After the headers are retrieved, you can mark which messages you want to download and which messages you want to delete without downloading. You can either download the selected messages immediately after retrieving the headers, or you can make another call later to download them.

- **Remote Network Access** Rather than using a specialized e-mail gateway for remote mail, Outlook Express relies on the standard Dial-Up Networking that is built into Windows 98. You can dial into another computer running Windows 98, Windows 95, Windows NT Server, or a third-party remote access server such as Shiva LanRover. Remote e-mail then becomes protocol-independent, because RNA supports standard network protocols such as TCP/IP, IPX, and NetBEUI.

- **Offline Use** As an Outlook Express user, you can compose messages while offline and have the messages queued up in the Outbox until the next time they connect to the appropriate mail service. For example, you can download new mail at an airport, read the messages and compose replies while on an airplane, dial in from a hotel, and then send the responses automatically.

- **Scheduled Connections** You can dial in as needed to retrieve mail remotely, or you can set up scheduled connections to dial in at specific times or on a regular basis. You might want to schedule a connection if the computer is permanently remote.

- **Telephony API (TAPI)** Outlook Express uses the Windows 98 TAPI facilities to dial in and retrieve mail remotely, allowing for effective sharing of modem resources between applications. For example, if you set your modem to listen for incoming faxes while still making a call to retrieve e-mail, TAPI handles the resource management between the relevant applications. Outlook Express also uses the TAPI Dial Helper feature to easily handle multiple locations, hotel dialing prefixes, and credit card calls.

Starting Outlook Express

To start Outlook Express and read new e-mail, follow these steps:

1. Click the Start button.
2. Select Programs to open the Programs menu.
3. Select Outlook Express Mail, as shown here:

No matter which application is active in Windows 98, new e-mail is announced by a notification appearing at the right end of the taskbar, as shown here:

These notifications also let you know whether the system is currently sending or receiving mail.

The Microsoft Mail Post Office

Windows 98 includes the workgroup edition of the Microsoft Mail Post Office, providing everything that is needed to set up and manage a complete e-mail system for a workgroup. Typically, one workgroup member, who is designated as the administrator, creates a Post Office by using the Workgroup Postoffice Admin applet in the Windows 98 Control Panel. The Post Office is simply a shared directory on the administrator's computer where e-mail is stored. A wizard leads the administrator through the process of creating the Post Office and is also used to add new users, delete users, and manage shared folders. After the administrator shares the Post Office directory, users can start Outlook Express, enter the shared directory name, and connect to the Post Office in order to send or retrieve mail.

The Microsoft Mail Post Office included in Windows 98 is a workgroup edition, meaning that it is limited to exchanging mail with users of a single Post Office. A single Post Office can potentially support dozens of users, depending on the server performance of the Post Office computer. However, a large group might need to be split up into separate workgroups, each accessing its own Post Office. In that case, a server is needed. The full edition of the Microsoft Mail Post Office allows mail to be routed between multiple Post Offices as well as to other e-mail gateways.

The Microsoft Mail Post Office that comes with Windows 98 can easily be upgraded to a Microsoft Exchange Server, a client/server messaging system that provides not only e-mail services but also personal/group scheduling, information sharing applications ("groupware"), and forms and application design tools.

Microsoft Fax

Windows 98, in conjunction with Outlook Express, provides PC users with the ability to send and receive faxes directly from their desktops. This capability, called Microsoft Fax, sets the standard for desktop faxing as an easy-to-use messaging facility that is well-integrated with Windows.

Microsoft Fax provides the following key features:

- High-resolution printed documents that are faxed from within Windows-based applications using a fax printer driver

- Microsoft At Work Binary File Transfer (BFT) capability, which sends original documents to users of Windows 98, Windows for Workgroups 3.11, and other Microsoft At Work–enabled platforms as e-mail attachments via fax

- The use of encryption and digital signatures, which makes the exchange of confidential documents secure

- Support for high-speed communications with popular Class 1 fax modems and the millions of traditional Group 3 fax machines worldwide. Microsoft Fax supports Error-Correction Mode (ECM) and transmission speeds of up to 14.4 Kbps

- For networked Windows 98 users, the ability to send and receive faxes through a network fax service on one of the Windows 98 workstations on the network

- A fax viewer, which allows users to browse multipage faxes using either "thumbnails" or full-page view mode

- A cover page designer that enables users to easily create new fax cover pages that incorporate graphics and text or to customize one of the predefined cover pages included with Microsoft Fax

- An easy connection to Faxback fax information services using a built-in "poll-retrieve" feature, which allows users to download faxes directly to their desktops

Microsoft Fax is integrated into Windows 98 as a MAPI transport service provider, leveraging Outlook Express's Universal Inbox, rich-text message creation, and browsing capabilities to deliver ease of use and consistency to the management of fax messages. The fax provider coexists with other information or messaging services that you might have installed and leverages Outlook Express's Personal Address Book and Inbox.

You can take advantage of Microsoft Fax innovations that provide the secure exchange of editable documents. You can send faxes from within mail-enabled Windows-based applications, such as Microsoft Word and Microsoft Excel, by using the File/Send command. Additionally, a fax printer driver lets you "print" documents to your local fax modems, either via the File/Print command or by dragging the documents to a Fax icon on the Windows 98 desktop.

Microsoft Fax takes advantage of the power of the Windows 98 operating system through the Win32 API. As a 32-bit application, Microsoft Fax integrates seamlessly with other Windows 98 applications through its support for MAPI, TAPI, and OLE. In addition to tight integration with Windows 98, Microsoft Fax incorporates Microsoft

At Work technologies that support BFT, security, and high-quality document rendering. These technologies put powerful desktop fax messaging at the fingertips of Windows 98 users.

When faxes are sent to other users of Windows 98 (or Windows 95 and other Microsoft Fax devices), the Microsoft At Work BFT capability can be used to send the original file over the fax connection. For example, you can attach a Microsoft Word document to an e-mail message and address the message to a customer's fax number. If the customer receives the fax via Microsoft Fax, the Word document is attached to an incoming e-mail message. By clicking the Word icon, the customer can open the original document. However, if the customer receives the fax via a traditional Group 3 fax machine, Microsoft Fax automatically renders the Word document as an appropriate Group 3 fax image. The highest speed and image compression that is supported by the customer's fax machine is used when transmitting the fax.

Working with Microsoft Fax

Microsoft Fax has been designed to allow Windows 98 users to exchange printed documents and binary files easily and with a minimum of setup. Because fax capabilities are provided as a core system service, they are always available from within Windows 98–based applications or through Outlook Express. Faxes can be transmitted using the Outlook Express e-mail client or by printing documents to a fax printer. Faxes that have been received from other sources are always delivered to Outlook Express.

You can identify a fax recipient by selecting a fax address from an address book—for example, the Personal Address Book—or by directly entering an address, such as [fax:555-1212]. The MAPI service provider architecture allows you to mix different types of recipients in the same message. For example, you can send a message simultaneously to Microsoft Mail, CompuServe, Internet, and fax users as long as Outlook Express contains profiles for these destinations.

Attaching a document to an Outlook Express e-mail message is the easiest way to fax original or editable documents from Windows 98. The Send command on the File menu within any MAPI-enabled application—for example, Microsoft Word or Microsoft Excel—displays the Outlook Express Send dialog box, in which fax users can address the intended recipient. The attached faxed document appears as an icon within the body of the message.

Microsoft Fax provides powerful features as well as ease of use. The Fax menu item under Accessories (shown in Figure 7-5) provides single-click access to most fax features. Selecting Compose New Fax activates a wizard that quickly guides you through the process of addressing, selecting a cover page, and attaching documents to a fax. The Cover Page Editor item provides an easy way to create personalized fax cover pages. The Request A Fax item puts the power of Faxback fax information services at your fingertips.

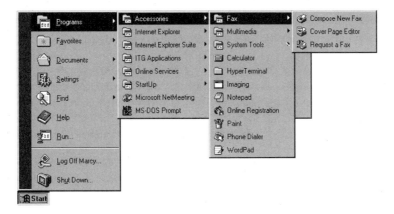

Figure 7-5   *Fax item on the Accessories menu allows users to send and retrieve fax messages*

Microsoft Fax also provides a "print to fax" interface. You can fax documents from within your favorite Windows applications by printing to the Microsoft Fax printer driver. Microsoft Fax will then activate the Compose New Fax wizard, shown in Figure 7-6, which will guide you through the addressing and transmission of the fax.

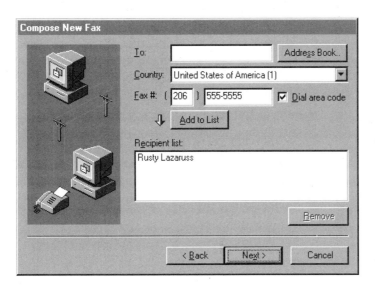

Figure 7-6   *The Compose New Fax wizard*

Rich-Text Messaging Capabilities

Microsoft Fax supports the rich-text capabilities of Outlook Express and the advanced capabilities provided by Microsoft At Work BFT and Rendering technologies. The Microsoft At Work capabilities are effective when a Microsoft Fax user connects to another Microsoft Fax user or to any Microsoft At Work-enabled fax machine. Microsoft Fax exchanges with the receiving device information about their respective capabilities to determine whether the receiving device is a Microsoft At Work–enabled device or a Group 3 fax machine. The transmission can then proceed according to one of these three scenarios:

- If the receiving fax device supports Microsoft Fax, an editable document attached to an e-mail message is transferred in its native format. In this case, faxing works exactly like electronic mail between the originator and recipient. This fax capability supports the Universal Inbox provided by Outlook Express, full-feature Outlook, and Microsoft Exchange.

- If the receiving fax device is a traditional Group 3 fax machine, Microsoft Fax converts the document to the most compact fax supported by the machine— that is, MH, MR, or MMR format—and transmits the image at the highest speed supported by the mutual connection (up to 14.4 Kbps).

- If the receiving fax device is Windows 98 or Windows 95, and the originating computer sent a printed document, the file is transmitted between the two computers using a special Microsoft At Work rendered (printed) document format. The exchange of printed documents between Microsoft At Work devices is always faster than between Group 3 fax machines because the Microsoft At Work rendered image format achieves greater compression ratios than Group 3 MMR.

Workgroup Fax Features for MIS Organizations

Microsoft Fax supports Windows 98 users on local area networks by providing a simple network fax service.

If a local fax modem is installed in one Windows 98 workstation, all other Windows 98 users who are on the same physical network can send and receive faxes through the shared modem. The Windows 98 workstation to which the modem is connected is called the "network fax server." Incoming faxes are stored on the network fax server. An administrator can use Microsoft Exchange to manually route faxes from the fax server to the final recipients via e-mail.

In a similar way, Windows users can connect to Microsoft At Work–enabled fax servers and fax machines over a network connection. Microsoft and a variety of hardware and software vendors are in partnership to develop fax products and services that incorporate Microsoft At Work technologies. These products and services will all be compatible with and leverage the capabilities of Microsoft Fax in Windows 98.

Easy Access to Fax Information Services

Microsoft Fax provides the capability to retrieve documents, software, binary files, and fax images from fax-on-demand systems and fax machines that support Group 3 poll-retrieve. The ability to easily download information directly into a Windows 98 workstation via fax vastly improves the capabilities of fax-on-demand systems as a way for companies and information services to cost-effectively distribute information.

For example, the distribution of information could include the automatic distribution of software updates. A Windows 98 workstation with Microsoft Fax could make a connection to a fax-on-demand server and request the name of a binary file via its poll-retrieve capability. The server would respond to the request by downloading the binary file to the Windows 98 workstation. This exchange could be accomplished using a single fax call to the fax-on-demand system. Figure 7-7 shows Microsoft Fax's Request A Fax wizard.

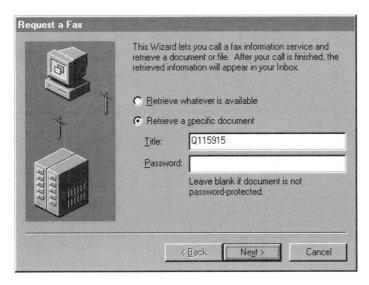

Figure 7-7   *Retrieving a document from a fax information service that supports poll retrieve*

The Fax Cover Page Editor

The Microsoft Fax Cover Page Editor lets you create customized fax cover pages or modify one of the predefined cover pages included with Windows 98. The Fax Cover Page Editor is an OLE application that makes it easy for you to create attention-grabbing cover pages.

Secure Faxing with Encryption and Digital Signatures

Microsoft Fax protects valuable and confidential documents through encryption and digital signature capabilities. The sender of a document or traditional fax can encrypt the fax using either a simple password or sophisticated RSA public/private key security. (See Figure 7-8.) The fax software includes the capability to exchange public keys with other users, and you can store and maintain the public keys you receive from other users in your Personal Address Book.

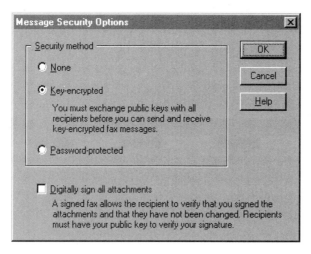

Figure 7-8   *The Message Security Options dialog box, showing encryption and digital signature support*

When an encrypted fax is transmitted to a recipient, it cannot be read unless the recipient knows either the password that was used to encrypt the file or the originator's public key, depending on the security mechanism used.

Faxed documents can be "signed" with a digital signature to ensure that the fax data is not modified during transmission. A sender uses a private key to sign the fax, and anyone with that sender's public key can read it, but with the knowledge that only the owner of that specific private key could have sent the fax.

Compatibility with Fax Modems and Fax Machines

To ensure fax connectivity with the widest possible variety of fax applications, fax machines, and fax modems, Microsoft Fax in Windows 98 supports the following:

- The ITU (International Telecommunications Union, formerly the CCITT) T.30 standard for Group 3 fax. Microsoft At Work capabilities such as BFT are implemented as T.30 nonstandard facilities (NSF), thereby maintaining compatibility with the installed base of Group 3 fax machines.

- The ITU V.17, V.29, and V.27ter standards for high-speed fax communications (up to 14.4 Kbps).

- Class 1 and Class 2 fax modems. A Class 1 modem is required for Microsoft At Work BFT and Security. Fax printing to traditional Group 3 fax devices is available on both Class 1 and Class 2 modems.

- MH, MR, and MMR compression for Group 3 fax communication. Microsoft Fax also supports Error Correction Mode (ECM) for reliable fax transmission over "noisy" telephone lines.

Coexistence with Windows-Based Telecommunications Applications

The ability of Outlook Express to support multiple simultaneous MAPI service providers in Windows 98 means that users will want to have available connections to the Internet, CompuServe, and Microsoft Fax. Well-behaved telecommunications applications that support the Windows Telephony API (TAPI) can coexist and share a local modem in a Windows 98 computer.

The implication of TAPI support for Microsoft Fax is that Fax can be listening to the phone line in auto-answer mode while other telecommunications applications and Outlook Express providers dial out to information sources over the phone network. TAPI provides the call arbitration to ensure that physical modem resources are allocated to the appropriate telephony applications when they are needed.

Microsoft Fax also leverages TAPI concepts such as locations and the Dial Helper dialog box to ensure that Fax calls are made consistently, whether the Fax user is connected to the network, is at home, or is on the road.

Integration of Fax and Applications

Microsoft Fax in Windows 98 is a powerful and extensible integration platform for Fax-enabled applications. The extensibility, through MAPI, of Fax and Outlook Express makes it easier for third-party software developers to deliver new Fax-enabled applications and enhanced Fax services.

Because Microsoft Fax is implemented in Windows 98 as a MAPI transport service provider, you can fax information to other users from any MAPI-enabled application by using the File menu's Send command. In addition, Fax features such as poll retrieve have been added to ensure that Fax is an excellent client for enhanced fax services.

8

Authoring and Publishing

AS PART OF THE MICROSOFT WINDOWS 98 and Microsoft Internet Explorer 4.0 package, you receive several tools for authoring and publishing your own Web pages, including these:

- Microsoft FrontPad for creating Web pages
- Personal Home Page Wizard for setting up a personal home page that Internet Explorer 4.0 displays when you start it
- Personal Web Server for creating a Web server on your own PC
- Web Publishing Wizard for posting your Web pages to any Web site

This chapter describes each of these authoring and publishing tools plus some additional ones that will make the Web developer's life a little easier.

Creating Your Own Web Pages with FrontPad

Although HTML has made it easier for many users to become Web publishers, HTML programming isn't a particularly intuitive method of creating Web pages. With FrontPad, one of the core components of Internet Explorer 4.0, even novice users can create Web pages. FrontPad is a WYSIWYG HTML editor with a graphical user interface that is based on the Microsoft FrontPage 97 editor.

FrontPad takes you step by step through the process of creating Web pages, and it's also a great tool for editing existing HTML documents. When you have FrontPad installed, you can open FrontPad by clicking the Edit button on the Internet

Explorer 4.0 toolbar and start editing the page you're viewing. Then you can use the Microsoft Web Publishing Wizard to post the modified page back to the server. Figure 8-1 shows the FrontPad window.

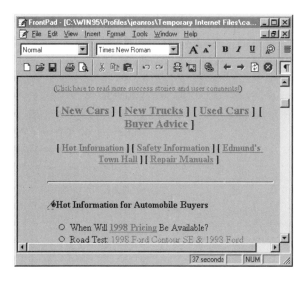

Figure 8-1 *The FrontPad window, in which you edit Web pages*

Key Features of FrontPad

FrontPad includes all the features of the FrontPage 97 editor except for these: editing frames, image maps, and proofing tools; support of Active Server Pages; Preview In Browser; most FrontPage WebBot components; and Microsoft Visual Basic, Scripting Edition (VBScript). Some of the key features included in FrontPad are the Include, Search, and Timestamp WebBot components; capabilities for editing tables, forms, plug-ins, Java Applets, and JavaScript; and some of the FrontPage page templates and wizards. Some of FrontPad's features are explained here:

- **Personal Home Page Wizard** This wizard takes you step by step through the process of creating a personal home page. (For more details about this wizard, see the section "Customizing Your Start Page with Personal Home Page Wizard" later in the chapter.)

- **Table creation and editing** You'll be able to insert a table into a Web page and then edit either the entire table or individual cells.

- **Forms** You can add forms to your Web page that can be filled out and returned. Your forms can include text boxes, checkboxes, drop-down menus, images, and more. (You must be connected to a server running FrontPage server extensions to use these forms-related features.)

- **Page templates and wizards** If you're connected to a server running FrontPage server extensions, you can also use forms-related wizards and templates that let you create the following items:

  o A form, by selecting the types of information you need to collect

  o A page to acknowledge that you've received a user's input

  o A survey to collect information from readers and store it on your Web server

- **Java applets, JavaScript, plug-in, and ActiveX support** FrontPad supports top Internet technologies to make your pages more engaging. As you can see here, inserting an ActiveX control with FrontPad is as easy as choosing a command:

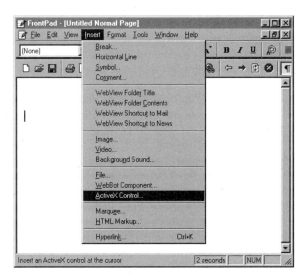

Benefits of Web Authoring

Writing your own Web pages offers two main benefits:

- **Fast Web page development** With FrontPad, you don't need to learn HTML; the application has a graphical user interface. FrontPad even lets novices insert Java applets, ActiveX controls, or scripts without knowing any programming. For those who still like to edit HTML directly, FrontPad offers a new color-coded HTML editing mode.

- **Tight suite integration**   As mentioned earlier, when you have FrontPad installed, the Edit button on the Internet Explorer 4.0 toolbar allows you to edit the currently viewed page. FrontPad has also been integrated into the Internet Explorer Web View wizard and includes specific commands that let you customize Web View folders.

How Web Authoring Works

On any Web page, you can click the Edit button on the Internet Explorer 4.0 toolbar to open FrontPad with all of the tables, controls, and pictures displayed inside the editor. FrontPad makes it easy to download pages from the Web locally because it lets you save an entire Web page (pictures included) in a single step.

FrontPad also helps you customize your environment using the Web View feature. When users or administrators customize a folder with HTML, the Customize This Folder wizard uses FrontPad. If they want their new Web page to include folder attributes—such as the folder's contents or name, or even links to other parts of the Internet Explorer 4.0 suite such as Microsoft Outlook Express—FrontPad makes it easy.

Most WebBot components are added to a page using the WebBot Component command on the Insert menu in the FrontPad editor. When you insert a WebBot component, dialog boxes help you configure it; a graphical representation of the WebBot component is then visible in the editor at that position in the page. A few of the WebBot components are specifically associated with forms and are accessed via the Form Properties dialog box rather than the Insert WebBot Component command.

When you view a page that includes a WebBot component, the interactive or programming properties of it are available. The WebBot components themselves are stored in a page using a specially formatted HTML comment, although the FrontPad author doesn't typically see this representation.

Customizing Your Start Page with Personal Home Page Wizard

Whenever you start the browser in Internet Explorer 4.0, the first page you see is the Internet Start page. This page always includes articles and features to help you get more out of the Internet. You can customize this page so that it also keeps you up to date with information about the topics that matter most to you—whether that's current events, the latest happenings in entertainment, sports, or technology, or up-to-the-minute financial information and stock prices. Those are just a few of the areas you can choose to receive information about through Internet Start's Personalization feature. Figure 8-2 shows the Personalization feature's (or Personal Home Page Wizard's) first screen.

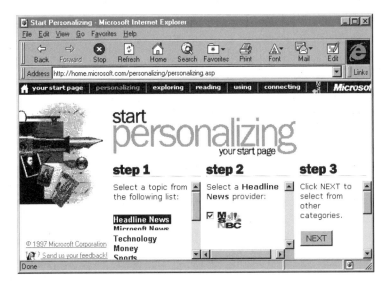

Figure 8-2   *The first panel of the Personal Home Page Wizard*

You can also add headlines from top news providers, including Wired, MSNBC, and Forbes. And you can search the Web from your Internet Start page and find everything from toll-free 1-800 numbers to e-mail addresses to concert and sporting event schedules.

Through its Exploring section, Internet Start also includes regularly updated links to the latest sites from around the world that qualify as the Best of the Web in categories such as sports, travel and entertainment, and computers and technology.

How the Personal Home Page Wizard Works

By default, your start page is set to Internet Start:

> *http://home.microsoft.com*

To personalize your Internet Start page, start Internet Explorer 4.0. When the Internet Start page at *home.microsoft.com* appears, click Personalizing on the toolbar at the top of the Internet Start page. Follow the instructions on the screen to select the type of content you want to see each time you start Internet Explorer 4.0.

Publishing with Personal Web Server

As millions of users flock to the Internet for information and entertainment, many decide that they want to give information to the world as well as receive it. The Microsoft Personal Web Server offers a way for users and corporations to publish Web pages on their own servers. The simplicity of Personal Web Server makes it perfectly suited to home users, schools, and corporate workgroups.

Personal Web Server for Windows 98 turns any Windows 98 computer into a Web server, enabling easy publication of personal or business Web pages onto the Internet or a corporate intranet. Easy to install and administer, Personal Web Server simplifies sharing information for all users on the Internet or a corporate intranet. It is designed for small-scale, peer-to-peer Web server usage. The software is fully integrated into the Windows 98 taskbar and Control Panel, making it easy for users to start and stop HTTP and FTP services at any time. Figure 8-3 shows the Personal Web Server's Properties dialog box.

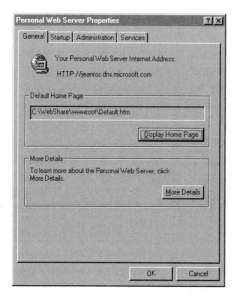

Figure 8-3   *The Properties dialog box for the Personal Web Server*

You can install Personal Web Server for Windows 95 onto your Windows 98 PC from the Internet Explorer Suite Components page at

http://www.microsoft.com/ie/ie40/download/addon.htm

Benefits of Personal Web Server

Personal Web Server offers the following benefits:

- **Integration** Personal Web Server turns a Windows 98–based personal computer into a low-volume Web server, making it as easy to share HTML and FTP files over the Internet and intranets as it is to share and print document files over a network. The software is fully integrated into the Windows 98 taskbar and Control Panel, allowing users to start and stop HTTP and FTP services whenever needed, administer the server, or change general options. Microsoft also designed Personal Web Server to complement its larger and fully compatible Web server products, such as Microsoft Windows NT Internet Information Server (IIS). Personal Web Server is also fully complementary to Peer Web Services included with Microsoft Windows NT Workstation version 4.0.

- **Easy to install, use, and manage** Personal Web Server installs easily in minutes and includes an intuitive HTML-based administration utility that also supports full remote administration. It supports both user-level and local security, ensuring flexible and effective protection of sensitive corporate information. Users can set up the Personal Web Server to support Windows NT Challenge/Response encrypted-password transmission.

- **Standards-based technology** Personal Web Server fully supports existing standards such as Common Gateway Interface (CGI) and includes the open Internet Server API (ISAPI) extension to the Win32 API that is up to five times faster than CGI-based applications. This technology enables any user to take advantage of ISAPI and CGI scripts.

- **Increased communication** Personal Web Server supports peer-to-peer publishing because of its support for file sharing over HTTP and FTP protocols.

How Personal Web Server Works

To share a folder through HTTP or FTP, open the Properties dialog box for the folder and click the Sharing tab. Turn on the Shared As option. Figure 8-4 on the following page shows the Sharing tab of the Properties dialog box, in which you see the Web Sharing button.

Click the Web Sharing button. (This button appears only if you have Personal Web Server installed.) In Figure 8-5, you'll see the dialog box in which you can select the kind of folder sharing you want.

Workgroups can share information with each other, or they can expose their projects to a wider audience, making sure that others are aware of their progress. Personal Web Server doesn't have the system requirements of a full Web server such as IIS.

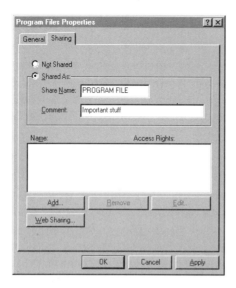

Figure 8-4   *The Sharing tab of the Properties dialog box*

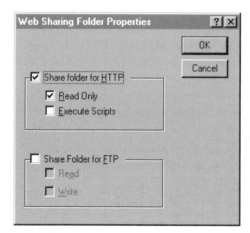

Figure 8-5   *The Web Sharing Folder Properties dialog box for HTTP and FTP sharing*

Personal Web Server supports multiple WebPost service providers such as CompuServe, SPRYNET, and America Online (AOL). The default WebPost Service Provider DLL can post to the most popular Internet servers, including the NCSA HTTPD, APACHE Web server, and Windows NT IIS. The Web Publishing Wizard connects to the Internet Service Provider (ISP), determines the protocol needed to copy the files, and then uploads the files to the appropriate directory on the ISP computer.

Personal Web Server is ideal for developing, testing, and staging Web applications. It supports many back-end programming APIs, such as CGI and ISAPI. It also supports all ISAPI extensions and CGI scripts and is optimized for interactive workstation use. This support enables Web site developers to host their test pages with complicated engines, such as forms or applications, on their own PC locally and then upload them to the Web server when they've debugged their code sufficiently.

Posting a Web Site with the Web Publishing Wizard

Internet Explorer 4.0's Web Publishing Wizard makes it easier than ever to post your own Web site to a server. The Web Publishing Wizard offers the opportunity to publish Web pages on their own or on a third-party server. The Web Publishing Wizard automates the process of copying files from your computer to the Web server—just follow the step-by-step instructions, and the wizard does the rest.

To begin publishing on the Internet with the Web Publishing Wizard, take the following steps:

● Create a Web page using your favorite authoring tool.

● Sign up for an account with an ISP.

● Use the Web Publishing Wizard to copy the Web pages to the Internet.

Figure 8-6 shows one of the Web Publishing Wizard's screens.

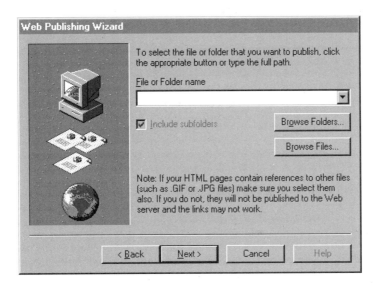

Figure 8-6   *The Web Publishing Wizard*

Key Features of the Web Publishing Wizard

The Web Publishing Wizard can automatically post to a variety of Web servers and offers support for standard protocols such as FTP, UNC, HTTP Post; third-party services such as CompuServe, AOL and America Online Primehost, and SPRYNET Primehost; and system-independent protocols such as CRS and FrontPage Extended Web.

The Web Publishing Wizard can post to local ISPs, IIS, intranet servers on your local area network, and FrontPage. It supports the following languages: English, French, German, Italian, Japanese, and Spanish.

ISPs that have their own protocol scheme for uploading files to their Web servers can write a custom WebPost provider DLL and distribute it from the Microsoft Web site at

http://www.microsoft.com/windows/software/webpost

If you want details about this procedure, send e-mail to *WebPost@lists.msn.com* expressing your interest in writing a provider DLL. Code for a sample WebPost provider is included in the ActiveX SDK.

Other Tools for Authors and Developers

In addition to delivering the industry's best browser, Internet Explorer 4.0 provides innovative new technology that you can use to increase interactivity and excitement for your customers—without slowing down server performance. Internet Explorer 4.0 includes the following technologies to help you create exciting and interactive Web pages and applications:

- **ActiveX scripting** Lets ActiveX controls "talk" to one another and to other Web applets.
- **ActiveX technology** Provides a means for creating innovative, Web-based software components using your existing knowledge and code base.
- **Dynamic HTML** Gives you more design options and control, plus the ability to add a new dimension of interactivity without slowing performance in the process. (For more detailed information about using Dynamic HTML, consult Chapter 4, "Introducing Internet Explorer 4.0.")
- **Java with AFC** Provides a powerful set of building blocks for developing Java applets and other Internet applications. Application Foundation Classes (AFC) deliver a rich suite of graphics as well as user interface and multimedia capabilities to authors who use Java in their Web pages.

The following sections will help you make the most of the innovations delivered with Internet Explorer 4.0.

The Site Builder Network: Key Resource for Improving Your Web Site

You'll be hard pressed to find a better source of information on Internet technologies than Site Builder Network, which you can find at the following address:

http://www.microsoft.com/sitebuilder/

The Site Builder Network offers documentation covering both familiar topics and new technologies such as Dynamic HTML's Object Model and Multimedia controls, plus strategic information to supplement the Internet Client Software Development Kit (described in the following section). Site Builder Workshop also provides a variety of samples—along with code—to help you create cutting-edge Web sites using Internet Explorer 4.0 tools and technologies.

Internet Client Software Development Kit

The Internet Client Software Development Kit (SDK) serves as the foundation for learning about Internet Explorer 4.0 technologies and the Active Platform. This comprehensive resource offers all the tools and information you need to make the most of the platform's innovations to create high-impact Web sites.

You don't have to be an expert programmer to develop compelling Web content. The Internet Client SDK is designed for authors of varying levels of experience and provides task-oriented documentation, samples, tools, and reusable components for authoring active content. The SDK also includes resources to enable traditional custom components and applications to run on the Internet and intranets. Here are the highlights of the Internet Client SDK:

- **Authoring for the desktop and the Web** Provides everything you need to author HTML pages that take advantage of the latest features of Internet Explorer 4.0, from cascading style sheets to scripting to ActiveX controls and Java applets

- **Component development** Provides the details you need to create ActiveX controls and Java applets

- **Internet application development** Describes features and technologies used by Internet Explorer 4.0 and explains how you can exploit them in your own applications

- **Component library** Provides downloadable components and the documentation for them

Extending Your Reach with Windows 98

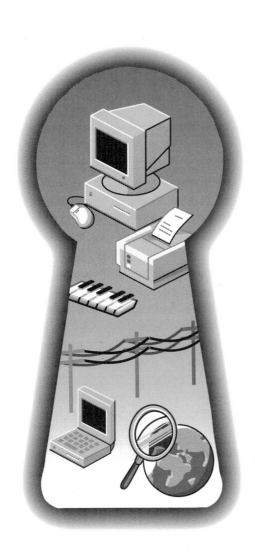

9

Networking in Windows 98

DEMANDS FOR BETTER NETWORK INTEGRATION, more sophisticated network and system management capabilities, and improved network performance and reliability are growing as more business-critical functions rely on PC networks. Because of these demands, companies are faced with increased costs to run PC networks and are investing in tools and staff to meet the challenge of day-to-day network management.

Microsoft Windows 98 is constructed to address the needs of corporate network administrators, with a well-integrated, high-performance, manageable 32-bit network architecture. Windows 98 is also designed with the Windows user in mind and makes access to and control of the network consistent and network browsing and printing easy. In addition, Windows 98 is designed to address users' mobility needs by enabling remote access to the network from portable PCs. (See Chapter 12, "Mobile Computing Services," for detailed information about mobile computer use.)

Given the amount of investment customers have made in Microsoft Windows and their PC network infrastructures, one overriding goal for networking in Windows 98 is compatibility. Compatibility involves ensuring continued support for existing real-mode components as well as making the new 32-bit protected-mode components in Windows 98 compatible with existing 16-bit MS-DOS–based applications and device drivers and existing 16-bit Windows-based applications and DLLs.

This chapter introduces the 32-bit, protected-mode networking architecture built into Windows 98 and shows how it provides well-integrated network support, manageability, improved performance, user-level network security, and dial-up access to the network.

Networking Features of Windows 98

The primary networking features in Windows 98 include the following:

- A robust, open, high-performance 32-bit network architecture, with 32-bit network client software, 32-bit file and printer sharing software, 32-bit network protocols, and 32-bit network card drivers

- Support for using multiple redirectors, multiple protocols, and multiple network card device drivers simultaneously to facilitate integrating the desktop into a heterogeneous network environment

- Support for industry standard connectivity and systems management solutions, including TCP/IP, IPX, SNMP, and DMI

- Tight integration with Novell NetWare, including high-performance, 32-bit protected-mode NetWare-compatible client software for connecting to NetWare 3.x and 4.x servers, and peer sharing for NetWare environments

- Tight integration with Microsoft Windows NT Server to support a powerful client/server solution

- Built-in support for systems management, including the ability to remotely administer, monitor, and view the configuration of PCs over the network

- Dial-up network access support, providing remote access to servers within Microsoft networks, Novell NetWare, and UNIX and support for remote protocols such as PPP, PPTP, and SLIP

- Easy connection and configuration of printers in network environments for network printing

Easy Networking with Windows 98

The Microsoft network support provides full interoperability with other Windows 98 PCs and PCs running Microsoft Windows 95, Microsoft Windows NT, Windows NT Server, LAN Manager, and any other Microsoft-compatible servers. Windows 98 includes support for client access and peer services capabilities on a Microsoft network. Additionally, other network servers and services are offered by third parties. For example, Artisoft, Banyan, Digital Equipment Corporation (DEC), Novell, and SunSelect provide Windows 98 support for their respective network servers.

This section summarizes the key features and concepts in Windows 98 that make networking easy to implement and use.

Novell NetWare Integration

Windows 98 has built-in support for two networks: Microsoft and Novell NetWare networks. Installing support for both kinds of networks is as simple as running the Setup program for Windows 98 or clicking the Network icon in the Control Panel. Both the Client for Microsoft Networks and the Microsoft Client for NetWare Networks are implemented as high-performance, high-reliability, 32-bit protected-mode components.

The "Well-Connected Client" Operating System

Today's networks are heterogeneous and becoming even more connected. Companies are linking their Windows PCs to multiple PC network servers, mainframe and minicomputer host systems, UNIX machines, and a variety of services like the Internet. The desktop operating system must meet this challenge and provide support for often disparate connectivity needs on the network. Windows 98 has multiple network support.

Because integrated networking support is a key focus of the design of Windows 98, it's much easier to install and manage support for a single network or even multiple networks simultaneously using Windows 98. Windows 98 can simultaneously support up to ten 32-bit, protected-mode network clients using its Network Provider Interface. This interface defines a set of APIs used by Windows 98 to access the network for tasks such as logging on to the server, browsing servers, connecting to servers, printing, and so on.

Installing network provider support is simple; you do it via the Network icon in the Control Panel or from the Network Setup dialog box when you're first installing Windows 98. A Windows 98 desktop can run client support for NetWare, Windows NT Server, Banyan, DEC Pathworks, and Sun NFS simultaneously.

PC users in a network environment that includes Apple Macintosh computers can use Windows 98 to exchange documents and share information with Macintosh users when Macintosh-compatible file services are used with Windows NT Server or Novell NetWare to connect to the common file server. (Long filename support in Windows 98 further simplifies the integration of the two systems.)

Internet Information with a Mouse Click

With Windows 98, you have easy access to the Internet, whether you dial into a commercial Internet provider or you gain access via your corporate network over TCP/IP. Windows 98 provides all the means you need to tap into the information on the Internet. Built-in support for TCP/IP; dial-up protocols such as Point-to-Point

Protocol (PPP), Point-to-Point Tunneling Protocol (PPTP), and Serial Line Internet Protocol (SLIP); and Windows Socket services make connecting to the Internet and the information highway just a mouse click away. (For more information about connecting to the Internet and intranets, see Chapter 4, "Introducing Internet Explorer 4.0.")

- TCP/IP, the protocol used on the Internet, is implemented in Windows 98 as a fast, robust, 32-bit Windows-based TCP/IP stack.

- Dial-up protocol support gives users flexibility in choosing the Internet access provider they want to dial into. Connection can be via a standard asynchronous modem or an ISDN connection.

- Support for Windows Socket services allows use of any of the large collection of third-party and public domain Internet utilities, such as Mosaic, winWAIS, and WinGopher to connect easily to the Internet and to access the thousands of worldwide information servers.

Additionally, Windows 98 includes Telnet and FTP to help users take advantage of the Internet. Windows 98 also supports sending and receiving e-mail messages over the Internet through the use of a provided mail driver that integrates with Microsoft Outlook Express. (For more information about Internet mail support in Windows 98, see Chapter 7, "Windows Messaging.")

Point and Click Networking

For users, running even one network client can be confusing—running multiple network clients is nearly unmanageable. Each server has unique client-side utilities and commands that are often difficult to remember and use. When the desktop PC has support for multiple networks loaded, the user is faced with at least twice the number of commands and utilities to remember and might have to remember multiple passwords to access network resources.

The easy-to-use Network Neighborhood introduced in Windows 95 continues to make it easy for users to perform common network operations on disparate servers. First, the network manager can establish one password to log a user on to the appropriate Windows 98 PC and network resources. These services can include, for example, e-mail, group scheduling applications, dial-in support, and database access. Additionally, common network actions, such as browsing servers, managing connections, and printing, are all performed identically through the graphical user interface in Windows 98, regardless of the type of server Windows 98 is connected to. As a result, users can locate, connect, and start print jobs on a NetWare print server as easily as they can with a printer attached to a Windows NT Server. All the common network actions can be accomplished visually, using the mouse to navigate through the network resources, the connections, and so on. Users aren't required to memorize any new network commands. For both the Client for Microsoft Networks and Microsoft

Client for Novell NetWare Networks, users can also run the corresponding command-line utilities. This ongoing backward compatibility is necessary to support batch files that are currently in use.

The Network Neighborhood also helps to manage the complexity of the network by showing it from the user's perspective—that is, the Network Neighborhood shows only what the user is interested in seeing. When the user initially opens the Network Neighborhood, the window contains only the servers the user has logged on to or the servers the user connects to most frequently unless the user has explicitly customized the network view by dragging and dropping the server into the Network Neighborhood. This context-sensitive view of the network reduces the number of network resources the user initially encounters to a more manageable number of objects. For Windows NT domains and NetWare 3.*x* and 4.*x*, the network context presented is the "login server" and any other connected servers.

For a more in-depth discussion of the Network Neighborhood and the user interface, see Chapter 3, "The Faces of Windows 98."

Easier Mobile Network Support

Two features in Windows 98 make connecting to a network easier for mobile PC users: Plug and Play and Dial-Up Networking.

Plug and Play

Plug and Play in Windows 98 solves several problems that face mobile PC users. Mobile users no longer have to maintain multiple configurations, such as desktop and portable configurations. Windows 98 recognizes when you add or remove peripherals, such as when you remove a network card and add a modem for dial-up network access. Because Windows 98 supports hot- and warm-docking, users don't have to reboot their systems each time they make a change to the configuration. In addition, Windows 98 has built-in Card and Socket services that allow for hot removal and insertion of PCMCIA cards, including network cards.

Network Plug and Play support in Windows 98 also includes application-level support. An application that is network-aware understands whether or not the network is available. If the network adapter is removed, the application automatically puts itself into "offline" mode to allow the user to continue to work or it shuts down gracefully.

Dial-Up Networking

Maintaining data access to their corporate network while working in a remote location is another challenge for mobile users. The Dial-Up Networking client in Windows 98 provides modular support for multiple dial-up providers, including Windows NT RAS servers and NetWare. It also supports several protocols, including

NetBEUI, IPX/SPX, and TCP/IP via PPP, PPTP, and SLIP. Support for dial-up can also be offered by third parties with support for the modular architecture of the Dial-Up Networking client in Windows 98.

For more information on these topics, see Chapter 12, "Mobile Computing Services," and Chapter 17, "Plug and Play."

Windows 98 Client: Designed for Manageability

Many corporations have rapidly growing networks that in some cases run worldwide. Keeping the networks and the ever-increasing number of systems connected to the networks running at peak performance is a challenge both for users and for network managers. Corporations are beginning to deploy network and desktop management tools to help their employees meet this challenge.

Windows 98 has built-in network and system management instrumentation to enable current and future management tools to remotely monitor, query, and configure Windows 98 PCs. Using these tools, network managers can quickly inventory the software and hardware used on their networks. Working from a Windows 98 PC, network managers can remotely diagnose and reconfigure Windows 98 systems as well as remotely monitor system and network performance on a Windows 98 PC. The following key components make Windows 98 very manageable:

- **SNMP agent** Windows 98 incorporates an agent that implements the Simple Network Management Protocol (SNMP). This agent complies with the Internet Engineering Task Force (IETF) SNMP specification, responding to queries and sending notifications of events that take place on the PC to an SNMP console. The SNMP console allows a network manager to remotely monitor and manage the Windows 98 PC. Events can be managed from a central SNMP management console.

- **SNMP MIB, MIB-II** The SNMP MIB (Management Information Base) describes what information about the system is available to the SNMP console. Windows 98 includes the MIB-II, which describes the Microsoft TCP/IP protocol and allows information about the protocol stack to be communicated back to the management console. For example, the management console can query the MIB-II for the IP address, the name of the user at this IP address, and IP routing information.

- **DMI agent** Desktop Management Interface (DMI) applications provide cross-platform desktop management capabilities. Microsoft, as a founding member of the Desktop Management Task Force (DMTF), will follow the ongoing evolution of the DMI specification. Windows 98 offers a DMI agent, with support for the agent built into the Registry.

- **Windows Management Infrastructure** The Windows Management Infrastructure collects a wealth of information about the configuration of devices and the system as a whole. This information is stored in the Registry and made available through API extensions. This software is the foundation of Microsoft's support for DMI and will provide device and system information to OLE Management Services (OLE MS) and SNMP. When this package is installed, a new key, HKEY_LOCAL_MACHINE\DesktopManagement, is created in the Registry. This key will contain numerous subkeys and values. Instrumentation code (which "mines" device information) will also be installed. However, there is no way to activate the instrumentation because this package contains just the infrastructure. If you're interested in testing this code or developing your own instrumentation, send e-mail to *WMI_INFO@microsoft.com* and request the WMI SDK.

- **Registry-based system management** Central to the operation of Windows 98 is the Registry, similar in design to the Registry in Windows 95 and Windows NT. The Registry contains information used by Windows 98 that describes the hardware configuration of the PC, user-defined preferences, and application-specific information. The Registry is a database containing keys and values. A special category of keys, called *dynamic keys*, are memory resident and can contain frequently changing data updated by system components, device drivers, or applications. For example, the network adapter device driver can register the number of packets sent per second.

  The Registry consists of two components: SYSTEM.DAT, which describes the PC configuration and computer-specific application information; and USER.DAT, which defines user preferences and user-specific application information. Each component is a file that resides on the PC or on a network server. The Registry is remotely accessible through an RPC-based interface. The Win32 Registry APIs are used to access the Registry, both locally and remotely.

Management tools for Windows 98

Several tools for Windows 98 make managing and administering the system or the network much easier:

- **Registry Editor** Allows local or remote editing of the Registry in Windows 98.
- **System Policy Editor** Used by network managers to set per-user or per-group "policy" overrides on Registry entries. It creates the POLICY.POL component of the Registry and contains a superset of those settings.
- **System Monitor** Allows local or remote viewing of the performance of the various I/O components of a local system or remote PC. For example, the

network administrator can use this tool to monitor the file system, the network components, or data from the network card. The data is updated dynamically using the Registry's dynamic keys.

- **NetWatcher** Allows local or remote viewing and management of the network connections of peer services in Windows 98.

Easy to set up and install

Some network managers install Windows on the network server for later installation onto users' PCs or to run Windows from the server. If network managers install Windows 98 on the network server for later installation on users' PCs, they have to decide on an approach for a number of variables: making the process appear transparent to the user; rolling out Windows using a "push" or "hands-free" installation; using specific settings for different categories of users; and updating these configurations when Windows, Windows applications, or device driver updates are available. If network managers want to run Windows 98 from the server, they have to manage variables such as having local swapping files and some local INIs and applications, allowing user-level configurations, supporting disparate hardware configurations, and handling roving users on the network.

Windows 98 addresses several elements of these problems with a Setup utility and the Registry. Setup streamlines the installation of Windows 98 on a network server for later installations onto users' PCs and for running Windows 98 from the server. The Windows 98 Setup utility has a scripting feature, making it possible to implement "hands-free" installation of Windows 98 from a network server to client PCs.

Running Windows 98 from a server becomes simple largely because of its Registry. The Registry is a centralized database of all hardware, software, and user information that is easy to maintain remotely on the server. The separation of hardware configuration and user profiles in the Registry means that if users move around on the network, their preferences follow them from PC to PC, regardless of the hardware configuration they're currently working on.

Network Architecture in Windows 98

The network architecture in Windows 98 provides high-level network support and integration. The key design points of the networking architecture in Windows 98 are the following:

- **Fast, 32-bit virtual device drivers (VxDs)** The networking components in Windows 98 are built as 32-bit VxDs, which have zero conventional memory footprint and are loaded dynamically when needed by the system. In addition, because the operating system and the VxDs are all running in protected-mode and overhead for mode switching and virtualization between protected and real-mode operation is not incurred, network I/O performance is fast.

- **Reliability** Because the networking components in Windows 98 run in protected-mode and are designed to a well-defined set of interfaces, they are reliable. Conflict in memory or attempts to exclusively chain the same set of interrupts, which commonly leads to system hangs or error conditions, don't occur with protected-mode network components because Windows 98 arbitrates the hardware resource allocation.

- **Modular, open design** The network architecture in Windows 98 is highly modular and includes a Network Provider Interface, an Installable File System (IFS) interface, and a version of Network Driver Interface Specification (NDIS) version 4.1 that has been enhanced for Plug and Play support.

  Windows 98 adds support for NDIS 4.1. The primary change between NDIS 4.0 and NDIS 4.1 is native support for ATM (asynchronous transfer mode) network cards. The standard NIC interfaces have not been modified. The specifications for all three interfaces are available to third-party network vendors.

- **Multiple network support** Windows 98 is designed to accept multiple network providers, multiple network redirectors written to the IFS interface, and multiple NDIS drivers as needed. As a result, client support for Microsoft Networks and Novell NetWare can be run simultaneously. Windows 98 can concurrently support the use of multiple 32-bit, protected-mode network clients and one real-mode network client.

- **Multiple protocol support** One of the NDIS components in Windows 98, the Protocol Manager, supports the loading of multiple transport protocols. The Protocol Manager enables Microsoft and third parties to independently write protocol stacks that coexist well for Windows 98. Windows 98 includes built-in support for IPX/SPX, TCP/IP, and NetBEUI.

- **Plug and Play** All the networking components in Windows 98 are designed for dynamic Plug and Play operation. For example, when a PCMCIA network card is inserted, the NDIS 4.1 network card driver is automatically loaded and the network is available. When either the PCMCIA network card or the network cable is removed, Windows 98 notifies any applications using the network that the network is no longer available and continues to run.

Figure 9-1 on the next page shows the general layout of the network architecture built into Windows 98. The following sections in this chapter describe key aspects of this architecture, including the Network Provider Interface, the IFS, and NDIS 4.1.

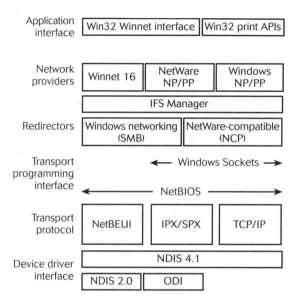

Application interface	Win32 Winnet interface	Win32 print APIs

Figure 9-1   *The layered network architecture of Windows 98*

Network Provider Interface: Concurrent Support for Multiple Network Servers

Windows 98 has an open, modular Network Provider Interface (NPI) to allow support for multiple networks to be installed in Windows 98 simultaneously. The NPI enables Microsoft or any third-party network provider to integrate various network services seamlessly into Windows 98. The NPI has the following key benefits:

- The open interface allows network vendors to supply tightly integrated support for their network servers for Windows.

- All supported networks are identically accessed and managed through the Windows 98 Network Neighborhood user interface.

The NPI abstracts the network services for the Windows 98 user interface components as well as for the various Windows 98 network and desktop management components. The NPI consists of two parts: the network provider API and the network providers. The network provider API is a single, well-defined set of APIs used by Windows 98 to request network services, such as those for browsing servers, connecting to and disconnecting from servers, and queuing a print job. These requests are then passed to the network providers. The network provider layer sits below the API layer and provides the network services requested by components of Windows 98. Conceptually, this model is similar to the design of the various device driver interfaces of Windows 98—a well-defined set of interfaces used by the operating system to request services, and the services themselves, which are provided by a device driver that is often written by a third party.

The most obvious abstraction of the various network services provided by the NPI is the Windows 98 system login. Each network provider can provide a unique logon dialog box to suit the needs of the network server's security model. For example, the logon dialog box shown in Figure 9-2 is for logging on to a Windows NT Server domain.

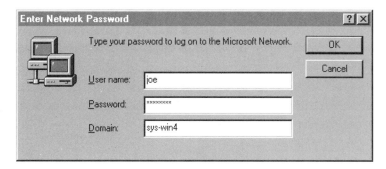

Figure 9-2   *The network logon dialog box for the Windows NT Server domain*

The dialog box for logging on to a Novell NetWare 3.*x* server, shown in Figure 9-3, offers additional information to allow users to log on as GUEST. This dialog box is invoked when a user first accesses a NetWare server.

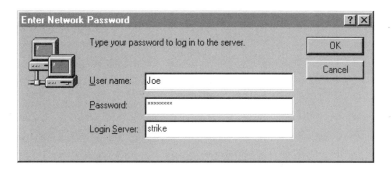

Figure 9-3   *The network logon dialog box for Novell NetWare 3.*x *or 4.*x

When the logon information from the dialog box has been validated against the requested server, the password is passed back to Windows 98, which can then use the password as the "password control" and unlock any linked system or network resources. In this fashion, Windows 98 can accommodate the various ways that network servers provide their services while offering the user a consistent interface.

Another example of support from the network provider that is visible to users occurs when they specify server name strings. For example, Microsoft-compatible networks use the Universal Naming Convention, which takes this form:

```
\\server-name\share-name
```

NetWare servers are specified in this form:

```
server-name/volume-name:directory-name
```

The respective network providers correctly parse the syntax of their server name strings, so users who are accustomed to using the NetWare server syntax can type name strings in that form wherever strings are required by the Windows 98 user interface to access NetWare server resources.

Installable File System: Support for Multiple Network Redirectors

The Installable File System (IFS) interface built into Windows 98 is a well-defined set of APIs that are used to implement all file systems in the operating system, including the VFAT (32-bit FAT), FAT32, and CD-ROM file systems. The IFS implementation in Windows 98 is functionally similar to the IFS implementations in Windows NT. For networking, the IFS is used to implement network redirectors. The IFS interfaces are documented for use by vendors of network servers when implementing their redirectors for Windows 98.

The IFS offers the following key benefits for network redirectors for Windows 98:

- **Multiple redirector support** The IFS interface was designed for multiple redirectors.
- **Increased reliability** The IFS model arbitrates resource requests, removing the source of many real-mode redirector conflicts.
- **Improved performance** Network redirectors benefit from the unified IFS cache, which makes client-side network redirector caching available.

The IFS consists of a set of file system APIs and loadable file system drivers (FSDs). Multiple FSDs can reside in the system simultaneously. The FSDs provide the logic necessary for the file system to provide a consistent view of devices and arbitrate access, update, and control of devices of different physical media types. For network redirectors, the FSDs provide mechanisms to locate, open, read, write, and delete files as well as services such as named pipes and mailslots.

To illustrate the flow of control, take as an example opening a file that is actually a link to a file on a server from a Windows 98 desktop. The user double-clicks the icon. The Windows 98 shell parses the link and determines that the file is a network object. The shell passes the filename to the NPI, which if necessary reestablishes the network connection to the server on which the object resides. The NPI then calls the network redirector to open the file on the file server. The network redirector translates the file request into a request formatted for the specified network file server, transmits the request to the server via its link through the NDIS layer, and returns to the NPI and the shell a handle to the open file.

The Microsoft-supplied redirectors for the Client for Microsoft Networks and the Microsoft Client for NetWare are implemented as IFS FSDs.

NDIS 4.1: Multiple Protocol Support

Network Driver Interface Specification (NDIS) version 4.1 is a superset of all earlier NDIS functionality that exists for Windows NT and Windows 95. NDIS 4.1 has features for Windows 98 in the following key areas:

- **Plug and Play enhancements to the Protocol Manager and Media Access Control layer** These enhancements enable network drivers to be dynamically loaded and unloaded.
- **ATM network cards** Windows 98 adds support for NDIS 4.1.
- **NDIS mini-driver model** The mini-drivers for use with Windows 98 are binary-compatible with the implementation used in Windows NT. The mini-driver model dramatically decreases the amount of code that a network adapter vendor must write.

Conceptually, the mini-driver model is similar to the driver models implemented for printers, disk drivers, and display drivers. Essentially the mini-driver divides the existing NDIS Media Access Control (MAC) layer into two halves. The mini-driver half implements only the code that is specific to the network adapter card, including specific implementation details—such as establishing communications with the card, turning electrical isolation on and off (if implemented) for Plug and Play, doing media detection, and enabling any value-added features the card might contain. The mini-driver is wedded to the NDIS wrapper, which implements the other half of the MAC functionality. This NDIS wrapper contains the code that is common to all NDIS drivers.

An NDIS stack is composed of three components: the protocol, the MAC or mini-port, and the mini-port wrapper. NDIS contains the Protocol Manager, which loads and unloads the protocol. This manager can manage multiple protocols loaded simultaneously. Immediately below the protocol is either the MAC or the mini-driver, if a mini-driver is used. Multiple MACs or mini-drivers can be loaded in systems in which multiple network adapter cards are loaded. Finally, the mini-port wrapper·layer below the mini-port does a mapping of Windows NT Hardware Abstraction Layer (HAL) APIs for I/O. This mini-port wrapper layer is very thin because Windows 98 can always assume that it's being run on an Intel architecture.

Novell NetWare Integration

Windows 98 provides a complete, Microsoft-supplied Microsoft Client for NetWare Networks for Windows. This client can be installed as the default network support for Windows 98 or it can coexist with the Client for Microsoft Networks, as shown in Figure 9-4. The Microsoft Client for NetWare Networks for Windows 98 provides interoperability with NetWare 3.*x* and 4.*x* servers.

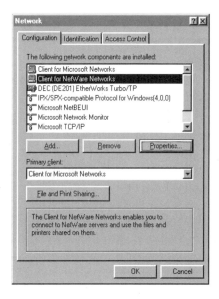

Figure 9-4   *The Control Panel's Network tool, showing the Client for Microsoft Networks and the Microsoft Client for NetWare Networks running simultaneously*

Microsoft Client for NetWare Networks

The Microsoft Client for NetWare Networks in Windows 98 provides interoperability for NetWare 3.*x* and 4.*x* servers. Systems running Windows 98 can use all NetWare server services, browse NetWare servers, connect to servers, and queue print jobs using either the user interface in Windows 98 or Novell's NetWare command-line utilities. The Microsoft Client for NetWare Networks in Windows 98 even runs "TSR clean" NetWare logon scripts. In addition, Windows 98 provides continued support for Novell NetWare real-mode components, thereby supporting both the NetWare 3.*x* NETX shell and the NetWare 4.*x* VLM shell.

The 32-Bit Microsoft Client for NetWare Networks

The Microsoft Client for NetWare Networks has the following key features:

- High performance
- Robust and reliable client support
- Zero conventional memory footprint
- An auto-reconnect feature
- Packet burst protocol support
- Client-side caching
- Plug and Play awareness
- Full integration with the user interface in Windows 98
- Full interoperability with Novell NetWare 3.*x* and 4.*x* clients and servers
- The ability to run NetWare command-line utilities
- Graphical logon to NetWare 3.*x* or 4.*x* via the NetWare bindery
- User-level security implemented using pass-through to the bindery
- A NetWare-compatible logon command processor
- Point and Print support

The client is fully implemented as 32-bit virtual device driver components. Designed to run in protected-mode and operate in a multitasking environment, the client is much more robust than real-mode networking components and takes no conventional memory.

The Microsoft Client for NetWare Networks has great performance characteristics. On large block transfers over the network, it is up to 200 percent faster than Windows 98 using the VLM shell. For most network operations that are a mix of reading and writing, the Microsoft Client for NetWare Networks is between 50 and 200 percent faster, depending on the mix of network I/O.

The Microsoft Client for NetWare Networks is enabled for Plug and Play. Portable computers that support this capability can be hot-docked or undocked, and the networking support is properly loaded and unloaded without hanging the system. (Hot-docking and undocking are the equivalent of connecting and disconnecting the network cable from a Windows 98 PC. Under Windows 98, the system continues to function.) PCMCIA network cards also function in the same manner.

Logon to Windows 98 is linked to a NetWare bindery, the NetWare server's security authority database. This link logs users on to both the Windows 98 system and their preferred NetWare server via a single graphical logon process.

As shown in Figure 9-5, users can specify that the Microsoft Client for NetWare Networks should process NetWare logon scripts. If drive mappings and search drives are specified in a logon script, the same user configuration is implemented under Windows 98, with no changes necessary. The Windows 98 logon processor can also parse conditional statements in NetWare logon scripts. Because the Windows 98 logon processor operates in protected-mode, it cannot load TSRs. Logon scripts that load TSRs must be updated to remove the TSR-loading commands, and the TSRs must be loaded in the 16-bit driver load prior to the protected-mode operation. (In some cases, these TSRs have protected-mode equivalents built into Windows 98, and loading them might not be necessary.)

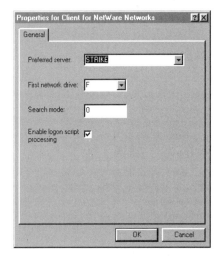

Figure 9-5   *The property sheet for the Microsoft Client for NetWare Networks, showing that a preferred server has been specified and logon scripts have been enabled*

File and Printer Sharing Services for NetWare Networks

Windows 98 provides NetWare-compatible peer services for file and printer sharing. These services feature user-level security by implementing a pass-through security link to an existing Novell NetWare server to leverage the existing user database. Windows 98 doesn't introduce a new security scheme; rather, it fully leverages the existing user-level security built into NetWare's bindery.

During the installation of Windows 98 and via the Network icon in the Control Panel, users can install either the NetWare Compatible Peer Services or Microsoft Network

Peer Services. The peer services in Windows 98 are meant to work in concert with an existing Novell NetWare server and add complementary sharing services.

The NetWare Compatible Peer Services enable the sharing of local files and printers on the Windows 98 system. For the NetWare Compatible Peer Services to be activated, a Novell NetWare server must be on the network. Without this server, file and printer sharing cannot be enabled because of the pass-through security model. Under this model, user-level security is implemented using the bindery, which passes the validation of users through to the NetWare server. (Unlike with file and printer sharing services for Microsoft networks, share-level security is not supported.)

Before sharing is enabled, a NetWare server must be specified via the Security tool in the Control Panel. The Control Panel's Network tool is then used to specify which server or domain controller is the PC's designated security authority, as shown in Figure 9-6.

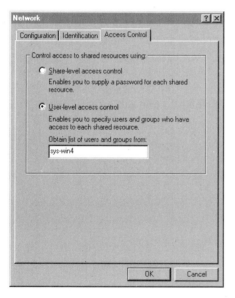

Figure 9-6   *Specifying user-level (pass-through) security from a Windows NT domain named SYS-WIN4*

Adding users to the list of those who can share the PC's hard drive is accomplished via an Add Users option on the hard disk's property sheet. Selecting this option displays the dialog box shown in Figure 9-7 on the following page, in which access privileges are specified. The list of users who can share the hard disk is obtained from the security authority specified in the Control Panel's Network tool—in this case, REDMOND.

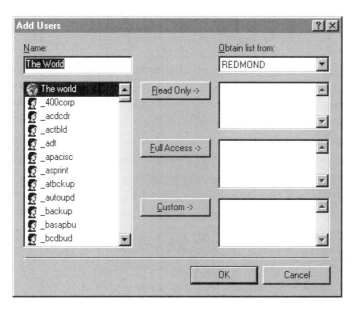

Figure 9-7 *Specifying access privileges for a user through user-level security*

When a user attempts to access a shared device on the Windows 98 system, the Windows 98 PC receives the connection request and validates the user name or group membership with the NetWare server. If the name or group membership is valid, the peer services in Windows 98 then check whether the name or group has been granted access rights to the shared resource and grants or denies the connection request accordingly.

The sharing-enabling process illustrates two points:

- User management is all done in the namespace of the existing NetWare server. Windows 98 doesn't add another namespace to administer, and the NetWare server is administered using the tools that are currently in use—for example, tools that the NetWare network manager currently uses, such as SYSCON, are used for user account management for Windows 98 user-level security.

- Only valid user accounts and groups can be shared with NetWare Compatible Peer Services.

Peer services in Windows 98 can be remotely administered through the NetWatcher. The network manager can monitor connections to any resource on any Windows 98 peer services PC on the network and can disconnect users and remotely change access rights for specific users. By default, remote administration is limited to user accounts with the administrator privilege.

The Microsoft print server for NetWare networks

In Windows 98, the file and printer sharing services for NetWare networks include a Win32-based PSERVER capability, which can despool print jobs from NetWare queues to printers on Windows 98 PCs. Consequently, a NetWare server queue can be serviced by a printer attached to a system running the file and printer sharing services for NetWare. One benefit of this capability is that because print queues can all be managed centrally from the NetWare server, users can print to one queue. If the network includes several systems running Windows 98 with peer services enabled, each system can despool from one queue, increasing overall network-based printer capacity. Alternatively, queues can be designated specifically for printers attached to a system running the file and printer sharing services for NetWare networks.

NetWare 4.x support

The Microsoft Client for NetWare Networks supports a NetWare 4.*x* server if it is running bindery emulation. The NetWare 4.*x* server is then browsable from the Network Neighborhood like any other NetWare server.

Client Support for NetWare Directory Services

NetWare Directory Services (NDS) offers the following benefits:

- Makes it easy to browse NDS resources
- Makes it easy to print to NDS print queues
- Enables processing of NetWare login scripts, NDS property pages, and NDS passwords

Microsoft service for NDS provides the functionality that Novell NetWare users need to connect to NDS servers and run many important utilities. Service for NDS provides the following networking features to support computers running on NetWare 4.*x* networks:

- Integrated logon to NetWare 4.*x* servers
- NDS authentication, including authentication to multiple NDS trees
- Full support for processing NetWare logon scripts, NDS property pages, and NDS passwords
- The ability to use Network Neighborhood to browse the directory tree and NDS resources
- The ability to print to NDS print queues
- Full support for 16-bit NDS-aware programs written for MS-DOS or Windows using documented calls from the NetWare Client Software Development Kit.

When the service is installed, it can be activated in the Network option on the Control Panel. Click Add on the Configuration tab, select Service from the list on the Select Network Component Type dialog box, click Add again, and then choose Microsoft and Service For NetWare Directory Services. This service is a supplement to the standard Windows 95 NetWare client software and includes the file and printer sharing update for NetWare networks originally shipped as part of the OSR-1 Service Pack for Windows 95.

Other NetWare Interoperability

Windows 98 offers these additional interoperability features:

- Full support for Novell command-line utilities (client and server) for NetWare 3.*x*
- Support for booting diskless workstations from NetWare servers
- Floppy boot capability
- Dial-up connectivity to Novell's NetWare Connect server

Microsoft Network Integration

Windows 98 includes a network client that implements support for Microsoft network functionality. This client allows Windows 98 to connect to Windows 95, Windows NT Server, and LAN Manager and interoperate with IBM LAN Server, DEC Pathworks, AT&T StarLAN, and LAN Manager for UNIX as well as other Server Message Block (SMB)–compatible networks.

The 32-Bit Client for Microsoft Networks

Key Client for Microsoft Networks features include the following:

- Robustness
- Zero conventional memory footprint
- An auto-reconnect feature
- Client-side caching
- Plug and Play awareness
- Full integration into the user interface in Windows 98
- Protocol independence
- Point and Print for one-click printer setup

The Client for Microsoft Networks is implemented as a collection of 32-bit protected-mode components. The Network Provider, the Redirector, and NDIS 4.1 drivers are implemented as VxDs, and because the components execute in protected-mode without the overhead of switching to real-mode, they provide great performance. The Network Provider implements client-side caching for an additional performance boost. The client's components are designed for operation in a multitasking environment, and they run in kernel Ring 0 context. As a result, they are not affected by errant Windows-based applications. And because they run in protected-mode, they have no conventional memory footprint.

The client is enabled for key features of Windows 98, such as long filenames, links, auto-reconnect to servers, Point and Print, and Plug and Play, and it is integrated tightly into the Windows 98 shell through the NPI. The client is protocol-independent, and it can use IPX/SPX (the default installed protocol), TCP/IP, or NetBEUI.

The client provides full interoperability with Windows 95, Windows NT Server, LAN Manager, and LAN Manager for UNIX. It also provides compatibility with AT&T StarLAN, IBM LAN Server, 3Com 3+Open and 3+Share, and DEC Pathworks.

For compatibility and to help customers implement floppy boot, a real-mode Client for Microsoft Networks is also included. The Microsoft real-mode components can be "unloaded" by the operating system after the protected-mode networking software is loaded.

The 32-Bit Microsoft Network Peer Services

Windows 98 includes peer services for Microsoft networks. The peer server in Windows 98 supports the user-level security model when used in conjunction with a Windows NT Server, and the peer services can be linked directly to domain-based user accounts. As a result, network administrators can centrally control access to peer services at the domain controller. This domain controller can be either a Windows NT Server or a LAN Manager.

User-level security begins with sharing a device on a Windows 98 system. The list of users that appears in the sharing dialog box is provided by the domain controller, so only validated domain users can share the device. After the share is established, user logons are specified for access rights. When a user requests access to a shared Windows 98 resource, the Windows 98 peer services check the user's logon name against the domain controller's list. If the user logon is valid, the peer services then check whether this user has access privileges for this resource. If the user has access privileges, the connection is established.

Windows 98 also includes share-level peer services. This level of security associates a password with a shared disk directory or printer. Share-level security can be implemented in a network consisting of only PCs running Windows 98 or in a network that includes other Microsoft networks–compatible servers.

Peer services in Windows 98 can be remotely administered through the NetWatcher. A network manager can monitor connections to any resource on any Windows 98 peer services PC on the network, disconnect users, and remotely change access rights for specific users. By default, remote administration is limited to user accounts with the administrator privilege.

IrDA Device Drivers and Utilities

Windows 98 supports Fast Infrared (FIR) and Serial Infrared (SIR) devices, which provides easy file transferring over infrared and LAN connectivity. Windows 98 includes the Microsoft Infrared Transfer applet that makes file transferring over infrared as simple as click and send.

Microsoft Infrared Transfer

To use Microsoft Infrared Transfer, simply right-click on the file you want to transfer and select Send To Infrared Recipient.

ATM Native Support

Windows 98 has native support for ATM network cards via NDIS 4.1 ATM miniport drivers.

Network Compatibility

Windows 98 includes built-in support for Microsoft networks and Novell NetWare networks. In addition, the Setup program in Windows 98 can correctly install and configure Windows 98 for a variety of existing real-mode networks, including but not limited to the following:

- Banyan VINES
- FTP Software, Inc., NFS Client
- DEC Pathworks
- Novell NetWare (Workstation shell 3.x NETX and Workstation shell 4.x VLM)
- SunSoft PC-NFS

Protocol Support

Protocols for networking components in Windows 98 are implemented as 32-bit protected-mode components. Windows 98 can support multiple protocols simultaneously. Protocol stacks can be shared among the installed networks. As an example, a single TCP/IP protocol stack can serve the needs of both the Client for Microsoft Networks and the Microsoft Client for NetWare Networks.

All three protocols included with Windows 98 (IPX/SPX, TCP/IP, and NetBEUI) are Plug and Play enabled. As a result, the Windows 98 system continues to run if the network is unavailable (whether because a portable computer has been undocked or a PCMCIA network card has been removed). If the network is unavailable, the protocol stacks unload themselves from the system after sending notification to any dependent applications. Plug and Play enabling also means protocols can be loaded automatically. For example, if a portable computer is undocked and attached to an infrared line-of-sight network, the TCP/IP protocol is unloaded and the appropriate infrared protocol is loaded.

The IPX/SPX-Compatible Protocol

The IPX/SPX stack is the default protocol for Windows 98 and is compatible with the Novell NetWare IPX/SPX implementation. This protocol stack can be used to communicate to either a NetWare server or a Windows NT Server. This protocol is routable and will run compatibly on most network infrastructures (such as bridges, routers, and so on) that are designed for IPX/SPX routing. The IPX/SPX protocol in Windows 98 includes support for "packet burst," which can offer improved network performance.

The Microsoft IPX/SPX implementation provides Windows Sockets programming interface support. The Windows Sockets interface is supported using IPX/SPX as the protocol. Hence, any WinSock applications can run on top of IPX/SPX with Windows 98. Support is provided for only Win32 WinSock applications.

The IPX/SPX implementation in Windows 98 also has support for the NetBIOS programming interface. Winsock 2.0 drivers are integrated into Windows 98 Setup.

The TCP/IP Protocol

The TCP/IP protocol is widely accepted for connectivity to the Internet and as an industry standard for many corporate networks. In Windows 98, TCP/IP is fully implemented as a 32-bit, high-performance VxD that consumes no conventional memory. It includes many of the more commonly used command-line utilities, such as Telnet, ftp, arp, ping, route, netstat, nbstat, ipconfig, tftp, rexec, rcp, rsh, and traceroute.

The TCP/IP protocol support in Windows 98 includes the Windows Sockets programming interface and a WinSock DLL. (A 16-bit WinSock is provided for compatibility with existing WinSock applications, and a 32-bit WinSock is provided for Win32-based WinSock applications.) Winsock 2.0 drivers are integrated into Windows 98 Setup.

NetBIOS programming interface support is also supplied with the TCP/IP support.

DHCP support

Working with other industry leaders, Microsoft has created a *bootp* backward-compatible mechanism for automatic allocation of IP addresses to make implementation of the TCP/IP protocol more manageable. The Dynamic Host Configuration Protocol (DHCP) runs from a Windows NT DHCP server and allows network managers to centrally establish a range of IP addresses per subnet for any Windows 98 TCP/IP client requesting an address. It also allows network managers to centrally establish a "lease time"—how long the allocated IP address is to remain valid. Unlike *bootp*, the address allocation is dynamic, not preconfigured. In this fashion, it is possible to move from subnet to subnet and always have a valid IP address mask. Windows 98 includes an *ipconfig* utility that allows a user or administrator to quickly examine the allocated IP address, its lease time, and other useful data about the DHCP allocation, as shown here:

```
Windows IP Configuration Version 0.1
  Host Name . . . . . . . . :
  DNS Servers . . . . . . :
  DNS Lookup Order. . . . :
  Node Type . . . . . . . : Mixed
  NetBIOS Scope ID. . . . :
  IP Routing Enabled. . . : No
  WINS Proxy Enabled. . . : No
  WINS Resolution For Windows Sockets Applications Enabled : No
  DNS Resolution For Windows Networking Applications Enabled : No

Adapter Address 00-AA-00-18-B0-C4:
  DHCP Enabled. . . . . . : Yes
  IP Address. . . . . . . : 11.105.43.177
  Subnet Mask . . . . . . : 255.255.0.0
  Default Gateway . . . . : 11.105.0.1
  DHCP Server . . . . . . : 11.105.43.157
  Primary WINS Server . . : 11.101.13.53
  Secondary WINS Server . : 11.101.12.198
  Lease Obtained. . . . . : Tue 10th. May 1994 6:44:40 am
  Lease Expires . . . . . : Wed 11th. May 1994 6:44:40 am
```

DHCP support can be specified at installation time or enabled via the Control Panel's Network tool. If DHCP support is disabled, an IP address can be entered in the Microsoft TCP/IP property sheet, as shown in Figure 9-8.

WINS support

The TCP/IP protocol stack in Windows 98 lets users choose to install support for either the Windows NT Windows Internet Naming Service (WINS) or the OSF DCE Domain Naming Service (DNS). These naming services provide name resolution by binding the node name and the currently allocated IP address, providing for correct addressing of any requests for resources from a node anywhere on the network. The amount of network traffic needed to locate the node on the network is thus minimized. Windows 98 supports a single DNS server and up to two WINS servers.

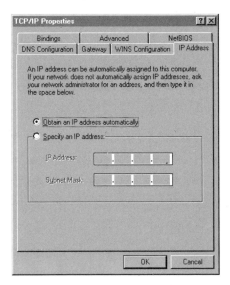

Figure 9-8   *The Microsoft TCP/IP property sheet, showing the DHCP configuration*

The NetBEUI protocol

Windows 98 includes a NetBEUI protocol stack that is compatible with existing networks using NetBEUI. This stack provides compatibility with Windows for Workgroups, Windows NT Server, LAN Manager, and other networks. A NetBIOS programming interface is also supported.

32-Bit Data Link Control

The Microsoft 32-bit Data Link Control (DLC) protocol stack upgrades the DLC protocol stack that shipped in the original Windows 95 disks with a protect mode implementation of the DLC protocol. This control can be used to provide enhanced connectivity and performance on Windows 98 systems and allows access to multiple host systems with a single network card.

The DLC protocol is used primarily to access IBM mainframe and IBM AS/400 computers. The 32-bit DLC protocol software built into Windows 98 enables a network administrator to add support for 32-bit and 16-bit DLC programs.

Host terminal emulation programs use this protocol to communicate directly with mainframe computers.

The 32-bit protocol software does the following:

- Supports Windows-based 32-bit programs that use CCB2.
- Supports 16-bit programs (MS-DOS and Windows) that use CCB1.

- Provides connectivity to local area printers connected directly to the network. For example, you can use DLC to print to a printer (such as a Hewlett-Packard LaserJet 4Si) that uses a Hewlett Packard JetDirect network adapter to connect directly to the network.
- Conforms to the Network Driver Interface Specification (NDIS) 3.1 and is compatible with Token-Ring, FDDI, or Ethernet network adapter drivers.

Client Support for Point-to-Point Tunneling Protocol

Point-to-Point Tunneling Protocol (PPTP) is a networking technology that supports multiprotocol virtual private networks, enabling remote users to access corporate networks securely over public networks such as the Internet. PPTP enables a low-cost, private connection that is particularly useful for people who work from home or travel and must access their corporate networks remotely to check e-mail or perform other activities. Rather than dial a long distance number to remotely access a corporate network, with PPTP a user can dial a local phone number (to an Internet Service Provider) and establish a secure connection to his or her corporate network via the Internet.

PPTP is a tunneling protocol defined by the PPTP Forum that allows Point-to-Point Protocol (PPP) packets to be encapsulated within IP packets and forwarded over any IP network, including the Internet itself.

Tunneling is a networking term to describe the encapsulation of one protocol within another protocol. Tunneling is typically done to join two networks using an intermediate network that is running an incompatible protocol or is under the administrative control of a third party.

PPTP and Windows Dial-Up Networking

PPTP is used to enhance the networking services provided by the Windows Remote Access Server (RAS) and Windows 98 Dial-Up Networking.

Windows Dial-Up Networking allows a computer to join and leave a network of computers over a dial-up connection. While connected to the network, the Windows client behaves exactly as if it had a local network connection. Except for speed differences over slow links, network applications are unaware that a Dial-Up Networking connection is in use.

Windows Dial-Up Networking uses the Internet standard PPP family to provide a secure, optimized multiple-protocol network connection over dialed telephone lines.

PPTP extends the service provided by Windows Dial-Up Networking. PPTP adds the ability to treat the Internet as a point-to-point Dial-Up Networking connection. All data sent over this connection can be encrypted and compressed, and multiple network-level protocols (TCP/IP, NetBEUI, IPX) can be run concurrently. Windows NT

Domain Login level security is preserved even across the Internet. PPTP can be used to connect to an intranet that is otherwise isolated from the Internet and can even have Internet address space conflicts.

PPTP appears as a new modem type that can be selected when setting up a connection in the Dial-Up Networking folder. The PPTP modem type doesn't appear elsewhere in the system.

When initiating a PPTP connection, use the DNS hostname of the destination computer or its IP address in dotted format (x.x.x.x) as the phone number. *Area Code* is not used for PPTP connections.

Windows 98 provides support for two concurrent outbound Dial-Up Networking connections. This support exists to allow a Dial-Up Networking PPTP connection to be established over a modem-based Dial-Up Networking connection to the Internet.

You don't need to have a Dial-Up Networking connection to the Internet to support PPTP. Reachability to the PPTP server over any IP network is the only requirement for a PPTP connection.

Technical details of PPTP

PPTP is a tunneling protocol defined by the PPTP Forum that allows PPP packets to be encapsulated within Internet Protocol (IP) packets and forwarded over any IP network, including the Internet itself. PPTP provides support for virtual LAN connection establishment/release and encapsulations of higher level protocol frames within the Generic Routing Encapsulation (GREv2) over IP. GREv2 is connectionless and is carried directly on top of IP. PPTP provides for congestion control using a sliding window mechanism and using the Internet as a PPP Media Type to Join Networks.

Since the Windows NT RAS server provides protocols and policies to dynamically connect two networks together, it is possible to provide this functionality over the Internet by using PPTP to establish a single PPP connection between a gateway computer on each network. A single computer joining an existing private network via PPTP and the Internet is a simple case of joining two networks together via PPTP gateways.

To exchange IP packets between the two gateway computers, both computers must already have Internet connectivity. You can join the two networks together by setting up the gateways as conventional Internet gateways and allowing the two networks to join the Internet. This setup requires that the IP addresses of all computers on both networks be consistent with the Internet address assignment and that routing information for all computers is propagated throughout the Internet. These requirements are difficult to achieve in practice. In addition, the security implications of direct Internet connectivity make this arrangement unsuitable for many networks.

When using PPTP to join the two networks together, the two gateways have limited visibility on the Internet and the networks behind them have none. This is accomplished by allowing only IP packets that contain PPTP packets to be forwarded from the Internet to the gateways on the Internet side adapter. A RAS connection between the two gateways is then established, and the new adapters created on each side of the RAS connection are used by the gateways to join the networks together. (See Figure 9-9.)

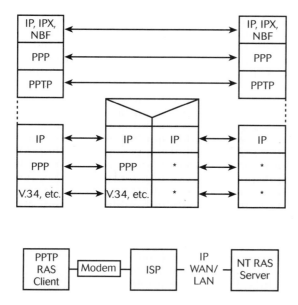

Figure 9-9   *Windows 98 PPTP RAS Client/Internet/NT RAS Server Protocol stack*

Establishing a PPTP connection between these two networks provides the following benefits over direct Internet connectivity:

- The private networks' IP address spaces don't have to be coordinated with the Internet address space.

- All network protocols supported by RAS are supported in the PPTP connection case. Private networks that are running combinations of TCP/IP, IPX, or NBF can be joined.

- RAS security protocols and policies are implemented to prevent unauthorized connections.

- All network packets being sent over the Internet can be encrypted.

Windows 98 support for PPTP
Windows 98 is a PPTP client. A single instance of a PPTP connection is supported over a LAN or WAN Internet connection.

Windows 98, unlike Windows NT, will not support the joining of networks in the sense that the connected networks will be able to route through Windows 98. Windows 98 will attempt to allow all connected networks to be visible from Windows 98. As described below, this isn't possible in all cases.

Network protocol issues

When a PPTP connection is established, the client network protocols will see an additional dial-up adapter become active. PPTP itself uses TCP/IP to tunnel network packets, so at least one adapter in the client must be bound to and running TCP/IP. When the client is connecting to a PPTP server on a LAN, this adapter can be a NIC. When the client is dialing into a RAS server or ISP and then connecting to a PPTP server across a private intranet or the public Internet, the TCP/IP adapter can also be a dial-up adapter. It is assumed that the PPTP client is connecting to an NT RAS/PPTP server.

- **NBF** NBF (NetBEUI Frame) will work as expected. The PPTP client will be able to see both the original network and the new network concurrently. The client will be visible to computers on both LANs, but the networks won't be joined through the client. The client's ability to see computers on the new network is provided by the Windows NT Server's NetBIOS gateway.

- **NWLink** Only one target network at a time will be visible with IPX. This configuration is unchanged from the way Windows 95 works today. Currently, when IPX is selected in a phonebook entry and IPX is active on a NIC, a dialog box is presented to the user (at dial time) indicating that NetWare servers on the LAN will no longer be visible. Users will see this same dialog box when establishing a PPTP connection.

- **TCP/IP** Several TCP/IP configurations will be examined. As a baseline, the first is the simple case of joining two routed IP networks together without PPTP.

The baseline: Two routed IP networks In this configuration, shown in Figure 9-10, IP packets generated by *Client* that are destined for hosts on the local subnet 1.1.1 are addressed at the MAC level directly to the target host and forwarded over interface *A*.

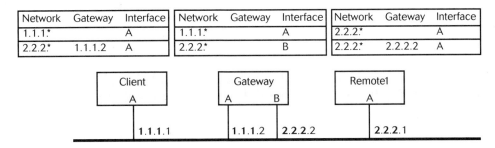

Figure 9-10 *Joining two IP networks without PPTP*

Client packets destined for *Remote1* are addressed at the IP level to *Remote1* and at the MAC level to host *Gateway*. *Gateway*, upon receiving these packets, changes the MAC address to be that of the target *Remote1* and forwards them on interface *B*.

The most common workstation configuration is a simple variation in which local subnet packets are sent directly to the target host and all other packets are forwarded to a default gateway. DHCP assigns client IP addresses and a default gateway address at boot time.

Any given host can have only a single active default gateway. This arrangement is ideal in the case of a host with a single adapter but doesn't work for hosts with multiple adapters. In the example below, both *Client* and *Remote1* could replace their route entry for the peer LAN with a default route, but *Gateway* requires explicit routes to each LAN in order to work properly.

PPTP effectively requires all hosts to have multiple adapters and exposes the limitations of default gateway-based routing schemes.

Using PPTP to securely bridge two networks   In the next scenario, shown in Figure 9-11, *Gateway* has been made a PPTP server and PPTP filtering has been enabled on interface *A*. PPTP filtering effectively makes *Gateway* invisible to *Client* without first establishing a PPTP connection. *Client*'s TCP/IP stack has a route to *Gateway* and uses this route to establish and maintain the PPTP connection. Since only PPTP packets are accepted on *Gateway*'s interface *A*, no applications can see *Gateway* at address 1.1.1.2.

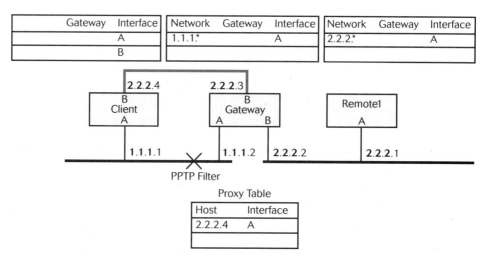

Figure 9-11   *Joining two IP networks with PPTP*

Once the PPTP tunnel has been established, *Client* has a second active adapter, with a new IP address assigned to it by the *Gateway* PPTP server. Since the Windows NT RAS server supports TCP/IP clients by proxy-ARPing (Address Resolution Protocol) for them on its local networks, *Client* is effectively bridged to the LAN side of *Gateway*.

Remote1 would send packets to *Client* by addressing them at the MAC level to *Gateway,* who would forward them over the PPTP adapter to *Client. Remote1* is completely unaware of *Gateway*'s role in this process since *Gateway* is pretending to be every PPTP client at the MAC level.

The issues associated with this configuration are identical to those of a conventional NT RAS server setup. This is no accident—a PPTP server is a RAS server that uses an IP network as a media type.

On the 1.1.1 network, *Client* has an IP address of 1.1.1.1. On the 2.2.2 network, *Client*'s IP address is 2.2.2.4. Named servers on each network must be configured correctly.

For hosts other than *Client* on the 1.1.1 network, to see hosts on the 2.2.2 network each host must be configured with a route entry that makes *Client* the gateway to network 2.2.2.

All hosts on the 2.2.2 network can automatically see *Client* but not other hosts on 1.1.1. In order for hosts on the 2.2.2 network to see hosts on 1.1.1, each host on the 2.2.2 network must be configured with a route entry that makes *Client* (2.2.2.4) the gateway to network 1.1.1. The packet path from a host on 2.2.2 to a host on 1.1.1 would then be the following:

1. Address the packet at the IP level to the target host and at the MAC level to *Client*.
2. *Gateway* steals the packet and forwards it to *Client* over the PPTP connection.
3. *Client* sees that its destination IP address is on 1.1.1 and forwards it on interface *A*.

Clearly, configuring a network by hand is a nontrivial process. PPTP, by virtue of making clients multihomed, further complicates the process. RIP or OSPF can help automate this process.

A typical case

The next network setup, shown in Figure 9-12 on the following page, represents most real-world networks. *Router1*, and probably *Gateway*, have been hand-configured by a system administrator to have explicit routing information. Clients are relying on the routing entries created locally (and automatically) derived from each NIC's IP address and subnet mask. These entries allow the client to reach hosts on the same subnet. Additionally, a single default gateway entry forwards all other packets to a router who hides the larger and more complex routing policy.

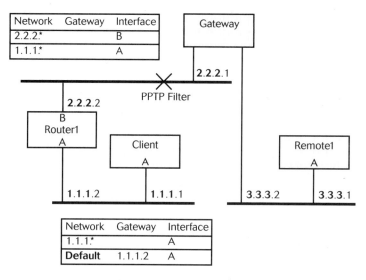

Network	Gateway	Interface
2.2.2.*		B
1.1.1.*		A

Network	Gateway	Interface
1.1.1.*		A
Default	1.1.1.2	A

Figure 9-12   *Joining two IP networks with PPTP: The problem case (before tunneling)*

Even if routers are dynamically exchanging RIP or OSPF routing information, in many cases the simple default gateway scheme will be used for clients. DHCP can easily assign IP addresses, subnet masks, and default gateways.

In Figure 9-12, *Client* can see all hosts on its local subnet, 1.1.1 by way of the 1.1.1 route table entry. It can see all hosts on the 2.2.2 network, including *Gateway*, by using the default gateway route. Note that PPTP filtering on *Gateway*'s interface *A* restricts traffic to *Gateway* to PPTP connections.

The multiple default gateway problem   After *Client* has established a PPTP tunnel to *Gateway*, as illustrated in Figure 9-13, it is effectively bridged to network 3.3.3 on the new interface *B*. As part of establishing this connection, RAS/PPTP normally changes the default gateway of *Client* to *Gateway*. In this example, it is not necessary to change the default to see hosts on the bridged network 3.3.3 but would be necessary if the other side of *Gateway* was attached to a more complex network.

Changing the default gateway entry has the unwanted side effect of making hosts that were visible on network 2.2.2, including *Gateway* itself, unreachable. In general, after establishing a PPTP connection from a host that was using a default gateway scheme, only hosts on local subnets (on the same LAN segment) will remain visible.

To prevent this problem from breaking the PPTP connection itself, Windows NT establishes a single host route entry to the PPTP gateway through the old default gateway, *Router1*. This solves the multiple default gateway problem for the PPTP connection but leaves some hosts on the originating network invisible.

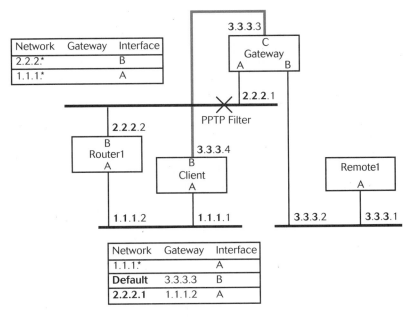

Figure 9-13 *Joining two IP networks with PPTP: The problem case (after tunneling)*

This problem occurs only when clients are using default gateways to reach some networks. Explicit host or network route table entries will continue to be valid when a PPTP connection is established. This means that clients that are receiving local RIP or OSPF routing updates will not have any problems.

Another common PPTP configuration will be affected by this problem. If a non-LAN-attached client dials into an ISP to get on the Internet and then establishes a PPTP tunnel to a corporate network, the client will lose connectivity to the rest of the Internet during the life of the PPTP connection.

Network Interprocess Communications Interfaces

Windows 98 includes support for a variety of distributed computing programming interfaces, including the following:

- Client-side named pipes
- Mailslots
- OSF DCE-compliant Remote Procedure Call (RPC)
- Network DDE
- The Windows Sockets interface

Windows Scripting Host

Windows 98 supports direct script execution from the user interface or the command line. (A script is simply a series of commands that can be automatically executed.) This support is provided by the Windows Scripting Host and allows administrators and users to automate many repetitive user interface actions, such as creating shortcuts, connecting to a network server, and disconnecting from a network server. The Windows Scripting Host is extremely flexible, with built-in support for Microsoft Visual Basic scripts, Java scripts, and a language-independent architecture, which allows software companies to build ActiveX scripting engines for languages such as Perl, TCL, REXX, and Python.

You can run the Windows Scripting Host from either the Windows-based host (WSCRIPT.EXE) or the command-shell–based host (CSCRIPT.EXE). When you double-click on a VBScript or a JavaScript file in Windows, the Windows-based host is used. To execute a script in command-line mode, click Run on the Start button menu, type *CSCRIPT filename* in the Run dialog box, and then click OK.

Long Filename Support

As in Windows 95, the network clients in Windows 98 support the use of long filenames. If the Windows 98 system is connected to a network server that supports long filenames, support for filenames on the server is identical to the local long filename support in Windows 98. (On some servers, the length of filenames and the list of restricted characters might differ from those of Windows 98.) Long filename support is possible both on the Windows NT Server and on NetWare servers if the servers are properly configured.

Network Printing

Windows 98 includes a number of enhancements designed to make printing easier over the network, including the following:

- **Point and print** A printer driver can be automatically installed when connecting to a printer attached to a Novell NetWare, Windows NT Server, or Windows 98 print server. As a result, Windows 98 printer drivers can be located on a Windows NT Server or Novell NetWare server and automatically installed by their Windows 98 clients.

- **The Microsoft Print Server for NetWare networks** For compatibility with NetWare's PSERVER functionality, Windows 98 peer services can despool print jobs from Novell NetWare print queues.

- **Deferred printing** When a Windows 98 PC is disconnected from the network, print jobs are deferred until the PC is once again attached to the network. Print jobs that have been deferred automatically start when the PC is reconnected.

- **Remote printing management** Print jobs can be held, canceled, or restarted remotely. In addition, on systems that have ECP ports, information about the print job status (such as paper tray status, paper jams, or other error conditions) can be returned.

Distributed Component Object Model

Distributed COM (DCOM) extends the Component Object Model (COM) infrastructure that underlies ActiveX, transparently and naturally adding support for reliable, secure, and efficient communication between ActiveX controls, scripts, and Java applets residing on different machines in a LAN, a WAN, or on the Internet. With DCOM, your application can be distributed across locations that make the most sense to your customer and to the application.

Because DCOM is a seamless evolution of COM, you can leverage your existing investment in all ActiveX applications, components, tools, and knowledge to move into the world of standards-based distributed computing. As you do so, DCOM handles the low-level details of network protocols so that you can focus on your real business: quickly providing great ActiveX solutions to your customers.

Network Security

Windows 98 implements a full user logon. The first thing most users encounter after booting their Windows 98 systems is a logon dialog box, which varies depending on the type of network. For example, the Windows NT Server logon dialog box might prompt for a user name, a password, and a domain name. The Novell NetWare 4.*x* logon dialog box might prompt for a user name, a password, and a preferred server name. When the user name and password pair has been validated against the network server's security authority, the Windows 98 user interface is displayed.

Network managers can configure the Windows 98 system to allow entry into the user interface with no network access if users fail to log on. (This configuration is the default.) As an alternative solution to this problem, network managers can specify guest accounts that have limited network access.

The Windows 98 user logon should not be construed as a mechanism to fully secure PCs. Because PCs are still vulnerable to a floppy boot, all data stored on their hard disks is potentially available. The underlying file system in Windows 98 is the MS-DOS FAT file system, which has no built-in encryption or other security mechanisms.

Network resources are secured under Windows 98 using the same security mechanisms employed by network servers on corporate networks. The user name and password in Windows 98 can be configured to be the same as those used by the network server. By doing this, the network manager can control network access, provide user-level security for access to shared resources on the local PC, and control the various agents in Windows 98 as well as limit who has remote administration authority on this Windows 98 system. In this fashion, Windows 98 leverages the existing investment in network servers, management tools, utilities, and infrastructure. Network managers can manage user accounts centrally on the server, just as they always have. They can also use familiar tools for managing user accounts.

Password Control: Unified Logon

The Password Control in Windows 98 can provide a unified logon for all system components requiring password authentication services as well as for any applications that choose to use the Password Control services. For example, protected spreadsheets or databases might use the Password Control services.

The Password Control associates the user name and password supplied at Windows 98 logon with other authentication-conscious programs or system components. For higher security, network managers can choose to associate other passwords with access to confidential corporate data or other sensitive network services.

Figure 9-14 shows the Passwords Properties property sheet, which is accessible from the Control Panel.

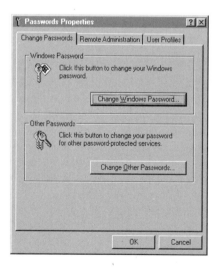

Figure 9-14   *The property sheet for security, showing the Password Control settings*

Password Control provides a mechanism to individually manage components that choose to use the unified password cache. Windows 98 can be configured to use the Windows 98 logon for authentication on a service-by-service or application-by-application basis, making it possible to access all resources on the Windows 98 system as well as on the network, using the Password Control in Windows 98. One example of how the Password Control service is used within Windows 98 is to provide a single logon to both the network and the Microsoft Outlook Express client, the mail client provided with Windows 98. Then when users log on to their PCs, the password they entered to log on to Windows 98 also automatically logs them on to e-mail. This single logon provides a solution for the problem of password proliferation.

User-Level Security

Windows 98 uses the logon process to provide user-level security for a variety of services beyond network resource access, including the following services that are remotely accessible:

- File and printer sharing
- Dial-up network access gateway control
- Backup agent
- Network and system management

Pass-through security

Pass-through security is implemented in Windows 98 as the mechanism to enable user-level security. *Pass-through* literally means that Windows 98 passes authentication requests through to a Windows NT Server or NetWare server. Windows 98 does not implement its own unique user-level security mechanism but instead uses the services of an existing server on the network.

File and printer sharing

For file and printer sharing using Windows 98 peer services, enabling pass-through security is a two-step process. First, user-level security must be enabled using the Control Panel. Second, the device must be shared and users with access privileges must be specified. Right-clicking the drive C icon in My Computer and selecting Properties from the context menu displays a property sheet that shows what shares already exist and which users have access and allows new devices to be shared and new users to be added to specific shares. The Windows NT Server domain, the NetWare bindery, or NDS supplies the user names listed in this property sheet.

Remote Administration

The Remote Administration function of a Windows 98 PC specifies the users or groups who have authority to manage the Windows 98 system, including the following.

- Dial-up network access gateway control
- Backup agent
- Remote access to the Registry
- Remote NetWatcher access
- Remote system performance monitoring

Remote Administration is controlled through the Network Security tool in the Control Panel. Figure 9-15 shows Remote Administration enabled. In this case, Remote Administration is limited to the Domain Admins network manager group—any user who is a member of this group can remotely administer this Windows 98 system. Individual users can also be designated as remote administrators—for example, sophisticated users could be given remote administrator access to their systems.

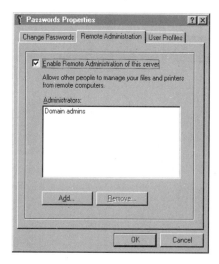

Figure 9-15   *The property sheet for security, showing the Remote Administration settings*

Remote Access Server

Windows 98 includes all the components necessary to enable your desktop to act as a Dial-Up server. This capability allows Dial-Up clients to remotely connect to a Windows 98 machine for local resource access or to an IPX/SPX and/or NetBEUI network. This remote connection will allow users to easily access information and manage their desktop machines no matter where the users are located.

Windows 98 supports a single-line, dial-in gateway that allows a Windows 98 PC with peer services enabled to serve as a gateway to the network. (Windows NT Server supports multiple concurrent dial-in users for additional capability.) The Remote Access Server is established through the property sheet shown in Figure 9-16.

Figure 9-16 *The Remote Access Server dial-in property sheet, which shows that dial-in access to the network is available on this PC running Windows 98*

Like the Dial-Up Networking client, the Remote Access Server supports the following protocols:

- TCP/IP through PPP and PPTP
- IPX/SPX through PPP and PPTP
- NetBEUI

The Remote Access Server supports pass-through security, so user-level security can be used to authenticate users to control access to dial-in services. After connecting to the Remote Access Server, Dial-Up Networking clients can access any network resource that they have privileges to use, including network server resources and peer services.

For more information about Dial-Up Networking, see Chapter 12, "Mobile Computing Services."

10

Printing

TO ADDRESS REQUESTS FROM CUSTOMERS and independent software and hardware vendors, Microsoft Windows 95 introduced several changes to the way printing is handled. The improvements focused on the following three major areas:

- **Better performance** Windows 95 had a new 32-bit printing architecture that supported preemptive multitasking and improved overall performance.

- **Easier to use** Improvements in the user interface in Windows 95 made printing easier, and Plug and Play support made installing new printers easier.

- **Better integration of network printing** Windows 95 extended the local printing architecture to the network environment and tied together installation enhancements to shared network printers.

This chapter describes the printing architecture used in Microsoft Windows 98, which is substantially the same as that in Windows 95. The primary improvements in printing for Windows 95, which carry over to Windows 98, were these:

- A 32-bit print subsystem modeled after the subsystem in Microsoft Windows NT, providing smooth background printing

- Increased printing performance through the use of enhanced metafile (EMF) spooling, which decreases the time needed to return control to the application

- Support for over 500 different printer models through the development of new printer mini-drivers (Windows 98 supports about 1300 printer models.)

- Support for PostScript Level II printers

- Spooling of MS-DOS–based application print jobs along with those from Windows-based applications, with conflict resolution when MS-DOS and Windows-based applications try to print at the same time

- Image color matching support, which provides better WYSIWYG between color in images displayed on the screen and color generated on an output device

- Deferred printing for mobile computer users, allowing users to issue the command to print while undocked and not connected to a printer, so that print jobs will be automatically started when the computer is docked into a docking station

- Simplified printer driver installation, configuration, ease of use, and ease of support through a consolidated user interface

- System support for bidirectional printers and ports, providing improved I/O performance with fast parallel ports (extended capabilities port, or ECP) and error status reporting

- Integration of network printing support, including Point and Print support for the automatic installation of printer drivers from Windows 95, Windows NT Server, or Novell NetWare servers

- Plug and Play support for printers, which allows easy installation and configuration

The 32-Bit Print Subsystem

Windows 98 has a 32-bit print subsystem that includes a multithreaded, preemptive spooler architecture and provides improved printing performance, smooth background printing, and quick return to the application after a print job is initiated by a user in an application. The architecture of the print subsystem is compatible with the Windows NT print subsystem.

The 32-Bit Preemptive Spooler

The Windows 98 print spooler is implemented as a series of 32-bit virtual device drivers, and the spooler functionality is consolidated into a single architecture that offers the following benefits:

- **Smooth background printing** The Windows 98 print spooler passes data to the printer only when the printer is ready to receive it. This strategy helps reduce jerkiness.

- **Quick return to the application** Because of the smooth background printing made possible by the new 32-bit print subsystem, Windows 98 spools EMFs rather than raw printer data when printing from Windows-based applications, resulting in a quicker return-to-application time. After it is spooled, the EMF is interpreted in the background by the printer driver, and output is then sent to the printer. For more details, see the following section, "Enhanced metafile spooling."

- **Power and flexibility** The architecture allows users to select printer attributes on a per-printer basis instead of requiring global printing attributes. For example, each printer can have a different separator page and the option of printing direct via a queue.

Enhanced metafile spooling

EMF spooling results in a quick return-to-application time and hence quicker return of control to the user after a print job is initiated in a Windows-based application.

Windows 98 spools high-level command information generated by the GDI Print API, collectively referred to as an EMF, rather than spooling raw printer data generated by the printer driver. For example, if a document contains a solid black rectangle, the EMF includes a command to draw a rectangle with the given dimensions that should be solidly filled with the color black. After the EMF is created, control is returned to the user, and the EMF file is interpreted in the background by the 32-bit print subsystem spooler and sent to the printer driver. This process, which is shown in Figure 10-1, results in control being returned to users in significantly less time because they don't have to wait for the print calls to be directly interpreted by the printer driver.

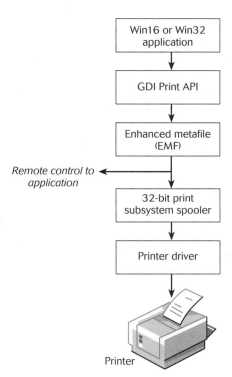

Figure 10-1 *The spooler's relationship to printing in Windows 98*

Support for MS-DOS–Based Applications

Microsoft Windows 98 supports printing from an MS-DOS–based application in the Windows environment by allowing MS-DOS–based applications to spool print jobs to the 32-bit print subsystem spooler. Windows 98 incorporates the functionality for an MS-DOS–based application to spool directly to the 32-bit print spooler. This support is integrated into a print spooler virtual device, which takes the output destined for a printer port and places it in the print spooler before sending the data to the printer. The print spooler is automatically installed and configured, and its handling is invisible to users. It works with all existing MS-DOS–based applications and results in a quicker return-to-application time. Although MS-DOS–based applications do not benefit from EMF spooling, which is supported only for Windows-based applications, the print spooler mechanism ensures that users won't encounter device contention issues and will benefit from smoother background printing and improved printing performance.

Deferred Printing Support

To benefit mobile computer users, the print subsystem in Windows 98 supports deferred printing. This capability allows users not connected to a printer to generate print jobs that are then stored on their local computers. Items not immediately printed are held in the print queue until the computer is connected to a printer. Using this feature, mobile users can create print jobs from Windows-based or MS-DOS–based applications while on the road and then print on a physical printer when they return to the office. This feature is also handy for times when users in the office temporarily lose printer connections because of network or printer problems.

Image Color Matching Support

Using technology licensed from Kodak, Windows 98 provides Image Color Matching (ICM) support, enabling applications to offer greater consistency between the color of images displayed on the screen and the color of images generated by an output device. ICM support is included for display, printer, and scanner devices.

ICM provides consistent (predictable) color rendering from input through monitor preview to output. With ICM functionality, color information is portable across applications that manipulate the information; across users, providing consistent use of colors; and across platforms, allowing the information to be easily moved to different systems in which ICM has been implemented.

ICM support in Windows 98 provides the following benefits to application developers, which in turn benefit users:

- Makes enabling color awareness in applications easy
- Allows for color
- Provides consistent color output across devices

Windows 98 includes ICM support as part of the operating system, allowing application developers to integrate ICM functionality into their applications and thus take advantage of this system service.

To provide support for device-independent color matching, colors used in applications are tied to international (CIE-based) colorimetric standards rather than to specific hardware devices. The operating system does the appropriate color transformations to map the device-independent color representations to the colors supported by the physical device.

The key to ICM support is the use of a profile that represents the color properties of a monitor, printer, or scanner device. The profile format used by the ICM support in Windows 98 is the work of InterColor 3.0, an industry consortium made up of many industry hardware vendors—Kodak, Microsoft, Apple Computer, Sun Microsystems, and Silicon Graphics, among others—and industry standard-setting bodies. The InterColor 3.0 efforts provide a consistent cross-platform color standardization process that will result in industry-wide standards for defining the ICM properties of output and display devices.

Microsoft's first implementation of color management support was released in the Windows 95 operating system as ICM 1.0. This version of ICM was designed to address the needs of applications that do not work in colors outside of RGB (such as CMYK) and that want color management to work fairly transparently for the user. ICM 1.0 requires ICC (International Color Consortium) profiles to be installed for all the color devices on the user's system, and it requires the application that wants to accurately portray colors to the user to support the ICM 1.0 APIs.

After meetings with multiple industry leaders in the field of color, Microsoft has designed ICM 2.0. The new APIs are a complete superset of the ICM 1.0 APIs and add a new range of capabilities:

- ICM 1.0 compatible
- ICC compliant
- Scalable: Simple APIs for applications such as Microsoft Office, complete control for applications such as Adobe PhotoShop
- Same APIs for Windows 95 and Windows NT operating systems
- Support for Profile management at API and user interface level
- Bitmap v5 header support

- Standard Color Space support: sRGB
- Broader color space support: RGB, CMYK, LAB, and others
- Broader support for bitmap formats
- Improved palette handling
- Device driver participation on the Windows 98 and Windows NT operating systems
- Support for multiple Color Management Modules (CMM)
- Faster default CMM that supports all ICC-compliant profiles
- Easier installation of profiles

Installing and Configuring a Printer

Windows 98 consolidates the printer and printing functions into a single Printers folder, shown in Figure 10-2. The Printers folder provides easy ways of adding new printers, configuring existing printers, and managing print jobs.

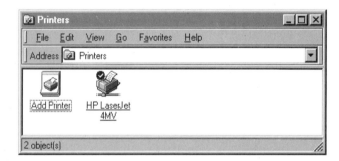

Figure 10-2   *The Printers folder in the new Web view*

Setting Up a Printer

Windows 98 makes it easy to install new printers by supporting the following installation mechanisms:

- **Plug and Play printer detection** For Plug and Play printers, Windows 98 automatically detects the printer at printer installation or during the boot process. The Plug and Play detection code prompts the user for the appropriate driver files if they do not reside in the Windows directory.
- **Add Printer Wizard** Windows 98 provides a wizard that walks users through the printer installation process. Whether the printer is connected to the local PC or shared on another PC on the network, installing it is simple. Figure 10-3 shows the Add Printer Wizard's first panel.

Figure 10-3   *The Add Printer Wizard, which walks users through the printer installation process*

- **Point and Print printing** The Point and Print feature lets users quickly connect to and use a printer shared on another Windows 98 PC, a Windows NT Server, or a Novell NetWare server. When users connect to a shared printer, Windows 98 automatically copies and installs the correct driver for the shared printer from the remote Windows 98 PC, the Windows NT Server, or the Novell NetWare server. Users can then simply begin printing. Point and Print printing is discussed in more detail in Chapter 9, "Networking."

Configuring a Printer

All printer configuration is consolidated onto a single property sheet for the printer that can be accessed from the Settings option on the Start menu. In the Settings submenu, click the Printers button to display the Printers folder. The property sheet, shown in Figure 10-4 on the following page, contains all printer parameters, such as the printer port (or network path) that the printer is connected to, the paper options for the printer, the fonts built into the printer, and device options specific to the printer model.

To further simplify printer configuration, Windows 98 supports bidirectional communications between compatible printers and printer ports. With this functionality, Windows 98 can query the characteristics and configuration options directly from the printer and can automatically configure the printer driver to match the configuration of the printer, including the amount of memory, the paper options, and the fonts installed in the printer.

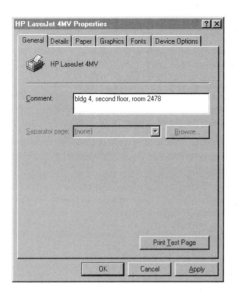

Figure 10-4 *The property sheet for the Hewlett-Packard LaserJet 4MV printer*

Managing Print Jobs

The Windows 98 print job management capabilities include the following:

- **Direct integration with the user interface in Windows 98** The Printers folder serves as the central location for interacting with or configuring printer devices. Opening a printer window and switching to Details view, as shown in Figure 10-5, displays detailed information about the contents of active print jobs or jobs that are waiting in the queue, including the name, status, and owner of the document; when the document was submitted to the print queue; the size of the document; and the priority of the print job.

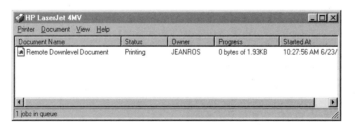

Figure 10-5 *A Details view of a remote print queue's status*

- **Local and remote management of print jobs** Users can pause or cancel the printing of print jobs residing in a remote print queue on a Windows 98 PC. Users with administrator access to a Windows 98 PC that is sharing a printer can remotely manage and administer the print queue with the same user interface and functionality available for a local printer.

Network Printing

Windows 98 also has enhancements for printing in a networked environment:

- **Network Point and Print functionality** Users can print to a shared network printer connected to a computer running Windows 98, Windows NT Advanced Server, or Novell NetWare and have the appropriate printer driver automatically copied from the remote computer and configured on the local Windows 98 computer. Point and Print simplifies the printer installation process and ensures that the correct printer driver is installed for the remote printer.
- **Remote administration of print jobs** Windows 98 provides full remote administration of print jobs for printers shared on computers running Windows 98. With the appropriate access privileges, operations such as holding a print job, canceling a print job, and resuming printing when the print queue is paused can be performed remotely.

You'll find more information about network printing in Windows 98 in Chapter 9, "Networking."

Plug and Play Support

Using bidirectional parallel communications, Windows 98 detects that a Plug and Play–compatible printer is connected to the PC (see Figure 10-6 on the following page) by means of a returned device ID value, as described in the USB, IEEE 1284, or IEEE 1394 specifications. Bidirectional parallel communications with the printer also enable Windows 98 to obtain information about other physical attributes of the device.

Windows 98 detects a Plug and Play printer in one of two ways: each time Windows 98 starts or when a user explicitly requests that a detection be made. When Windows 98 starts, a Plug and Play printer connected to a bidirectional communications port attempts to identify itself by sending its detection code. If the connected printer isn't presently configured in the Windows 98 system, the user is asked whether the printer should be installed. If the user clicks Yes and the appropriate printer driver

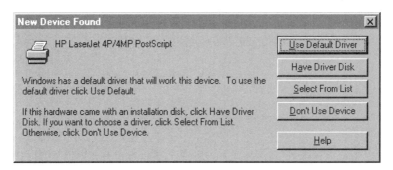

Figure 10-6   *The New Device Found dialog box, showing detection of a Plug and Play printer*

is already present on the system, Windows 98 automatically installs and configures the driver for the printer. If the printer driver is not on the system, Windows 98 prompts the user for the appropriate Setup And Installation disk for Windows 98. If the system doesn't recognize the printer, Windows 98 prompts the user to insert a disk containing the printer driver provided by the printer manufacturer.

11

Communications

MICROSOFT WINDOWS 98 FEATURES a 32-bit communications subsystem that provides high throughput, reliability, and device independence for communications operations. This subsystem provides a powerful, robust, and flexible underlying communications architecture on which Windows 98 provides communications services that support telecommuting and dial-up network access, Microsoft Fax services, access to online information services, computer-telephone integration, conferencing, and remote access to mail.

Benefits to the Windows 98 User

The kernel and communications architecture results in the following benefits to Windows 98 users:

- Robust and reliable high-baud-rate communications throughput
- Multitasking of communications applications
- Simple centralized setup and configuration
- Broad device support
- Support for sharing communication devices, such as modems, among different communications applications
- Telephone network independence

The Communications Architecture

Around the time Microsoft Windows 3.0 was developed, 2400-baud modems were the norm and 9600-baud modems were just becoming affordable. Windows 3.0 was able to handle receiving data at these relatively slow rates without much difficulty. However, as mechanisms to transfer communications information at faster rates—for example, by using higher baud rates or data compression—became more popular, the communications architecture of Windows needed to be examined closely.

When Windows 3.1 was released, 9600-baud modems were extremely popular, but because of communications barriers under Windows 3.1, the overall effectiveness of reliable high data throughput was limited, and the efficiencies of multitasking were eroded when communications applications were running. These communications barriers included high interrupt latency and overhead that affected high-speed communications and a monolithic driver architecture that made it necessary for some third parties to replace the communications driver provided with Windows 3.1 to allow their devices to run efficiently on the system.

Windows 98 supports communications applications and high-speed communications and provides a modular architecture that allows third parties and device manufacturers to easily plug in new communications device drivers. This section describes the communications architecture used in Windows 98.

Communications Goals of Windows 98

The goals of communications support in Windows 98 are to deliver better performance and to enhance ease of use through Plug and Play communications. The communications architecture of Windows 98 delivers the following performance benefits:

- **Reliable high-speed communications** Windows 98 supports reliable high-speed communications by keeping up with data coming in from the communications port, thereby incurring no lost characters because of interrupt latency. In addition, the use of a 32-bit protected-mode file system and network architecture has less impact on the communications system because required mode transitions and interrupt latency are reduced.

- **High data throughput** The 32-bit communications subsystem uses the preemptive multitasking architecture of Windows 98 to provide responsiveness to communications applications and support high data throughput. Communications transfers in 32-bit applications are not affected by other tasks running in the system.

- **Support for time-critical protocols** The communications architecture provides support for time-critical protocols and allows for real-time serial device control.

- **Independence of underlying telephone networks** Windows 98 allows application developers to build telephony applications that can run on a wide variety of telephone networks, including analog, proprietary digital PBXs, key systems, ISDN, and cellular.

The Plug and Play initiative provides ease-of-use enhancements throughout Windows 98, and communications support is no exception. Plug and Play support for communications has the following benefits:

- **Broad device support** Windows 98 features a communications driver architecture that makes it easy for third parties to extend the communications support provided as part of the operating system without sacrificing functionality or stability. In addition, this communications architecture features APIs that support more robust communications devices beyond base RS-232 devices—for example, ISDN.

- **Easy-to-install and easy-to-use communications devices** Windows 98 features centralized modem installation and configuration to simplify setup for users and to simplify communications development efforts for application developers. Windows 98 uses a single universal modem driver (Unimodem) to provide a consistent mechanism for communicating with modem devices. It also provides detection support for Plug and Play modems and supports existing hardware by including mechanisms for detecting legacy modems.

- **Device sharing among communications applications** Windows 98 provides consistent, device-independent mechanisms for controlling communications devices for operations such as dialing outgoing calls and answering incoming calls through the use of the Telephony API (TAPI). Arbitration for the sharing of communications ports and devices is also handled through TAPI. For example, while dial-up networking in Windows 98 is waiting for an incoming call, a TAPI-aware fax communications application can send an outgoing fax without having to first terminate the communications application that is already running.

The rest of this section examines the components that comprise the communications support for the 32-bit communications subsystem in Windows 98.

Kernel Architecture

When data comes into the system from a serial communications port, an interrupt tells the system that a piece of data has been received. Whereas disk I/O and network I/O manipulate blocks of information at a time, serial communications I/O generates one interrupt on the system for *each* incoming character. The burden on the communications driver to keep up is high. To support high-speed throughput of information from a communications device, the system must be able to respond quickly to incoming data. To improve performance and the rate at which the system can reliably accept incoming data, the code that can be used by only one process at a time (critical sections) is kept small; interrupt latency in the core system is also kept small. In addition, the use of 32-bit protected-mode components for the implementation of the file system and network subsystem improves the system responsiveness. Windows 98 is limited in baud rate only by PC hardware characteristics, such as the processor speed and type of communications port.

Driver Architecture

The Windows 98 communications subsystem consists of a modular, 32-bit protected-mode architecture with new communications drivers. A layer called VCOMM provides protected-mode services that allow Windows-based applications and device drivers to use ports and modems. To conserve system resources, communications device drivers are loaded into memory only when in use by applications. VCOMM uses the Windows 98 Plug and Play services to assist with configuration and installation of communications devices.

Windows 98 provides a flexible communications architecture, separating communications operations into three primary areas: Win32 communications APIs and TAPI, the universal modem driver, and communications port drivers. Figure 11-1 shows the relationship that exists between the VCOMM communications driver and the port drivers to communicate with hardware devices. The flow path for a Win16-based application is also illustrated to show how compatibility is maintained for Windows 3.x–based applications.

Here are the primary areas that make up this architecture:

- **Win32 communications APIs and TAPI** The Win32 communications APIs in Windows 98 provide an interface for using modems and communications devices in a device-independent fashion. Applications call the Win32 communications APIs to configure modems and perform data I/O through them. Through TAPI, applications can control modems or other telephony devices for operations such as dialing, answering, or hanging up a connection in a standard way. TAPI-aware communications applications no longer need to provide their own modem support list because interaction with a modem is centralized by Windows 98. The communications functionality provided with Windows 98 utilizes these services.

- **Universal modem driver** The universal modem driver, Unimodem, is a layer that provides services for data and fax modems and voice. Users don't have to learn (and application developers don't have to maintain) difficult modem AT commands to dial, answer, and configure modems. Unimodem handles these tasks automatically, using mini-drivers written by modem hardware vendors. Application developers can use TAPI to perform modem control operations in a modem-independent manner.

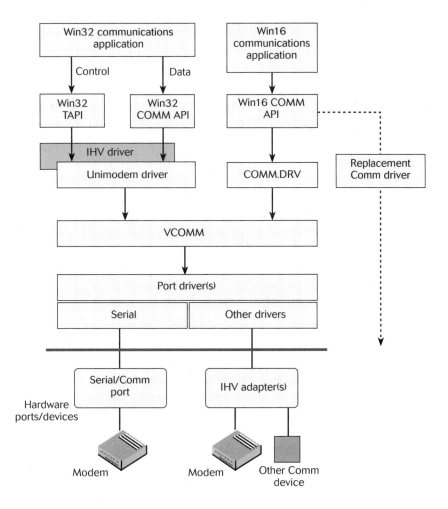

Figure 11-1 *The communications architecture of Windows 98*

- **Port drivers** Port drivers are responsible for communicating with I/O ports, which are accessed through the VCOMM driver and provide a layered approach to device communications. For example, Windows 98 provides a port driver to communicate with serial communications and parallel ports, and third parties and IHVs can provide port drivers to communicate with their own hardware adapters, such as multiport communications adapters. With the port driver model in Windows 98, third parties don't have to replace the communications subsystem.

The Telephony API

The Windows Telephony API (TAPI) is part of the Microsoft Windows Open Services Architecture (WOSA). WOSA encompasses a number of APIs, providing application and corporate developers with an open set of interfaces to which applications can be written and accessed. WOSA also includes services for data access, messaging, software licensing, connectivity, and financial services.

Like other WOSA services, the Windows Telephony API consists of two interfaces: the applications programming interface (API) that developers write to and the service provider interface (SPI) that is used to establish the connection to the specific telephone network. This model is similar to the one whereby printer manufacturers provide printer drivers for Windows-based applications. Figure 11-2 shows the relationship between the "front-end" Windows Telephony API and the "back-end" Windows Telephony SPI.

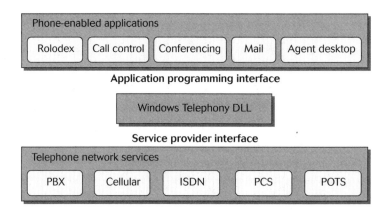

Figure 11-2   *The seamless integration of applications and telephone networks by means of the Windows Telephony API and the Windows Telephony SPI*

The Windows Telephony API provides a standard way for communications applications to control telephony functions for data, fax, and voice calls. TAPI manages all signaling between a PC and a telephone network, including such basic functions as establishing, answering, and terminating a call. It also includes supplementary functions, such as hold, transfer, conference, and call park, found in PBXs, ISDN, and other phone systems. In addition, TAPI provides access to features that are specific to certain service providers, with built-in extensibility to accommodate future telephony features and networks as they become available.

TAPI supports four models for integrating Windows 98 PCs with telephone networks, as illustrated in Figure 11-3. Applications using TAPI can work in any of these four connection models, whether they involve a physical connection between a PC and a phone on the desktop, as in the phone-centric or PC-centric model, or a logical connection, as in either of the client-server models.

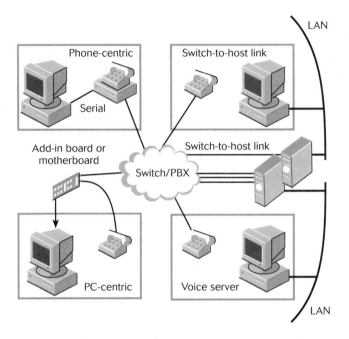

Figure 11-3   *Four models for integrating Windows 98 PCs with telephones*

Through the use of the TAPI services, applications that support communications services have a device-independent means for interacting with telecommunications networks. TAPI also provides a common access mechanism for requesting the use of communications ports and devices, thus providing a means for multiple communications applications to share a single modem—data, fax, or voice—in the computer.

Windows 98 includes TAPI support in the base operating system, allowing application developers to leverage this functionality in their Windows 98–aware applications. In addition, all communications components included as part of Windows 98 are TAPI clients.

Sharing Communications Devices

Through the TAPI interface, communications applications can ask for access to the modem or telephone device, allowing the communications subsystem in Windows 98 to arbitrate device contention and enable applications to share the communications device in a cooperative manner.

Win32-based applications can utilize TAPI functionality to allow some applications to make outgoing calls while others are waiting for inbound calls. For example, while a dial-up network service that is configured for auto-answer mode is waiting for an incoming call, a Win32-based communications application can call the TAPI services to request the use of the modem to perform an outgoing call. Only one call can be performed at a time, but users no longer have to terminate other applications that are using a communications port in order to run a different application. The TAPI services arbitrate requests to share communications ports and devices.

Centralized Modem Setup and Configuration

Windows 98 provides central configuration of communications devices through a tool on the Control Panel. Win32-based applications that take advantage of the TAPI services implemented in Windows 98 can completely leverage the users' configuration of their communications hardware, making subsequent configuration of communications applications easy.

Windows 98 brings the following benefits to modem configuration:

- Easy modem configuration of new communications applications that the entire system can use
- Centralized communications port status and configuration
- Support from TAPI and Win32 communications APIs
- Support for 100+ modems

Modem Configuration in Windows 98

As with support for printers, the support for modems in Windows 98 is centralized. When users first start Windows 98 after installation, they are prompted to detect or identify the modem device they have connected to or installed in their computer. When a modem has been selected and configured, any communications application that supports TAPI services can interact with the modem in a device-independent way. Users don't need to know or understand AT command sequences to customize their communications application.

Configuring a modem under Windows 98 involves performing three simple steps: identifying the new modem device, configuring the modem device, and configuring the telephony services.

Identifying a new modem device

If a modem is not selected when Windows 98 is started the first time after installation, you can use the Modem Wizard to identify a new modem. You get to the Modem Wizard in one of three ways: by using the Add New Hardware shortcut in the Settings Wizard, by using the Modems tool in the Control Panel, or by using the Add New Hardware tool in the Control Panel.

In the Modem Wizard, you can have the wizard detect the modem connected to the PC or you can manually select a modem from the list of known manufacturers and modem models. The detect option uses Plug and Play to configure the correct device. If the wizard can't detect the device, you can still manually select the correct modem.

Configuring a modem device

After you have selected the correct modem, you can optionally change configuration parameters—such as the volume for the modem speaker, the time to wait for the remote computer to answer a call, and the maximum baud rate to use—on a property sheet like the one shown in Figure 11-4. (The maximum baud rate is limited by the speed of the PC's CPU and the speed supported by the communications port.)

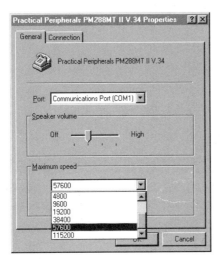

Figure 11-4   *A Modem property sheet*

Configuring telephony services

In addition to configuring the modem device, you can configure telephony services to identify the various dialing parameters associated with the different locations at which the PC will be used. For each location, information is stored for use by TAPI-aware applications, including information needed to dial a local call and a long distance call, the location's area code (for use in determining whether the call is inside or outside the calling area code), and calling card information. For a desktop PC, you would typically use the default location—you could change the default name to *in the office*. For a portable computer, a mobile user might add several different locations to accommodate those at which the computer is commonly used. For example, a mobile user might use the computer in the office, on the road, and in a remote city. Figure 11-5 shows two location configurations that are selectable depending on the location at which the computer is being used.

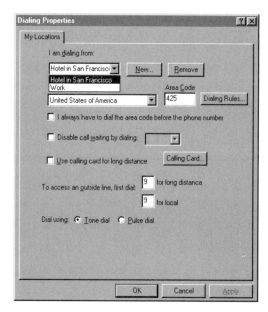

Figure 11-5   *Dialing Properties for configuring location calling information*

Device/Hardware Support

Windows 98 provides communications device and hardware support in a variety of areas, a few of which are discussed on the next page.

Support for 16550A UART FIFO

Windows 98 provides robustness and performance at high baud rates for MS-DOS–based and Windows-based communications applications using local serial ports with 16550A-compatible UARTs. The 16550A UART contains a 16-byte FIFO buffer to prevent character overflow resulting from interrupt latency and to help reduce overall interrupt overhead.

Support for More Ports

The communications APIs in Windows 98 support the same number of logical ports as MS-DOS does: 128 serial ports and 128 parallel ports. Obviously, the number of usable ports is a function of the number of physical ports available to the system.

Support for Parallel Port Modems

Windows 98 supports Enhanced Capabilities Ports (ECPs) to facilitate higher-speed communications than is possible over a serial device. This support provides for the use of parallel port modems.

Plug and Play Support

Plug and Play support for communications devices in Windows 98 facilitates the detection of connected modem devices and the assignment of system resources (for example, IRQs and I/O addresses for communications ports), which simplifies configuration and setup. In addition to Plug and Play detection, Windows 98 provides manual detection of non–Plug and Play communications devices, such as modems. Because no standard for automatically obtaining device information using the AT modem command strings presently exists, detection of legacy modems is handled manually by querying the modem device and checking the information returned against a database of known modem information. As part of a Telecommunications Industry Association (TIA) proposed standard called IS-131, Microsoft is working with other leading industry manufacturers to standardize the modem command set. When this proposal is adopted, Windows 98 will support the standardized command set, which will aid detection of legacy modems.

Modems

External modems require new firmware to return the required Plug and Play ID information, whereas internal modems utilize the ISA Plug and Play specification. PCMCIA communications devices are supported as part of the Plug and Play services for the PCMCIA specification. Some modem manufacturers will improve their communications product offerings by revising their existing modem lines, while others will produce a new line of Plug and Play modems.

Detection of Plug and Play serial devices, such as modems, is handled during the Windows 98 boot process or when a new modem device is connected to the system. As with other Plug and Play devices, the user is notified that the new device has been detected and is asked to confirm the installation and configuration of the device.

Support for legacy modems is provided by using device-specific information to provide a manual detection mechanism or by displaying a list of supported modems from which a user can choose the appropriate one. After a modem has been identified for a system, it can be used by TAPI-enabled communications applications, including dial-up networking, Microsoft Fax services, and the HyperTerminal communications application.

HyperTerminal

Windows 98 includes a 32-bit communications application named HyperTerminal that has all the qualities of a good Windows 98 communications application. HyperTerminal offers base communication capabilities, but integrates well with the user interface in Windows 98.

Good communications applications utilize the Windows 98 services and capabilities to offer a robust and powerful product in the following ways:

- They are Win32-based applications that use the Win32 communications APIs.
- Their internal architecture uses multiple threads of execution to provide good responsiveness to the user and great error-free high-speed communications. Multiple threads allow full preemptive multitasking of communications tasks and support concurrent interaction with the user, downloading of remote data, and display of communications status.
- They take advantage of TAPI services for making remote connections and controlling the modem device.

Phone Dialer

The Phone Dialer application in Windows 98 provides basic support for making telephone calls. As shown in Figure 11-6, it includes a telephone dial pad and user programmable speed dials; it also includes a call log.

New communications hardware supports voice communications as well as data and fax. This next generation of modems supports the AT+V standard (TIA IS-101), which adds voice support to the standard AT command set, effectively turning the modem into a telephone designed to be a PC peripheral. Other devices, such as those built on digital signal processors (DSPs), also include voice telephony support.

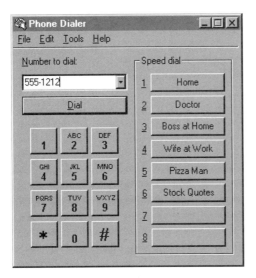

Figure 11-6 *Phone Dialer application*

Windows 98 communications applications bring control of the telephone to the PC, enabling programmable "smart" answering machines, dynamic call filtering and routing, dialing from any PC application or directory, drag-and-drop setup of conference calls, and other types of computer-telephone integration.

12

Mobile Computing Services

AS MORE AND MORE BUSINESSPEOPLE HAVE increased their mobility—whether because they telecommute or because they need to travel or move around to do their jobs—portable computers have become increasingly critical tools. Portable PCs currently make up a significant proportion of all new computers sold. Microsoft knows that mobile computing support can't be implemented as an afterthought or as a set of utilities but must be built into the operating system, optimizing the core networking, device support, and communications architectures for the mobile environment. Microsoft has designed Microsoft Windows 98 with mobile computing in mind. The goals of mobile computing support in Windows 98 are to help portable PC users be more productive and to reduce the support costs associated with using portable PCs.

Three Observations About Mobile Computer Users

Microsoft has made three observations about mobile computer users that provide key insights into the problems of designing an effective operating system to run on portable PCs:

- **Mobile computing encompasses anyone who moves computing capabilities away from a traditional desktop PC.** The Windows 98 vision for mobile computing includes everyone who uses an Intel-based portable PC (including "luggables" and notebook and subnotebook computers, but not PDAs [Personal Digital Assistants])—from users who move from meeting to meeting in an office building, to those who telecommute between their homes and offices, to business travelers, to road warriors who have no office at all and move from customer site to customer site.

- **The tasks users want to perform away from their desks are fundamentally similar to those that they perform on their desktops.** While they're in the office, users want to draft memos, review budget spreadsheets, query databases, browse e-mail messages, peruse presentations on the network, send faxes, and look at their schedules. Away from their offices and their desktop PCs, users want to continue performing these same tasks.

- **The mobile computer environment is fundamentally different from the desktop environment.** When users move away from their offices, their computing environment changes dramatically. Their hardware environment is dynamic, as they plug in and unplug different components to deal with the tasks at hand. Portable PC users might be operating in a power-constrained environment with video displays half the size of their desktop displays. They can't easily access files on a server or receive e-mail. As a result, users can find the mobile computing environment to be constrictive.

These observations are confirmed by extensive research, including quantitative surveys of portable PC users, discussions with corporate implementers of mobile computing technology, and periodic focus groups with mobile users. The remainder of this chapter explains Windows 98 support for mobile users.

Three User Challenges

According to portable PC users, mobile computing presents three main challenges: getting the most out of their portable PC hardware; staying in touch with, or connected to, information resources they need; and keeping data organized while they're away from the office. Windows 98 delivers system services and user functionality that address these challenges and dramatically enrich the mobile computing experience.

- **Getting the most out of portable PC hardware** Rapid advances in portable PC hardware technology and innovations by OEMs have minimized the functionality and performance differences between desktop and portable PCs, and many users are turning to mobile form-factor PCs as replacements for or complements to their desktop PCs. Users expect their portable PC's hardware to work well and not to require time-consuming setup hassles or elaborate reconfiguration for different work environments. And they don't want to buy a new portable PC every time an enhancement shows up in the marketplace. Given the cost of portable PCs, users hope to preserve their investment and extend the lifetime of their portable machines.

- **Staying in touch** At their desks, users have access to a wide array of communications capabilities that keep them connected to data and to other people, both inside and outside their organizations. They have access to the local area network (LAN) and all its services, such as e-mail, file sharing, and print sharing. A telephone, a fax machine, and a modem are close at hand. Away from their desks, users become communications islands. They are cut off from their network and all its services. Phones, faxes, and modems are often unavailable. Mobility entails a constant struggle to stay in touch with needed information and contacts. The ideal for most mobile users is to be as productive while mobile as they are at their desks. To achieve this goal, users must have easy access to powerful communications tools, regardless of location. They must be able to readily access channels of communication between their portable and desktop PCs and among themselves, the rest of their workgroup, and the broader community of computer and fax users.

- **Keeping organized** Mobile users can also spend inordinate amounts of time making sure that files stay in sync between a portable PC and a desktop PC or file server, without corrupting or losing data. They also need to be able to manage print jobs created out of the office and easily transfer data between a desktop and portable PC. In short, the nature of the mobile work environment introduces significant, time-consuming organizational challenges—many of which can be addressed through software.

Getting the Most Out of Portable PC Hardware

Windows 98 is designed to enable computer users to get the most out their portable PC hardware. Windows 98 includes native, designed-in support for innovations such as PC Cards (PCMCIA), docking stations and port replicators, and Advanced Power Management. A key component of support in Windows 98 for portable PC hardware is an architecture that enables applications and system programs to be "mobile aware." Under Windows 98, system software and application programs can take an active role in conserving battery power and managing configuration changes, dramatically enhancing the users' experience. For the first time, portable computer users can take advantage of all the features of their machines in a robust, stable, easy-to-support environment.

PC Card (PCMCIA) support

PC Cards have been one of the most exciting innovations in the portable computer market. Through the Plug and Play architecture, Windows 98 delivers power, compatibility, ease of installation, and dynamic card insertion and removal to PC Card users. PC Card drivers in Windows 98 are robust, 32-bit, dynamically loadable virtual device drivers with zero conventional memory footprint. Windows 98 ships with an integrated version of card and socket services.

With Plug and Play, installing a PC Card device is as simple as inserting the card. For example, when you plug in a PC Card network adapter, the portable computer detects the network card, loads the network drivers, and establishes a network connection. The shell then updates its user interface to reflect that the network is now active. When the card is ejected, Windows 98 closes down the network connection and unloads the network drivers.

Windows 98 PC Card support extends to hundreds of devices from leading manufacturers, including modems, network adapters, storage devices, audio adapters, SCSI interfaces, and more. The native PC Card support in Windows 98 is compatible with the majority of popular PC Card devices currently on the market. However, Windows 98 requires a 32-bit, protected-mode driver for any card it supports via the Plug and Play architecture. Windows 98 can utilize existing real-mode PC Card driver solutions, but at the expense of performance, dynamic driver loading, and system awareness of card insertion and removal. Real-mode PC Card drivers and protected-mode PC Card support cannot coexist on the same system.

When upgrading a Microsoft Windows 95 system, Windows 98 preserves any existing PC Card support software as a safety measure. (The Windows 98 Setup program doesn't want to risk disabling access to a device.) Windows 98 provides a PC Card Wizard to manage the transition from real-mode Card and Socket services to the Windows 98 protected-mode support.

PCMCIA enhancements
PCMCIA enhancements in Windows 98 improve the battery life of portable PCs and enable more functionality from a limited number of PCMCIA slots.

PC Card32 (CardBus)
Windows 98 includes support for PC Card32 (CardBus). CardBus brings 32-bit performance to the small PC Card form factor. It enables notebooks to implement high-bandwidth applications such as video capture and 100 Mbs networking.

PC Cards that operate at 3.3 volts
Windows 98 also supports 3.3V/5V cards. This support enables hardware manufacturers to lower the power consumption of their devices to 3.3 volts rather than 5 volts.

Multifunction PC Cards
Multifunction PC Card support allows two or more functions (such as LAN and modem, or SCSI and sound) on a single physical PC Card. Supporting multifunction cards helps decrease the cost per function of PC Cards and makes better use of the limited number of slots on most PCs, permitting more functions per PC. Although support for multifunction cards was available with Windows 95, these devices could not be configured and enabled independently. Windows 98 treats each function on a multifunction PC Card independently.

Advanced Power Management 1.2 support

Portable PC users unanimously name "limited battery life" as the bane of their existence. While true innovation in battery life depends in large part on physics and hardware engineering, Windows 98 supports Advanced Power Management (APM) 1.2. From a user perspective, APM 1.2 support delivers five major benefits:

- Plug and Play APM messages allow application software to react to changes in the power state and battery life. For example, applications can now prompt users to save their work and avoid data loss when battery power runs low; programs that do background disk accesses can disable these features when running on battery power.

- The Windows 98 shell includes a battery meter that accurately measures and shows the remaining battery life. APM 1.2 can display power information for two batteries at the same time.

- Users can put their systems in Suspend mode directly from the Start menu, as opposed to having to go to a hardware control. Users also have the option of automatically powering their PCs off when they shut down Windows instead of having to shut down Windows and then use the hardware power switch to shut off the PC. Software-managed power control enables Windows to properly deactivate and reset peripheral devices to prevent data loss and conserve power.

- For convenience, many laptop users leave their PC Card modems in their laptops. This practice can cause shorter battery life because the modem is still receiving power even though it's not being used. Windows 98 turns off PC Card modems when they're not in use. This feature provides a noticeable gain in battery life, not only while the computer is running but also when it is suspended.

- From a suspended state, Windows 98 provides modem wake-on-ring so that users can receive an incoming fax without having to run the computer at full power.

From a software-developer perspective, Windows 98 dramatically simplifies the process of making an application "power aware." APIs for power management enable virtually any developer (including corporate developers coding in Microsoft Visual Basic or Microsoft Visual Basic for Applications) to make applications sensitive to the power status of the machine. For example, a corporate data-collection application running on a portable PC can automatically save data and exit when the computer's power reaches critical levels, thereby preventing inadvertent loss of data. Commercial applications such as word processors can make "smart" moves, such as turning off background auto-save (which requires a power-intensive disk access) when running on a battery-powered machine.

Windows 98 depends on a quality implementation of the APM BIOS to provide power management support. Windows 98 is compatible with portable PCs that adhere to the APM 1.0, 1.1, and 1.2 BIOS standards. If the BIOS in a particular machine is incompatible with the APM specifications or is poorly implemented, Windows 98 might provide a limited level of power awareness or might need to disable power management support altogether. Most new portable PCs have high-quality APM BIOS implementations, and Windows 98 Setup can detect many of the older machines that require special treatment.

Hot-docking and port replicator support

Docking stations and port replicators provide users with the mobility of the portable PC and the storage, extensibility, and versatile display capabilities of a desktop PC. Many corporations are turning to portable PC/dock combinations as replacements for desktop PCs.

Microsoft has forged partnerships with leading portable vendors, such as Toshiba and Compaq, and BIOS vendors, such as Phoenix Technologies, to achieve integration between hardware and software. On the hardware side, PC vendors have enabled docking and undocking operations without powering off the computer. On the software side, Windows 98 detects the impending changes in configuration and anticipates the resulting changes in hardware, manages any conflicts (such as open files on an external hard drive or network), and loads and unloads the hardware drivers appropriate to each configuration.

Instead of rebooting and fooling with configuration files, users can now simply click the Start button and choose Eject PC (or, depending on their hardware, Suspend) from the Start menu. Windows 98 checks for any potential problems and then prepares the computer for undocking, without users having to shut down Windows. After undocking, Windows 98 automatically reconfigures itself for the different hardware—for example, changing the video resolution to match the resolution of the built-in display—and continues running.

Windows 98 is dependent on a machine's underlying BIOS to support hot-docking or hot port-replicator operations. In particular, the BIOS must reliably and consistently inform Windows 98 when the machine is about to change state, must enable Windows 98 to control any motorized docking hardware, and must rapidly perform any tasks associated with changing configuration (such as entering or exiting suspend mode or resetting on-board devices). The performance of configuration support in Windows 98 on these new machines is directly dependent on the quality of the BIOS the various OEMs create.

Configuration-change message support

Plug and Play provides a set of Windows messages that work in concert with configuration-change support in Windows 98 to enable applications and device drivers to react intelligently to changes in the hardware. These messages include the following types.

Configuration change and docking

- About to change configuration (for example, when the user is about to un-dock)
- Configuration changed (for example, when the user just undocked)
- Device about to be removed
- Device about to be added

Power management

- System about to suspend
- System suspended
- System resumed
- Change in power status

PC Card support

- Device inserted
- Device removed

These messages enable applications and system services to support portable PC users. Windows 98 takes full advantage of these messages. For example, here are some of the ways that applications shipped with Windows 98 use the "Configuration changed" message:

- The Briefcase uses it to try to start updating.
- The print spooler uses it to print all deferred print jobs.
- Mail uses it to try to reestablish a network connection.

Applications "Designed for Windows 95" or "Designed for Windows 98" can take advantage of these messages as well. With older applications, no special behavior is possible; the necessary Windows messages, APIs, and other programming support were new in Windows 95 and are carried on in Windows 98.

Integration with the Registry

The Registry provides centralized, dynamic data storage for all Windows settings. The Registry defines a "current-configuration" branch to enable ISVs to better serve the needs of mobile users. This branch stores information on a per-configuration basis. For example, in the Control Panel, the Display tool stores per-configuration information about video resolution changes, and Print Manager stores per-configuration information about the default printer. Applications can access and store information for each of the different hardware configurations used by mobile users. This Registry support enables applications to adapt gracefully to the different hardware environments a portable PC encounters.

Configurations are created when Windows 98 queries the BIOS for a hardware serial ID (which changes when the machine is docked or attached to a port replicator),
asks the user for a name for the configuration, and then stores information about hardware and software associated with this configuration. The user can also create multiple configurations manually through the Hardware Profile manager. (Select System
from the Control Panel, and then click on the Hardware Profiles tab.) This functionality enables users to create different configuration settings for the same hardware
setup and choose between them at boot time.

Built-in support for Infrared Data Association standard

A key requirement for the success of infrared is compatibility. Windows 98 includes
support for the Infrared Data Association (IrDA) standard for wireless connectivity
between PCs and other devices and networks. IrDA support enables Windows 98
users to connect easily to peripheral devices or other Windows 98-based PCs without using connecting cables. For example, the user of an infrared-equipped portable PC can simply walk up to an infrared printer and print. Or two portable PC
users can quickly exchange a file or other data without physically connecting their
computers.

This driver set provides infrared-equipped laptop or desktop computers with the
capability of networking, transferring files, and printing wirelessly with other IrDA-
compatible infrared devices. IrDA connectivity is designed to take advantage of the
mobile computing features already built into Windows 98.

The IrDA driver in Windows 98 (IrDA 2.0) includes a new feature, named IrLan Access
Point Mode, that enables a computer with an IrDA adapter to attach to a LAN through
an access point device that acts as the network adapter for the computer. The infrared driver architecture also includes provisions for emulating traditional parallel and
serial ports, which provides backward compatibility with existing software.

IrDA device drivers and utilities

Windows 98 supports Fast Infrared (FIR) and Serial Infrared (SIR) devices, which
provide easy file transferring over infrared and LAN connectivity. Windows 98 also
includes the Microsoft Infrared Transfer applet, which makes file transferring over
infrared as simple as click and send. To use the Microsoft Infrared Transfer applet,
simply right-click on the file you want to transfer and select Infrared Recipient from
the Send To submenu.

ISDN 1.1 Accelerator Pack support

ISDN is a service of your telephone company that can provide up to 128-Kbps access to the Internet and other networks. To learn about ISDN and to determine if ISDN
service is available in your area, visit the Get ISDN Web page at

http://www.microsoft.com/windows/getisdn

The ISDN Accelerator Pack adds multilink, which allows you to bond two B channels together for 128-Kbps performance. The ISDN Accelerator Pack is required to configure your system to use an internal ISDN adapter card. External adapters don't require any additional software.

To use ISDN 1.1 Accelerator Pack, you need ISDN 1.1–compatible driver software provided by your ISDN adapter manufacturer. Certified Windows 98 compatible ISDN 1.1 adapter drivers are available for download from the Hardware Compatibility List. The ISDN 1.1 Accelerator Pack won't work correctly with 1.0-compatible drivers. Do not install version 1.1 without getting updated drivers that support ISDN 1.1. To check on driver availability, check the ISDN Accelerator Pack Web page at

http://www.microsoft.com/windows/common/aa2720.htm

If a driver for your ISDN adapter is not listed, contact your ISDN adapter manufacturer or check the Hardware Compatibility List at a later date. New ISDN driver software is added to the list when the drivers pass Windows Hardware Quality Labs (WHQL) certification.

DriveSpace disk compression

Many older portable computers have small disk drives. Although these machines might still function for word processing, checking e-mail, or other non-compute-intensive tasks, the lack of disk space is a major constraint. Disk compression is a great example of how Windows 98 helps users get the most out of *any* portable PC. DriveSpace increases disk capacity to usable levels and provides ancillary performance benefits as well.

All disk compression in Windows 98 is handled by 32-bit protected-mode code integrated into the file system. In addition to the inherent performance advantages, such tight integration with the underlying device driver code means that all compression operations are transparent to the user.

A version of DriveSpace 3 is included with Windows 98 that handles drives up to 2 GB. DriveSpace has been revised to recognize FAT32 drives. However, DriveSpace does not—and will not—support compressing FAT32 drives.

The updated DriveSpace is compatible with Microsoft Plus! When you install Plus! on Windows 98, you won't actually install any DriveSpace 3 files. However, you will enable the DriveSpace 3 advanced features, including Compression Agent, when you install Plus!

IMPORTANT

If you compressed your hard disk with Microsoft Plus! and then upgraded to Windows 98 and you need to reinstall Plus!, do *not* use the Re-Install All option in Plus! Setup. If you need to reinstall Plus! and your disk is compressed, you must delete your Setup.STF file (which should be in your \Program Files\Plus!\Setup folder) and then rerun Plus! Setup.

Document viewers

Like other PC users, portable PC users often exchange documents with customers or other users in different work environments. Because of limited disk space or lack of network access, however, mobile users often don't have the applications they need to view the files they receive.

An extensible, replaceable File Viewer technology has been seamlessly integrated into the Windows 98 shell. Simply select a file and choose Quick View. Windows 98 directly supports more than 30 of the most common application file types and publishes interfaces to allow applications to add support for additional formats (and even to add their own viewers). Systems Compatibility Corporation, for example, offers an enhanced viewer program as well as a library of viewer drivers for additional application software.

Keeping in Touch

Windows 98 provides powerful, easy-to-use user communications capabilities and an open, extensible set of services for applications, which enable mobile computer users to stay in touch with essential information resources. Dial-Up Networking support is integrated into the Windows 98 network architecture and user interface; accessing a network by modem is as convenient and reliable as using a hard-wired network adapter. Similarly, the Microsoft Outlook Express e-mail client and Microsoft Fax system are optimized to enable portable computer users to easily send and receive e-mail messages and faxes while mobile. The goal of the mobile communications support in Windows 98 is to offer as great a level of access to information while mobile as is provided on the desktop, with no additional user training or support requirements.

Windows 98 Dial-Up Networking

In the office, well over 50 percent of PC users have become accustomed to full workgroup computing capabilities—printing to a network printer, sending and receiving e-mail messages, and accessing shared files. When users leave the office, however, they can't take all the shared resources from their workgroup environment with them. The Dial-Up Networking features in Windows 98 automate connections to Bulletin Board Services and other online services and provide faster remote network connections (including Internet connections), giving users complete workgroup computing capabilities while mobile. Dial-Up Networking is smoothly integrated into the Windows 98 network architecture and shell. Whether you're running a client/server application, accessing a customer database, downloading or browsing e-mail messages, or accessing shared files, network access while mobile looks and works exactly like network access in the office (except for speed, of course).

Windows 98 Dial-Up Networking provides support for a single client Point-to-Point Tunneling Protocol (PPTP) connection, support for internal ISDN adapters, and connection time scripting to automate nonstandard logins. All fixes included in the OSR2 release of Windows 95 and the ISDN 1.1 Accelerator Pack have been included in Windows 98.

Windows 98 treats the Dial-Up Networking software and modem combination as just another instance of a network adapter, making it easy to access network resources while on the road. (See Figure 12-1.) Windows 98 supports the notion of multiple, concurrently operating network adapters, clients, and protocols. If one protocol, client, or adapter cannot satisfy a network request, Windows 98 tries each component in turn. If no physical network adapter can resolve a network request (as is the case when a user is mobile), Windows 98 drops down to the Dial-Up Networking adapter and attempts to resolve the network request by creating a Dial-Up Networking connection. Windows 98 creates a Dial-Up Networking connection whenever the user implies that one is needed (by referencing a resource not available via any local network). Such automatic connections are therefore referred to as *implicit* connections.

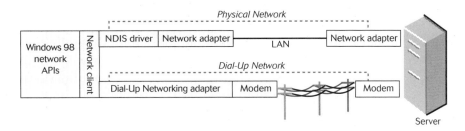

Figure 12-1   *Dial-Up Networking support in Windows 98*

Establishing a remote connection works the same as establishing a connection in the office, courtesy of support in Windows 98 for implicit connections. You simply double-click the desired network object, and Windows 98 takes whatever steps are necessary to establish a connection to that object. Similarly, if you double-click Mail or another client/server application, a remote connection is automatically established.

The Dial-Up Networking client software component, like the rest of networking in Windows 98, provides an open architecture and connects to a broad set of networks, including Microsoft Windows NT, NetWare, and the Internet. Support is built in for TCP/IP, IPX, and NetBEUI network protocols. (See Figure 12-2.)

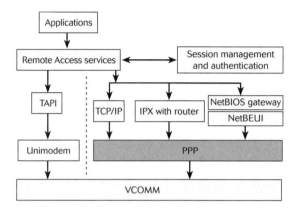

Figure 12-2   *The Windows 98 remote access architecture in its default configuration*

The Remote Access API, a component of the Win32 API, provides ISVs with services to initiate and resume a remote connection as well as to gather information about the type and status of the connection. These APIs enable applications to adjust their behavior depending on the transmission speed and other characteristics of the network connection.

Third parties can easily add additional network protocols. Using industry standard Point-to-Point Protocol (PPP) and PPTP, any of these underlying protocols can be routed over a Dial-Up Networking connection. (See Figure 12-3.)

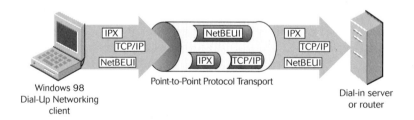

Figure 12-3   *Windows 98 support for industry standard PPP connections, enabling multiprotocol connectivity*

In addition to PPP and PPTP, Windows 98 can also communicate with NetWare Connect servers using the NRN protocol and Windows NT servers using the RAS protocol. As with PPP and PPTP, third parties can add additional over-the-wire protocols. For example, Microsoft provides an implementation of the SLIP (Serial Line Internet Protocol) as part of the Windows 98 Resource Kit.

Because remote access is part of the dynamic 32-bit, protected-mode network architecture of Windows 98, you don't have to reconfigure or reboot your computers to continue working after establishing or ending a connection.

You can use a Windows 98 desktop PC equipped with the Dial-Up Server component as a convenient access point to a small LAN or simply to the desktop PC itself. When used as a host computer—that is, the computer you dial into—a Windows 98 PC provides an easy-to-use, single-port host, capable of multiprotocol routing for IPX and NetBIOS with pass-through user-level security. (See Figure 12-4.) Windows NT Server supplements the remote network access functionality in Windows 98 to provide a large network solution that allows for as many as 256 simultaneous dial-in sessions.

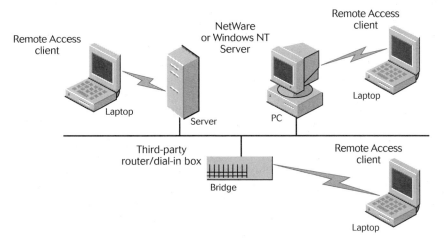

Figure 12-4 *Windows 98 remote connectivity options*

The Windows 98 security scheme employs the Windows NT or NetWare authentication mechanism and user database to validate the user. Share-level security is also available. Using the desktop management capabilities in Windows 98, an administrator can disable dial-up access so that users can't dial into a particular desktop PC or remotely access the entire network. If the user dials into a host system, such as Windows NT, Shiva NetModem or LanRover, or NetWare Connect, Windows 98 offers full connectivity, depending on the permissions and security schemes in place on the server.

Support for dial-up scripting

Many Internet Service Providers and Online Services require you to enter information (such as your user name and password) manually to establish a connection. With the dial-up scripting support built into Windows 98, you can write a script to automate this process.

A script is a text file that contains a series of commands, parameters, and expressions required by your Internet Service Provider or Online Service to establish the connection and use the service. You can use any text editor, such as Microsoft Notepad, to create a script file.

For added flexibility, dial-up scripting properties are included as a property sheet for each individual Dial-Up Networking connection. (See Figure 12-5.)

Figure 12-5 *Scripting tab of property sheet for Dial-Up Networking connection*

Dial-Up Networking user interface enhancements

User interface improvements were also made to the Settings option available from the Connections menu (shown in Figure 12-6), which now features these enhancements:

- Set the Show A Confirmation Dialog After Connected option.

- If the Prompt For Information Before Dialing option is unchecked, Dial-Up Networking will not stop to request a password or dialing location. If you use your system from a fixed location, such as a home PC, this saves a dialing step.

- Set the automatic reconnect with a short delay. This capability is particularly useful for busy connections to large banks of modems where redialing immediately is the best way to get connected.

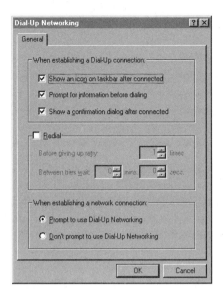

Figure 12-6 *The Dial-Up Networking settings*

Support for multilink channel aggregation

As mentioned earlier, Windows 98 supports Multilink PPP connections. Now you can combine the bandwidth of two or more physical communications links to increase your remote access bandwidth and throughput using Dial-Up Networking Multilink. Based on the IETF standard RFC 1717, RAS Multilink lets you easily combine analog modem paths, ISDN paths, and even mixed analog and digital communications links on both your client and server PC. When used with two or more modems or ISDN B channels, Multilink PPP supports simultaneous data transfer across multiple connections. This will speed up your access to the Internet or to your intranet and cut down on the amount of time you have to be remotely connected, so it can reduce your costs for remote access and effectively double, triple, or even quadruple the speed of your transfer rates.

For example, Windows 98 with four 33.6-Kbps modems can connect to a Windows NT Server with multiple modems and maintain a sustained transfer rate of 134,400 bps. This example can be extended across any number of modems or ISDN lines to achieve even greater bandwidth. The speeds of the modems and ISDN lines can vary, but Multilink coordinates transfer across the various links to achieve performance equal to the combined speed of the devices.

The Remote Access subsystem

The Remote Access subsystem is a key component of the Windows 98 architecture. This subsystem is network-independent and device-independent to enable universal connectivity. For example, Windows 98 supports ISDN boards, PBX modems, and so on. This capability is accomplished through service providers—software components that manage physical connections and network traffic over the remote media.

The Remote Access subsystem includes a modular authentication provider that can be supplemented or replaced to provide custom security services. For example, if a company wants to provide custom services, it can replace the authentication DLL in Windows 98 with its own to take advantage of company-specific security features.

Dynamic network architecture

To adapt to changes in link speed and configuration, the network architecture in Windows 98 is completely dynamic, regardless of whether users are using the NetWare-compatible components or the Microsoft networking components. All the underlying drivers, transports, and redirectors are robust, 32-bit, dynamically loadable, protected-mode virtual devices that support Plug and Play. This architecture enables Windows 98 to load and unload components of the network stack in response to hardware events. For example, when the user docks a portable PC or inserts a PC Card network adapter, the appropriate network components are loaded and connections are established without user interaction. Even assigning a TCP/IP address is now dynamic, using the Dynamic Host Configuration Protocol (DHCP) servers to allocate addresses on demand.

As with other components of Windows 98, the dynamic nature of the network architecture is dependent on the availability of 32-bit, protected-mode drivers and the general robustness of other network components. The default network components in Windows 98 (Windows NT Server and NetWare clients, TCP/IP, IPX, and NetBEUI protocols) are all implemented as 32-bit, protected-mode code. Any of these components can be loaded or unloaded on the fly. If a particular network architecture is dependent on real-mode, nondynamically loadable drivers, the dynamic nature of the network architecture will obviously be compromised.

Telephony API

To communicate in a mobile environment, users and applications must dial phones or modems. Windows 98 provides the Telephony API (TAPI) to deal with telephone devices.

TAPI provides Dialing Properties to guide users through the process of defining a correct phone number, given their location and telephone system. Dialing Properties gives users the opportunity to define phone numbers in a location-independent fashion. Users enter an area code and phone number, and Dialing Properties applies location-specific parameters to the number, such as a prefix to get an outside line. When users dial this same number from a different location, they simply switch their location and Dialing Properties automatically adjusts the prefixes, area codes, and other parameters. (See Figure 12-7.)

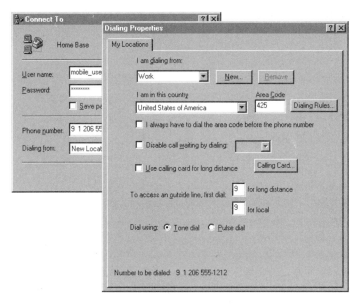

Figure 12-7   *TAPI, which provides telephone-line management services to Dial-Up Networking*

TAPI provides services that allow applications to share a line so that more than one application can wait for an incoming call while another dials out. Because TAPI itself is extensible, third-party developers can write TAPI service providers to extend dial support to new devices. One such TAPI service provider is Unimodem, which is discussed in detail below.

TAPI 2.1
Windows 98 contains TAPI 2.1, which is based on TAPI 2.0 support as shipped in Windows NT 4.0.

Unimodem

Windows 98 provides an easy, central, extensible mechanism for installing and configuring modems. (This mechanism is similar to the Window 98 infrastructure for printers.) Windows 98 automatically detects the modem and provides a default configuration for it. After the modem is installed, it is available to all applications, which no longer need to store modem commands or data about the capabilities of different modems. Windows 98 ships with support for over 1300 modems worldwide. Adding new modems is as simple as supplying the appropriate installation data (INF) file.

As part of the "Designed for Windows 98" logo certification process, an independent testing laboratory will examine the INF files for each new modem and certify it as compatible with Windows 98.

Unimodem/V
In Windows 98, Unimodem has been updated to add support for the following:

- VoiceView modems
- Sierra modems (for example, Prometheus, Motorola, and some PC systems)
- SpartaCom modem pooling
- Denmark support
- Intel H.324 support
- Lucent controller-less modems

Remote mail
Historically, when users left the office they left behind robust e-mail capabilities. Windows 98 delivers the next generation of remote mail so that you can simply connect a phone line to your modem and start using e-mail. The remote connection is established automatically using Remote Access services.

Windows 98 has optimized Mail to gracefully handle remote network connections and slow network links. Performance over the wire has been enhanced, and using Remote Mail functionality, users can browse message headers and download only the specific messages they want to read. This mobile-aware approach to electronic mail dramatically improves the productivity of mobile users.

Messaging API
More than any other class of users, mobile users need access to multiple messaging providers and the ability to move seamlessly among these providers. Whereas desktop users receive most of their electronic mail through a corporate-based or network-based electronic mail system, mobile users frequently connect to several different messaging providers—for example, both CompuServe and their corporate network.

The Windows 98 Messaging API (MAPI) makes the communications abilities of mobile users powerful. MAPI is an open, extensible messaging infrastructure standard that ensures complete independence of Windows applications and client software from underlying messaging systems, while enabling vendors to supply a wide array of providers. (See Figure 12-8.) To the user, each messaging provider looks more or less the same. MAPI provides the support to dynamically switch between providers and associate multiple providers and preferences with a "profile."

Inbox integration and remote mail functionality depend on the availability of MAPI Service Providers. Without the appropriate MAPI driver, the Inbox doesn't know how to access a particular mail provider. The depth and robustness of the functionality provided by the Inbox depends largely on the quality of the MAPI driver. Some drivers might provide excellent performance and a wide variety of options (including Remote Mail), whereas the performance and feature set provided by other drivers might be more limited.

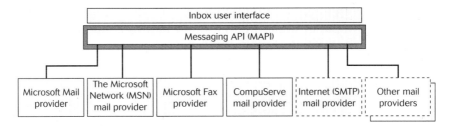

Figure 12-8 *MAPI provides unified support for the use of multiple mail providers*

Microsoft is shipping full-function MAPI drivers with Windows 98 for Microsoft Mail, The Microsoft Network, and Microsoft Fax. A full-function MAPI driver for CompuServe Mail is included on the CD version of Windows 98, and an Internet (SMTP) mail driver is included with Microsoft Plus! Other messaging vendors are also at work on MAPI providers for their respective services.

Microsoft Fax

Fax is one of the most common tools mobile users employ to send messages and documents. Rich fax services are seamlessly integrated into the e-mail client provided with Windows 98. Users of Windows 98 can send or receive fax messages the same way they send or receive any other electronic message. New fax documents are received by fax modem directly into the Inbox, where they can be viewed online using standard, built-in tools. The tight integration between facsimile messaging and electronic messages significantly enhances the user experience relative to separate fax solutions.

If users want to send faxes when they are not connected to a phone line or network, they can spool them to their outbox. When a fax modem becomes available, the queued messages are automatically transmitted.

Microsoft Fax uses the open, extensible architecture of MAPI, plugging in as a transport provider and then leveraging the user interface provided by the Windows 98 client. Users are more productive since they don't need to learn how to operate a separate fax software package.

For more information about Microsoft Fax, see Chapter 7, "Windows Messaging."

Staying Organized

The mobile computing environment presents significant data-management challenges for users. Since many portable PCs typically exist in at least two states—on the network and off—portable users need to contend with the possibility that they and their data will be separated. Most portable computer users deal with this possibility by making copies of important documents on their portable PCs. This practice introduces the problem of file synchronization. What happens to the portable PC user if the original copy of the document changes? What if the portable PC user edits his or her copy of the document? Windows 98 attempts to address these issues through the metaphor of a Briefcase.

Windows 98 also addresses the problem of getting a portable PC connected to a desktop PC or network to transfer files. Direct Cable Connection enables a standard parallel cable, serial cable, or infrared link to serve as a simple PC-to-PC, or network pass-through, connection.

Deferred printing support handles the problem of creating print jobs while users are on the road. Instead of forcing users to contend with error messages when printers are unavailable or to manually record which documents to print, Windows 98 is smart about managing the printing process in different environments.

The Briefcase

The Windows 98 Briefcase minimizes the headaches of keeping the information on a portable PC up to date by keeping track of the relationships among different versions of a file on different computers. Portable PC users who also have desktop PCs (or who connect to a network) need to keep the most up-to-date files on the computer they are currently using. Users most often stay up to date by comparing the dates stamped on files and manually copying files from one machine to another—a tedious, unintuitive, and error-prone process. The user interface for this feature employs a simple metaphor that users are already comfortable with: a physical briefcase. (See Figure 12-9.)

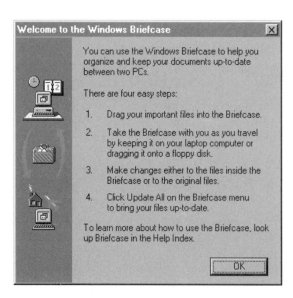

Figure 12-9   *The initial Briefcase screen outlining the Briefcase process*

You can specify which files and directories you want to keep up to date by dragging and dropping those objects into the Briefcase. When you reconnect your portable PC to a network or your desktop PC, the Briefcase updates unmodified files on the host with the recently modified files from the portable computer, and vice versa. (See Figure 12-10.)

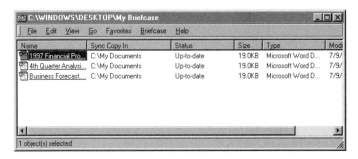

Figure 12-10 *Sample Briefcase contents, showing document status*

In Figure 12-10, notice the additional information maintained by the Briefcase, such as the location of the original file and the synchronization status for each document.

Windows 98 includes a set of ActiveX interfaces that allow applications to define *reconciliation handlers*. When both the file in the Briefcase and the corresponding original document have changed, Windows 98 calls the appropriate reconciliation handler to merge the two files. For example, Microsoft Access 97 uses these interfaces to provide database replication through the Briefcase.

By default, the Briefcase provides file-level synchronization. It doesn't attempt to understand different applications' file formats or to make changes to the contents of the files it is managing. This was a deliberate design decision; given the pace of application upgrades and the many file formats in use, it would be impossible for the Briefcase to stay current. Supporting sub–file-level reconciliation would also put Microsoft in the business of interpreting or reverse-engineering the file formats of many other vendors' applications—not the best use of development resources.

If the Briefcase determines that either the Briefcase copy or the original copy of a file has been changed, it will suggest a copy operation to put the newest version of the file in both places (original location and in the Briefcase). The Briefcase, by itself, cannot handle the situation where both the Briefcase copy and the original copy of a file have changed, since resolving this situation would involve sub–file-level reconciliation. In situations like this, the Briefcase has two options. It first checks the Registry to see whether a reconciliation handler for the file in question is available. In the case of a Microsoft Access MBD file, for example, the answer is "yes," and Briefcase passes control to a module supplied by Microsoft Access, which synchronizes the two MDB files. If no reconciliation handler is available, the Briefcase doesn't change either copy of the file but instead flags the situation for the user (who can decide to keep both files, select one over the other, or do nothing).

Direct cable connection

Roughly 70 percent of portable PC users also use a desktop PC. As a result, they constantly need to transfer files and other data between the two machines. A simple way to effect these transfers is via a direct parallel, serial, or infrared connection.

With Direct Cable Connection, Windows 98 makes connecting two PCs easy. The process of establishing a PC-to-PC connection is integrated into the shell and provides full participation for the client on a variety of networks. The services provided by a direct cable connection are much the same as those provided by a dial-up connection, only faster. The Direct Cable Connection application provides a connection to the host PC, much as Dial-Up Networking provides a connection to the dial-in server. The client can use shared files and directories on the host PC, or if properly configured, the host PC can be used as a pass-through server to provide full network access for the client PC. Direct Cable Connection provides a simple, cost-effective solution when a portable PC needs infrequent or low-intensity network access.

The support for Direct Cable Connection in Windows 98 presents market opportunities for peripheral manufacturers. Using the ECP (Enhanced Capabilities Port), parallel ports found on newer computers along with a special "active" cable can provide data throughput rates in excess of 1 Mbps over the parallel link. Parallel Technologies, for example, supplies a line of DirectParallel cables designed to optimize the performance of direct cable connection links.

Deferred printing

Users generate print jobs regardless of where they are. Windows 98 supports deferred print jobs, enabling users to generate print jobs even if a printer isn't currently available. The print jobs are spooled to disk by the system until a printer becomes available, at which time Windows 98 detects the connection and automatically prints the jobs as a background process.

Windows 98 switches to deferred printing mode whenever an installed printer is not available (whether because of a change in configuration, a network failure, or a printer hardware problem). When in deferred printing mode, Windows 98 periodically checks (in the background) the connection to the printer to see if it has been reestablished. If the printer comes back online, Windows 98 switches out of deferred printing mode and begins spooling any documents that have queued up. When switching out of deferred printing mode, Windows 98 prompts you to begin printing—this enables you to continue in deferred printing mode if desired.

To better support mobile users, Windows 98 stores the default printers on a per-configuration basis. If you have a different printer at home than you do at the office, Windows 98 changes the default printer when it detects the computer's change in location—for example, from docked status to undocked status.

13

Multimedia Services

MICROSOFT WINDOWS 98 DELIVERS a high-performance platform for PC multi-media. Here are some of the exciting contributions Windows 98 makes to the world of multimedia computing:

- Windows 98 is a complete multimedia upgrade that allows you to turn any PC into an easy-to-use multimedia playback machine. Because all the architectural support for digital video, audio, and the Musical Instrument Digital Interface (MIDI) is built into Windows 98, users and developers are relieved of the challenges of device-driver installation and publishers can reduce their support costs. The Plug and Play architecture makes it simple to install and operate compatible multimedia devices. And Windows 98 is compatible with multimedia titles and tools created for earlier versions of Windows.

- Windows 98 is designed to help entertainment software developers create fun, state-of-the-art, fast, highly graphical games quickly and easily. Windows 98 supports major technology advances in 2-D raster graphics, 3-D rendering, and digital audio, which are crucial to game developers.

For developers, Windows 98 offers a powerful platform for professional multimedia authoring:

- The 32-bit architecture in Windows 98 squeezes multimedia performance out of PCs, so developers can capture digital video and sound that is big and bold. The multitasking architecture of Windows 98 makes for a convenient working environment for multimedia authors.

- The streamlined architecture of digital video, digital audio, MIDI, and file handling subsystems in Windows 98 enables authors and toolmakers to create professional-quality sound, video, and animation effects. Windows 98 is an attractive platform for the professional development of multimedia effects and footage beyond the realm of the PC—for example, TV commercials.

Making Multimedia Easier

Microsoft is committed to making Windows the leading force in multimedia technologies and systems for PCs. This commitment takes many forms, the most important being an ongoing investment in multimedia-related research and development. Some of the results of the last few years' research and development are described in this chapter. Multimedia technologies are evolving rapidly, and Microsoft continues to press ahead in providing tools and architectural enhancements to enable developers and consumers to take advantage of innovations.

Windows 98 includes built-in support for essential multimedia technologies. No longer are users, resellers, or vendors required to add or distribute software components such as CD-ROM file systems, digital video support, or audio compression. Digital video playback (multiple codecs) and audio (compressed WAVE and MIDI), CD-ROM, and joystick support are all built directly into the Windows 98 operating system. All of these subsystems have been developed in high-performance 32-bit code to ensure smooth playback and quick response times.

Multimedia technology in Windows 98 is fully compatible with 16-bit multimedia titles. Testing has shown that the 32-bit improvements in file access speed and stream handling result in performance improvements even for 16-bit multimedia applications. The biggest improvements, however, will be realized in full 32-bit titles designed for Windows 98.

Plug and Play Support

As multimedia applications, titles, tools, and games have become more and more compelling, consumers have begun buying add-on multimedia components, such as CD-ROM drives and sound cards. These devices have become relatively inexpensive and are easy to install and use.

Support of Plug and Play in Windows 98 makes adding a new multimedia device to a PC simple. Just plug in a Plug and Play–enabled sound card, and it plays. Windows 98 even makes the prospect of installing *old* multimedia devices less daunting because it includes tools that make identifying and resolving conflicts between legacy devices that are not Plug and Play–enabled easy. To make this process as painless as possible, Windows 98 includes built-in drivers for the most popular sound cards.

Plug and Play rewrites the rules for multimedia on PCs. Here are three effects of Plug and Play that multimedia users will enjoy:

- It allows the base of multimedia-capable PCs to grow through Plug and Play upgrade kits. User won't have to buy more powerful CPUs just to support multimedia. Because Windows 98 includes the basic architecture for handling sound, MIDI, and digital video, every PC running Windows 98 can easily be transformed into a multimedia PC by the simple act of the user plugging in a sound card and/or a CD-ROM drive.

- It substantially decreases the cost of installing and supporting multimedia devices, making their adoption for business use much more feasible.

- As multimedia standards, such as CD-ROM speed, continue to improve, Plug and Play allows consumers to upgrade multimedia components conveniently, without having to replace their entire PC. Plug and Play support is vital to the success of new multimedia devices, such as MPEG (Moving Pictures Experts Group) cards.

AutoPlay

In various ways, titles and games that run off a CD-ROM feel different than other applications. First, just starting CD-ROM programs differs from starting hard disk–based applications. You have to open a drawer, extract the right disk, and place it in the CD-ROM drive before you can run the program—assuming, of course, that you can find the icon you created when you first installed the program. Second, unlike hard disk–based applications, you're more likely to use CD-ROM products irregularly.

When you put a disk in a CD-ROM drive, you want either to install the program or, if you've already installed it, to run the program. In Windows 98, a feature called AutoPlay allows software developers to make their products easier for users to install and run. When the user puts a disk in a CD-ROM drive, Windows 98 automatically spins it and looks for a file named AUTORUN.INF. If this file exists, Windows 98 opens it and follows the instructions. This feature makes the setup instructions for a Windows 98-based multimedia game or title almost absurdly easy, reducing them to something like this:

1. To play this program, insert the disk in your CD-ROM drive.
2. Have a nice day!

Built-In Support for Digital Video

For several years, Microsoft has been developing a high-performance architecture for digital video: Microsoft Video for Windows. In the past, Video for Windows was distributed separately (principally as a Software Development Kit). Since the release of Windows 95, Video for Windows has been built into every copy of Microsoft Windows, including Windows NT. The widespread ability to play digital video has the following implications:

- Users and ISVs can use the AVI file format to distribute digital video files with the same confidence they have when distributing files of other Windows-supported formats, such as TXT, WRI, BMP, PCX, and WAV.

- The barriers to entry for would-be multimedia title and tool developers are lowered because the issues of licensing and installing Video for Windows disappear.

Built-In Support for Sound and MIDI

MIDI is the computer equivalent of sheet music. Using sheet music, an arranger can describe how to play Beethoven's *Moonlight Sonata* in a few pages; but to play the piece, a person who knows how to read music must have a piano. The sound quality of the music performed from the sheet music varies depending on the quality of the instrument—for example, when played on a concert grand piano, the sonata will sound better than when played on an old upright.

Similarly, a MIDI file can contain the electronic instructions for playing the *Moonlight Sonata* in just a few kilobytes, but playing the piece requires a device, such as a sound card, that knows how to "read" MIDI instructions and can produce a piano-like sound. And just as the sound of real pianos varies somewhat, so does the piano sound produced by sound cards.

At the high end, MIDI is used as a development tool for musicians. Virtually all advanced music equipment today supports MIDI, and MIDI offers a convenient way to control equipment precisely. At the low end, MIDI is becoming an increasingly popular tool for multimedia product developers because it offers a way to add music to titles and games with a tiny investment of disk space and data rate. The majority of sound cards currently on the market have on-board MIDI support built in. Windows 98 includes built-in support for both MIDI and waveform audio (WAV).

The CD Player

To accommodate the many people who like to play audio CDs in their CD-ROM drives while working, Windows 98 includes the CD Player. As Figure 13-1 shows, the controls on this player look just like those on a regular CD player. The Windows 98 CD Player supports many of the same features found in sophisticated CD players, such as random play, programmable playback order, and the ability to save programs so that users don't have to re-create their playlists each time they pop in a CD.

Figure 13-1 *The CD Player, which will play uninterrupted in the background*

Built-In Support for Fast CD-ROMs

The development of faster CD-ROM drives (up to 12x speed) has been essential for the growth of multimedia computing because faster reading of CD-ROM data helps make video and audio playback from CD-ROM drives look and sound better.

To get the best possible performance from these new devices, Windows 98 includes a 32-bit CD-ROM file system (CDFS) for reading files from CD-ROM drives as quickly and efficiently as possible. (The Windows 3.1 system for reading files from CD-ROM drives [MSCDEX.DLL] is also included in Windows 98, to provide compatibility with products that rely on it.) CDFS is an important component of the overall multimedia performance in Windows 98.

Windows 98 also extends its support for CD-ROM to drives that read XA-encoded disks, such as Kodak PhotoCD and video CDs.

An Ideal Platform for Home Entertainment

With Windows 98, PCs become better multimedia machines, so software developers can produce more engaging and speedier titles and games.

3-D Graphics Development Support

Windows 98 includes Microsoft DirectX 5, a new set of graphics development APIs. The most common use of these APIs is by games developers, although DirectX is also a valuable tool in the development of graphical applications such as Internet publishing and real-time communications.

DirectX 5 is composed of the following components:

- DirectDraw (2-D graphics)
- Direct3D (3-D graphics)
- DirectSound (sound-mixing and playback)
- DirectPlay (Internet multiplayer game connectivity)
- DirectInput (joysticks and other input devices)
- DrawPrimitive (Direct3D extensions)

DirectX 5 brings a number of new features to the Windows environment. The DirectX 5 APIs allow access to new hardware capabilities, including multimonitor support, universal serial bus support for gaming and audio devices, MMX optimizations, 3-D sound acceleration, rendering features such as anti-aliasing and anisotropic texture filtering, optimized texture support, and force feedback joystick support.

DirectX 5 is designed to be easy for developers to learn and use. The performance and quality of the DirectX 5 APIs are greatly improved over previous versions of graphics APIs.

Built-In CD Plus Support

In addition to making it easy for users to play their favorite audio CDs, Windows 98 supports the new Sony Corporation and Philips International CD Plus (also called Enhanced Music CD) format, which enables integrated audio and data on the same CD. Microsoft is working with the music industry to help define a specification for these music CDs.

Because data and audio information can be combined on the same CD, the CD Plus format opens a broad category of CD titles that can be enjoyed fully as music CDs and, when inserted into a PC running Windows 98, can also provide digital information in the form of music videos, song lyrics, biographies, and other text. The CD Plus discs can even promote online exchanges with musicians.

CD Plus uses multisession drive technology to solve the "track one" problem that has prevented convenient use of CD-ROMs in audio CD players. Until this technology became available, CD-ROM titles used the first track of a compact disc for data, thus producing static—and potential speaker damage—when played on audio CD players. Sony and Philips International implement multisession technology under the brand name CD Plus. Other music industry companies can license the CD Plus brand from them or create their own multisession implementations. Windows 98 accommodates all compatible implementations of the CD Plus technology.

The CD Plus format takes advantage of a range of features included in Windows 98 to help make multimedia more engaging, including the AutoPlay feature and the 32-bit multimedia subsystems in Windows 98, which enable high-fidelity playback performance.

Multimedia Support

Multimedia includes far more than games and entertainment. Many of the technology advances in Windows 98 were pioneered in games applications but then implemented in new categories of applications. Multimedia technologies in Windows 98 enable groundbreaking possibilities in education, corporate training, reference, and business applications.

DirectShow

DirectShow (formerly known as ActiveMovie) is a new media-streaming architecture for Windows that delivers high-quality video playback while exposing an extensible set of interfaces on which multimedia applications and tools can be built. DirectShow enables playback of popular media types, including MPEG and WAV audio and MPEG, AVI, and Apple QuickTime video.

Because DirectShow uses and is integrated with Microsoft DirectX technology, it automatically takes advantage of any accelerating video and audio hardware to deliver the highest possible performance for a given machine configuration. For example, DirectShow utilizes DirectDraw and features present on many standard graphics cards to improve video playback quality of AVI and QuickTime movies. Additionally, DirectShow is capable of decoding MPEG entirely in software and playing it back at high quality.

With DirectShow, corporations can begin rolling out video-based training and other exciting solutions from their corporate intranet or Internet sites.

For the highest possible playback quality on machines with adequate processing power, the Moving Pictures Experts Group (MPEG) compression/decompression specification has long been recognized as a leader. Microsoft reached agreement with Mediamatics in May 1995 to include software-based MPEG support in Windows.

Software-based MPEG support in Windows offers developers at least two distinct benefits:

- MPEG squeezes surprisingly good-looking video into very small files, so a significant amount of high-quality footage can fit on a single CD.
- MPEG is well suited to data rates that a high-speed CD-ROM drive can sustain reliably, which covers the vast majority of CD-ROM drives installed today.

Although the MPEG codec generates high-quality playback results, it's extremely calculation-intensive. In most cases today, the practical use of MPEG requires specialized hardware. The widespread availability of MPEG hardware for Windows is one of the distinctive advantages of the Windows platform, but the installed base of these boards is far from universal. Software-based MPEG decompression, such as that provided by the Mediamatics MPEG Arcade Player, further increases the momentum of MPEG, especially on Pentium systems. Other codecs, such as Indeo and Cinepak, continue to be important because of their lower system requirements and greater flexibility.

Windows 98 delivers the ability to play high-quality, full-screen video on today's personal computers. It makes possible new applications such as video-based reference works and education and training titles.

Surround Video

At the 1995 Winter Consumer Electronics Show, Microsoft unveiled Surround Video— a Windows-based technology that enables full-screen, interactive multimedia titles. Titles created with this technology allow users to interact with objects, images, and live-action video within a 360-degree photorealistic scene. Unlike most multimedia experiences, in which the user's interactive role is limited to a rectangular screen, Surround Video surrounds the user in an interactive environment.

Like a photographer looking through a camera's viewfinder, the user of a Surround Video title can turn at will to see more of the software environment. Surround Video offers developers many possibilities to take advantage of this technology, such as adventure-style games authored with photorealistic backgrounds. Other opportunities include guided tours of major cities, museums, and real-estate listings.

Developers can easily create Surround Video titles because the development tools are based firmly on popular, well-known authoring technologies. For example, Surround Video backgrounds can be captured easily with a 360-degree panoramic camera. Similarly, the foreground video images can be added using the same blue screen or chroma-key techniques that are used by television weather forecasters.

Opportunities for Great-Sounding Audio

A MIDI file of just a few kilobytes can contain electronic instructions for playing a composition of piano music. Playing the piece, however, requires a device, such as a sound card, that can read MIDI instructions and produce a piano sound. Built-in MIDI support means that developers can distribute an increased variety of sounds in less space and that users can hear richer-sounding music with their applications.

At the high end, MIDI is a popular development tool for musicians. Virtually all advanced music equipment today supports MIDI, which offers a convenient way to control equipment precisely. The built-in support for MIDI in Windows 98 makes the

Windows platform viable for audio development or equipment control. At the low end, MIDI is an increasingly popular tool for multimedia product developers because it offers a way to add music to titles and games with a small investment of disk space and bandwidth. The majority of sound cards today have on-board, built-in MIDI support.

With built-in support in Windows 98 for both MIDI and WAV, developers can be assured that MIDI-developed music will play on PCs with little or no configuration effort on the part of the user. Consumers will readily enjoy richer sound from their multimedia titles simply by running Windows 98.

WinToon

WinToon is an animation playback tool for Windows 98 that facilitates the creation of full-screen, animated multimedia titles and improves the quality and speed of animation playback. WinToon provides high-speed playback of animation cels without forcing animators to change their standard animation production techniques. It can be incorporated easily into CD-ROM multimedia titles. Support for WinToon in Windows means consumers can choose from a broader range of high-quality animated titles.

Support for Intel MMX Technology

MMX is a major enhancement to the Intel architecture that gives PCs more robust multimedia and communication capabilities—in other words, faster audio and video functionality. The MMX technology enhancements include 57 new CPU instructions designed specifically for high parallel operations with multimedia and communications data types. The new instructions include a technique known as SIMD (single instruction, multiple data). SIMD delivers better performance and response for multimedia and communications calculations.

Windows 98 not only supports the running of MMX-aware applications and drivers but, via DirectX APIs, can take direct advantage of MMX processors.

A Powerful Development Environment

Because of its new 32-bit, multitasking architecture, Windows 98 is an attractive platform for the professional development of multimedia titles.

Sound Compression for CD-Quality Sound

Sound can take up a lot of disk space. Full CD-quality, uncompressed stereo audio contains a lot of data—about 176 KB for every second of sound! An entire CD-ROM can contain only a little over an hour of music. Sound can also eat up a fair-sized chunk of the data rate that a CD-ROM drive is capable of sustaining.

To lessen the burden of storing and playing sound from an application, Windows 98 includes a family of sound compression technologies. These codecs can be divided into the following two groups:

- Music-oriented codecs, such as IMADPCM, allow close to CD-quality sound to be compressed to about one-quarter of its original size.
- Voice-oriented codecs, such as TrueSpeech, allow extremely efficient compression of voice data.

This support for compressed sound is two-way: sound can be played from a compressed sound file, or a sound file can be compressed using the built-in sound recording and editing utility. If users have microphones, they can turn on voice compression when recording so that the file is compressed in real time.

In addition to the codecs that come with Windows 98, the audio architecture of Windows multimedia is designed to be extensible through other installable codecs. (The Windows 98 video architecture can be extended in the same way.)

Polymessage MIDI Support for Better Sound

Windows 98 comes with Microsoft's implementation of MIDI, including a technology called "polymessage MIDI support." This support allows Windows 98 to communicate multiple MIDI instructions simultaneously within a single interrupt. As a result, playing MIDI files requires little computing power and allows developers to process MIDI instructions alongside graphics and other data successfully.

Multitasking

Multitasking makes Windows 98 an attractive platform for multimedia authoring. Creating multimedia content is CPU-intensive work that can take a long time. For example, compressing a digital video file can take hours, depending on the complexity of the file and what type of system is doing the compression. Moreover, digital video files have to be compressed one at a time using the traditional platforms. As a result, video authors have been virtually chained to their desks monitoring their work.

Because of the Windows 98 multitasking capabilities, authors can still retain control of their PCs, even when an enormous compression operation is underway. But with Windows 98, digital video authors can initiate several compression operations at once—and then head home.

Professional Quality

The digital video, digital audio, MIDI, and file handling subsystems in Windows 98 make it an ideal platform for developing high-quality video, sound, and animation effects.

Capture and Compression of Bigger Digital Video

The grim reality is that video contains an enormous amount of data. Capturing digital video is even more data-intensive than playing it back because raw digital video footage is uncompressed. A single frame of full-color video at 640 pixels by 480 pixels contains close to a megabyte of data. At 30 frames per second, you can fill up a 1-GB hard drive with uncompressed video data in less than a minute. This data can be compressed to make storage go further, but for multimedia developers, the rate at which they can write data to disk is still an important concern.

The 32-bit file access of Windows 98 is every bit as important to digital video authors as it is to digital video users. Because data can be written to disk more quickly in Windows 98, authors can capture better-looking video—bigger, more frames per second, and more colorful. After the raw footage is captured, the potentially time-consuming process of compression begins. Both Cinepak and Indeo are available in 32-bit versions for Windows 98 to make the compression process considerably more efficient.

General MIDI for Specific Sounds

One of the early challenges for MIDI was that it was, in a way, too flexible. Any instrument can be "connected" to any MIDI channel so that a "sequence" (song) written for a piano might accidentally end up being played on a tuba. Windows 98 supports the General MIDI specification, an industry-standard way for MIDI authors to request particular instruments and sounds.

Built-In Support for Multimedia Devices

Windows 98 includes built-in support for common multimedia authoring devices, such as laser disks and VCRs. This support simplifies the process of setting up a system for "step capture," a process in which the author captures digital video data one frame at a time, usually to be compressed later. Step capture is a slow process, but it is the best way to capture the highest quality digital video. Frame-accurate control of the VCR is also important for recording broadcast-quality special effects for use in commercials, movies, television programs, music videos, and so on.

DVD Support

Windows 98 supports DVD devices. The acronym DVD originally stood for either Digital Video Disc or Digital Versatile Disc but has now become a stand-alone name. DVD is a method of storing many different types of data digitally. These data types include audio, video, and computer data. Windows 98 has a DVD Player you can run to view the data on DVD discs.

14

Accessibility

MICROSOFT IS COMMITTED TO MAKING computers easier for everyone to use. As long as the computers themselves are accessible, personal computers are powerful tools that enable people to work, create, and communicate in ways that might otherwise be difficult or impossible. The vision of making computers easier for everyone can be realized only if people with disabilities have equal access to the world of personal computing.

The issue of computer accessibility in the home and workplace for people with disabilities is increasingly important. Out of every 10 major corporations, 7 to 9 of them employ people with disabilities who might need to use computers as part of their jobs. In the United States alone, an estimated 30 million people have disabilities that potentially limit their ability to use computers. In addition, as the population ages, more people experience functional limitations, making more acute the issue of computer accessibility for the population as a whole.

Legislation, such as the Americans with Disabilities Act (which affects private businesses with more than 15 employees) and Section 508 of the Rehabilitation Act (which addresses government spending), also brings accessibility issues to the forefront in both the public and private sectors.

Microsoft already offers a number of products specifically for users with disabilities and includes features in its mainstream software products to help make them easier for people who have disabilities to use. Microsoft's two most prominent accessibility products are Access Pack for Microsoft Windows and AccessDOS. Both were developed by the Trace Research and Development Center at the University of Wisconsin-Madison using research funded by the National Institute on Disability and Rehabilitation Research. Also available is Access Pack for Microsoft Windows NT.

These products enhance the Windows, MS-DOS, and Windows NT operating systems by adding a variety of features that make the computer more accessible to users with limited dexterity or hearing impairments. Microsoft distributes these utilities at no charge to customers and announces their availability in each of its new products.

Microsoft Windows 98 offers several features designed to make the system more useful to people with disabilities. In recent years, Microsoft has established close relationships with users who have disabilities, organizations representing disabled people, workers in the rehabilitation field, and software developers who create products for this market. Based on their combined input, the following specific design goals were defined for Windows 95:

- Integrate and improve the features from Access Pack that compensate for the difficulties some people have using the keyboard or the mouse.
- Make the visual user interface easier to customize for people with limited vision.
- Provide additional visual feedback for users who are deaf or hard of hearing.
- Provide new APIs and "hooks" for ISVs developing third-party accessibility aids, including those that allow blind people to use Windows.
- Make information on accessibility solutions more widely available and increase public awareness of these issues.

Enhancements designed to meet these goals were included throughout Windows 95 and are carried forward in Windows 98. This chapter describes these enhancements.

Accessibility Features in Microsoft Windows 98

Windows 98 enhances a user's system for accessibility (or allows the user to adjust the enhancements) in the following ways:

- Make UI elements scalable
- Compensate for difficulties using the keyboard
- Emulate the mouse with the keyboard
- Support alternative input devices that emulate the keyboard and mouse
- Provide visual cues to let users know when an application is making sounds
- Advise applications when the user has a vision impairment
- Advise applications when the user needs additional keyboard support because the user has difficulty using a mouse
- Advise applications when the user wants visual captions displayed for speech or other sounds
- Advise applications when they should modify their behavior to be compatible with accessibility software utilities running in the system
- Optimize keyboard layouts for users who type with one hand, one finger, or a mouthstick

- Include audible prompts during setup for users with vision impairments
- Optimize color schemes for users with visual impairments
- Include accessibility information in Microsoft product documentation

To provide information about accessibility features and to provide ways of controlling these features, Windows 98 includes several capabilities, briefly described in the following sections.

Online Help

An Accessibility section in the contents and index of Windows 98 online Help provides a quick reference and a pointer to topics that can help users adjust the behavior of the system for people with disabilities.

Controlling the Accessibility Features

In Windows 98, most of the accessibility features described in this chapter are adjusted through the Accessibility Options icon in the Control Panel. Clicking this tool displays the property sheet, shown in Figure 14-1, which enables users to turn the accessibility features on or off and customize timings, feedback, and other behavior for their particular needs.

Figure 14-1 *The Accessibility property sheet*

Emergency Hotkeys

Most of the accessibility features described in this chapter are adjusted through the Control Panel. But if users can't use the computer until an accessibility feature is turned on, how can they use the Control Panel to activate it? Providing emergency hotkeys with which users can temporarily turn on the specific feature they need solves this chicken-and-egg problem. After a feature is turned on, users can navigate to the Control Panel and adjust the feature to fit their own preferences or turn it on permanently.

If a feature gets in the way or if another person needs to use the computer, the same hotkey can be used to temporarily turn off the feature.

Microsoft has worked hard to ensure that the emergency hotkeys don't get in the way of users who don't need them. Each hotkey is an obscure key combination or key sequence that shouldn't conflict with applications. If a conflict does arise, the hotkeys can be disabled, but the features will still be available as needed.

As an additional precaution, each emergency hotkey plays a rising tone and displays a confirmation dialog box that briefly explains the feature and how it was activated. If users pressed the hotkey unintentionally, this notification allows them to deactivate the feature. It also provides a quick path to a more detailed Help topic and the Control Panel settings for that feature, allowing users who don't need the hotkey to disable it permanently.

The Accessibility TimeOut

The Accessibility TimeOut feature turns off Accessibility functionality after the system has been idle for a certain period of time. It returns the system to its default configuration. This feature is useful on machines shared by multiple users. The Accessibility TimeOut can be adjusted using the Control Panel.

The Accessibility Status Indicator

Windows 98 provides an optional visual indicator, shown in Figure 14-2, that tells users which accessibility features are turned on, helping users unfamiliar with the features to identify the cause of unfamiliar behavior. The indicator also provides feedback on the keys and mouse buttons currently being "held down" by the StickyKeys and MouseKeys features (described later in this chapter). The status indicator can be displayed on the taskbar or as a free-floating window.

Figure 14-2 *The Accessibility status indicator*

Features for Users with Limited Vision

Windows 98 offers several enhancements designed to make the system more accessible and easier to use for people with impaired vision.

Scalable User Interface Elements

Users who have limited vision or who suffer eyestrain during their normal use of Windows can adjust the sizes of window titles, scroll bars, borders, menu text, and other standard screen elements. These sizes are completely customizable through the Control Panel in Windows 98. Users can also choose between two sizes for the built-in system font.

A Customizable Mouse Pointer

Users who have difficulty seeing or following the mouse pointer can now choose from three sizes: normal, large, and extra large. They can also adjust the color or add animation, both of which can increase the pointer's visibility.

High-Contrast Color Schemes

The Windows color schemes allow users to choose from several well-designed sets of screen-color options designed both to match users' individual tastes and to meet their visual needs. The new color schemes in Windows 98 include high-contrast colors designed to optimize the visibility of screen objects, making it easier for users with visual impairments to see them.

High-Contrast Mode

Many users with limited vision require a high contrast between foreground and background objects to be able to distinguish one from the other. For example, they might not be able to easily read black text on a gray background or text drawn over a picture. Users can set a global flag to advise Windows 98 and applications that they need information to be presented with high contrast.

Windows 98 also provides an emergency hotkey that allows users to set the computer in high-contrast mode when they can't use the Control Panel or when the current color scheme makes the computer unusable for them. Pressing this hotkey—Left Alt+Left Shift+Print Screen—allows users to choose an alternate color scheme that better meets their needs.

Windows 98 Features for Easier Keyboard and Mouse Input

Windows 98 offers several features designed to make entering information via the keyboard and mouse easy.

StickyKeys

Many software programs require users to press two or three keys at one time. For people who type with a single finger or a mouthstick, that just isn't possible. StickyKeys allows users to press the keys of a key combination one at a time and instructs Windows to respond as if the keys had been pressed simultaneously.

When StickyKeys is turned on, pressing any modifier key—that is, Ctrl, Alt, or Shift—latches that key down until either the mouse button or a nonmodifier key is released. Pressing a modifier key twice in a row locks it down until it is pressed a third time.

The functionality of StickyKeys is adjusted using the Control Panel, or it can be turned on or off using an emergency hotkey (pressing the Shift key five consecutive times).

SlowKeys (FilterKeys)

The sensitivity of the keyboard can be a major problem for some people, especially if they often press keys accidentally. SlowKeys instructs Windows to disregard keystrokes that are not held down for a minimum period of time, allowing users to brush against keys without any ill effect. When you put a finger on the correct key, you can hold the key down until the character appears on the screen.

The functionality of SlowKeys is adjusted using the Control Panel, or it can be turned on or off using an emergency hotkey (holding down the Right Shift key for 8 seconds).

RepeatKeys (FilterKeys)

Most keyboards allow users to repeat a key just by holding it down. This feature is convenient for some but can be a major annoyance for people who can't lift their fingers off the keyboard quickly. RepeatKeys lets users adjust the repeat rate or disable it altogether.

The functionality of RepeatKeys is adjusted using the Control Panel, or it can be turned on or off using an emergency hotkey (holding down the Right Shift key for 8 seconds).

BounceKeys (FilterKeys)

For users who "bounce" keys and produce double strokes of the same key or similar errors, BounceKeys instructs Windows to ignore unintended keystrokes.

The functionality of BounceKeys is adjusted using the Control Panel, or it can be turned on or off using an emergency hotkey (holding down the Right Shift key for 8 seconds).

MouseKeys

The MouseKeys feature lets people control the mouse pointer using the keyboard. Users don't need a mouse to use this feature. Windows 98 is designed to allow users to perform all system actions without a mouse, but some applications require one, and a mouse can be more convenient for some tasks. MouseKeys is also useful for graphic artists and others who need to position the pointer with great accuracy.

When MouseKeys is turned on, the following keys navigate the pointer on the screen:

- Press any number key except 0 or 5 on the numeric keypad—these keys are also called the direction keys—to move the pointer in the directions indicated in Figure 14-3.

- Press the 5 key for a single mouse-button click, and press the Plus (+) key for a double-click.

- To drag an object, point to the object, press the Ins key to begin dragging, move the object to its new location, and press the Del key to release it.

- Select the left or right mouse button or both mouse buttons for clicking by pressing the Divide (/), Minus (–), or Multiply (*) key, respectively.

- Hold down the Ctrl key while using the direction keys to "jump" the pointer in large increments across the screen.

- Hold down the Shift key while using the direction keys to move the mouse a single pixel at a time for greater accuracy.

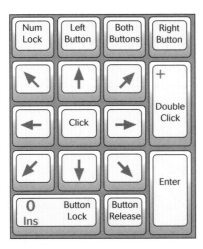

Figure 14-3   *The keys on the numeric keypad that control the mouse pointer*

The functionality of MouseKeys can be adjusted using the Control Panel, or it can be turned on or off using an emergency hotkey (Left Alt+Left Shift+Num Lock).

ToggleKeys

ToggleKeys provide audio cues—high and low beeps—to tell users whether a toggle key is active or inactive. It applies to the Caps Lock, Num Lock, and Scroll Lock keys.

The functionality of ToggleKeys can be adjusted using the Control Panel, or it can be turned on or off using an emergency hotkey (holding down the Num Lock key for 5 seconds).

Features for Users Who Are Hearing Impaired

Windows 98 offers several features designed to make the system accessible and easy to use for people who are hearing impaired.

ShowSounds

Some applications present information audibly, as waveform files containing digitized speech or through audible cues, each of which conveys a different meaning. These cues might be unusable by a person who has impaired hearing, or someone who works in a very noisy environment, or someone who turns off the computer's speakers in a very quiet work environment. In Windows 98, users can set a global flag to let applications know they want visible feedback, in effect asking the applications to be "close captioned."

SoundSentry

SoundSentry tells Windows to send a visual cue, such as a blinking title bar or screen flash, whenever the system beeps. Turning on this feature allows users to see messages that they might not have heard.

Support for Alternative Input Devices

Windows 98 provides support for the use of alternative input devices, such as head-pointers or eye-gaze systems, with which users can control the computer.

SerialKeys

The SerialKeys feature, in conjunction with a communications aid interface device, allows users to control the computer using an alternative input device. These devices can send coded command strings through the computer's serial port to specify keystrokes and mouse events that are then treated like normal keyboard and mouse input.

Support for Multiple Pointing Devices

The Plug and Play architecture in Windows 98 inherently supports multiple cooperating pointing devices. This capability allows seamless addition of alternative pointing devices, without requiring users to replace or disable the normal mouse.

Features for Software Developers

As you can see, Windows 98 contains many built-in features designed to make the computer more accessible to people with disabilities. To make a computer running Windows 98 truly accessible, however, application developers must provide access to their applications' features, taking care to avoid incompatibilities with accessibility aids.

Accessibility Guidelines for Software Developers

As part of the *Win32 Software Development Kit* and *Windows Interface Guidelines for Software Design,* Microsoft provides developers with documentation that not only outlines these important concepts but also provides technical and design tips to help ISVs produce more accessible applications. Most of these tips involve very little additional work for developers, as long as they are aware of the issues and incorporate accessibility into application designs at an early stage. By providing this information to application developers, Microsoft hopes to increase the general level of accessibility of all software running on the Windows platform.

Methods for Simulating Input

Windows 98 now allows developers of voice-input systems and other alternative input systems to easily simulate keyboard and mouse input using fully documented and supported procedures.

Chaining Display Drivers

Some accessibility aids, such as screen review utilities for users who are visually impaired, need to detect information as it is drawn to the screen. Windows 98 supports chaining display drivers that allow these utilities to intercept text and graphics being drawn, without interfering with the normal computer operation.

New Common Controls

Many accessibility aids have difficulty working with applications that implement nonstandard controls. Windows 98 provides a whole new set of controls for mainstream software developers, and these standardized implementations are designed to cooperate with accessibility aids.

15

Applications and Utilities in Windows 98

MICROSOFT WINDOWS 98 INCLUDES applications and utilities designed to take advantage of 32-bit preemptive multitasking, long filenames, new visual elements and common dialog boxes, OLE, TAPI, MAPI, and other Win32 API features. This chapter describes some of the new applications and utilities.

The Windows 98 applications and utilities are designed to ensure that even novice users will be able to run them with no problems. Experienced users will find the applications both powerful and flexible, though the applications were not necessarily designed to satisfy all the needs of advanced users. Third-party developers should be inspired by many of the applications and utilities to further utilize technology included in Windows 98.

The Quick Viewers

The Quick Viewers included in Windows 98 allow you to view files in most popular file formats without opening the application used to create the files. For example, the Quick Viewers are convenient for looking at attachments sent in e-mail messages or browsing files on a network. Figure 15-1 on the following page shows the right-click shortcut menu with the Quick View command selected and the resulting Quick View window, which shows the contents of a Microsoft Excel worksheet.

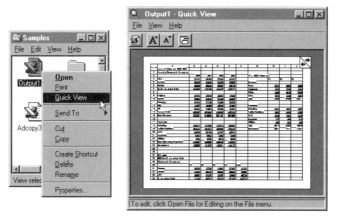

Figure 15-1   *An Excel worksheet in a Quick View window*

The Quick Viewers support the ability to drag and drop a file from Microsoft Windows Explorer or from your desktop into an open Quick View window. You can also access Quick View from the Open With dialog box. If you try to open a file that has an extension that isn't associated with a known application, the Open With dialog box is displayed so that you can specify whether you want to view the file in a Quick View window or to open the selected file with an application.

You can choose Options from Windows Explorer's View menu and specify Quick View as the default Open command for any file type, which is convenient when you want to view a particular file type but don't have the corresponding application on your hard disk. You can customize the Quick View window to display in the following ways:

- View files in standard view or page view, in both landscape and portrait modes
- View files in different fonts and font sizes
- Rotate bitmap files so that documents such as fax messages are oriented correctly

Jointly developed by Microsoft and Systems Compatibility Corporation (SCC), the Quick Viewers are available for most popular file formats. SCC offers additional viewers and features in its Outside In for Windows product. ISVs are encouraged to include Quick Viewers for the file formats they support in future releases of their software. Quick Viewers for the file formats listed in the table on the facing page are available for use with Windows 98 and are shipped on the CD-ROM. (Floppy disk users can download the Quick Viewers from online sources or can obtain fulfillment disks from Microsoft.)

Quick Viewer File Formats

File Format	Description
ASC	ASCII files
BMP	Windows bitmap graphics files
CDR	CorelDraw files
DIB	Windows bitmap graphics files
DLL	Dynamic-link libraries
DOC	Files created by Microsoft Word for MS-DOS; Word for Windows; and WordPerfect
DRW	Micrographix Draw files
EXE	Executable files
INF	Setup files
INI	Configuration files
MOD	Files created by Multiplan
PPT	Microsoft PowerPoint files
PRE	Freelance for Windows files
RLE	Bitmap files (run-lengthen coding)
RTF	Rich Text Format files
SAM	AMI and AMI PRO files
TXT	Text files
WB1	Quattro Pro for Windows spreadsheet files
WDB	Microsoft Works database files
WK1	Lotus 1-2-3 release 1 and 2 files
WK3	Lotus 1-2-3 release 3 files
WK4	Lotus 1-2-3 release 4 spreadsheet and chart files
WKS	Lotus 1-2-3 files and Works files
WMF	Windows Metafiles
WPD	WordPerfect demo files
WPS	Works word processing files
WQ1	Quattro Pro for MS-DOS files
WQ2	Quattro Pro version 5 for MS-DOS files
WRI	Windows Write files
XLC	Excel 4 chart files
XLS	Excel spreadsheet and chart files

WordPad

Microsoft WordPad is a 32-bit editor that can be used in place of Write and Notepad. Although it is not a full-blown word processor, WordPad makes it easy to create simple documents and memos. The WordPad window is shown in Figure 15-2.

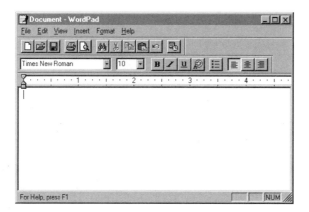

Figure 15-2   *The WordPad application*

WordPad exemplifies the user interface style that applications written for Windows 98 should have. It uses the new common dialog boxes for opening, saving, and printing files, which makes it easy to use long filenames.

As an ActiveX server and client application, WordPad provides easy integration with other ActiveX-enabled applications provided with Windows 98 or available from third parties. WordPad uses the same native file format as Word for Windows version 6 but also supports the reading and writing of rich text files (RTF) and text files, and the reading of Write (WRI) files.

WordPad is MAPI-enabled, so it is easily integrated with Microsoft Exchange and Microsoft Outlook, allowing users to send files over e-mail or by fax from directly within WordPad.

Paint

Microsoft Paint is a 32-bit Windows 98 application that replaces Paintbrush. The Paint window is shown in Figure 15-3.

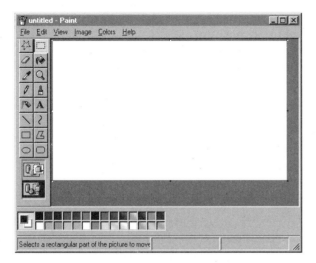

Figure 15-3   *The Paint application*

Paint is an ActiveX server, allowing you to create ActiveX object information that you can embed or link into other documents. Paint is also MAPI-enabled, so you can easily integrate it with Exchange and Outlook for sending images as e-mail or fax messages. Paint can read PCX and BMP files and can write BMP files.

HyperTerminal

HyperTerminal is a 32-bit communications application included with Windows 98 that provides asynchronous connectivity to host computers (such as online services) or to other PCs. HyperTerminal replaces Terminal and provides advanced features and functionality not supported by Terminal.

HyperTerminal is completely integrated with, and takes full advantage of, the Telephony API and Unimodem subsystems built into Windows 98. HyperTerminal uses the 32-bit communications subsystem and provides error-free data transfer by leveraging the architecture components in Windows 98, including multithreading and preemptive multitasking. The HyperTerminal user interface reflects the document-centric nature of Windows 98 and focuses on the communications connection that users make rather than on the main application. As with the other applications and utilities included with Windows 98, HyperTerminal uses common dialog boxes and supports the use of long filenames.

HyperTerminal makes connecting to remote computers easy for all levels of PC users. Through the use of innovative autosensing technology, HyperTerminal automatically determines complex communications settings (such as baud rate, number of stop bits, parity, and terminal emulation type). Users don't ever have to deal with these settings.

HyperTerminal provides mainstream communications program functionality, including terminal emulation and binary file transfer capability. Terminal emulation support includes emulation of ANSI, TTY, VT52, and VT100 terminals. Binary file transfer protocol support includes Xmodem, Ymodem, Zmodem, and Kermit file transfer protocols. Figure 15-4 shows HyperTerminal in action.

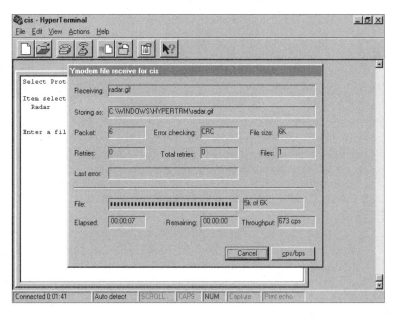

Figure 15-4 *The HyperTerminal application, which makes connecting to host computer services and performing error-free downloading of files easy*

The MS-DOS Editor

Windows 98 includes an MS-DOS–based text editor, EDIT.COM. The editor makes it easy for users to work with text files if the Windows 98 shell can't be loaded for some reason.

EDIT.COM is small and fast. It allows you to open up to nine files at the same time, split the screen between two files, and easily copy and paste information between files. You can also open files as large as 4 MB. In addition, EDIT.COM supports long filenames and allows you to open files and navigate through directory structures just as you can in the Windows 98 user interface. Figure 15-5 shows the new MS-DOS Editor window.

Figure 15-5 *The MS-DOS Editor, which supports a split screen and the use of long filenames*

Disk Utilities

Windows 98 includes disk utilities designed to keep your system error-free and performing optimally. In addition to the DriveSpace disk compression tool (which is discussed in Chapter 16, "Base System Architecture"), Windows 98 provides a Backup applet, which is both a disk optimizer tool and a disk checking and repair tool.

Backup

Backup is a 32-bit utility for Windows 98 that makes it easy to back up information from your computer to another storage medium, such as floppy disk or tape. As shown in Figure 15-6 on the next page, the Backup user interface takes full advantage of the Windows 98 user interface. Because the Backup user interface uses standard controls such as the tree and list view controls, both novices and users familiar with these controls in the Windows Explorer can perform backups quickly and simply.

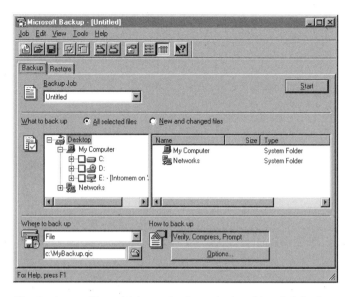

Figure 15-6   *The Backup utility, which can back up the local hard disk, floppy disks, or network drives*

Backup includes the ability to drag and drop file sets and backup sets onto a short-cut link to the Backup utility, which you can place on your desktop to make starting a backup operation a simple click-and-drag procedure. You can also run the Backup utility in the usual way through the user interface or by selecting the Backup option on the Tools tab of the disk's property sheet.

Backup is extremely flexible and allows backing up, restoring, and comparing of files on the following media:

- Hard disks
- Network drives
- Floppy disks
- QIC 40, 80, 3010, and 3020 tape drives connected to the primary floppy disk controller
- QIC 40, 80, and 3010 tape drives, manufactured by Colorado Memory Systems, which connect to the parallel port
- Parallel, IDE/ATAPI, and SCSI devices; devices supported include QIC-80, QIC-80 Wide, QIC-3010, QIC-3010 Wide, QIC-3020, QIC-3020 Wide, TR1, TR2, TR3, TR4, DAT (DDS1&2), DC 6000, 8mm, and DLT; this includes drives from Conner, Exabyte, HP/Colorado, Iomega, Micro Solutions, Seagate, Tandberg, WangDAT, and Wangtek; backup supports backup to floppy-based and network drives

Backup also supports compression of files to maximize storage space. The on-tape format is the industry-standard QIC-113 format. The Backup utility can read tapes created with other backup utilities that use this standard, both with and without file compression.

Other standard options include differential and full backup, redirection of files on restore, and always erasing floppies or tapes before a backup. Backup includes a full-system backup/restore feature that allows users simply to select the full-system backup file set (which is automatically created when Backup is first launched), perform the backup, and then restore files later. This feature works even if you replace your hard disk with a completely different type of hard disk. Because the Backup utility does all the necessary merging of Registry settings and manages the replacement of files in use, novice users don't have to understand all the technical details associated with this fairly complex operation.

Backup even enables you to rebuild the operating system and the latest full backup without having to reinstall the operating system or the backup software. You do this by creating Emergency Recovery Disks, which enable you to restore your files even if Windows 98 won't start.

Disk Defragmenter

Disk Defragmenter, which is a graphical utility that runs under Windows 98, optimizes a hard disk by rearranging information so that it is better organized. Properly organized information helps minimize the hard disk area Windows 98 needs to search to load requested information.

For convenience, you can defragment disks in the background while other applications are running on the system. You can also see details of the defragmentation process and watch its progress, or you can display a minimal status, as shown in Figure 15-7, which simply shows the status of the defragmentation process.

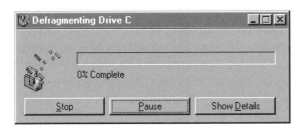

Figure 15-7   *The Disk Defragmenter utility, which helps optimize disk performance*

New Disk Defragmenter Optimization Wizard

The new Disk Defragmenter Optimization Wizard, shown in Figure 15-8, uses the process of disk defragmentation to increase the speed with which your most frequently used applications run. (For a definition of disk defragmentation, see the Note below.) To accomplish this, the Wizard creates a log file that identifies your most commonly used programs. Once this log file has been created, it can be used by Disk Defragmenter to store the files associated with your most frequently run programs in a single location. Placing all the files associated with a given application in the same location on your hard disk will optimize the speed with which the application runs.

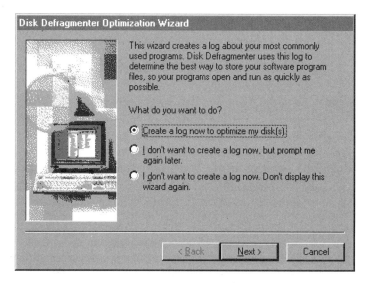

Figure 15-8   *Disk Defragmenter Optimization Wizard opening screen*

NOTE

A file is fragmented when it becomes too large for your computer to store in a single location on a disk. When this happens, your computer splits up the file and stores it in pieces. You can use fragmented files, but it takes your computer longer to access them. Disk Defragmenter speeds up disk access by rearranging the files and the free space on your computer so that files are stored in contiguous units and free space is consolidated in one contiguous block.

ScanDisk

The ScanDisk disk checking and repair utility included with Windows 98 is designed to help you check the integrity of your disks and to remedy any problems that are detected. ScanDisk is a graphical utility. As shown in Figure 15-9, you can run either

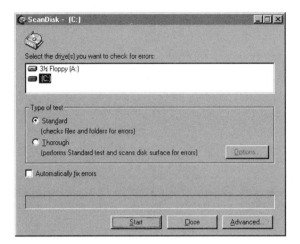

Figure 15-9   *The ScanDisk utility, which performs Standard or Thorough scans to check the integrity of files and disks*

a Standard scan, in which ScanDisk checks the files on your system for errors only, or a Thorough scan, in which ScanDisk checks the files for errors and performs a disk surface test to check for additional errors.

As with the Disk Defragmenter, you don't need to exit any running applications to run ScanDisk. As a result, checking the integrity of a disk system and thereby preventing possible catastrophic errors in the future is easy and convenient.

Automatic ScanDisk after improper shutdown

Windows 98 runs ScanDisk automatically in the event the operating system is shut down improperly or your hard disk suffers a hard error. This addition helps you ensure that your hard drive is in proper working order and free of lost clusters, cross-linked files, and other disk problems.

With Automatic ScanDisk, any files damaged after improper shutdown are automatically and immediately corrected and unused disk space is regained.

System File Checker Utility

System File Checker is a new utility that provides an easy way to verify that the Windows 98 system files (such as *.dll, *.com, *.vxd, *.drv, *.ocx, *.inf, and *.hlp) have not been modified or corrupted. The utility also provides an easy mechanism for restoring the original versions of system files that have become corrupt or modified via application/utility installation.

When a system file is identified as having changed, System File Checker will allow you to choose from several courses of action:

- Restore the original version of the file from its original location

- Restore the original version of the file from a user-defined location

- "Record" the change and continue, if you're aware of the differences in a file or know what caused them (You won't be prompted again about the specific change.)

- Ignore the difference and continue (You won't be prompted again about the specific change.)

For added flexibility, this utility not only monitors specific Windows 98 system files but can also be set up to monitor any type of file from any location on your hard drive. This flexibility allows you to monitor, verify, and restore files associated with other applications and utilities.

System File Checker will be extremely valuable in helping users and support personnel to track changes (such as file corruption, application installation, application removal, and accidental deleting of files) made to Windows 98 systems and to restore original files in the event a change causes a conflict.

Hardware and Software Support

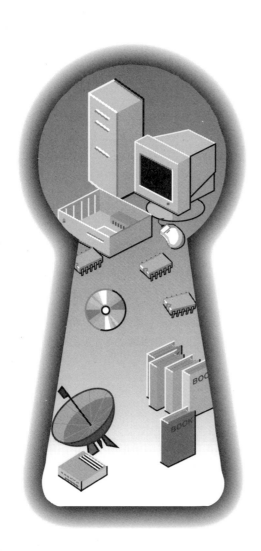

16

Base System Architecture

EASE ON THE SURFACE REQUIRES POWER and speed at the core, and the modern, 32-bit architecture of Microsoft Windows 98 meets these requirements. In Windows 98, 32-bit components preemptively multitask and deliver increased robustness and protection for applications. Windows 98 also provides the foundation for a generation of easier, more powerful, multithreaded 32-bit applications. And most important, Windows 98 delivers this power and robustness while scaling itself to take advantage of additional memory and CPU cycles.

The mission of Windows 98 is to deliver a complete, integrated operating system that offers modern, 32-bit operating system technology and includes built-in connectivity support. In addition to the high-level mission of Windows 98, market requirements dictate delivery of a high-performance, robust, and completely backward-compatible operating system that provides a platform for a generation of applications.

Windows 98 is built on the same code base as Microsoft Windows 95. Our goal is to provide the same level of compatibility as Windows 95, while improving hardware support, system stability, and robustness; reducing support and administration costs; and updating Internet applications and other utilities. We have added a limited set of NT Kernel services for the Win32 Driver Model (WDM), and the same real-mode MS-DOS components, Windows 95 Kernel, USER, GDI, and VMM are still available for existing application compatibility. Removing or redesigning these components would introduce significant compatibility and performance problems. By continuing to use these, while adding common services between NT and Windows 98, we're able to support the best of both worlds.

This chapter describes the base system architecture used by Windows 98. The base architecture covers low-level system services for managing memory, accessing disk devices, and providing robust support for running applications.

Important Base Architecture Components of Windows 98

The base architecture of Windows 98 results in many benefits to users. Following is a summary of some of the key components:

- **A fully integrated 32-bit protected-mode operating system** The need for a separate copy of MS-DOS is eliminated.

- **Preemptive multitasking and multithreading support** These capacities enable system responsiveness and smooth background processing.

- **32-bit installable file systems** Systems such as VFAT, CD-ROM file system (CDFS), FAT32, and network redirectors provide high performance, use of long filenames, and an open architecture that supports future growth.

- **32-bit device drivers** Available throughout the system, these drivers deliver high performance and intelligent memory use.

- **A complete 32-bit kernel** Included are memory management, scheduler, and process management.

- **Systemwide robustness and cleanup** This stable and reliable operating environment cleans up after an application ends or crashes.

- **Dynamic environment configuration** The need for users to tweak their systems is reduced.

- **Improved system capacity** Included are better system resource limits when running multiple applications.

A Fully Integrated Operating System

Windows 98 is a tightly integrated operating system that features a preemptive multitasking kernel, which boots directly into the graphical UI and also provides full compatibility with the MS-DOS operating system.

A Preemptive Multitasking Operating System

The job of the operating system is to provide services to the applications running on the system and, in a multitasking environment, to provide support that allows more than one application to run concurrently. Windows 95 uses a preemptive multitasking mechanism for running Win32-based applications, and the operating system takes control away from or gives control to another running task depending on the needs of the system. Unlike Win16-based applications, Win32-based applications don't need to *yield* to other running tasks in order to multitask in a friendly manner.

(Win16-based applications are still cooperatively multitasked for compatibility reasons.) Windows 98 provides *multithreading,* a mechanism that allows Win32-based applications to take advantage of the preemptive multitasking nature of the operating system and that facilitates concurrent application design. In operating-system terms, a running Win32-based application is called a *process.* Each process consists of at least a single thread. A thread is a unit of code that can get a time slice from the operating system to run concurrently with other units of code. It must be associated with a process, and it identifies the code path flow as the process is run by the operating system. A Win32-based application can spawn (or initiate) multiple threads for a given process. Multiple threads enhance the application for the user by improving throughput and responsiveness and aiding background processing.

Because of the preemptive multitasking nature of Windows 98, threads of execution allow background code to be processed in a smooth manner. For example, a word processing application (process) can implement multiple threads to enhance operation and simplify interaction with the user. The application might have one thread of code responding to the keys pressed on the keyboard by the user entering characters in a document, while another thread is performing background operations, such as spelling checking or pagination, and yet another thread is spooling a document to the printer.

Some available Win16 applications provide functionality similar to that just described, implemented by the application developer. The use of threads in Windows 98 facilitates the adding of asynchronous processing of information to applications by their developers.

Applications that use multithreading techniques can also take advantage of improved processing performance available from a *symmetric multiprocessing* (SMP) system running Windows NT, which allows different portions of the application code to run on different processors simultaneously. (Windows NT uses a thread as the unit of code to schedule symmetrically among multiple processors.)

For information about how Windows 98 runs MS-DOS–based applications in a preemptive manner, Win16-based applications in a cooperative manner, and Win32-based applications in a preemptive manner (as Windows NT does), see later sections in this chapter.

No CONFIG.SYS or AUTOEXEC.BAT

Windows 98 doesn't need the separate CONFIG.SYS or AUTOEXEC.BAT files. Instead, Windows 98 is intelligent about the drivers and settings it requires and automatically loads the appropriate driver files or makes the appropriate configuration settings during its boot process. If a CONFIG.SYS or AUTOEXEC.BAT file is present, the settings in these files are used to set the global environment. For example, the default search path or the default appearance of the command prompt can be defined by using the appropriate entries in the AUTOEXEC.BAT file. While Windows 98 itself doesn't need a CONFIG.SYS or AUTOEXEC.BAT file, compatibility is maintained with existing software or environments that might require one or both of these files.

No MS-DOS

Windows 98 isn't dependent on real-mode operating system components for its interaction with the file system. However, the Windows 98 boot sequence does begin by loading real-mode operating system components that are compatible with MS-DOS. During the boot sequence, support for loading any real-mode drivers and terminate-and-stay-resident programs (TSRs) that are identified in a CONFIG.SYS or AUTOEXEC.BAT file is processed. Because these drivers explicitly look for or use MS-DOS application support, the real-mode operating system components of Windows 98 help maintain compatibility with software that users already have on their system. After the real-mode drivers are loaded, Windows 98 begins loading the protected-mode operating system components. In some cases where a protected-mode Windows-based driver is provided, Windows 98 actually removes real-mode drivers from memory. More information about this subject is given later.

If you look at the system services that Windows 98 supplies, you'll find categories like these:

- Process and thread management
- Interprocess communications and synchronization
- Fully preemptive Win32 subsystem
- CD-ROM and hard disk I/O services
- Network I/O services
- Printing services
- High-level graphics operations
- Window management

In Windows 98, none of these services are provided by any MS-DOS code. Windows 98 does, however, implement some low-level functions in virtual 8086 mode (not real-mode) for backward compatibility. All of these functions require setting or retrieving of some global data structures, and all of these must be propagated down so that existing real-mode programs or other device drivers that rely on these functions continue to work.

32-Bit vs. 16-Bit Components

To provide a good balance between delivering compatibility with existing applications and drivers, decreasing the size of the operating system working set, and offering good system performance, Windows 98 uses a combination of 32-bit and 16-bit code. In general, 32-bit code is provided in Windows 98 to maximize the performance of the system, while 16-bit code balances the requirements for reducing the size of the system and maintaining compatibility with existing applications and drivers. System reliability is maintained without a cost in terms of compatibility or increased size.

The design of Windows 98 deploys 32-bit code wherever it significantly improves performance without sacrificing application compatibility. Existing 16-bit code is retained where it's required to maintain compatibility or where 32-bit code would increase memory requirements without significantly improving performance. All of the I/O subsystems and device drivers in Windows 98, such as networking and file systems, are fully 32-bit, as are all the memory management and scheduling components (the kernel and virtual memory manager). Figure 16-1 depicts the relative distribution of 32-bit code vs. 16-bit code present in Windows 98 for system-level services.

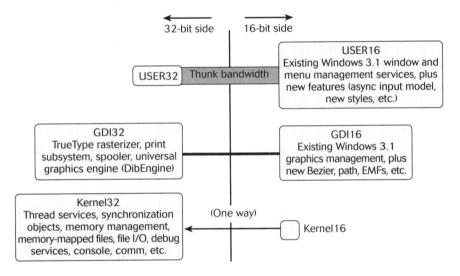

Figure 16-1   *The relative code distribution in Windows 95*

As shown in Figure 16-1, the lowest-level services provided by the operating system kernel are provided as 32-bit code. Most of the remaining 16-bit code consists of hand-tuned assembly language, delivering performance that rivals some 32-bit code used by other operating systems available on the market today. Many functions provided by the Graphics Device Interface (GDI) have been moved to 32-bit code, including the spooler and printing subsystem, the font rasterizer, and the drawing operations performed by the universal graphics engine (DibEngine). Much of the window management code (USER) remains 16-bit to retain application compatibility.

In addition, Windows 98 implements many device drivers as 32-bit protected-mode code. Virtual device drivers in Windows 98 assume the functionality provided by many real-mode MS-DOS–based device drivers, eliminating the need to load them in MS-DOS. This technique results in a minimal conventional memory footprint, high performance, and reliability and stability of the system.

Virtual Device Drivers

A virtual device driver is a 32-bit, protected-mode driver that manages a system resource, such as a hardware device or installed software, so that more than one application can use the resource at the same time. To understand the significance of this, it helps to have a basic understanding of what virtual device drivers (VxDs) are and the role they play in the Windows 98 environment.

The term *VxD* refers to a general virtual device driver, with *x* representing the type of device driver. For example, VDD is a virtual device driver for a display device, a VTD is a virtual device driver for a timer device, a VPD is a virtual device driver for a printer device, and so on. Windows uses virtual devices to support multitasking for MS-DOS–based applications, virtualizing the different hardware components on the system to make it appear to each MS-DOS virtual machine (VM) that it is executing on its own computer. Virtual devices work in conjunction with Windows to process interrupts and carry out I/O operations for a given application without disrupting how other applications run.

Virtual device drivers support all hardware devices for a typical computer, including the programmable interrupt controller (PIC), timer, direct-memory-access (DMA) device, disk controller, serial ports, parallel ports, keyboard device, math coprocessor, and display adapter. A virtual device driver can contain the device-specific code needed to carry out operations on the device. A virtual device driver is required for any hardware device that has settable operating modes or retains data over any period of time. In other words, if switching between multiple applications can disrupt the state of the hardware device, the device must have a corresponding virtual device. The virtual device keeps track of the state of the device for each application and ensures that the device is in the correct state whenever an application continues.

Although most virtual devices manage hardware, some manage only installed software, such as an MS-DOS device driver or a TSR. Such virtual devices often contain code that either emulates the software or ensures that the software uses only data applicable to the currently running application. ROM BIOS, MS-DOS, MS-DOS device drivers, and TSRs provide device-specific routines and operating system functions that applications use to indirectly access the hardware devices. Virtual device drivers are sometimes used to improve the performance of installed software—for example, the 80386 and compatible microprocessors can run the 32-bit protected-mode code of a virtual device more efficiently than the 16-bit real-mode code of an MS-DOS device driver or TSR. In addition, eliminating ring transitions that result in executing 32-bit applications that access 16-bit real-mode services enhances performance. With virtual device drivers, the system can stay in protected mode.

Windows 98 benefits from providing more device driver support implemented as a series of VxDs in the Windows environment instead of using the device drivers previously available as real-mode MS-DOS device drivers. Functionality supported as VxDs in Windows 98 includes the following components:

- MS-DOS FAT file system
- SmartDrive
- CDFS
- Network card drivers and network transport protocols
- Network client redirector and network peer server
- Mouse driver
- MS-DOS SHARE.EXE TSR
- Disk device drivers including support for SCSI devices
- DriveSpace (and DoubleSpace) disk compression

In summary, in Windows 98, VxDs provide the following advantages:

- High performance as a result of a 32-bit code path
- Small conventional memory footprint by providing device driver and TSR functionality as protected-mode components that reside in extended memory
- System stability and reliability

Virtual device drivers in Windows 98 can be identified by VxD extensions.

Win32 Driver Model (WDM)

The Win32 Driver Model (WDM) is a unified driver model for Windows 98 and Windows NT. The benefits of WDM are the following:

- It reduces complexity by having one driver for both Windows 98 and Windows NT.
- It exemplifies new driver development.

WDM enables new devices to have a single driver for both operating systems. WDM has been implemented by adding selected NT Kernel services into Windows 98 via a special virtual device driver (NTKERN.VXD). This allows Windows 98 to maintain full legacy device-driver support while adding support for new WDM drivers. Windows 98 has extensive support for WDM devices and buses, including these:

- **Human input devices** Keyboards, keypads, mice, pointing devices, joysticks, and game pads
- **Communications devices** Modems
- **Image capture devices** Scanners, still cameras, and video cameras
- **Other devices** Digital Video Disc (DVD), speakers, amplifiers, and so on
- **Buses** Universal Serial Bus (USB) and IEEE 1394

Connect to *http://www.microsoft.com/hwdev* for design information about WDM, buses, and classes in Windows 98.

USB support

Windows 98 includes support for USB hubs, Universal and Open host controller interfaces, and HID compliant USB devices. (For more information on this topic, see the next section, "Human Input Devices (HID)." The new WDM Stream–class support in Windows 98 provides infrastructure for USB audio and camera devices.

Human Input Devices (HID)

HID equivalents to legacy input devices (for example, keyboards, keypads, mice, pointing devices, joysticks, and game pads) that are compliant with the Human Interface Device firmware specification are supported by Windows 98 when connected via the Universal Serial Bus (USB). Input from these HID devices is routed to applications through the legacy input driver architecture in a totally transparent way. Multiple keyboards can be connected and used simultaneously, but the multiple input streams are merged and passed to the single active application window in focus. Similarly, multiple mice and pointing devices can be connected and used simultaneously, but the input streams are merged to control the movement of the single pointer on the screen. Joysticks and gamepads, however, are treated as distinct devices so that applications can distinguish which input comes from which device or user and react appropriately.

Windows 98 supports input devices that are compliant with the HID firmware specification. HID functionality that goes beyond the capabilities of the legacy input devices just listed, however, isn't automatically supported by Windows 98. Other sorts of human input devices require additional vendor and/or application specific software (drivers, special applications, and so on). Device vendors and developers should consult the Windows 98 DDK for details.

IEEE 1394

Support for the IEEE 1394 bus includes the 1394 bus class driver, and mini-drivers for both the Texas Instruments PCI-LYNX, and the Adaptec 8940 200 MBPS host controllers. A Stream class driver for the Sony desktop camera (CCM-DS250) is also provided.

WDM digital audio

Windows 98 contains support for audio over USB speakers. (Altec Lansing Multimedia and Philips Semiconductors are manufacturing USB speakers.)

If you aren't planning to use USB speakers, this section is probably of no use to you. Conventional sound cards that operated prior to Windows 98 should continue to operate exactly as they did before Windows 98. The features mentioned in the following paragraphs are of no relevance to systems with conventional audio systems installed.

WDM audio includes a Sound Blaster emulator for DOS games running under Windows 98. There won't be any support for real-mode DOS Sound Blaster register sets for USB audio. DOS games will run in "DOS Boxes" or DOS virtual machines that run under Windows 98. Some games won't run in DOS emulation mode.

This emulation is the original Sound Blaster. This is also known as Sound Blaster 2.1. Sound Blaster 2.1 supports only monaural 8-bit audio. Windows 98 supports Sound Blaster Pro. This is also known as Sound Blaster 3.2 and features stereo audio.

Neither OPL-2 nor OPL-3 music synthesis is emulated. These are the FM synthesis chips manufactured by Yamaha. The OPL-2 was used in the Adlib and Sound Blaster boards. The OPL-3 is used in Sound Blaster Pro and Sound Blaster 16 hardware. Emulation of these music synthesis chips isn't now and won't in the future be supported by USB audio.

The MPU-401 is a music synthesis hardware interface defined by Roland. Most recent DOS computer games support this register interface for generating music. The MIDI emulation today supports General MIDI (GM) wavetable music synthesis.

Normally RedBook or CD audio is supported by sending a command to the CD drive that causes the CD to play audio out an onboard digital-to-analog converter (DAC). This DAC is connected to the system sound card that controls volume levels. This is impractical for USB audio, so Windows 98 reads bits off the CD over the computer interface (SCSI or ATAPI) and sends them out to the USB speakers.

Normally, CD audio will play out headphone jacks on the front of the CD drive. Usually there is a volume control near the headphone jack. Playing audio through this headphone jack is supported in Windows 98.

Most Windows applications use 16-bit APIs to play audio. These APIs are supported exactly as they have been in earlier versions.

The mixer is used to set volume controls. CD audio, wavetable music synthesis, and 16-bit Windows applications can all play through a USB speaker simultaneously.

DirectSound is supported for USB audio in Windows 98. Windows 98 supports DirectSound 5.

DirectShow (formerly known as Active Movie) is the preferred 32-bit API for audio. DirectShow is supported natively by USB audio. This is the native mode for USB audio support.

DirectMusic will be the preferred music interface to Windows. Future versions of DirectMusic will support downloadable samples. As versions of DirectMusic are released, USB audio will support them. Today MIDI under Windows is supported by USB audio in the form of the 16-bit MIDI APIs.

MIDI in and MIDI out are supported. Patch caching is supported and is an important memory optimization feature of Windows 98.

Wavetable music synthesis is supported with kernel resident software. The quality is better than earlier FM synthesis hardware.

DVD storage and UDF file system

DVD-ROM drives as storage media are being supported for the first time in Windows 98. In order to be able to use a DVD-ROM drive, you must have a drive that is compliant with the Mt. Fuji specification (also called SFF8090). The CD-ROM class driver that existed in Windows 95 has been updated to support DVD-ROM drives as well.

Windows 98 has a new file system, called Universal Disk Filesystem (UDF). It's currently a read-only file system; you can't write UDF to a disc. This is implemented because DVD movies will always have an UDF file system on them, while they might or might not have an ISO9660 file system on them. You can tell that you have UDF support installed on your system if you have the binary UDF.VXD somewhere on your system.

All DVD-ROM drives are required to support DMA.

DVD movie playback

DVD movie playback requires the following components:

Hardware

- DVD-ROM drive
- DVD movie media
- DVD (MPEG/AC-3) decoder

Software

- DVD storage support
- WDM Stream class driver
- Stream mini-driver specific to your decoder hardware (not written by Microsoft)
- Active Movie filtergraph specific to your decoder
- DVD Movie playback application

The components in the preceding list allow DVD movie playback on an NTSC or PAL display, if the decoder card has such an output. If output on a VGA is desired, then there should be a physical connection between the decoder card and the graphics adapter, and a DirectDraw HAL with VPE support should be written for the graphics adapter.

Decoders can be in software rather than hardware on faster processors.

Microsoft isn't yet providing DVD movie content.

WDM still image capture

This device class includes scanners and digital still cameras.

WDM video capture

This device class includes video cameras on USB or 1394 busses, analog video digitization hardware, and TV tuners.

The System Architecture Layout in Windows 98

Figure 16-2 illustrates the layout of the base system architecture for Windows 98. Components of the system are divided between Ring 0 and Ring 3 code, offering different levels of system protection. The Ring 3 code is protected from other running processes by protection services provided by the Intel processor architecture. The Ring 0 code consists of low-level operating system services, such as the file system and the virtual machine manager.

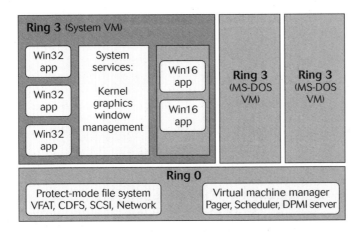

Figure 16-2 *The integrated architecture of Windows 98, which supports running MS-DOS–based, Win16-based, and Win32-based applications*

Figure 16-2 also depicts the way that MS-DOS–based, Win16-based, and Win32-based applications run in the system. The following section discusses the provisions that the system makes for running these applications.

Support for Win16-Based Applications

Win16-based (16-bit) applications run together within a unified address space and run in a cooperatively multitasking manner. Win16-based applications benefit from the preemptive multitasking of other system components, including the 32-bit print and communications subsystem, and from system robustness and protection from the system kernel in Windows 98.

Based on customer needs, resource needs, and market needs, three goals drove the architectural design of Win16-based application support: compatibility, size, and performance. Functionality adjustments, such as preemptively running Win16-based applications together in the Win16 subsystem or running Win16-based applications in separate VMs, were considered, but each of the options considered failed to meet the three design goals. The following discussion provides some insight into the architecture of Windows 98 as far as running Win16-based applications in a fast, stable, and reliable way is concerned.

Compatibility

First and foremost, Windows 98 needs to run existing Win16-based applications without modification. This factor is extremely important to existing users who want to take advantage of the functionality offered in Windows 98, such as 32-bit networking, but don't want to have to upgrade to Windows 98–enabled applications.

Windows 98 provides support for running existing Win16-based applications and using existing Windows-based device drivers, while also providing support for 32-bit applications and components.

Size

While many newer computer purchases are Intel Pentium–based computers with 16 MB (or more) of memory, a high percentage of 80486DX–based computers with 8 MB of memory are still in use. To support the needs of the market, Windows 98 must run on a base platform of an Intel 80486DX–based computer with 8 MB of RAM and provide the equivalent level of performance for the tasks that users are performing, while also providing access to new features and functionality.

To meet its goals, Windows 98 is designed to occupy a working set of components that ensure that any Win16-based application running at a perceived speed on an 8-MB (or greater) computer runs at the same (or higher) speed under Windows 98 without suffering performance degradation. To meet the size goals of Windows 98, Win16-based applications run within a unified address space. Running in a unified address space allows Windows 98 not only to fit on an 8-MB computer but also to perform well. The architecture of Windows 98 includes design features, such as dynamically loadable VxDs, to decrease the working set of components and memory requirements used by the operating system.

Meeting the size design goal (as well as meeting the compatibility goal) precluded the strategies of running Win16-based applications in a separate VM (by running a separate copy of Microsoft Windows 3.1 on top of the operating system, which would involve paying a several megabyte "memory tax" for each application) as OS/2 does or of emulating Windows 3.1 on top of the Win32 subsystem (which would also involve paying a "memory tax" for running Win16-based applications) as Windows NT does.

Running Win16-based applications in separate VMs is very expensive in terms of memory. This strategy would require separate GDI, USER, and KERNEL code in each VM that is created, increasing the working set by as much as 2 MB for each Win16-based application that is running (as is the case with OS/2 for Windows). On a computer with 16 MB or more, this increase might not appear significant. However, bearing in mind the existing installed base of computers, running Win16-based applications in their own separate VMs in 8 MB with the expected level of performance observed is very difficult.

Performance

Users expect their existing Win16-based applications to run fast. Both Win16-based applications and MS-DOS–based applications benefit from the 32-bit architecture of Windows 98, including the increased use of 32-bit device driver components and 32-bit subsystems.

Win16-based applications run within a unified address space. Running Win16-based applications in separate VMs requires either mapping Win16 system components in each address space as Windows NT does or providing a separate copy of each system component in each address space as OS/2 for Windows does. The additional memory overhead required for Win16 system components in each VM to run a Win16-based application has a negative impact on system performance.

Windows 98 balances the issue of system protection and robustness with the desire for high system performance and system robustness. This area is briefly discussed in the next section and is described in greater detail in Chapter 21, "Robustness."

Protection

Windows 98 provides a more stable and reliable operating environment. An errant Win16-based application is unlikely to bring the system down or affect other running processes. While Win32-based applications benefit the most from system memory protection in Windows 98, several things have been done systemwide for the robustness of the operating system.

Win16-based applications run within a unified address space and cooperatively multitask. Overall systemwide robustness enhances the system's ability to recover from an errant application, and improved cleanup of the system lessens the likelihood of application errors. General protection faults (GPFs) are most commonly caused by an application overwriting its own memory segments rather than by an application overwriting memory belonging to another application. When a GPF causes the system to halt an application, the system commonly leaves allocated resources in memory, causing the system to degenerate. Windows 98 tracks these resources and cleans up the system should an error occur. (See Chapter 21, "Robustness," for a more thorough description.)

Other protections include the use of separate message queues for each running Win32-based application. The use of a separate message queue for the Win16 address space and for each running Win32-based application provides for recovery of the system and doesn't halt the system if a Win16-based application hangs.

Support for Running MS-DOS–Based Applications

Support for MS-DOS–based applications, device drivers, and TSRs is maintained in Windows 98. Windows 98 allows users to launch an MS-DOS command prompt as an MS-DOS VM. The functionality supported in an MS-DOS VM is the same as that available under the latest version of MS-DOS, allowing users to run the same intrinsic commands and utilities.

Windows 98 delivers support for running MS-DOS–based applications that enables almost all applications to run properly. This support allows MS-DOS–based applications to coexist peacefully with the rest of the Windows 98 environment.

Summary of Support for Running MS-DOS–Based Applications

Support in the system provides the following benefits for running MS-DOS–based applications in the Windows 98 environment:

- Zero conventional memory footprint for protected-mode components
- Compatibility for running MS-DOS–based applications
- Robustness for MS-DOS–based applications
- Support for running MS-DOS–based games, including in a window
- Support for running existing MS-DOS–based applications without exiting Windows 98 or running MS-DOS externally
- Consolidated attributes for customizing the properties of MS-DOS–based applications
- The availability of the toolbar when running an MS-DOS–based application in a window, providing quick access to features and the functionality for manipulating the window environment
- A user-scalable MS-DOS window through the use of TrueType fonts
- The ability to gracefully end an MS-DOS–based application without exiting the application
- The ability to specify local VM environment settings on a per-application basis through the use of a separate batch file
- Support for new MS-DOS commands, providing tight integration between the MS-DOS command line and the Windows environment

Zero Conventional Memory Footprint Components

Windows 98 helps make the maximum amount of conventional memory available for running existing MS-DOS–based applications. Windows 98 replaces many of the 16-bit real-mode components with 32-bit protected-mode counterparts to provide the same functionality while improving overall system performance and using no conventional memory.

32-bit virtual device drivers are provided to replace their 16-bit real-mode counterparts for functions such as those listed in the table below.

The memory savings that result from using 32-bit protected-mode components can be quite dramatic. For example, if a PC were configured with the NetWare NetX client software and used a SCSI CD-ROM drive, SmartDrive, the MS-DOS mouse driver, and DriveSpace disk compression, the conventional memory savings that would result from using Windows 98 would be over 262 KB.

Functions Carried Out by 32-Bit Device Drivers in Windows 98

Description	File(s)	Conventional Memory Saved
Microsoft Network client software	NET.EXE (full)	95 KB
	PROTMAN	3 KB
	NETBEUI	35 KB
	EXP16.DOS (MAC)	8 KB
Novell NetWare client software	LSL	5 KB
	EXP16ODI (MLID)	9 KB
	IPXODI.COM	16 KB
	NETBIOS.EXE	30 KB
	NETX.EXE	48 KB
	VLM.EXE	47 KB
MS-DOS extended file sharing and locking support	SHARE.EXE	17 KB
Adaptec SCSI driver	ASPI4DOS.SYS	5 KB
Adaptec CD-ROM driver	ASPICD.SYS	11 KB
Microsoft CD-ROM Extensions	MSCDEX.EXE	39 KB
SmartDrive disk caching software	SMARTDRV.EXE	28 KB
Microsoft Mouse driver	MOUSE.COM	17 KB
Microsoft DriveSpace disk compression driver	DRVSPACE.BIN	37 KB

Compatibility

Some MS-DOS–based applications require lots of free conventional memory to be available and thus were prevented from running in an MS-DOS VM by large real-mode components, such as network drivers or device drivers. Other MS-DOS–based applications require direct access to the computer hardware, which can conflict with Windows internal drivers or other device drivers.

The MS-DOS support goal of Windows 98 is to run "clean" MS-DOS–based applications as well as the "bad" MS-DOS–based applications that try to take over the hardware or unavailable require machine resources.

Many MS-DOS–based games assume that they are the only application running on the system and access and manipulate the underlying hardware directly. Games are the most notorious class of MS-DOS–based applications that write to video memory directly, manipulate hardware support resources such as clock timers, and take over hardware resources such as sound cards.

A number of strategies have been used to provide support for running MS-DOS–based applications that interact with the hardware, including virtualization of computer resources such as timers and sound devices. In addition, the use of 32-bit protected-mode device drivers provides DOS-based applications with plenty of free conventional memory, so that memory-intensive applications run properly.

Different MS-DOS–based applications require varying levels of support from both the computer hardware and from the operating system. For example, some MS-DOS–based games require close to 100 percent use of the CPU to perform properly. Other MS-DOS–based applications modify interrupt addresses and other low-level hardware settings. Windows 98 provides several different levels of support for running MS-DOS–based applications. These levels of support take into account that different applications interact with the hardware in different ways, and that some behave well whereas others expect exclusive access to the PC system and hardware. By default, MS-DOS–based applications are preemptively multitasked with other tasks running on the system and can run either full-screen or in a window. (CPU-intensive MS-DOS–based applications might not perform well in a window but can be run in full-screen mode to get the best response level.)

APPS.INF

Windows 98 provides an INF file that contains program settings for many MS-DOS–based applications. These program settings specify special configuration-related settings that are necessary to allow the application to run under Windows 98.

The APPS.INF file is processed when the user attempts to execute an MS-DOS–based application from the Windows 98 user interface. If a program information file (PIF) doesn't exist for the MS-DOS–based application, the system examines the APPS.INF file for information about the specified MS-DOS–based application. If the application is listed in the APPS.INF file, the system will read the contents and create a PIF that will be used when the application is executed.

MS-DOS mode

To provide support for the most intrusive set of MS-DOS–based applications that work only under MS-DOS and require 100 percent access to the system components and system resources, Windows 98 provides a mechanism that is the equivalent of running an MS-DOS–based application in real-mode MS-DOS. This mechanism, called MS-DOS mode, provides an "escape hatch" for applications that run only under MS-DOS. In this mode, Windows 98 removes itself from memory (except for a small stub) and provides the MS-DOS–based application with full access to all the resources in the computer. Relatively few MS-DOS–based applications need to run in single MS-DOS application mode because of the compatibility support provided by Windows 98.

To run an MS-DOS–based application in this mode, the user sets the MS-DOS Mode property on the Advanced Program Settings dialog box (from the Advanced button on the Program tab) of the MS-DOS property sheet for the application. To create a unique environment tailored to an application's needs and system requirements, the user can also specify a CONFIG.SYS or AUTOEXEC.BAT file to run for the application. When the user runs an MS-DOS–based application in this mode, Windows 98 asks whether running tasks can be ended. With the user's approval, Windows 98 ends all running tasks, configures the machine to use the CONFIG.SYS and AUTOEXEC.BAT files for the MS-DOS mode session, restarts the computer, loads a real-mode copy of MS-DOS, and launches the specified application. When the user exits the MS-DOS–based application, Windows 98 restarts and returns the user to the Windows 98 shell. This solution is much more elegant than requiring users to dual-boot between different operating systems in order to run desired applications.

Some entries in the APPS.INF file contain setting information that instructs Windows 98 to run an MS-DOS–based application in MS-DOS mode. These applications will run only in MS-DOS mode due to problems they have running in the protected-mode environment of Windows 98 or due to assumptions they make about the environment (e.g., addressing of extended memory for loading their information) that prevent them from running under Windows 98.

Support for Graphic-Intensive MS-DOS–Based Applications

Windows 98 provides support for running graphic-intensive MS-DOS–based applications in the Windows environment. MS-DOS–based applications that use VGA graphic video modes can now be run in a window; they do not have to be run in full-screen mode. Users can still choose to run graphic-intensive MS-DOS–based applications in full-screen mode for the best level of performance.

Memory Protection

To support a higher level of memory protection for running MS-DOS–based applications, Windows 98 includes on the Program tab of the application's property sheet a global memory protection attribute that allows the MS-DOS system area to be protected from errant MS-DOS–based applications. When the global memory protection attribute is set, the MS-DOS system area sections are write-protected so that applications can't write to this memory area and corrupt MS-DOS support and MS-DOS–based device drivers. In addition to system area protection, enhanced parameter validation is performed for file I/O requests issued through the MS-DOS INT 21H function, providing a higher degree of safety.

This option isn't enabled by default for all MS-DOS–based applications—because of the additional overhead associated with providing improved parameter and memory address checking. Users can set this flag if they constantly have difficulty running a specific MS-DOS–based application.

Defaults for Running MS-DOS–Based Applications

By default, Windows 98 runs MS-DOS–based applications in a window and enables the background-execution setting, allowing the application to continue to run when it isn't the active application. This default behavior provides integration of running MS-DOS–based applications and Windows-based applications without requiring users to change or customize the state of the system.

Consolidated Customization of MS-DOS–Based Application Properties

Each MS-DOS–based application has different characteristics and mechanisms for using machine resources such as memory, video, and keyboard access. Windows 98 understands how to run Windows-based applications because requests for system services are handled through the use of the Windows API. However, MS-DOS–based applications include only minimal information about their requirements in the format of their EXE headers. To provide additional information about applications' requirements to the Windows environment, PIFs are used to specify the necessary configuration settings.

Windows 98 defines properties for running MS-DOS–based applications with PIF files (located in the PIF directory where Windows 98 is installed). This arrangement provides easy access to property information for an application (right-clicking the application's icon or window) and for providing better organization of properties (through the use of a tabbed property sheet, shown in Figure 16-3). By means of this arrangement, Windows 98 provides flexibility and control for running MS-DOS–based applications.

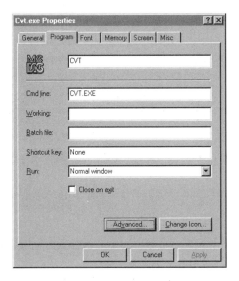

Figure 16-3   *The property sheet for configuring an MS-DOS–based application*

Toolbars in MS-DOS Windows

Many Windows-based applications provide one or more toolbars for quickly accessing common features and functionality. Windows 98 extends this simple but powerful feature to provide easy access to the functionality associated with an MS-DOS–based application, as shown in Figure 16-4.

Figure 16-4   *A toolbar in a windowed MS-DOS box*

Optionally, users can enable the display of a toolbar in the window of a running MS-DOS–based application to provide the user with quick access to the following functionality:

- Access to cut, copy, and paste operations for integrating text or graphic MS-DOS–based applications with Windows-based applications
- Switching from windowed to full-screen mode
- Access to property sheets associated with the MS-DOS–based application
- Access to MS-DOS VM tasking properties, such as exclusive or foreground processing attributes
- Access to font options for displaying text in a windowed MS-DOS VM

Scalable MS-DOS Windows

Windows 98 supports the use of a TrueType font in a windowed MS-DOS VM, which allows users to scale the MS-DOS window to any size. When the font size is set to Auto, the contents of the MS-DOS window are sized automatically to display the entire window within the user-specified area.

Ending MS-DOS–Based Applications Gracefully

Windows 98 provides support for gracefully closing an MS-DOS VM through a property sheet setting that is available on an application-by-application basis. When this setting is enabled, users can close an MS-DOS–based application just as they would a Windows-based application—by clicking the Close Window button.

In addition to gracefully ending an MS-DOS–based application, the Windows 98 system ensures that system cleanup is completed properly and that all allocated resources are freed. As a result, memory used by an MS-DOS–based application running under Windows 98 is deallocated properly and made available for use by other applications.

Local Virtual Machine Environment Settings

Under Windows 98, a batch file can be optionally specified for a given MS-DOS–based application, allowing customization of the VM on a local basis before running the application. The batch file is specified on the Program tab of the MS-DOS–based application's property sheet, as shown in Figure 16-5. Using a batch file allows MS-DOS environment variables to be set or customized for individual MS-DOS–based applications and for TSRs to be loaded in the local VM only. This mechanism is like having different AUTOEXEC.BAT files for different MS-DOS–based applications.

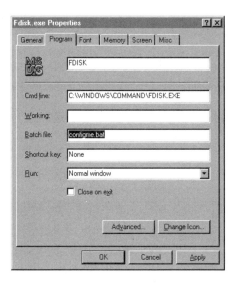

Figure 16-5 *Specifying a batch file on the Program tab of the MS-DOS–based application's property sheet*

Support for Accessing Network Resources with UNC Pathnames

Windows 98 makes accessing network resources from the MS-DOS command prompt easier by supporting the use of universal naming conventions (UNC). UNC provides a standard naming scheme for referencing network servers and shared directories. It uses the following syntax:

```
\\servername\sharename[\pathname]
```

The Windows 98 shell allows users to browse and connect to network servers without mapping a drive letter to the network resource. Windows 98 supports the same functionality at an MS-DOS command prompt and allows you to do the following:

- View the contents of shared directories on network servers from both Microsoft Network servers and Novell NetWare servers by typing *dir\\servername\sharename[\pathname]*

- Copy files from the contents of shared directories on network servers from both Microsoft Network servers and Novell NetWare servers by typing *copy\\servername\sharename\pathname\file destination*

- Run applications from shared directories on network servers for both Microsoft Network servers and Novell NetWare servers by typing *\\servername\sharename\pathname\filename*

MS-DOS Prompt Commands

The MS-DOS command processor and utilities provide integration between MS-DOS functionality and the Windows environment. Commands that manipulate files support long filenames, and other commands provide access to capabilities supported by the system.

For example, the **start** command has the following syntax:

```
start <application name> | <document name>
```

The **start** command allows users to start an MS-DOS or Windows-based application from the command prompt in one of the following ways:

- Start an application by specifying the name of a document to open, and Windows 98 launches the application associated with the given file type. For example, typing *start myfile.xls* starts the application associated with the specified file, if there is a valid association.

- Start an MS-DOS–based application in a different MS-DOS VM instead of the current one.

- Start a Windows-based application from an MS-DOS command prompt. Typing the name of a Windows-based application is essentially the same as typing *start <application>*.

Support for Long Filenames

Many MS-DOS intrinsic commands and utilities support the use of long filenames. For example, the following commands are among those that support long filenames:

- The **dir** command has been extended to show long filenames in the directory structure, along with the corresponding 8.3 filename. Also, the **dir** command now supports a verbose mode so that users can display additional file details by typing *dir/v*.

- The **copy** command has been extended to allow mixing of long and short filenames in copy operations. For example, typing *copy myfile.txt "this is my file"* creates a new file with a long filename.

Support for Win32-Based Applications

Win32-based applications can fully exploit and benefit significantly from the design of the Windows 98 architecture. In addition, each Win32-based application runs in its own fully protected, private address space. This strategy prevents Win32-based applications from crashing each other.

Win32-based applications feature the following benefits over Win16-based applications in Windows 98:

- Preemptive multitasking
- Separate message queues
- Flat address space
- Compatibility with Windows NT
- Long filename support
- Memory protection
- Robustness improvements

Preemptive Multitasking

Win32-based 32-bit applications are preemptively multitasked in Windows 98. The operating system kernel is responsible for scheduling the time allotted for running applications in the system, and support for preemptive multitasking results in smooth concurrent processing and prevents any one application from utilizing all system resources without permitting other tasks to run.

Win32-based applications can optionally implement threads to improve the granularity at which they multitask within the system. The use of threads by an application improves the interaction with the user and results in smooth multitasking operations.

Separate Message Queues

Under cooperative multitasking, the system uses the point when an application checks the system message queue as the mechanism to pass control to another task, allowing that task to run in a cooperative manner. If an application doesn't check the message queue on a regular basis or if the application hangs and thus prevents other applications from checking the message queue, the system keeps the other tasks in the system suspended until the errant application ends.

Each Win32-based application has its own message queue and is thus not affected by the behavior of other running tasks on their own message queues. If a Win16-based application hangs or if another running Win32-based application crashes, a Win32-based application continues to run preemptively and can still receive incoming messages or event notifications.

Message queues are discussed in more detail in Chapter 21, "Robustness."

Flat Address Space

Win32-based applications can access memory in a linear fashion, rather than being limited to the segmented memory architecture used by 16-bit systems. To provide a means of accessing high amounts of memory using a 16-bit addressing model, the Intel CPU architecture provides support for accessing 64-KB chunks of memory, called segments, at a time. Applications and the operating system suffer a performance penalty under this architecture because of the manipulations required by the processor for mapping memory references from the segment/offset combination to the physical memory structure.

The use of a flat address space by the 32-bit components in Windows 98 and by Win32-based applications allows application and device driver developers to write software without the limitations or design issues inherent in the segmented memory architecture.

Compatibility with Windows NT

Win32-based applications that exploit Win32 APIs common to Windows 98 and Windows NT can run without modification on either platform on Intel-based computers. The commonality of the Win32 API provides a consistent programmatic interface and allows application developers to leverage a single development effort to deliver software that runs on multiple platforms. It also provides scalability of applications and broadens the base of platforms available for running ISV or custom applications with minimal additional effort.

Application developers are encouraged to develop applications either under Windows 98 or under Windows NT and to test compatibility on both platforms.

Long Filename Support

Win32-based applications that call the file I/O functions supported by the Win32 API benefit from the ability to support and manipulate filenames of up to 255 characters with no additional development effort. To ease the burden of the application developer, the Win32 APIs and common dialog support handle the work of manipulating long filenames and the file system provides compatibility with MS-DOS and other systems by automatically maintaining the traditional 8.3 filename.

Memory Protection

Each Win32-based application runs in its own private address space and is protected by the system from other applications or processes that are running in the system. Errant Win32-based applications under Windows 98 only affect themselves, instead of bringing down the entire system if they attempt to access memory belonging to another Win32-based application.

The use of separate message queues for Win32-based applications also ensures that the system continues to run even if an application hangs or stops responding to messages or events, thus allowing the user to switch away from or shut down the errant task.

32-Bit File System Architecture

The file system in Windows 98 supports the characteristics and needs of the multi-tasking nature of its kernel. The 32-bit file system present in Windows 98 provides many benefits to users and has the following results:

- **Improved ease of use** Ease of use is improved by the support of long filenames because users no longer need to reference files by the MS-DOS 8.3 filename structure. Instead they can use up to 255 characters to identify their documents. Ease of use is also improved by hiding the filename extensions.

- **Performance** File I/O performance comes from 32-bit protected-mode code for reading information from and writing information to the file system, reading from and writing to the disk device, and intelligent 32-bit caching mechanisms. A full 32-bit code path is available from the file system to the disk device.

- **System stability and reliability** File system components implemented as 32-bit protected-mode device drivers offer system stability and reliability because they can remain in protected-mode for code execution and because they leverage existing driver technology first implemented in Windows NT.

Architecture Overview

Windows 98 features a layered file system architecture that supports multiple file systems and provides a protected-mode path from the application to the media device, resulting in a high level of file and disk I/O performance. The following features are included in the new file system architecture:

- Win32 API support
- Long filename support
- 32-bit FAT file system
- 32-bit CD-ROM file system
- Dynamic system cache for file and network I/O
- Open architecture for future system support
- Disk device driver compatibility with Windows NT

Figure 16-6 on the next page depicts the file system architecture used by Windows 98, which is made up of the following components:

- **Installable File System (IFS) Manager** The IFS Manager is responsible for arbitrating access to different file system components.

- **File system drivers** The file system drivers layer includes access to file allocation table (FAT)–based disk devices, CD-ROM file systems, and redirected network device support.

- **Block I/O subsystem** The block I/O subsystem is responsible for interacting with the physical disk device.

Components of each of these layers are examined in the next three sections.

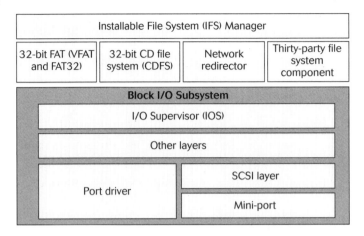

Figure 16-6   *The file system architecture*

The Installable File System Manager

Under MS-DOS and Windows 3.1, the MS-DOS INT 21H interrupt is responsible for providing access to the file system to manipulate file information on a disk device. To support redirected disk devices, such as a network drive or a CD-ROM drive, other system components, such as the network redirector, would hook the INT 21H function so that it could examine a file system request to determine whether it should handle the request or whether the base file system should. Although this mechanism provided the ability to add additional device drivers, some add-on components were ill-behaved and interfered with other installed drivers.

Another problem with the MS-DOS–based file system was the difficulty in supporting the loading of multiple network redirectors to provide concurrent access to different network types. Microsoft Windows for Workgroups provided support for running the Microsoft network redirector at the same time as an additional network redirector, such as Novell NetWare, Banyan VINES, or SUN PC-NFS. However, support for running more than two network redirectors at the same time was not provided.

The key to friendly access to disk and redirected devices in Windows 98 is the Installable File System (IFS) Manager. The IFS Manager is responsible for arbitrating access to file system devices as well as to other file system device components.

File System Drivers

Windows 98 includes support for the following file systems:

- 32-bit file allocation table (VFAT and FAT32) driver
- 32-bit CD-ROM file system (CDFS) driver

- 32-bit network redirector for connectivity to Microsoft network servers, such as Windows NT Server, along with a 32-bit network redirector to connect to Novell NetWare servers

In addition, third parties will use the IFS Manager APIs to provide a clean way of concurrently supporting multiple device types and adding more disk device support and network redirector support.

The 32-bit protected-mode FAT file system

The 32-bit VFAT driver provides a 32-bit protected-mode code path for manipulating the file system stored on a disk. It is also reentrant and multithreaded, providing smoother multitasking performance. The 32-bit file access driver is compatible with more MS-DOS device drivers and hard disk controllers.

Benefits of the 32-bit file access driver over MS-DOS–based driver solutions include the following:

- Dramatically improved performance and real-mode disk caching
- No conventional memory used (replacement for real-mode SmartDrive)
- Better multitasking when accessing information on disk with no blocking
- Dynamic cache support

Under MS-DOS and Windows 3.1, manipulation of the FAT and writing to or reading from the disk is handled by the INT 21H MS-DOS function and is 16-bit real-mode code. Being able to manipulate the disk file system from protected-mode removes or reduces the need to transition to real mode to write information to the disk through MS-DOS, which results in a performance gain for file I/O access.

The 32-bit VFAT driver interacts with the block I/O subsystem to provide 32-bit disk access to more device types. Support is also provided for mapping to existing real-mode disk drivers that might be in use on a user's system. The combination of the 32-bit file access and 32-bit disk access drivers results in significantly higher disk and file I/O performance.

The 32-bit cache

The 32-bit VFAT works in conjunction with a 32-bit protected-mode cache (VCACHE) driver and replaces and improves on the 16-bit real-mode SmartDrive disk cache software provided with MS-DOS. The VCACHE driver features a more intelligent algorithm for caching information read from or written to a disk drive than SmartDrive, resulting in improved performance when reading information from cache. The VCACHE driver is also responsible for managing the cache pool for the CD-ROM File System (CDFS) and the provided 32-bit network redirectors.

Another big improvement VCACHE provides over SmartDrive is that the memory pool used for the cache is dynamic and is based on the amount of available free system memory. Users no longer need to statically allocate a block of memory to set aside as a disk cache because the system automatically allocates or deallocates memory used for the cache based on system use. Because of intelligent cache use, the performance of the system also scales.

FAT32

FAT32 is an improved version of the File Allocation Table file system that allows disks over 2 GB to be formatted as a single drive. FAT32 also uses smaller clusters than FAT drives, resulting in a more efficient use of space on large disks. FAT32 offers the following benefits:

- Reduces complexity by representing very large disks with a single driver letter
- Saves disk space by storing data more efficiently
- Allows existing FAT users to regain unused disk space

Cluster sizes

The cluster size used on all FAT partitions depends on the size of the drive. For the original version of FAT, the default cluster sizes are those shown in the following table:

Original Default Cluster Sizes

Drive Size	FAT Cluster Size
< 32 MB	512 bytes
32 – 63 MB	1 KB
64 – 127 MB	2 KB
128 – 255 MB	4 KB
256 – 511 MB	8 KB
512 – 1023 MB	16 KB
1024 – 2048 MB	32 KB

For FAT32, the default cluster sizes are shown here:

FAT32 Default Cluster Sizes

Drive Size	FAT32 Cluster Size
< 260 MB	512 bytes
260 MB – 8 GB	4 KB
8 GB – 16 GB	8 KB
16 GB – 32 GB	16 KB
> 32 GB	32 KB

These are the defaults you will get if you FDISK and format a drive using FAT32 or if you convert an existing FAT drive in place using CVT.EXE.

> **NOTE**
>
> FDISK offers to enable FAT32 support only on drives over 512 MB.

FAT32 drives have a different on-disk format than existing FAT drives. Most disk utilities (for example, disk defragmenting tools) have already been revised to work on FAT32 volumes; this includes all of the major disk utility vendors. You might need to update your disk utilities if you have older versions. The disk utilities included with Windows 98 have already been revised to include FAT32 support, including FDISK, Format, ScanDisk, Disk Defragmenter, and DriveSpace. Note, however, that DriveSpace does not—and will not—support compressing FAT32 drives.

In addition, support for FAT32 affects many of the internal data structures that the real-mode DOS kernel and the protected-mode file system components use. As a result, some device drivers and disk utilities might encounter compatibility problems with Windows 98, whether or not FAT32 drives are used. To support FAT32, many new low-level disk APIs are provided with Windows 98 and some old ones will fail or behave differently on FAT32 drives. The new and changed APIs are summarized in the Win32 SDK, available via a subscription to MSDN.

Note that most applications are unable to display free or total disk space over 2 GB. Windows 98 includes new DOS and Win32 APIs (GetDiskFreeSpaceEx) that applications can use to obtain the correct amounts of space. The Windows Explorer and the MS-DOS command prompt have been modified to use these new APIs, so they should display the correct amount of free space. File Manager won't display more than 2 GB of free space.

> **NOTE**
>
> If you use FAT32 with anti-virus software, converting your drive requires updating your partition table and boot record. If you have anti-virus software enabled, it might intercept the request to update the partition table and/or the boot record and ask you whether to allow them to be updated. If this occurs, you must instruct the anti-virus software to enable these structures to be updated. Also, when rebooting your system after converting the drive, your anti-virus software might detect that the partition table and/or boot record have changed and offer to "repair" it for you. *DO NOT allow the anti-virus software to restore the boot record or partition table, or your drive and all of the data on it will become inaccessible.*

FAT32 conversion utility

For added flexibility, Windows 98 includes a graphical FAT32 conversion utility, which can quickly and safely convert a hard drive from the original version of FAT (which shipped with all versions of MS-DOS and Windows 95) to FAT32. This utility can be run from the Start menu by choosing Programs, Accessories, System Tools, FAT32 Converter. After the conversion process, Disk Defragmenter will run on the drive during your next reboot. Depending on the size of the drive, the defragmenting process can take some time. You can stop the defragmenter and run it at another time, but your system performance might be degraded until you allow the defragmenter to complete on this drive.

A benefit of the FAT32 conversion utility is that it allows existing FAT users to gain the benefits of FAT32 without reformatting.

> **NOTE**
>
> Windows 98 does not include a utility for converting a drive *back* to FAT16 once you've converted it to FAT32. There are several third-party utility products on the market now that *do* support converting back from FAT32 to FAT16, however.

How to enable FAT32

> **WARNING**
>
> Before converting your drive to FAT32, it is recommended that you make a backup of any important data and also make a Windows 98 Emergency Startup Disk.

Converting an existing FAT drive in place is easy. On the enclosed CD, there is a batch file called FAT32.BAT. Run this batch file from within Windows, and it will do the following:

- Copy a conversion utility into your C:\ directory
- Prompt you for a drive to convert
- Restart your system in MS-DOS mode
- Check the drive you are converting for errors using ScanDisk
- Convert the drive to FAT32
- Defragment the drive upon rebooting into Windows

FAT32 questions and answers

Q   *Will FAT32 be faster than FAT16?*

A   In general, no. FAT32 performance will usually be about the same as FAT16, but in some cases, it might be a bit slower. Typically, there's no noticeable performance difference. The major benefits of FAT32 are that it's more efficient than FAT16 on larger disks (sometimes by as much as 20 to 30 percent), and that it can support drives larger than 2 GB without having to use multiple partitions.

In real-mode MS-DOS or when running Windows 98 in Safe Mode, FAT32 will be considerably slower than FAT16. If you need to run applications in MS-DOS mode, loading SMARTDRV.EXE in AUTOEXEC.BAT will be beneficial.

Q   *Can I dual boot Windows NT if I use FAT32?*

A   In general, no. Windows NT (including version 4.0) can't access or boot from a FAT32 drive, so if you need to dual boot Windows NT, you shouldn't use FAT32 except on a nonboot drive that you don't need to access from NT.

Q   *Why didn't Microsoft just add NTFS to Windows 98 rather than introduce another file system?*

A   We certainly considered NTFS, but it didn't meet three requirements that we felt were critical for Windows 98: Windows 98 boots using real-mode MS-DOS and supports MS-DOS mode for games and other applications that can't run under a multitasking OS. Supporting NTFS under DOS would have taken a significant amount of very limited DOS memory and thus would have impaired Windows' ability to continue to support these applications. Implementing NTFS without DOS support would have meant that two disk partitions would have been required—a FAT partition to boot from, plus the main NTFS partition. We felt that for Windows 98 customers a solution that allowed a single drive letter was critical. Secondly, based on feedback from PC and disk drive manufacturers, it's clear that a significant percentage of new PCs are currently shipping with drives larger than 2 GB. Given the sophistication and complexity of NTFS, we felt that it would have been impossible to complete and test an NTFS implementation until well after this problem had become acute. Finally, because NTFS has such a different on-disk format than FAT, we felt that FAT32 was much less likely to introduce application compatibility problems.

Q   *Is the FAT16 to FAT32 converter part of Windows 98?*

A   Yes. The conversion tool is part of Windows 98.

Q   *How can I tell if my drive is FAT32?*

A   In My Computer, right-click on the drive and select Properties. The Type field should indicate whether a drive is FAT or FAT32.

Q   *Can I use disk compression on FAT32 drives?*

A   No. The DriveSpace included with Windows 98 has been modified to recognize FAT32 drives, but it won't compress them. We don't plan to make further modifications to DriveSpace.

Q   *Can I use FAT32 on drives that are* not *visible in real-mode MS-DOS?*

A   Yes. The CVT.EXE utility can convert protected-mode-only drives while Windows is running. Most drives, however, are visible in MS-DOS mode, and you must shut down to MS-DOS mode in order to convert them with CVT.

Notes for FAT32

- **Dual boot and FAT32** You can't use FAT32 on a machine that you need to dualboot to another operating system, such as the original releases of Windows 95, Windows NT, and Windows 3.1 or MS-DOS 6.*x*. Other operating systems are unable to access a FAT32 partition. This is simply because these older operating systems don't understand the new data structures. You *can* dual-boot to another operating system if drive C: is FAT16, but if you have other partitions that are FAT32, they won't be visible to other operating systems. Windows 98 also supports dual-booting between Windows 98 and older MS-DOS operating systems, such as MS-DOS 6.22, using the same "F4" dualboot that Windows 95 supports, provided you're using FAT16. You can't at this time; however, multiboot between Windows 95 and Windows 98 because Windows 98 replaces Windows 95.

- **FAT32 and disk free space** Some applications are unable to display free or total disk space over 2 GB, even on larger FAT32 drives. These applications will show the correct free space up to 2 GB, but at that point they'll max out and show only 2 GB. This is typically due to limitations in those applications that assumed that free space could never exceed 2 GB because of the previous FAT16 limitations. Windows 98 provides new DOS and Win32 APIs that applications can utilize to determine free or total disk space over 2 GB.

- **FAT32 converter** You can convert a hard drive from FAT16 to FAT32 by running CVT.EXE *x*: (where *x*: represents the drive letter you wish to convert). After running the FAT32 converter, Disk Defragmenter runs on that drive during your next boot. Defragmenting your drive after it has been converted might take several hours. You *can* stop the defragmenter and run it at another time, but your system performance might be degraded until you allow the defragmenter to complete on this drive.

- **InterLnk from MS-DOS 6.*x*** The InterLnk networking product contained in MS-DOS 6.*x* won't function properly in MS-DOS mode if you are using FAT32.

- **Ontrack Systems' Disk Manager** If you use Ontrack Systems' Disk Manager product on a system booting from a FAT32 drive, it might result in a long pause at boot time and/or that the drive will be set to run in compatibility mode. With version 7.0*x*, you can use the /L=0 option with Disk Manager to avoid this pause. If you're running an earlier version of Disk Manager, you should update to at least version 7.04 and use the /L=0 switch if you use FAT32.

- **SyQuest SQATDRV.SYS and SQDRIVER.SYS drivers** The SQATDRV.SYS driver might cause systems containing FAT32 drives to hang during boot. Remove this driver from the CONFIG.SYS file if you are using FAT32 drives on a system with this device driver. Versions of these drivers that are compatible with FAT32 boot drives will be added to the Windows Driver Library (on the Windows CD and downloadable from the Internet) shortly.

The 32-bit protected-mode CD-ROM file system

The 32-bit protected-mode CD-ROM file system (CDFS) in Windows 98 provides high CD-ROM access performance and is a full 32-bit ISO 9660 CD file system. The CDFS driver replaces the 16-bit real-mode MSCDEX driver and features 32-bit protected-mode caching of CD-ROM data. The CDFS driver cache is dynamic and shares the cache memory pool with the 32-bit VFAT driver, requiring no configuration or static allocation on the part of the user.

Benefits of the 32-bit CDFS driver include the following:

- No conventional memory used (replaces real-mode MSCDEX)
- High performance
- Multitasking when accessing CD-ROM information, with no blocking
- Dynamic cache support to provide a balance between providing memory to run applications vs. memory to serve as a disk cache

If MSCDEX is specified in the AUTOEXEC.BAT, the 32-bit CDFS driver takes over the role played by the MSCDEX driver and communicates with the CD-ROM device. The use of MSCDEX is unnecessary under Windows 98.

Users of CD-ROM multimedia applications benefit greatly from the 32-bit CDFS. Their multimedia applications run smoothly and information is read from the CD-ROM quickly for high performance.

The Block I/O Subsystem

The block I/O subsystem in Windows 98 provides high performance for the entire file system and a broad array of device support.

As shown in Figure 16-7 on the next page, the components of the block I/O subsystem include the following:

- High-level I/O Supervisor (IOS) layer, which provides an interface to the block I/O subsystem for the higher layer components
- The port driver, which represents a monolithic disk device driver
- The SCSI layer, which provides a standard interface and driver layer to provide device-independent control code for SCSI devices
- The SCSI mini-port driver, which contains the device-dependent control code responsible for interacting with individual SCSI controllers.

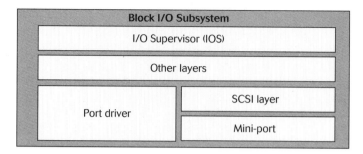

Figure 16-7   *The architecture of the block I/O subsystem*

The block I/O subsystem provides the following support in Windows 98:

- A fully Plug-and-Play-enabled architecture
- Support for mini-port drivers that are binary compatible with Windows NT
- Support for Windows 3.1 fast disk drivers for backward compatibility
- Protected-mode drivers that take over real-mode MS-DOS device drivers when safe to do so
- Support for IDE drive spin down
- The ability to support existing MS-DOS real-mode disk device drivers for compatibility

The following sections examine the different areas that make up the block I/O subsystem. The explanations are provided to facilitate an understanding of the components, bearing in mind that the configuration of the disk device driver layers is isolated from the user.

The I/O supervisor

The I/O Supervisor (IOS) provides services to file systems and drivers. The IOS is responsible for the queuing of file service requests and for routing the requests to the appropriate file system driver. The IOS also provides asynchronous notification of file system events to installed drivers.

The port driver

The port driver is a monolithic 32-bit protected-mode driver that communicates with a specific disk device, such as a hard disk controller. This driver is specifically for use with Windows 98. In Windows 98, the driver that communicates with IDE/ESDI hard disk controllers and floppy disk controllers is implemented as a port driver. A port driver provides the same functionality as the combination of the SCSI manager and the mini-port driver.

The SCSI layer

The SCSI layer applies a 32-bit protected-mode universal driver model architecture to communication with SCSI devices. The SCSI layer provides all the high-level functionality that is common to SCSI-like devices and then uses a mini-port driver to handle device-specific I/O calls. The SCSI Manager is part of this system and provides compatibility support for using Windows NT mini-port drivers.

The mini-port driver

The mini-port driver model used in Windows 98 simplifies the task of writing device drivers for disk device hardware vendors. Because the SCSI Stub provides the high-level functionality for communicating with SCSI devices, disk device hardware vendors need to create only a mini-port driver that is tailored to their own disk device. The mini-port driver for Windows 98 is 32-bit protected-mode code and is binary compatible with Windows NT mini-port drivers, another factor that simplifies the task of writing device drivers. Binary compatibility with NT also results in a stable and reliable device driver because hardware vendors need to maintain only one code base for device support. Users of Windows 98 also benefit because many mini-port drivers are already available for Windows NT.

Support for IDE, ESDI, and SCSI controllers

Through the use of either a port driver or a mini-port driver, support for a broad array of disk devices is available for Windows 98, including popular IDE, ESDI, and SCSI disk controllers. Users won't have to decide whether to use a port driver or a mini-port driver because the driver is provided by the hardware vendor and configuration of the driver is handled by the Windows 98 system.

Support for IDE drive spin down

Drive spin down allows Windows 98 machines to stop a computer's hard drive when the drive isn't in use. Drive spin down reduces power consumption and noise.

The real-mode mapper

To provide binary compatibility with real-mode MS-DOS–based disk device drivers for which a protected-mode counterpart doesn't exist in Windows 98, the block I/O subsystem provides a mapping layer to allow the protected-mode file system to communicate with a real-mode driver as if it were a protected-mode component. The layers above and including this real-mode mapper (RMM) are protected-mode code, and the real-mode mapper translates file I/O requests from protected mode to real mode so that the MS-DOS device driver can perform the read or write operation you want from or to the disk device. The real-mode mapper would come into play when, for example, real-mode disk-compression software is running and a protected-mode disk-compression driver isn't available.

Long Filename Support

The use of long filenames of up to 255 characters in Windows 98 overcomes the sometimes cryptic 8.3 MS-DOS filename convention and allows more user-friendly filenames. MS-DOS 8.3 filenames are maintained and tracked by the system to provide compatibility with existing Win16-based and MS-DOS–based applications that manipulate only 8.3 filenames, but as users migrate to Win32-based applications, the use of 8.3 filename conventions is hidden from the user.

Long filenames are supported by extending the MS-DOS FAT file system and using bits and fields that were previously reserved by the operating system to add special directory entries that maintain long filename information. Extending the MS-DOS FAT layout, rather than creating a new format, allows users to install and use Windows 98 on existing disk formats without having to change their disk structure or reformat their drives. This implementation provides ease of use and allows future growth while maintaining backward compatibility with existing applications.

Because Windows 98 simply extends the FAT structure, long filenames are supported on disks as well as hard disks. If a file on a disk that has a long filename is viewed on a computer that's not running Windows 95 or Windows 98, only the 8.3 filename representation is seen.

The following disk directory listed from the command prompt shows long filenames and their corresponding 8.3 filename mappings on a computer running Windows 98:

```
Volume in drive C is MY HARDDISK
Volume Serial Number is 1E30-830F
Directory of C:\Long Filename Directory

. <DIR> 07-11-94 10:02a .
.. <DIR> 07-11-94 10:02a ..
4THQUART XLS 147 05-11-94 12:25a 4th Quarter Analysis.xls
BOSS'SBI TXT 147 05-11-94 12:25a Boss's birthday card.txt
1994FINA DOC 147 05-11-94 10:35a 1994 Financial Projections.doc
FISCALYE <DIR> 07-11-94 10:02a Fiscal Year Information
COMPANYL BMP 478 03-27-94 12:00a Company Logo.bmp
SHORTC~2 PIF 967 02-16-95 4:55p Shortcut to MS-DOS Application.pif
NEWWAVES WAV 0 06-14-94 1:14p New Wave Sound.wav
NEWVID~1 AVI 0 06-14-94 1:15p New video.avi
DIRECTIO DOC 147 05-11-94 12:25a Directions to company picnic.doc
 8 file(s) 2,033 bytes
 3 dir(s) 134,643,712 bytes free
```

Support for existing disk management utilities

For existing disk management utilities to recognize and preserve long filenames, utility vendors need to revise their software products. Microsoft documents long filename support and its implementation as an extension to the FAT format as part of the Windows 98 Software Development Kit (SDK).

Existing MS-DOS–based disk management utilities that manipulate the FAT format, including disk defragmenters, disk bit editors, and some tape backup software, might not recognize long filenames as used by Windows 98 and might destroy long filename entries in the FAT format. However, no data is lost if the long filename entry is destroyed because the corresponding system-defined 8.3 filename is preserved.

Hidden File Extensions

Windows 95 uses file extensions to associate a given file type with an application. However, to make it easier to manipulate files, file extensions are hidden from users in the Windows 98 shell and in the Windows Explorer, and instead, icons are used in the UI in Windows 98 to differentiate the documents associated with different applications. Information about file type associations is stored in the Registry, and the associations are used to map a given file with the icon that represents the document type. (For compatibility reasons, Windows 98 must track filename extensions for use with existing MS-DOS and Win16-based applications.)

In addition to hiding filename extensions in the Windows 98 shell and the Windows Explorer, application developers can hide filenames from users in their applications. Mechanisms for hiding filenames are documented in the Windows 98 SDK. A good Windows 98 application makes use of these mechanisms for handling files to be consistent with the rest of the Windows 98 environment.

Additional File Date/Time Attributes

Windows 98 maintains additional date/time attributes for files that MS-DOS doesn't track. Windows 98 tracks the date and time when a new file was created, the date and time when a file was modified, and the date when a file was last opened. These file attributes are displayed in the file's property sheet, as shown in Figure 16-8 on the next page.

Utilities vendors can take advantage of this additional date and time information to provide enhanced backup utilities—for example, to use a better mechanism when determining whether a given file has changed.

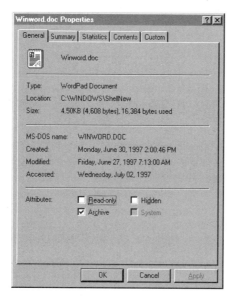

Figure 16-8 *The properties for a file, showing the new file date/time attributes*

Coordinated Universal Time Format

MS-DOS has traditionally used the local time of the computer as the time stamp for the directory entry of a file and continues to use local time for files stored on the local system. However, Windows 98 supports the use of the coordinated universal time (UTC) format for accessing or creating information on network file servers. This format provides the superior, more universal tracking of time information required by networks that operate across time zones.

Exclusive Access for Disk Management Tools

Disk management utilities, such as disk defragmenters, disk-compression utilities, and sector editors, and file system programs, such as CHKDSK and DEFRAG, require exclusive access to the file system to minimize the disk access complexities that are present in a multitasking environment where disk I/O occurs. For example, without exclusive access to the disk, data corruption might occur if a user requests that a disk operation move information on the disk at the same time that another task is accessing that information or writing other information to disk.

The file system in Windows 98 supports the use of Windows-based disk management utilities by permitting exclusive access to a disk device. Exclusive disk access is handled as part of the file system through an API mechanism and can be used by utilities vendors to write Windows-based disk management utilities. Microsoft encourages third-party utilities vendors to use this API mechanism and is also using it to deliver disk management utilities as part of Windows 98.

For example, this mechanism is used by the Disk Defragmenter utility delivered as part of Windows 98. The Disk Defragmenter in Windows 98 can be run from the Windows 98 shell and can even be run in the background while users continue to work on their systems.

DriveSpace Disk Compression

Windows 98 provides built-in support for DriveSpace disk compression. Windows 98 provides base compression in the form of a 32-bit virtual device driver that delivers high performance and frees conventional memory for use by MS-DOS–based applications. Users of MS-DOS–based DoubleSpace and DriveSpace don't need to change their existing compressed volume file (CVF) and thus don't need to take any special actions when they install Windows 98.

> **NOTE**
>
> The DriveSpace included with Windows 98 has been modified to recognize FAT32 drives, but it won't compress them. We don't plan to make further modifications to DriveSpace.

As shown in Figure 16-9, the DriveSpace disk compression tool provided with Windows 98 is GUI-based and provides the ability to compress a physical hard drive or removable floppy drive. The Compress A Drive dialog box, shown in Figure 16-10 on the next page, graphically depicts the amount of free space available before compression and the estimated space available after compression.

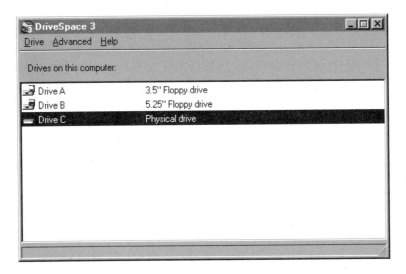

Figure 16-9   *The DriveSpace disk compression tool*

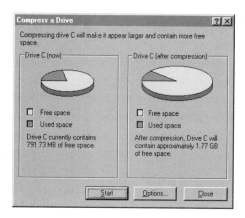

Figure 16-10   *The Compress a Drive dialog box, which graphically displays free space*

System Resources

Prior to Windows 95, many users encountered "Out of Memory" error messages when running multiple Windows-based applications, even though the system still reported several megabytes of available free memory. Typically these messages appeared because the system couldn't allocate an internal memory resource in a Windows API function call due to lack of available space in a region of memory called a *heap*.

Windows maintains heaps for system components named GDI and USER. Each heap is 64 KB in size and is used for storing GDI or memory object information allocated when an application calls a Windows API function. The amount of space available in the combination of these two heaps is identified as the percentage of system resources that are free.

The percentage of free system resources is calculated using an internal algorithm to represent the aggregate percentage of free memory in the GDI and USER heaps. When the free system resources percentage gets too low, users commonly see an "Out of Memory" error message, even though the amount of free memory is still high. This error can result from low memory in either the GDI or USER heap (or both).

To help reduce this system resource limitation, a number of the data structures stored in the 16-bit GDI and USER heaps were moved out of these heaps and stored in 32-bit heaps, providing more room for the remaining data elements to be created. As a result, system resources decrease less rapidly.

For compatibility, not all objects were removed from the 16-bit GDI or USER heap and placed in a 32-bit heap. For example, some Windows-based applications manipulate the contents of the GDI heap directly, bypassing the published API mechanisms for doing so because their developers think direct manipulation increases performance. However, because these applications bypass the Windows API mechanisms, moving their data from the existing heap structures and placing them in 32-bit heaps would cause these applications to fail because of memory access violations.

Win16-based and Win32-based applications use the same GDI and USER heaps. The impact of removing selected items from the heaps was closely examined and objects were selected based on the biggest improvement that could be achieved while affecting the fewest number of applications. For example, the GDI heap can quickly become full because of the creation of memory-intensive region objects that are used by applications for creating complex images and by the printing subsystem for generating complex output. Region objects were removed from the 64-KB 16-bit GDI heap and placed in a 32-bit heap, benefiting graphic-intensive applications and providing for the creation of more small objects by the system. Windows 98 system capacity for the USER heap expanded when menu and window handles moved to the 32-bit USER heap. Windows 98 allows 32,767 menu handles and an additional 32,767 window handles *per process* rather than systemwide. The following table identifies other system limits.

Windows 98 System Limits

Resource	Size*
Windows Menu handles	32 KB
Timers	Unlimited
COM and LPT ports	Unlimited
Items per list box	32 KB
Data per list box	Unlimited
Data per edit control	Unlimited
Regions	Unlimited
Physical pens and brushes	Unlimited
Logical pens and brushes	All in 64-KB segment
Logical fonts	750–800
Installed fonts	1000 (or more)
Device contexts	16 KB

* Systemwide resources, unless noted otherwise.

In addition to moving information from the GDI and USER heaps, robustness improvements in Windows 98 that facilitate system cleanup of unfreed resources also relieve system resource limitations. When Windows 98 determines that the owner and other ended processes no longer need the resources in memory, Windows 98 cleans up and deallocates leftover data structures. The robustness improvements in Windows 98 are discussed in Chapter 21, "Robustness."

Memory Management

Windows 98 uses linear memory addressing to provide access to physical memory, as well as improves upon the swap file implementation provided in Windows 3.1 to support virtual memory supplementation of physical memory.

Linear Memory Addressing for Win32-Based Applications

To support a 16-bit operating environment, the Intel processor architecture uses a mechanism called a *segment* to reference memory by using a 16-bit segment address and a 16-bit offset address within the segment. A segment is 64 KB in size, and applications and the operating system pay a performance penalty when they access information across segments. For 32-bit operating system functionality and Win32-based applications, Windows 98 addresses this issue by using the 32-bit capabilities of the Intel 80386 (and above) processor architecture to support a flat, linear memory mode. A linear addressing model simplifies the development process for application developers, removes the performance penalties imposed by the segmented memory architecture, and provides access to a virtual address space that permits the addressing of up to 4 GB of memory. Windows 98 uses the flat memory model internally for 32-bit components and virtual device drivers.

Compatibility with the Windows NT Memory Model

Windows 98 uses the same memory model architecture as Windows NT, providing high-end operating system functionality for the mainstream system. Windows 98 allows full use of the 4 GB of addressable memory space to support even the largest desktop application. The operating system provides a 2-GB memory range for applications and reserves a 2-GB range for itself.

Virtual Memory Support (Swap File)

Virtual memory can use either a temporary swap file or a permanent swap file. Deciding how much memory to allocate to the swap file and whether to use 32-bit disk access to access the swap file are important decisions. A temporary swap file doesn't need to be contiguous, and Windows dynamically allocates hard disk space when it starts and frees up the space when it's terminated. A permanent swap file provides the best performance, but it has to be contiguous, has to be set up on a physical hard disk, and is statically specified and is not freed up after exiting Windows.

The swap file implementation in Windows 98 simplifies configuration and, because of improved virtual memory algorithms and access methods, combines the best features of a temporary swap file and a permanent swap file. The swap file in Windows 98 is dynamic and can shrink or grow based on the operations performed on the system. The swap file can occupy a fragmented region of the hard disk and it can be located on a compressed disk volume.

Windows 98 uses intelligent system defaults for the configuration of virtual memory. Figure 16-11 shows the virtual memory configuration settings.

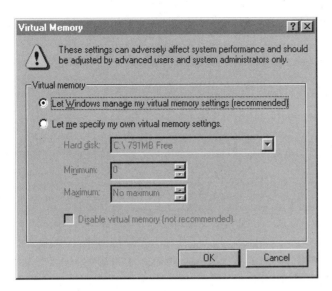

Figure 16-11   *The virtual memory settings*

The Registry: A Centralized Configuration Store

Windows 98 uses a mechanism named the *Registry* to serve as the central configuration store for user, application, and computer-specific information. The Registry is a hierarchical database that stores systemwide information in a single location, making it easy to manage and support.

Registry Improvements in Windows 98

We've rewritten the Registry handling code to be faster and more robust. The in-memory data structures are better optimized. You won't see any changes in the registry structure as exposed through the APIs or REGEDIT. But how it's handled in code has been significantly improved.

Some new Registry entries have been added to support advanced power management and multiple displays. See Chapter 18, "Display Support," and Chapter 19, "Device Support," for more information on those topics.

Windows Management Infrastructure

The Windows Management Infrastructure collects a wealth of information about configuration of devices and the system as a whole. This information is stored in the Registry and made available through extensions to the Registry API. This software is the foundation of Microsoft's support for DMI and, in the future, will provide device and system information to OLE Management Services (OLE MS) and SNMP.

The package can be installed through Add/Remove Programs in the Control Panel. The package is named Desktop Management and is selected from the Accessories option on the Windows Setup tab.

When this package is installed, a new key, HKLM\DesktopManagement, is created in the Registry. You'll find lots of entries there which locate where instrumentation code (which "mines" device information) will be installed. However, there's no way to activate the instrumentation because this package contains just the infrastructure. If you're interested in testing this code or in developing your own instrumentation, send e-mail to *WMI_INFO@microsoft.com* and request the WMI SDK.

Solutions to INI Problems

Using initialization (INI) files to store system-specific or application-specific information about the state or configuration of the system poses a number of problems. Problems using INI files for configuration management include the following:

- Information is stored in several different locations, including CONFIG.SYS, AUTOEXEC.BAT, WIN.INI, SYSTEM.INI, PROTOCOL.INI, private INI files, and private GRP files.
- INI files are text-based and limited in total size to 64 KB, and APIs allow for get/write operations only.
- Information stored in INI files is nonhierarchical and supports only two levels of information: key names broken up by section headings.
- Many INI files contain myriad switches and entries that are complicated to configure or are used only by operating system components.
- INI files provide no mechanism for storing user-specific information, thus making it difficult for multiple users to share a single computer.
- Configuration information in INI files is local to each system, and because no API mechanisms are available for remotely managing configuration, managing multiple systems is difficult.

To solve these problems, the Registry was designed with the following goals in mind:

- Simplify the support burden
- Centralize configuration information
- Provide a means to store user, application, and computer-specific information
- Provide local and remote access to configuration information

The Registry is structured as a database of keys in which each key can contain a value or other keys (subkeys). As shown in Figure 16-12, the Registry uses a hierarchical structure to store text or binary value information and maintains all of the configuration parameters normally stored in the Windows system INI files such as WIN.INI, SYSTEM.INI, and PROTOCOL.INI. The Registry serves not only as a central repository for file associations and OLE registration information but also supports keys that can have more than one value and also supports data of different types.

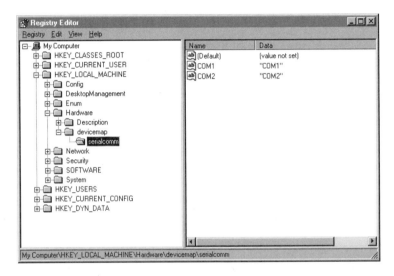

Figure 16-12 *The hierarchy of the Registry, as displayed by the Registry Editor*

The Registry is made up of several DAT files that contain system-specific information (SYSTEM.DAT) or user-specific information (USER.DAT). System-specific information, such as the static reference to loading virtual device drivers, is moved as appropriate from the SYSTEM.INI file to the Registry.

System switches

Windows supports several hundred different system configuration switches. With intelligent enhancements to the system and dynamic configuration properties, Windows 98 reduces the number of system switches that must be set. These reductions don't result from simply moving system switch entries to the Registry but by examining and justifying the presence of each and every one.

The Role of INI Files

Like CONFIG.SYS and AUTOEXEC.BAT, WIN.INI and SYSTEM.INI and application-specific INI files still exist for compatibility reasons. The Win16 APIs for manipulating INI files still manipulate INI files, but developers of Win32-based applications are encouraged to use the Registry APIs to consolidate application-specific information.

Many existing Win16-based applications expect to find and manipulate the WIN.INI and SYSTEM.INI files to add entries or load unique device drivers, so Windows 98 examines INI files during the boot process. For example, the [386Enh] section of SYSTEM.INI is checked for virtual device drivers during startup.

Role in Plug and Play

One of the primary roles of the Registry in Windows 98 is to serve as a central repository for hardware-specific information for use by the Plug and Play system components. Windows 98 maintains information about hardware components and devices that have been identified through an enumeration process in the hierarchical structure of the Registry. When new devices are installed, the system checks the existing configuration in the Registry to determine which hardware resources—for example, IRQs, I/O addresses, DMA channels, and so on—aren't being used. This way, the new device can be properly configured without conflicting with a device already installed in the system.

Remote Access to Registry Information

Many of the Win32 Registry APIs use the remote procedure call (RPC) mechanism in Windows 98 to provide remote access to Registry information across a network. As a result, desktop management applications can aid in the management and support of Windows-based computers, and the contents of the Registry on a given PC can be queried over a network. Industry management mechanisms, such as SNMP or DMI, can easily be integrated into Windows 98, simplifying the management and support burden of an MIS organization. For more information about manageability and remote administration, see Chapter 9, "Networking."

Font Support

Font support in Windows 98 is integrated with the UI and is optimized for the 32-bit environment.

The 32-Bit TrueType Rasterizer

The rasterizer component for rendering and generating TrueType fonts in Windows 95 is written as a 32-bit component and delivers fidelity from the mathematical representation to the generated bitmap, as well as high performance for rendering TrueType fonts.

In addition, the 32-bit rasterizer provides support for generating complicated glyphs—for example, Han—and results in a fast initial boot time in Windows 98, even when many fonts are installed.

17

Plug and Play

PERSONAL COMPUTERS HAVE REVOLUTIONIZED the way people work. Today, PCs are being used extensively both at work and home for various tasks—for personal productivity, information exchange, and education and entertainment ("edutainment"). Furthermore, as hardware technology has advanced in the areas of graphics, audio, networking, storage, imaging, and communication, PCs have become more powerful and less expensive, accelerating their adoption on a worldwide basis. The widespread adoption of the Microsoft Windows operating system has gone hand in hand with the advances in hardware technology.

With these innovations, however, have come new industry challenges. Specifically, configuring PC hardware and operating systems to work with different networks and peripheral devices can pose a significant problem. Changing the hardware configuration of a machine is a task that few end users attempt and even trained technicians can find difficult, time-consuming, and frustrating. This problem is compounded by the growing use of mobile computers because users of mobile computers typically need to change their PC configurations more frequently. Mobile devices are often unplugged from corporate networks and peripheral devices in the office and reconfigured to allow computing and remote communication from home or while on the road.

Whether related to changing the configuration of a notebook computer from an office to a mobile setting or simply adding a CD-ROM or other device to an existing desktop computer, PC configuration difficulties can result in low customer satisfaction and high support costs. The Plug and Play framework architecture in Microsoft Windows 98 reduces the cost of owning PCs while increasing their ease of use and value.

What Is Plug and Play?

Plug and Play is both a design philosophy and a set of PC architecture specifications. Microsoft's goal for Plug and Play is to make the PC, add-in hardware devices, drivers, and operating system work together automatically without user intervention. To achieve this goal, all the components need to be Plug and Play compatible. The components of a complete Plug and Play system consist of the following:

- A Plug and Play operating system
- A Plug and Play Basic Input/Output System (BIOS)
- Plug and Play hardware devices with drivers

Levels of Plug and Play Support

The system's ease of use and dynamic operation depend on how many of the three main components—the operating system, system BIOS, and hardware devices with drivers—support Plug and Play. At the lowest level, when none of the components supports Plug and Play, the user needs to set card jumpers and switches manually, and load drivers from floppies.

At the next level, when the operating system supports Plug and Play but is used with legacy or non–Plug and Play hardware, user intervention is reduced but not completely eliminated. To aid the user in hardware setup, the Plug and Play operating system provides tools such as the Add New Hardware Wizard, the Device Manager, and the Registry. (See the section entitled "Plug and Play Architecture in Windows 98" for a description of these features.) In addition, drivers are installed, loaded, and unloaded automatically.

At the highest level, when all three components support Plug and Play, installing new devices is as easy as plugging them in and turning on the system. Hardware identification and configuration is completely automated and invisible to users. And because of the Plug and Play BIOS, the system supports full dynamic operation, including hot docking, Advanced Power Management (APM) 1.1, automatic configuration of boot devices, and programming of motherboard devices.

Benefits of Plug and Play

A complete Plug and Play system provides substantial benefits to both users and computer-industry vendors. The PC is easier to use because users don't have to worry about switches, jumpers, hardware conflicts, or loading drivers manually. For example, to turn a desktop-computer system into a great multimedia system, all the user has to do is plug in a Plug and Play audio card, CD-ROM drive and SCSI adapter, turn on the system, and play a video clip.

Users also have great mobility. For example, hot-docking stations that support Plug and Play enable the user to remove a portable system while it's running and bring the system to a meeting without having to close or reboot the computer. The system automatically senses its removal from the station, reconfigures itself to work with a new display, and adjusts for the absence of a network card and large disk drive.

For PC vendors, Plug and Play can provide cost reductions. As many as 50 percent of support calls to PC vendors result from installation and configuration problems. By making operations easier and automatic, manufacturers can achieve lower support costs and pass these savings to the user. Easy installation and configuration during setup also benefit original equipment manufacturers (OEMs) who offer systems with Windows preinstalled; they, too, can pass cost savings to the user. Similarly, Plug and Play's Universal Driver simplifies device-driver development, which enables a developer to create a single driver that works across multiple bus types and eliminates the need to include bus-specific code in several drivers.

Finally, Plug and Play provides a common platform that enables PC vendors to develop innovative features and differentiate their products from others. This effort can have the effect of expanding the overall PC market.

Market Momentum

Microsoft, Intel, and Compaq Computer formally introduced the Plug and Play effort in March 1993 at the Windows Hardware Engineering Conference to more than 1300 attendees. At COMDEX/Fall 93, 18 Plug and Play devices were demonstrated. Today, acceptance of Plug and Play is widespread throughout the PC industry. More than 300 Plug and Play products from over 80 vendors have been demonstrated and made available.

In addition, Plug and Play hardware specifications for BIOS, APM, ISA, SCSI, LPT, COM, ESCD, PCI, PCMCIA, VL, and VESA DDC have been completed and are publicly available to PC vendors. These specifications were generated using an open-design process via CompuServe. The PLUGPLAY forum on CompuServe was used to distribute the specifications and solicit feedback from more than 3000 participants.

Finally, Plug and Play is an integral part of PC vendors' product plans. Vendors are using the specifications, in addition to the *Hardware Design Guide for Microsoft Windows 98*, to build all three components of Plug and Play systems. These components are tested during Plug and Play interoperability workshops (or "PlugFests").

Configuration Process in a Plug and Play System

A certain amount of configuration must first be performed by the system BIOS during the power-up phase. For the system to boot, the BIOS must, at a minimum, configure a display device, an input device, and a device for initial program loading. Then, it must pass the information about each of these devices to the operating system for additional system configuration.

When devices are added and removed, the three components of a Plug and Play system coordinate and perform the following basic tasks:

- Identify installed devices
- Determine device-resource requirements
- Create a nonconflicting system configuration
- Program devices
- Load device drivers
- Notify the operating system of configuration changes

The operating system first identifies every installed device in the system and determines the resource requirements for each device. Each nonbooting device is inactive upon power-up so that the operating system can identify any conflicts between the resource requirements of different devices before configuring them. The operating system then identifies and creates a nonconflicting system configuration. Once any resource conflicts have been resolved, the operating system programs each hardware device automatically with its working configuration, then stores all configuration information in the central database. Finally, the operating system loads the device drivers for each device and notifies these drivers of the resource assignments. This process, which is centrally managed by the Plug and Play operating system, is repeated as devices are added or removed.

If a change occurs to the system configuration during operation, the hardware must be able to notify the operating system of the event so that the operating system can configure the new device. In addition, applications must be able to respond to configuration changes to take advantage of new devices and to cease calling devices that have been removed. Such dynamic configuration events might include the insertion of a PCMCIA card, the addition or removal of a peripheral such as a mouse, CD-ROM drive, or printer, or a docking event for a notebook computer.

Plug and Play Support in Windows 98

The Plug and Play specifications are designed to be implementation-independent and aren't tied to a specific operating system. It's up to the operating system developer to define the level of support the system provides. Windows 98 is designed and built with Plug and Play support. It supports both existing market requirements and future PC growth to enable the following:

- **Compatibility with legacy hardware** With over 140 million MS-DOS–based and Windows-based PCs used throughout the world, providing compatibility with legacy hardware is a requirement. Compatibility with existing hardware ensures that neither Windows 98 nor the new Plug and Play peripherals require the purchase of completely new hardware.

- **Automatic installation and configuration of Plug and Play devices** With Plug and Play, initial PC configuration is automatic. Users don't need to configure their systems and make system-resource assignments, such as those for IRQs, I/O ports, and DMA addresses. These assignments are handled by the BIOS and operating system, which avoids configuration conflicts. Installation and configuration of add-on devices and peripherals is also automatic.

- **A dynamic operating environment that supports mobile computing environments** Dynamic Plug and Play properties in Windows 98 include support for the following, all of which have the effect of allowing users to reconfigure their PCs on the fly and have the changes take effect immediately without rebooting:

  - Hot-docking and undocking of mobile computers to change the state of the system dynamically

  - Hot-plugging and unplugging of Plug and Play devices on the fly

  - "Dynaload drivers," which are loaded by the operating system for devices that are present and removed from memory when the device is no longer available

  - Unified messaging mechanism for dynamically notifying other operating system components and applications about changes to the state of the system

- **A universal driver model that simplifies device driver development** To simplify the development of device drivers for independent hardware vendor (IHV) hardware devices, Windows 98 incorporates the use of a universal driver model in various components of the system. Windows 98 provides support for printer drivers, communications drivers, display adapter drivers, mouse drivers, and disk device drivers. The universal driver model ensures that IHVs can easily write peripheral drivers, thus increasing the number of Plug and Play devices available on the market.

- **An open and extensible architecture that supports new technologies** The Plug and Play implementation in Windows 98 is flexible and extensible enough to support future technologies as they emerge on the market. The Plug and Play Initiative will spur the creation of new and innovative technologies, and Windows 98 will support them.

- **The availability of configuration information for simplified systems management** The sharing of configuration information not only helps users solve configuration problems but also helps MIS organizations support and manage PCs within corporate environments, which might have hundreds or thousands of PCs. Through the use of the Registry, configuration information is easily available to the system and to applications, both locally and remotely.

Plug and Play Architecture in Windows 98

To provide complete Plug and Play functionality in Windows 98, Microsoft has included the following components:

- Configuration Manager
- Hardware tree and Registry
- Bus and port enumerators
- Resource arbitrators
- Setup and device installer

Configuration Manager

The Configuration Manager is the central software component that handles all phases of the configuration process. It orchestrates the entire flow of operations performed by all the components involved in the configuration process, and it accepts and responds to communications from the BIOS and hardware devices during the configuration process. It also responds to dynamic events during operation, including the insertion or removal of devices and the docking or undocking of mobile computers. As these events occur, the Configuration Manager communicates the information to the applications.

Hardware Tree and Registry

The hardware tree is a record of the current system configuration. The tree information is drawn from the Registry, a central database of configuration information for all devices. The Registry is stored locally for each computer and holds information about all device types, whether they are currently installed or not. The Configuration Manager creates the hardware tree each time the system boots or a run-time change occurs to the system configuration. The existence of the Registry eliminates the need for most device-specific initialization files. The hardware tree is displayed to the user on the Device Manager property sheet page, as shown in Figure 17-1.

Bus and Port Enumerators

Bus enumerators are responsible for building (enumerating) the hardware tree on a Plug and Play system. Bus enumerators are a type of driver. Enumerators are based on specific bus architectures and understand the implementation details of their bus types. Therefore, an ISA enumerator can identify the devices on an ISA bus, read their resource requirements, and configure them as instructed by the Configuration Manager. Other enumerators include those for VLB, PCI, SCSI, PCMCIA, serial ports, and parallel ports. During installation, Windows determines automatically which bus enumerators are applicable to a given computer.

Figure 17-1   *The Device Manager property sheet*

Resource Arbitrators

Resource arbitrators allocate specific types of resources to devices and resolve conflicts between devices that request identical resource assignments. The functional separation of resource arbitrators and the Configuration Manager provides for future extension of the Windows operating system to address new types of resources.

Setup and Device Installer

The operating system Setup program creates the central configuration database during initial system startup. Although under normal circumstances the system won't require user intervention to perform any initial-setup configuration operations, there are some exceptions. For example, if the system fails to detect a non-Plug and Play device, the user can force an installation by using the Add New Hardware Wizard in the Control Panel, shown in Figure 17-2 on the following page. At times, the system might be unable to generate a nonconflicting configuration for a non–Plug and Play device. In this case, a Windows user-interface component communicates the event to the user and presents the user with several options to resolve the problem.

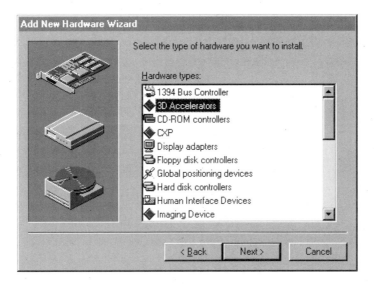

Figure 17-2   *Add New Hardware Wizard*

Plug and Play Hardware Design

PC 98 hardware is optimized for Windows 98 and takes full advantage of Plug and Play. PC 98 hardware meets certain requirements that are listed in the *Hardware Design Guide for Microsoft Windows 98* and the Plug and Play specifications.

The Windows 98 Logo Program

To help users easily identify PC 98 hardware and software that is optimized for Windows 98, a "Designed for Microsoft Windows 98" logo is available. This new logo replaces the old "Designed for Microsoft Windows 95," "Windows Ready-to-Run," and "Windows Compatible" logos. PCs, peripherals, and software that bear the Windows 98 logo must be qualified and authorized by Microsoft to do so.

Building PC 98 hardware is the first of three essential steps PC hardware vendors must follow to qualify for the Windows 98 logo. The other two steps are passing the Windows 98 Hardware Compatibility Tests (HCTs) and returning a signed logo-license agreement to Microsoft. (See the Windows 98 Logo Program for PC Hardware Vendors Backgrounder for more information.) PC 98 hardware covers all the major busses (ISA, PCI, VLB, USB, and IEEE 1398); connectors (PCMCIA, PC Card32 (Cardbus), and SCSI); ports (LPT, COM, keyboard, and mouse); systems (desktops and mobiles);

motherboard devices; and add-on devices (such as monitors, display adapters, and network adapters, as well as SCSI, IDE, and floppy storage devices, printers, and other LPT devices, fax/modems, and other COM devices).

For More Information

Additional information, including Plug and Play specifications, catalogs, and general information, can be obtained via CompuServe from the libraries in the PLUGPLAY forum or from the *ftp://ftp.microsoft.com/developr/drg/Plug-and-Play* subdirectory.

18

Display Support

MICROSOFT WINDOWS 98 INHERITED STRONG support for video display adapters from Microsoft Windows 95 and now adds strong support for multiple displays. Multiple display support allows you to use more than one monitor and more than one graphics adapter on a single PC at any one time. The ability to have your work displayed on multiple monitors can be extremely beneficial in many areas, including desktop publishing, Web development, video editing, and gaming environments. You'll find out more about multiple display support later in the chapter.

Windows 98 consolidates display properties into a common Display icon in the Control Panel, allowing easy customization of the colors, wallpaper, screen saver, and display adapter settings from a single location. Access to display properties is as easy as clicking Display in the Control Panel or by right-clicking the desktop and selecting Properties to display the appropriate property sheet, which is shown in Figure 18-1 on the next page.

With the addition of the new consolidated display properties, users can now do the following:

- See the appearance of display changes modeled on screen before the changes are applied. This capability has been referred to as *What You See Before You Get It* (WYSBYGI).
- Change background settings to select patterns or wallpaper for the desktop.
- Select a screen saver to be activated after the computer is idle for a specified amount of time.
- Change window appearance properties for displaying text in title bars or menus, such as the font, font style (including bold or italic), and font size.

- Change the display settings, such as the number of colors to use with the display driver, or change the size of the desktop area on the fly (if the display driver and display adapter supports this functionality).

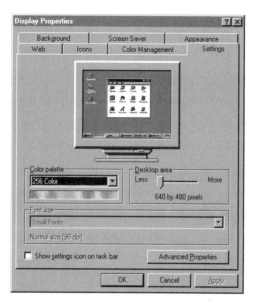

Figure 18-1 *The Display property sheet*

Display Settings

The Display property sheet has been enhanced to support new display driver technology. It contains the following new features:

- **Settings icon on the taskbar** From this icon, you can automatically change resolution and color depth. You can use a check box to turn on the taskbar icon for quick resolution and color depth switching.

- **Advanced Properties button** The Settings tab on the Display property sheet includes an Advanced Properties button that provides access to additional configuration options. (See Figure 18-2.)

- **Resolution and color depth switching without rebooting** This option on the Performance tab located in the Advanced Display property sheet gives you the ability to switch display color depths without rebooting. (You still need to reboot if you change font size.) Many applications and display drivers will work with this automatically, but some might need to be updated. This feature is a great utility for game developers who want to use a specific color depth.

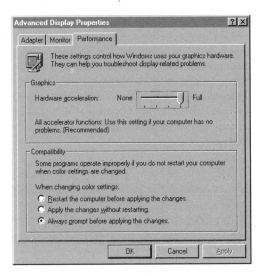

Figure 18-2   *The Advanced Display property sheet*

- **Hardware panning** Hardware panning is now enabled on lower-resolution displays such as VGA-only monitors or laptop LCD panels where the chip set supports it. If the chip set supports this and you have a monitor selected in the Monitor settings that doesn't support resolution greater than 800 by 600, hardware panning will be enabled. Hardware panning is disabled on monitors capable of 1024-by-768 resolution because it isn't normally needed. If hardware panning is enabled and the display device is capable of 800-by-600 resolution, two graphics sliders are available—one for the screen resolution and one for the virtual desktop resolution. The screen slider isn't shown for 640-by-480-only displays because it would be fixed at one setting only.

- **Display Adapter Performance slider** This slider is now accessible from the Performance tab of the Advanced Display property sheet. Users no longer have to go to the System property sheet. This slider is used to diagnose and solve display driver incompatibilities.

- **Multiple display support** If multiple displays are enabled, the Settings tab is replaced with a Monitors tab. This Monitors tab allows you to control relative screen placement by dragging and to set individual adapter settings as described above by selecting the appropriate adapter. (For more details, see the "Multiple Display Support," section later in the chapter.)

TIP

On some chip sets (older S3 chip sets such as 801 and Cirrus Laguna), lower-resolution modes might cause some older monitors to lose sync. This happens because the lower-resolution modes are driving the pixel clock too high. It might help to reset your display settings to VGA settings (640 by 480 by 16 color).

Energy Star Monitor Support

Energy Star is an effort inspired by the Environmental Protection Agency (EPA) to develop computer hardware and peripherals that conserve power when in idle states. This idea is similar to the standby mode commonly implemented in laptop computers to save power.

In a PC system, the video display monitor is typically one of the power-hungry components. Manufacturers of newer display monitors have incorporated energy-saving features into their monitors based on the VESA Display Power Management Signaling (DPMS) specification. Based on signals from a video display adapter, software can place the monitor in standby mode or even turn it off completely, thus reducing the power it uses when inactive.

Users typically display screen savers to prevent burn-in of a monitor image. Windows 98 extends this screen saver mechanism to provide both a time-delay setting that allows the user to put the display monitor in a low-power standby mode and a delay setting for turning the monitor off completely.

For example, a user might want to set options to display a specific screen saver after 5 minutes of inactivity, to set the PC to standby after the screen saver has displayed for 10 minutes, and to turn off the monitor after 15 minutes of standby.

To take advantage of the Energy Star power-consumption mechanisms, users need both a monitor that meets the DPMS/Energy Star specifications and a video card that meets the VESA DPMS specifications. The video display driver must support the extensions necessary to control the monitor device. Several manufacturers are presently shipping monitors designed to support the Energy Star goals.

Multiple Display Support

As mentioned at the beginning of the chapter, multiple display support allows you to connect more than one monitor and more than one graphics adapter to a single PC. For maximum efficiency, the user interface has been modified to recognize a desktop that spans multiple monitors, with no restrictions on size or position. For monitors attached to the same system but showing different images simultaneously, the different displays might have differing resolution and refresh rates in addition to differing display capabilities.

APIs have been added to the Win32 API set to allow any application to take full advantage of multiple monitors. Applications don't need to be modified to work on a PC with multiple monitors, but some application developers might want to take special advantage of this feature by utilizing the new APIs.

These are the most obvious benefits of multiple display support:

- Easy development of Web sites through multiple simultaneous views of content
- Enhanced experiences in multimedia, gaming, and desktop publishing

Enabling Multiple Display Support

The primary requirement for multiple display support is that both of the display adapters must be PCI devices. The Setup instructions vary according to two scenarios, which are described in this section.

This is the first scenario: Your computer has a PCI display adapter on the motherboard and you have additional PCI display adapters to plug in.

If your computer has a built-in PCI display adapter on the motherboard, follow these steps exactly when setting up Windows 98:

1. Run the Windows 98 Setup program with *only* the motherboard video in the computer.
2. After Setup has completed successfully, shut down and add additional display adapters.
3. Boot the computer, and restart when prompted.
4. In the Display property sheet, you should see a Monitors tab replacing the Settings tab.
5. Select the secondary display/monitor combination, and check the box entitled Use This Device As Part Of The Desktop.

Notice that you can independently set the resolution and color depth for each display by clicking the Settings button when the desired monitor/adapter pair is selected. Also keep in mind the following notes about systems with built-in motherboard display adapters:

- The built-in display will usually become your secondary display (or tertiary, and so on, depending on the number of graphics boards you have in the system). The system will disable the onboard video at boot time, and the add-in card will become your primary display. This is a function of the BIOS and isn't under your control.
- It's important that you set up Windows 98 for the first time with only your onboard video in the system. If another adapter is present before you start Windows 98 for the first time, your system probably won't be able to initialize your onboard video properly until you run Setup without the additional graphics boards installed.

- If you follow the instructions and your onboard video doesn't function correctly as the secondary display, it probably never will. It's likely the system is unable to find and read the complete ROM of the adapter to initialize it properly. You'll have to use two add-in adapters for multiple monitor support.

This is the second scenario: You have two separate plug-in PCI display adapters.

If your computer's display adapter is an add-in card (in other words, none of the display adapters in the system are on the motherboard or built-in), you have the option of installing the additional graphics cards *before* setting up Windows 98. The instructions for the first scenario will also work.

General Notes About Multiple Display Support

Virtually any display adapter can function as a primary display. Any PCI display adapter with a Windows 95 or later driver (with the noted exception of motherboard or onboard video) can be a primary display. In order to function as a secondary display, however, the display adapter must be a PCI device supported by Windows 98 as an additional display adapter. Currently, the following display adapter chip sets are supported as additional displays:

- ATI Mach64
- S3 764 (Trio) and 764V+ (765)
- Cirrus 5436, 5446, and 7548
- Imagine 128, series 1 and 2
- S3 ViRGE
- ET6000

Display Driver Support in Windows 98

Windows 98 display drivers provide high functionality and easy setup and configuration. Benefits of the display driver support in Windows 98 include the following:

- Stable and reliable video display adapter drivers
- Support for many video cards
- Support for the ability to change video resolution on the fly without restarting Windows 98 (important for hot-docking and warm-docking support)
- Video driver support for mobile computer docking and undocking, providing the functionality to switch automatically between the video card in the portable computer and the video card in the base unit
- Consistent and unified installation and configuration of display drivers and of display properties, such as colors, wallpaper patterns, and screen savers

- Image color matching support for device-independent color usage, which Microsoft works with Kodak to offer
- Support for hardware and device functionality, such as Energy Star monitors conforming to the VESA DPMS specification, and detection of monitor properties, such as the maximum resolution supported when used with monitors that support the VESA Display Data Channel (DDC) specification

Driver Stability and Reliability

By using a mini-driver architecture for video display adapter drivers, Windows 98 supports the range of products offered by IHVs and provides stable and reliable drivers. Windows 98 provides a universal driver to support device-independent code and functionality normally handled by a monolithic video display driver and supports device-dependent code in a display mini-driver. The mini-driver uses a graphics device-independent bitmap (DIB) engine, providing a high-quality mechanism for manipulating memory bitmaps and delivering high performance.

Because mini-drivers are simpler than monolithic display drivers, they are easier to write and debug. Extensive testing on a less complex driver results in better stability and reliability in the overall operating system.

Furthermore, to ensure broad display adapter–device support in Windows 98, Microsoft developed many display drivers with the cooperation of all major display controller IHVs. Microsoft also worked closely with IHVs to write additional display drivers and assisted IHVs with optimizing their display drivers and performance, tuning them for the speed of information display by the driver.

The use of the mini-driver architecture for display drivers in Windows 98 leverages Microsoft's development experience in writing fast, reliable graphics code with the IHVs' engineering experience, allowing IHVs to concentrate on delivering high-performance hardware accelerated display adapters.

Video Display Performance

Not only are the video display adapters in Windows 98 stable and reliable, but the display drivers show high performance. The mini-driver architecture for display drivers in Windows 98 is centered on a 32-bit DIB engine that features optimized code for fast, robust drawing for high-resolution and frame buffer–based display adapters. The use of a universal driver to provide the device-independent display adapter support, instead of requiring each IHV to redesign this code, allows base functionality to be optimized and thus benefits all mini-driver display drivers.

Windows 98 includes drivers for nearly all popular graphics accelerators.

Robustness

The video drivers provided with Windows 98 are stringently tested to ensure reliability and stability.

Windows 98 includes mechanisms to ensure that bad or incompatible video drivers can't prevent users from accessing the system. If a video driver fails to load or initialize when the system starts, Windows 98 defaults to the generic VGA video driver. Because driver configuration is handled through a graphical interface, users can then at least get into Windows 98 to fix the system.

Image Color Matching Support

Windows 98 provides image color matching (ICM) support for mapping colors displayed on screen and colors generated on output devices to provide consistency.

Microsoft's first implementation of color management support was released in the Windows 95 operating system as ICM 1.0. This version of ICM was designed to address the needs of applications that don't work in colors outside of RGB (such as CMYK) and that want color management to work transparently for the user. ICM 1.0 requires International Color Consortium (ICC) profiles to be installed for all of the color devices on the user's system, and it requires the application to accurately portray colors to support the ICM 1.0 APIs.

After meetings with a number of industry leaders in the color field, Microsoft has designed ICM 2.0. The new APIs are a complete superset of the ICM 1.0 APIs and add a new range of capabilities:

- ICM 1.0 compatible
- ICC compliant
- Scalable: Simple APIs for applications such as Microsoft Office, complete control for applications such as Adobe PhotoShop
- Same APIs for Windows 95 and Microsoft Windows NT operating systems
- Support for Profile management at API and UI level
- Bitmap v5 header support
- Standard Color Space support: sRGB
- Broader color space support: RGB, CMYK, LAB, and others
- Broader support for bitmap formats
- Improved palette handling
- Device driver participation on the Windows 98 and Windows NT operating systems
- Support for multiple Color Management Modules (CMM)
- Faster default CMM that supports all ICC-compliant profiles
- Easier installation of profiles

19

Device Support

MICROSOFT WINDOWS 98, LIKE MICROSOFT Windows 95, features improved support over earlier versions of Windows for hardware devices and peripherals, including disk devices, video display adapters, mice, modems, and printers. This support is provided through a mini-driver architecture, which provides device-independent code in a universal driver written by Microsoft and device-dependent code for direct communication with the printer written by the independent hardware vendors (IHVs). The mini-driver architecture increases the stability of driver support for devices and decreases the amount of time needed for device manufacturers to develop driver support for a new device. Although IHVs can still write monolithic drivers, Microsoft recommends using the mini-driver model because of the advantages it provides.

Device Driver Philosophy

The device driver philosophy of Windows 98 is based on a mini-driver/mini-port layered model that provides the following benefits:

- **Leverages IHVs' hardware knowledge** IHVs know their hardware. They understand the various I/O mechanisms that their hardware supports, and they know the commands that their hardware devices will respond to. The mini-driver model allows IHVs to implement the device-dependent portion of the code used to interact with their hardware devices.

- **Leverages Microsoft's Windows knowledge** Microsoft developed the universal driver code, which is the layer of code that sits between the API layer of device interaction (as used by other Windows components) and the device-dependent code that controls the device. The development team that wrote the Windows components above the API layer understands the mechanisms available from the operating system for interacting with the code. This model leverages Microsoft's knowledge of the operating system with the IHVs' knowledge of their hardware.

- **Increases system stability and reliability** Because the universal driver is the mechanism through which the Windows components communicate with the device, this driver receives a high level of scrutiny and debugging. Through extensive use and testing, the universal driver code is made stable and reliable. Because IHVs no longer have to write the code that would be considered device-independent (as they did when they wrote monolithic drivers), the code required for driver-dependent functions for interacting with the hardware device is minimized. The complexity of the necessary code is reduced, and the driver development process is simplified. A less complex driver is presumably more stable and reliable than a traditional monolithic driver.

- **Increases forward compatibility** Forward compatibility is ensured by allowing the device-independent code to continue to evolve and by encapsulating the device-dependent code in a mini-driver. If an IHV develops new functionality in a hardware device, the mini-driver model also simplifies modifications to the driver. The IHV doesn't need to completely rewrite the entire device driver; the new functionality can simply be added to the mini-driver (if it's even necessary).

- **Supports OEM/IHV innovation** The mini-driver model provides mechanisms for IHVs to add special device functionality support beyond what would be considered the base set of required functionality. The mini-driver model doesn't require IHVs to sacrifice any flexibility to simplify the driver development process.

Windows 98 uses the mini-driver/mini-port layered model for components throughout the operating system, including printers, display devices, modems, communication devices, and mice.

Power Management Improvements

Windows 98 provides the following improvements in power management:

- Support for Advanced Configuration and Power Interface and the OnNow design initiative
- Support for Advanced Power Management 1.2
- Support for IDE drive spin down (Refer to Chapter 16, "Base System Architecture," for a description of this support.)
- Powering down inactive PCMCIA modems

The improvements in power management bring you the following benefits:

- Conserve power
- Allow instant access to your PC
- Enable automated tasks even when the system is powered down

Support for Advanced Configuration and Power Interface and the OnNow Design Initiative

Windows 98 includes built-in support for Advanced Configuration and Power Interface (ACPI). ACPI is an open industry specification proposed by Intel, Microsoft, and Toshiba that defines hardware interfaces that allow for standard power management functionality throughout a PC system.

Working to extend the hardware interfaces defined in ACPI, Microsoft proposed the OnNow design initiative. OnNow is a comprehensive approach to system and device power control. OnNow is a term for a PC that is always on but appears off and responds immediately to user or other requests. The OnNow design initiative relies on the changes defined in the ACPI version 1.0 specification.

OnNow design initiative background

For the PC to become a more integral part of daily life in the office and the home, it must be instantly available to answer the phone, display new e-mail, or browse the Internet. The PC must always be on and ready for use but appear to be off when not in use. The PC hardware and software must be capable of responding immediately to the On button, network or communication events, and other actions. Finally, the PC must be capable of returning to its "off but ready" state automatically and must be able to survive the abuse served up in daily life.

The goal of the OnNow design initiative is to advance the PC platform to a level of usability and robustness that will enable the PC to deliver these new capabilities. For the OnNow design initiative, the term *PC Platform* involves not only the PC hardware but also the software running on the PC. The key to creating the OnNow PC is integration. The hardware, the operating system, and the applications must work well together to ensure that the PC operates as the user expects.

The OnNow PC platform functions in these ways:

- The PC is ready for use immediately when the user presses the On button.
- The PC is perceived to be off when not in use but is still capable of responding to wake-up events. A device receiving input, such as a phone ringing or software that has requested the PC to wake up at some predetermined time, might trigger wake-up events.

- Software adjusts its behavior when the PC's power state changes. The operating system and applications work together intelligently to operate the PC in a manner that delivers the kind of power management the user currently needs. For example, applications won't inadvertently keep the PC busy unnecessarily and instead will participate in shutting down the PC to conserve energy and reduce noise.

- All devices have a part in the device power management scheme, whether they were originally installed on the PC or later added by the user. Any new device can have its power state changed as system use dictates.

Support for Advanced Power Management 1.2

Windows 98 supports enhancements made available through Advanced Power Management (APM) 1.2, including multiple batteries (displaying power information for two batteries at the same time) and modem wake-on-ring.

Powering Down Inactive PCMCIA Modems

For convenience, many laptop users leave their PC Card modems in their laptops. This habit can cause shorter battery life because the modem is still receiving power even though it isn't being used. Windows 98 turns off PC Card modems when they aren't in use. This feature provides a noticeable gain in battery life, not only while the computer is running but also when it's suspended.

Disk Device Support

Windows 98 features a block I/O subsystem that provides broad 32-bit disk device support as well as improved disk I/O performance. In addition, disk mini-port device drivers written for use with Windows 98 are compatible with Microsoft Windows NT, and vice versa.

Windows 98 also provides support in the following areas:

- **Support for large media using logical block addressing** Extensions to the Int 13h disk controller support are provided in the protected-mode disk handler drivers to support disks with cylinder numbers greater than 1024.

- **Better support for removable media** Windows 98 provides better support for removable media devices and allows the system to lock or unlock the device to prevent the media from being removed prematurely. Windows 98 also provides an eject mechanism for devices that support it, which means that users can use software control to eject media from a device—for example, new floppy drives that support software-based media ejection.

Win32 Driver Model

The Win32 Drive Model reduces complexity by having one driver for both Windows 98 and Windows NT and simplifies new driver development. You can find more information on this topic in Chapter 16, "Base System Architecture."

New Device Drivers

The following sections describe device drivers new to or updated in Windows 98.

Display

These are DirectX 3 and DirectX 5 drivers with multiple display support enabled. New for Windows 98 are ET6000, 3Dfx VooDoo, and 3Dlabs (not yet available). Updated for Windows 98 are ati3d, chips, cirrus, cirruslg, cirrusmm, i128, mach64, mgamm, rendition, s3mm, and s3v.

> **NOTE**
> The ATI Rage and Rage II chips will be supported in drivers in the release version of Windows 98. In the meantime, ATI has provided, as a courtesy to Microsoft's beta testers, a version of its driver that appears to work on Windows 98. It's located in the \betaonly\atirage directory. You'll have to copy the VDD.VXD file to your \windows\system directory manually to use this driver.

Audio

The Windows Sound System driver from DirectX 3 has been updated for DirectX 5.

Modems

Approximately 300 new modems are supported, bringing Windows 98 up to compatibility with Windows NT 4.0. Microsoft is now adding the current crop of new modem drivers.

Disk drives

The disk drives described below are new or updated in Windows 98.

Floppy disk driver

Windows 98 includes an all new, from scratch HSFLOP.PDR floppy disk driver. This new driver offers significantly enhanced performance on many machines. It also works on some portable machines that used to require custom HSFLOP.PDR files. This new driver works on all known hardware.

> **NOTE**
> The current version will hit the floppy disk on boot; this is a diagnostic test that will be removed before Windows 98 is released.

LS 120 support

The real-mode MS-DOS kernel, the protect-mode file system components, and the various formatting utilities have been updated to support the LS-120 (120 MB) floppies built into some newer PCs.

IDE disk driver

This updated IDE hard-disk driver includes support for the following hardware:

- Bus mastering chipsets such as Intel Triton and Opti Viper M
- SMART (Self-Monitoring Analysis and Reporting Technology), a hard-drive fault prediction system developed by Compaq and several hard-drive vendors
- IDE Tape backup units
- ATAPI-CD Changers (with up to seven CD slots), including the Sanyo/Torisan 3CD changer

Bus mastering

Bus mastering should be enabled only for specific hard-drive models that are certified by their manufacturers to work properly with a Windows bus master driver. The drives in question must indicate that they support Direct Memory Access (DMA) in the drive ID data (both in ATA and in ATAPI drives).

CAUTION

During joint Intel and Microsoft testing, some hard drives that were originally designed to support this DMA functionality were found to contain firmware bugs that can cause data corruption. Only OEMs should enable the DMA feature when they ship compatible hard-disk drives. Users should *not* enable the DMA feature on their PCs if their PC manufacturer did not enable it originally.

To determine whether bus mastering is available, take these steps:

1. Open to the Control Panel.
2. Open the System icon.
3. Click the Device Manager tab.
4. Select the individual Disk Drive (not drive controller), and click Properties.

If a check box for DMA shows up under Int 13 Unit in the Options box on the Settings tab, you can try the Bus Master DMA transfers. If no check box appears, your motherboard chip set doesn't support a compatible bus master interface.

NOTE

If the check box isn't checked after your system reboots, your hard drive probably doesn't support bus mastering and it's been automatically disabled again.

CD-ROM changers

CD-ROM changer support is now available for ATAPI-CD changer compliant CD-ROM drives with up to seven CD slots. CD-ROM devices with more than seven slots are generally considered "CD jukeboxes" and are not supported with these drivers. This driver set also includes support for the Sanyo/Torisan 3CD changer.

CD disk driver

CDFS.VXD and CDVSD.VXD have been updated:

- ISO-9660 format CDs greater than 4 GB are now supported.
- CDFS read-ahead behavior is now more intelligent and better supports slower hardware and applications that access the CD randomly.
- CDI disks are now supported (with appropriate application software).

NOTE

At present, Enhanced Music CD (CD+) works properly only on the first assigned drive letter. CD+ audio won't be recognized on CD+ discs in slots not assigned to the first drive letter. For example, on a system that has slots assigned to D:, E:, F:, and G: drives, CD+ audio will play only on drive D:. This problem does not affect standard audio CDs.

Monitors

Microsoft has added approximately 175 new monitors to the built-in list.

Human input (keyboard, joystick, mouse, gamepad)

Look for new drivers built in for these devices in the final release.

Still image capture

Look for new drivers built in for these devices in the final release.

Video capture

Look for new drivers built in for these devices in the final release.

Support for IDE Drives and Controllers

Windows 98 provides support for IDE drive configurations, including these:

- **Support for large IDE disk drives** Some new IDE drives support a logical block addressing scheme that allows them to exceed the 0.5-GB (528-MB) size limitation. Support for IDE disk drives as large as 137 GB is provided by the Windows 98 operating system. Windows 98 provides this support in a protected-mode disk driver.

- **Support for an alternate IDE controller** Windows 98 allows the use of two IDE controllers in a PC or the combination of an IDE controller in a laptop and an alternate controller in a laptop docking station—available, for example, in some Compaq laptop/docking station combination products. Windows 98 provides this support in a protected-mode disk driver.

- **Support for IDE-based CD-ROM drives** The majority of disk devices in PCs use an IDE-based hard-disk controller. Adding a CD-ROM drive typically requires adding an additional controller card to provide either SCSI or a proprietary interface for connecting to the CD-ROM drive. Inexpensive CD-ROM drives that connect to IDE-compatible disk controllers are widely available. Windows 98 recognizes and supports these devices.

Support for SCSI Devices and Controllers

Windows 98 also supports SCSI disk devices:

- **Broad support for popular SCSI controllers** Windows 98 includes 32-bit disk device drivers for popular SCSI controllers from manufacturers such as Adaptec, Future Domain, Trantor, and UltraStor, providing great support right out of the box.

- **Compatibility with Windows NT mini-port drivers** Windows 98 supports the use of Windows NT mini-port SCSI drivers without modification or recompiling. Compatibility with Windows NT–based mini-port drivers ensures broad device support for disk devices under Windows 98 while simplifying driver development efforts for hardware manufacturers.

- **ASPI/CAM compatibility for MS-DOS–based applications and drivers** Windows 98 provides support for the Advanced SCSI Programming Interface (ASPI) and Common Access Method (CAM), which allow application and driver developers to submit I/O requests to SCSI devices. As a result, MS-DOS–based applications and drivers that use the ASPI or CAM specification work properly under Windows 98.

- **16-bit and 32-bit ASPI for Windows-based clients and applications** In addition to MS-DOS–based compatibility with ASPI, Windows 98 includes 16-bit and 32-bit drivers to support Windows-based ASPI clients and applications.

Support for ESDI Controllers

In addition to supporting IDE and SCSI disk devices, Windows 98 provides 32-bit disk driver support for ESDI controllers.

The High-Speed Floppy Disk Driver

As with hard-disk controller support, Windows 98 provides protected-mode support for communicating with floppy disk controllers. Windows 98 provides Int 13h hard-disk controller support as 32-bit device drivers, resulting in improved performance, stability, and robustness of the system. Windows 98 provides floppy disk controller support as a 32-bit device driver, resulting in high performance for file I/O to floppy disk drives plus high system reliability.

Users can format a disk or copy files to and from a disk while performing other tasks.

Built-In Support for Infrared Data Association

Windows 98 includes support for the Infrared Data Association (IrDA) standard for wireless connectivity. IrDA support enables Windows 98 users to connect easily to peripheral devices or other Windows 98–based PCs without using connecting cables. This driver set provides infrared-equipped laptop or desktop computers with the capability of networking, transferring files, and printing wirelessly with other IrDA-compatible infrared devices. IrDA connectivity is designed to take advantage of the mobile computing features already built into Windows 98.

The IrDA driver in Windows 98 (IrDA 2.0) includes a new feature, named IrLan Access Point Mode, that enables a computer with an IrDA adapter to attach to a local area network (LAN) through an access point device that acts as the network adapter for the computer. See Chapter 12, "Mobile Computing Services," for more on IrDA.

Mouse and Pointing Device Support

As with other device drivers, the mini-driver architecture of Windows 98 simplifies mouse driver development and improves virtualization in a protected-mode mouse driver to better support MS-DOS–based applications in the Windows environment.

Mouse support in Windows 98 yields the following benefits:

- Smooth, reliable input support through the use of protected-mode drivers.
- Support for numerous devices, which makes it easier for IHVs to write drivers, and support for a mini-driver architecture model.
- Support for Plug and Play makes mouse and pointing devices easy to install and use.
- You can implement mouse driver functionality in a single driver, and you won't need to use MS-DOS–based mouse drivers, which will increase robust-ness and save conventional memory.
- Support for connecting a mouse *after* Windows 98 has started means that mobile computer users who forget to connect a mouse before turning on their computer can connect a mouse without restarting the computer.

Windows Mouse Driver Features

Windows 98 provides mouse support as a protected-mode virtual device driver. Virtualization of mouse interrupt services allows protected-mode Windows-based mouse drivers to provide mouse support for Windows-based applications, for MS-DOS–based applications running in a window, and for MS-DOS–based applications running in full-screen mode. The features result in a zero conventional memory footprint for mouse support in the Windows 98 environment.

In addition to these mouse services, Windows 98 provides robust device support to allow the use of serial ports COM1 through COM4 for connecting a mouse or other pointing device.

Mouse Control Panel

Windows 98 consolidates mouse configuration and customization support into a single Control Panel icon and uses a tabbed property sheet, shown in Figure 19-1, to provide easy access to all the possible settings. Such settings control the behavior of the mouse buttons, the look of the mouse pointer, and the behavior of the wheel on the IntelliMouse.

Figure 19-1   *The IntelliMouse mouse property sheet*

Built-In Support for Microsoft IntelliMouse

The Microsoft IntelliMouse, with the wheel on top, allows users to concentrate on their document or spreadsheet rather than moving to icons or scroll bars to navigate the program. The following support features are built into IntelliMouse for applications that can take advantage of its design:

- Just rotating the wheel causes text to scroll several lines (default 3) per wheel detent.

- In Microsoft Office 97, rotating the wheel while holding down the Ctrl key zooms the monitor image in or out (causing the document to be displayed larger or smaller).

- The wheel itself acts as a middle mouse button if pressed.

- By pressing the wheel button in a wheel-aware application (Office 97 and Microsoft Internet Explorer, for example), you get to "panning mode." This mode is indicated by the mouse cursor changing to a special panning cursor. While panning mode is active, just dragging the mouse forward or backward will cause the document to auto-scroll. The speed at which the document scrolls is determined by how far the mouse is dragged away from the position where panning mode was enabled. To exit panning mode, simply press any mouse button.

20

International Language Support

WITH THE GROWTH OF THE WORLDWIDE PC market, Microsoft Windows and Windows-based applications have made PCs easier to use around the globe. The fact that Windows and Windows-based applications are sold and used worldwide poses some unique problems for Microsoft as an operating system vendor and for ISVs as application developers.

When a new software application or operating system intended for a world market is developed, efforts must be made to localize the software to the countries and written languages in which it will be used. In many cases, localization is a simple matter of translating the names of menus, menu items, and strings displayed by the software into the language used in the locale. However, as the features and functionality of a software product grow, so does the complexity required to tailor the application to characteristics of the native country. Since the start of the design work for the Microsoft Windows NT operating system, Microsoft has been adding to the level of support for international languages and cultural conventions in the 32-bit editions of the Windows family of operating systems.

Major Features Supporting International Use of Windows 98

Built-in support in Microsoft Windows 98 for international use of the Windows operating system provides benefits for users and software developers alike. Major features supporting the global utility of Windows are summarized in the following two lists, benefits to users being the first.

- **Easy switching from one language to another, even within one document** Windows 98 makes the use of multiple language fonts and character sets as well as the task of switching among the different keyboard layouts required to support them easy.

  Included in the CD-ROM version of Windows 98 (all languages) is an option that lets any application *write text* in not only western European but also in all eastern European languages. (Note that you can only *write text* in these languages. If you need to run, for example, a Russian version of Microsoft Excel, you will need either the Russian or the Pan European Edition of Windows 98.) To install multilingual support in Windows 98, you either choose it when you set up Windows 98 or install it later through the Control Panel (by choosing Multilanguage Support on the Windows Setup tab of the Add/Remove Programs property sheet).

  With Windows 98, users can easily switch among all available languages and corresponding keyboard layouts configured on their system by using the Left Alt+Shift key combination or by clicking on the language indicator on the taskbar, making the creation and integration of information in a multilingual document easy.

- **Font substitution** When a user switches among different languages, Windows 98 substitutes matching fonts for each new language if the font used to create the document in its original language isn't available. As a result, users can read and use the text for a similar character set, even if they don't have the font in which the information was first created.

- **Correct sorting and formatting rules** Different locales and cultures have different rules for interpreting information. For example, cultures use different sequence algorithms for sorting information, use different comparison algorithms for finding or searching for information, and use different formats for specifying time and date information. Win32-based applications that use the National Language Support (NLS) APIs allow users to easily exchange information on a global basis, while preserving the integrity of the information.

The benefits for developers include the following:

- **Easy addition of international language support to applications** Developers can use the Win32 NLS APIs for sorting, searching, and manipulating information in a locale-independent way. NLS services in Windows 98 ensure that information is handled correctly for the given culture or locale. The correct national format is automatically supplied based on the international settings specified by the user in the Control Panel. For example, to obtain the current date format information to match the current locale, the application calls an NLS API and the system returns the correct format. Likewise, to sort information in the proper sequence in French, Norwegian, or Spanish, the application calls a corresponding culture-independent NLS API.

- **Automatic switching of fonts and keyboard layouts** Windows 98 provides services that application developers can use to ensure that as users move through a multilingual document the correct fonts and keyboard layouts are used. For users who create or edit multilingual document content—for example, translators—a Win32-based application using the international services in Windows 98 automatically activates the correct fonts and corresponding keyboard layouts for the edit point in the text. This feature allows easy editing of information contained within multilingual documents.

- **Preservation of language-specific attributes on the Clipboard** Windows 98 provides additional services for application developers so that information can be passed through the Clipboard for easy exchanges of information between internationally aware applications while preserving all language-formatting characteristics.

- **Switching of languages by multilingual-aware applications** Windows 98 provides services that application developers can use to automatically switch the language that the system uses to match attributes in a document. For example, as a user scrolls through a multilingual document, the application can automatically switch the system language to match the format of the information contained within the document.

- **Storage of international language information in RTF format** Extensions have been provided to the Rich Text Format (RTF) specification to support saving language-relevant information in RTF from a multilingual-aware application.

The Localization of Windows 98

As a result of the success of Microsoft Windows around the world, Windows and Windows-based applications have been localized into many different languages. To support a global market, Microsoft plans to localize Windows 98 into at least 29 different language versions, including German, French, Spanish, Swedish, Dutch, Italian, Pan European Edition (an English version that supports running eastern European applications), Norwegian, Danish, Finnish, Portuguese (Brazilian and Iberian), Japanese, Chinese, Korean, Russian, Czech, Polish, Hungarian, Turkish, Greek, Arabic, Basque, Hebrew, Thai, and Catalan (as well as several variations of these languages). The localized versions of Windows 98 are being released on a planned development schedule that doesn't exceed 120 days following the release of the English version—exceptions being Arabic and Hebrew, which will release about 180 days after the English version.

International Language Issues

Localization is only a small part of the effort that goes into ensuring that an operating system can be used effectively in a worldwide environment. A worldwide operating system must also provide services to support the use of international applications and to support the global market by making the application developer's job easier. Following are some of the language issues that international users and application developers face:

- **From the user's perspective** Some users need to include more than one language in a document. For example, they might be translating from English into Russian, or they might be writing a product instruction manual in many different languages. When using more than one language, users must deal with a series of obstacles. For example, they might need repeatedly to switch from one keyboard layout to another in order to continue writing in a different language. When using a database, users face the problem of sorting the information in the correct order for a given language.

- **From the developer's perspective** When localizing a product into different languages, developers are faced with several questions, such as the following: "What is the correct sorting order for French?" "How is a date represented in German?" "Are the characters Å, Ä, and Ö used in Swedish?" "If a document contains text in more than one language, is there some way for the software to know which part of the document is in which language?" "Can information in a multilingual document be passed to another application via the Clipboard?" Many developers try to address these issues in their applications and fall short, creating problems for the users, their support organization, and their own development teams.

Before the mainstream Windows platform offered international language support as an operating system service, many application vendors had hard-coded global characteristics into their applications. Hard coding allows their applications to be used in a given locale but prevents the applications from being used easily in a different cultural environment. As a result, users have needed to depend on application developers to provide a version of the application that specifically matches the attributes of their language and culture.

In Windows 98, Microsoft offers international language support at the operating system and API level. This support provides functionality for using software and exchanging documents around the world, despite regional differences in conventions for presenting data. (See more about this in the section "Multilingual Content Support," later in this chapter.) Providing international language support services in

Windows 98 makes it easy for application developers to solve international language issues related to presenting or manipulating information in their applications. The next few paragraphs describe some of these issues.

Date and Time Formats

Date and time information needs to be represented in different formats, depending on the custom where the information is being used. For example, date information presented in American English places the day between the month and year, as in "March 9, 1994," whereas a New Zealander customarily represents the same date as "9 March 1994."

Sorting and Searching

Other international language issues are much more complex than the matter of representing date and time information in the correct format. Sorting and searching algorithms in applications must correspond to the proper language rules for the locale in which the information is being used and manipulated. The following examples illustrate the subtle differences in language rules:

- In French, diacritics are sorted from right to left instead of from left to right, as in English.

- In Norwegian, some extended characters (diacritically marked characters) follow the Z character in the alphabet because they are considered unique characters rather than ordinary characters merely equipped with the extra baggage of a diacritic.

- In a Spanish alphabet, CH is a unique character between C and D, and Ñ is a unique character between N and O.

As a further example, if a database in Swedish were sorted with an English-language sort algorithm, the names would be sorted as shown in the left column of this table:

How Are Names Sorted?

English Sorting	Correct Swedish Sorting
Andersson	Andersson
Åkesson	Karlsson
Ärlingmark	Magnusson
Karlsson	Turesson
Magnusson	Åkesson
Turesson	Ärlingmark

The English-language system treats both the Å and Ä as an A and therefore sorts them after A at the top of the list. However, in the correct Swedish sort order, the Å and Ä are sorted after Z because they are separate vowels that occur at the very end of the Swedish alphabet. Anyone with a comprehensive knowledge of Swedish would be confused to find "Ärlingmark" near the beginning, instead of at the end, of a list of names.

Multilingual Content Support

Windows 98 resolves many problems related to international language issues by integrating multilingual content support in the core of the operating system. Windows 98 also offers national language support to application developers as a series of APIs that are part of the Win32 API set.

Multilingual content support is the ability to display and edit text of various languages and scripts in a single document. Multilingual content support is a core feature of Windows 98.

Multilingual content support in an application provides the following two major benefits:

- Users can create and edit document content in multiple languages and scripts and exchange these documents with users of other language systems. This feature is important within the European Union, for example, where Greek-based and Latin-based languages must coexist in documents.

- An application that supports multilingual content supports the native content of any market into which it is sold.

Easy Switching Among Languages and Keyboards

Windows 98 allows users to add support for multiple keyboard layouts to match different international conventions. In the Control Panel, the Keyboard icon provides the ability to configure the system to support the preferred keyboard layouts, as shown in Figure 20-1.

In Windows 98, switching keyboard layouts is easy. Figure 20-2 shows a sample word processing document that illustrates the ability to integrate text by using the Tahoma font in different languages within the same document. The language identifier in the status area of the taskbar allows users to easily switch the system language among the available language options. A Windows 98 application that uses NLS APIs would incorporate the ability to switch the preferred language directly on the toolbar of the application.

Figure 20-1 *The Keyboard property sheet, showing international layout support*

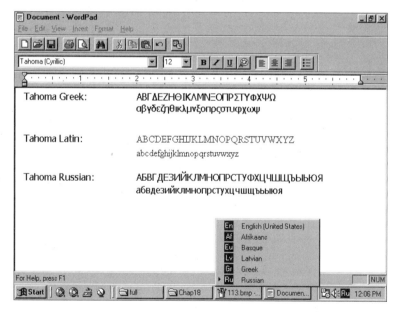

Figure 20-2 *Switching among different languages to create a multilingual document*

Multilingual Extensions to the Font Common Dialog Box

The Font common dialog box includes a list box showing the character set scripts supported by a particular font. This mechanism ensures the correct representation of fonts for a given language.

Figure 20-3 shows the Font common dialog box, illustrating the integration of font script selection options. The Script drop-down list shows the script names for each of the character sets covered by the font selected in the Font list. The Sample box displays a font sample that is dependent on the script selected, as well as the other font attributes. The sample preview string, which is specific to the selected character set, shows what each of the different scripts looks like.

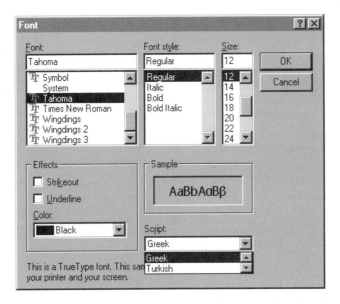

Figure 20-3 *The Font common dialog box, showing the Script drop-down list*

Multilingual-aware applications can support multilingual font selection by allowing users to select fonts via the Font common dialog box and by recognizing the extensions to the ChooseFont data structures in Windows 98. Even Windows-based applications—which in not having been originally designed for Windows 98 support formatted text but not multilingual messages—can gain some basic level of support for multilingual content. If an application uses the Font common dialog box, it benefits from the enhancements, allowing users to select from the full range of character sets and fonts configured in the system. As long as the application saves the complete logical font data structure representation for fonts, an existing Windows-based application can get by without being aware that the font selected by the user includes a possible change of character set. (Applications generally do save this data when saving text in their native format, but not all save this data when writing to interchange formats, such as RTF.)

Multilingual Support for Exchanging Information via the Clipboard

A good multilingual-aware application can exchange multilingual content with other aware applications and can exchange appropriate flat text with unaware applications within the limitations of the ASCII text formats. Windows 98 provides special support in the data exchange APIs to pass language information along with the rich text data.

The Win32 National Language Support APIs

When users install Windows 98 on a freshly formatted hard disk, they specify a locale preference. Installing Windows 98 over Windows 95 preserves the locale preferences set in Windows 95. (This preference can be changed later via the Control Panel.) The Win32 NLS APIs can use either this default locale setting or a specific locale setting. Using the Win32 NLS APIs offers the following benefits to developers:

- Developers can easily integrate international language support into their Win32-based applications. These APIs, which are supported on both the Windows 98 and Windows NT platforms (with limited support available for Win32-based applications under Microsoft Windows 3.1), allow applications to correctly retrieve regional and language settings, format date and time, sort lists according to cultural rules, compare and map strings, and determine character type information. Application developers in the U.S. can be sure that the sorting order and date formats that Microsoft provides with the operating system are correct, so all they have to do to sort or display information is use the appropriate Win32 NLS APIs.

- They can more easily develop applications for new global markets. Using this API set lowers development costs by eliminating the need for proprietary sorting methods, parsing the WIN.INI file or Registry, and locale-specific coding.

Perhaps more important for developers, the API set provides a mechanism for accurate and consistent behavior on all 32-bit Windows platforms.

Users benefit because the API set ensures that information is handled and displayed correctly for a given locale-specific format. In addition, users don't have to worry about whether their international text is being sorted properly.

21

Robustness

MICROSOFT WINDOWS 98 ROBUSTNESS provides great support for running MS-DOS–based, Win16-based, and Win32-based applications and provides a high level of system protection from errant applications.

Microsoft Windows 3.1 provided a number of mechanisms to support a more robust and stable environment than Windows 3.0, including the following:

- **Better resource cleanup** When an MS-DOS–based or Windows-based application crashed, users could continue running in a way that allowed them to save their work.
- **Local reboot** Users could shut down an application that hung.
- **Parameter validation for API calls** The system could catch many common application errors and fail the API call rather than allow bad data to be passed to an API.

Just as the improvements in Windows 3.1 provided a more robust and stable environment than Windows 3.0, the improvements in Microsoft Windows 95 provided an even better environment.

Windows 98 is built on the same code base as Windows 95. Its goal is to provide the same level of compatibility as Windows 95 while improving hardware support, system stability, and robustness; reducing support and administration costs; and updating Internet applications and other utilities. A limited set of NT Kernel services for the Win32 Driver Model (WDM) have been added, but the same real-mode MS-DOS components, Windows 95 Kernel, USER, GDI, and VMM are still available for existing application compatibility. Removing or redesigning these components would introduce significant compatibility and performance problems. By continuing to use these while adding services common to both Microsoft Windows NT and Windows 98, you get support for the best of both worlds.

In the descriptions of robustness in the rest of this chapter, the features are the same in Windows 98 as they are in Windows 95. Features carried forward from Windows 95 are described as Windows 98 features.

Features Supporting Robustness in Windows 98

Features resulting in a robust operating system environment in Windows 98 include the following:

- Better local reboot
- Virtual device driver thread cleanup when a process ends
- Per-thread state tracking
- Virtual device driver parameter validation

Local Reboot

The capability enabling a user to end an application or VM that hangs is called a *local reboot*. Windows 98 local reboot support provides a means to end an MS-DOS–based application running in a VM, a Win16-based application, or a Win32-based application without bringing down the entire system. Moreover, the process of cleaning up the system after a local reboot is complete. (This process is described later in this chapter.)

When a user requests a local reboot in Windows 98, the system displays the Close Program dialog box, which identifies the tasks that are running and the state that the system perceives each one to be in, as shown in Figure 21-1. This level of detail affords the user flexibility and control over the local reboot.

Applications are identified as "not responding" when they haven't checked the message queue for a period of time. Although some applications don't check the message queue while performing computationally intensive operations, well-behaved applications check the message queue frequently. In Windows 98, as in Windows 95 and Windows 3.1, Win16-based applications must check the message queue to relinquish control to other running tasks.

Figure 21-1 *The Close Program dialog box*

Virtual Device Driver Thread Cleanup

Local reboot support is also aided by VxD thread cleanup when a given process ends. Windows 98 supports system cleanup by providing each system VxD with the ability to track the resources it allocates on a per-thread basis. Because most computer system functionality and support is handled in Windows 98 by VxDs rather than by real-mode code or BIOS routines, Windows 98 can recover from errors or situations that previously required that the computer be rebooted.

When Windows 98 ends a given thread (because the user exited the application, a local reboot was requested, or the application ended abnormally), each VxD receives notification that the thread is ended. This notification allows the VxD to safely cancel any operations it is waiting to finish and frees any resources that the VxD previously allocated for the thread or application. Because the system tracks each VM, Win16-based application, and Win32 thread as a separate per-thread instance, the system can clean up properly at each of these levels without affecting the integrity of the system.

Per-Thread State Tracking

As just mentioned, for system cleanup, Windows 98 tracks resources on a per-thread basis by system VxDs. Resources such as memory blocks, memory handles, graphics objects, and other system items are allocated and also tracked by system components on a per-thread basis. Tracking these resources on a per-thread basis allows the system to clean up safely when a given thread ends, either normally—at the user's request—or abnormally. Resources are identified and tracked by both a thread ID and the major Windows version number that's stored in the EXE header of the application.

For a description of how the thread ID and the Windows version number are used to facilitate cleanup of the system and recovery of allocated resources for Win16-based and Win32-based applications, see the robustness sections for these applications later in this chapter.

Virtual Device Driver Parameter Validation

Virtual device drivers are an integral part of the Windows 98 operating system and have an important role because many operating system components are implemented as VxDs. To provide a stable and reliable operating system, Windows 98 provides support for parameter validation of virtual device drivers. The debug version of Windows 98 system files provided as part of the Windows 98 SDK and Windows 98 DDK can be used by VxD developers to debug their VxDs during the course of development, ensuring that their VxDs are stable and robust.

In addition to systemwide robustness, Windows 98 provides robustness for running MS-DOS–based, Win16-based, and Win32-based applications, which ensures that Windows 98 is a stable and reliable environment.

Robustness for MS-DOS–Based Applications

Several improvements that provide great robustness for running MS-DOS–based applications are described in the next two sections.

Virtual Machine Protection Improvements

Each MS-DOS–based application runs in a separate VM and is configured by default to execute preemptively and run in the background when another application is active. Each VM is protected from other tasks running in the system, so an errant Win16-based or Win32-based application can't crash a running MS-DOS–based application, and vice versa.

Windows 98 provides memory protection for running MS-DOS–based applications by preventing the applications from overwriting the MS-DOS system area in real mode. If users want the highest level of system protection, they can configure their MS-DOS–based applications to run with general memory protection enabled. (This mode isn't enabled by default because of the overhead required to validate memory access requests.) In addition, parameter validation of INT 21H operations on pointers increases the robustness of the system.

Better Cleanup When a Virtual Machine Ends

When a VM ends in Windows 98—either normally, because the user exited the application or VM or requested a local reboot, or abnormally, because the application hung—the system frees all resources allocated to the VM. These resources include not only those allocated and maintained by the system VxDs but also those allocated for the VM by the Virtual Machine Manager, including any DPMI and XMS memory that the VM requested.

Robustness for Win16-Based Applications

Windows 98 provides robust support for Win16-based applications as well as compatibility with existing Windows-based applications, while keeping memory requirements low. The next two sections describe support for Win16-based applications running under Windows 98.

Per-Thread State Tracking

For resource tracking under Windows 98, each Win16-based application runs as a separate thread in the Win16 address space. When a Win16-based application ends, Windows 98 doesn't immediately release the resources allocated to the application but holds them until the last Win16-based application has ended. (Windows 98 determines that no more Win16-based applications are running by associating the Windows version number of the application with the thread ID for the running process.) When the last Win16-based application has ended and it is safe to free all resources allocated to Win16-based applications, Windows 98 begins releasing the resources.

Parameter Validation for Win16 APIs

Windows 98 provides parameter validations for all Win16-based APIs and checks incoming data to API functions to ensure that the data is valid. For example, functions that reference memory are checked for NULL pointers, and functions that operate on data within a range of values are checked to ensure that the data is within the proper range. If invalid data is found, an appropriate error number is returned to the application and it's then up to the application to catch the error condition and handle it accordingly.

The Windows 98 SDK provides debug system components to help software developers debug their applications. The debug components provide extensive error reporting for parameter validation to assist developers in tracking common problems related to invalid parameters during the course of development.

Robustness for Win32-Based Applications

Although robustness for running MS-DOS–based and Win16-based applications is provided by Windows 98, even greater support for robustness is available for running Win32-based applications. Win32-based applications also benefit from preemptive multitasking, a linear (rather than segmented) address space, and support for a feature-rich API set.

Robustness support for Win32-based applications includes the following:

- A private address space for each running Win32-based application, segregating and protecting one application from others that are running concurrently
- Win32 APIs that support parameter validation and provide a stable and reliable environment
- Resource tracking by thread and the immediate freeing of resources when the thread ends
- Separate message queues for each running Win32-based application, ensuring that a hung Win32-based application doesn't suspend the entire system

A Private Address Space for Each Win32-Based Application

Each Win32-based application runs in its own private address space so that its resources are protected at the system level from other applications running in the system. This strategy also prevents other applications from inadvertently overwriting the memory area of a given Win32-based application and prevents that Win32-based application from inadvertently overwriting the memory area of another application or of the system as a whole.

Parameter Validation for Win32 APIs

As it does for Win16-based applications, Windows 98 provides parameter validation for Win32 APIs used by Win32-based applications. The Windows 98 SDK helps software developers debug errors resulting from attempts to pass invalid parameters to Windows APIs. For additional information about parameter validation for Win16 APIs, see the description of robustness for Win16-based applications presented earlier in this chapter.

Per-Thread Resource Tracking

Windows 98 tracks the resources allocated to Win32-based applications by thread. Unlike resources allocated to Win16-based applications, resources allocated to Win32-based applications are automatically released when a thread ends processing. This immediate freeing of system resources ensures that the resources are available for use by other running tasks.

Resources are cleaned up properly when threads end execution, either on their own—for example, if the application developer inadvertently failed to free allocated resources—or when the user requests a local reboot that ends a given Win32-based application thread or process. Win32-based applications free up their allocated resources immediately when a separate thread or the application itself ends.

Separate Message Queues for Win32-Based Applications

The Windows environment performs tasks based on the receipt of messages sent by system components. Each message is generated based on an action, or *event,* that occurs on the system. For example, when a user presses a key on the keyboard and releases it or moves the mouse, a message is generated by the system and passed to the active application to inform it of the event that occurred. Windows-based applications call specific Windows API functions to extract event messages from message queues and perform operations on the messages—for example, accept an incoming character typed on the keyboard, or move the mouse cursor to another place on the screen.

Windows 98 provides separate message queues for each running Win32-based application. (Each thread in a Win32-based application can have its own message queue.) As shown in Figure 21-2, the system takes messages from the input message queue and passes them to the appropriate Win32-based application or to the Win16 Subsystem if the message is destined for a Win16-based application. If a Win32-based application hangs and no longer accepts and processes its incoming messages, other running Win16 and Win32-based applications aren't affected.

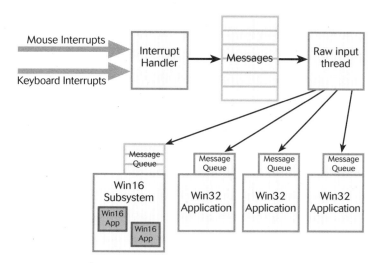

Figure 21-2 *Win32-based applications use separate message queues for increased robustness*

If a Win32-based application ends or the user requests a local reboot for a Win32-based application, having separate message queues improves the robustness of the operating system by making it easier to clean up and free the system resources used by the application. It also provides greater reliability and recoverability if an application hangs.

Local Reboot Effectiveness

Because of robustness for Win32-based applications, including the use of a private address space, separate message queues, and resource tracking by thread, users should be able to request a local reboot to end almost any ill-behaved Win32-based application without affecting the integrity of the Windows system or other running applications.

When Windows 98 ends a Win32-based application, its resources are immediately deallocated and cleaned up by the system. Because Win32-based applications run in their individually allocated environments, this method is even more robust than the method for reallocation of Win16-based application resources. For more details on the robustness of Win16-based applications, see the appropriate section earlier in this chapter.

Structured Exception Handling

An *exception* is an event that occurs during the execution of a program and requires the execution of software outside the normal flow of control. Hardware exceptions can result from the execution of certain instruction sequences, such as division by zero or an attempt to access an invalid memory address. A software routine can also explicitly initiate an exception.

The Win32 API supports a mechanism called *structured exception handling* for handling hardware-generated and software-generated exceptions. Structured exception handling gives programmers complete control over the handling of exceptions. The Win32 API also supports termination handling, which enables programmers to ensure that whenever a guarded body of code is executed, a specific block of termination code is also executed. The termination code is executed regardless of how the flow of control leaves the guarded body. For example, a termination handler can guarantee that cleanup tasks are performed even if an exception or some other error occurs while the guarded body of code is being executed. Structured exception and termination handling is an integral part of the Win32 system, and it enables a very robust implementation of system software.

Windows 98 provides structured exception and termination handling for Win32-based applications. By using this functionality, applications can identify and rectify error conditions that might occur outside their realm of control, providing a robust computing environment.

22

Systems Management

MICROSOFT WINDOWS 98 IS DESIGNED for manageability. The design ensures that a privileged network manager can manage PCs running Windows 98 both locally and remotely. Network security is used to determine administrator-privileged accounts using pass-through security. Windows 98 also provides for PC users to be logically separated from the underlying configuration of their PCs so that the PC and user configurations and privileges can be managed independently. As a result, network managers can allow users to "rove" on the network—that is, log on from virtually any PC on the network and then operate from a desktop that has the correct settings and network privileges. The logical separation also means that multiple users can share a single PC, each with a different desktop configuration and different network privileges.

Given the proliferation of PCs connected to corporate networks, the Windows 98 PC must be able to participate in any networkwide management schemes. Windows 98 is designed to meet various network management criteria by providing built-in support for several of the key network management standards. With this infrastructure built into Windows 98, network management applications can provide tools for network managers to keep PCs and networks running more efficiently and cost-effectively.

Open management interfaces are key to the management implementation in Windows 98. Where a standard exists, Windows 98 implements an enabling technology to embrace the standard—for example, a Simple Network Management Protocol (SNMP) agent is supplied to enable remote management of Windows 98 PCs via any number of third-party SNMP consoles. Where no standard exists, the management interfaces are documented in the Win32 API set. Management software is available for Windows 98 from a wide range of vendors.

The following list outlines the key components of the system management infrastructure in Windows 98:

- Internet System Update
- System File Checker utility
- Microsoft System Information utility
- New Dr. Watson utility
- New Backup utility
- Automatic ScanDisk after improper shutdown
- The Registry
- The Registry Editor
- User profiles (the user component of the Registry)
- Hardware profile (the system component of the Registry)
- System policies (the network and system policy component of the Registry)
- The System Policy Editor
- Remote Administration Security (the remote admin authentication scheme)
- Remote Procedure Call (the mechanism used to administer Windows 95 remotely)
- NetWatcher
- The System Monitor
- The SNMP Agent
- The Desktop Management Infrastructure (DMI) Agent
- Backup agents, such as Cheyenne ARCserve and Arcada Backup Exec with MTF (Microsoft Tape Format)

The discussion of the management infrastructure in Windows 98 is organized as follows:

- The Registry
- User management
- System management

NOTE

System utilities are also part of the management infrastructure in Windows 98, and they're now faster and better than ever. The new and improved system utilities are described in other chapters: Internet System Update, Microsoft System Information utility, and Dr. Watson utility (Chapter 2); System File Checker utility, Windows Tuneup Wizard (which includes the Disk Defragmenter Optimization Wizard), Backup utility, and Automatic ScanDisk after improper shutdown (Chapters 2 and 15).

The Registry

The Windows 98 Registry hasn't changed significantly from the Windows 95 Registry. It is the central repository in which Windows 98 stores all its configuration data. The Windows 98 system configuration, the PC hardware configuration, Win32-based applications, and user preferences are all stored in the Registry. For example, any Windows 98 PC hardware configuration changes that are made with a Plug and Play device are immediately reflected in a configuration change in the Registry. Because of these characteristics, the Registry serves as the foundation for user, system, and network management in Windows 98.

The Registry essentially replaces the configuration files AUTOEXEC.BAT, CONFIG.SYS, WIN.INI, SYSTEM.INI, and the other applications' INI files. However, instances of CONFIG.SYS, WIN.INI, and SYSTEM.INI files can exist on a Windows 98 PC for backward compatibility with either 16-bit device drivers or 16-bit applications that must run on Windows 98. For example, 16-bit applications will probably continue to create and update their own INI files.

The Registry is a single configuration datastore built directly into the operating system. Although it is logically one datastore, physically it consists of three different files to allow maximum network configuration flexibility. Windows 98 uses the Registry to store information in the following three major categories:

- User-specific information, in the form of user profiles, is contained in the USER.DAT file.

- Hardware or computer-specific settings (the hardware profile) are contained in the SYSTEM.DAT file.

- System policies are designed to provide an override for any settings contained in the other two Registry components. System policies can contain additional data specific to the network or corporate environment, as established by the network manager. The system policies themselves are contained in the POLICY.POL file. Unlike SYSTEM.DAT and USER.DAT, POLICY.POL is not a mandatory component of a Windows 98 installation.

Breaking the Registry into these three logical components provides the following benefits:

- The Registry components can be located in physically different locations. For example, the SYSTEM.DAT component and other Windows 98 system files might be located on the PC's hard disk, and the USER.DAT component might be located in the user's logon directory on a network server. With this configuration, users can log on to various PCs on the network and still have their unique network privileges and desktop configuration, allowing the "roving user" network configuration for Windows 98.

- All of the Registry files and the rest of the system files in Windows 98 can be installed on a network server. This configuration enables Windows 98 to be run on a diskless or remote initial program load (RIPL) workstation or from a floppy-disk boot configuration. With this scenario, Windows 98 can be configured to page to a local hard disk but still load all its system files from a server.

- The Registry and all of the system files can be installed on the local hard disk. With this configuration, multiple users can share a single Windows 98 PC. Each user has a separate logon user name, separate user profile, separate privileges, and separate desktop configuration.

- The network manager can administer an entire network's user privileges by having a single, global POLICY.POL file. Or the network manager can establish these policies on a server basis or on a per-user basis. In this fashion, a network manager can centrally enforce a "common desktop configuration" for each user type. For example, a data-entry Windows 98 PC can be configured so that only two applications—the data entry application and e-mail—can be run. Additionally, the network manager can specify that data-entry users cannot modify this desktop configuration. In spite of this configuration, the Windows 98 PC can fully participate in the network and is fully configurable if a different user with more network privileges logs on to the same PC.

- Separate privileges can be assigned to users and to a PC. For example, if a user who has sharing privileges logs on to a Windows 98 PC that has no sharing (no peer services), the user cannot access the PC's resources. This feature is useful if certain PCs contain sensitive data that should not be available to everyone on the corporate network.

The Registry contains ordered pairs of keys and their associated values that are manipulated via the Win32 Registry APIs. For example, the Registry might have a Wallpaper key with an associated value of WORK.BMP, meaning that the current desktop background is configured to use the Work bitmap.

Additionally, a special category of keys known as *dynamic keys* points to either a memory location or a callback function. Dynamic keys are used by device drivers or Windows 98 subsystems that want to register a dynamic data type, such as a counter, in the Registry. In the case of network cards, the dynamic keys represent data such as data transfer rates, number of framing errors, packets dropped, and so on. In general, dynamic keys are used for data that is updated frequently and is therefore not well suited for storage in the disk-based Registry. Because the dynamic keys exist in memory, their data can be quickly updated and quickly accessed. The data can be accessed by the system performance tools in Windows 98, which call the Registry for the data they are monitoring.

Keys and values can be created either programmatically or by using the Registry Editor (REGEDIT) tool. The APIs for programmatically managing the Registry are the Win32 Registry APIs, which can be remotely invoked via the Microsoft RPC (DCE-compliant) support built into Windows 98. Windows 98 includes both the client and server portions of Microsoft RPC (Remote Procedure Call), making the Registry manageable remotely from another Windows 98 PC. In this scenario, the network manager's system is the RPC client. It accesses the Registry APIs on the target Windows 98 PC through the RPC server running on the target machine. This RPC access to the Registry is secure, and network managers can limit access to either named privileged users or a group of network managers.

The Registry is also editable using the Registry Editor utility, shown in Figure 22-1. The Registry consists of various parallel "trees." The Registry Editor is built on the RPC support and can edit the local Windows 98 Registry as well as the Registries on remote Windows 98 PCs. Although the Registry Editor is powerful, it is fairly rudimentary in design and is intended for use by knowledgeable PC and network support staff or power users. Most users will never use the Registry Editor because Registry entries are usually modified through the Control Panel, by applications, or by Plug and Play. Assigning an incorrect value to a Registry entry or adding or deleting certain entries can result in a completely disabled operating system.

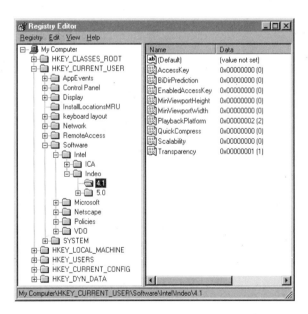

Figure 22-1   *The Registry Editor, showing the settings stored in the Registry, which can be accessed remotely*

As Figure 22-2 illustrates, the Registry is the central datastore on which all system management services build. The Registry unites all key subsystems, and Windows 98 implements "agents" for standard management protocols, such as SNMP, using the Registry and Registry services.

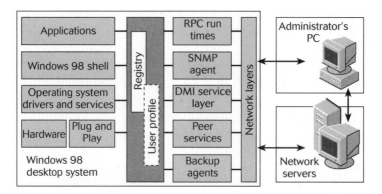

Figure 22-2   *The Windows 98 management architecture, showing the central role of the Registry*

Registry Improvements in Windows 98

Microsoft has rewritten the Registry-handling code to be faster and to improve robustness. The in-memory data structures are optimized. You won't see any changes in the Registry structure as exposed through the APIs or the Registry Editor—but how the code handles the structure has been improved significantly.

Registry Tools

The primary user management tools in Windows 98 are the Registry Editor and the System Policy Editor. For most other types of user administration, network managers use the same user accounts tools on their PC servers that they used with and even before Microsoft Windows 95.

Registry Editor

The Registry Editor allows network managers to directly read and write values that are contained in the user profiles and the hardware profile in the Registry. Using this tool, network managers can read current settings, modify them, create new keys and values, and delete current keys and values in the Registry.

The Registry Editor can edit remote Registries using the RPC-enabled Win32 Registry APIs built into Windows 98. In the case of a user profile residing on a network server, the network manager simply connects to the network server and opens the file using normal file I/O—no RPC connection is needed between the Windows 98 client and the network server.

System Policy Editor

The System Policy Editor generates the System Policies file, POLICY.POL. This tool allows network managers to specify specific network policies or user configurations for Windows 98. The tool is extensible by third parties; the ADF (administration configuration files) format is a text file that can be extended by network tool vendors or by network managers as needed. The System Policy Editor works via local file I/O and is not RPC-enabled. Because the system policies file is located centrally on a network server, each server usually needs a copy. All the network manager needs to do is connect to the network server and edit the system policies file.

User Management

Windows 95 was the first version of Windows to implement functionality for management of user-specific configurations and user-specific privileges. User management under Windows 98 is the same.

User management is most evident in the user logon dialog box that minimally prompts users for their logon names and passwords each time they reboot a Windows 98 PC. This logon dialog box captures the user name and password, which can trigger Windows 98 to dramatically reconfigure the desktop and, as needed, limit access to either network resources or sharing capabilities from this Windows 98 PC. Windows 98 can also pass the user name and password through to registered applications and network services that use the Windows 98 logon information as a "master key" for granting or denying access.

The user management capabilities in Windows 98 are built on the following components:

- User profiles
- System policies
- Server-based security

User Profiles

User management in Windows 98 is integral to the system and is implemented in a feature known as user profiles. User profiles are part of the Registry, and they contain system, application, and network data that is unique to individual users of a Windows 98 PC. The user, the network manager, or the Help desk staff can set the user profile characteristics. The user profiles in Windows 98 are contained within a single file named USER.DAT. By keeping all user-specific data in one file, Windows 98 can provide a means to manage the user of the PC separately from the configuration of the Windows 98 operating system and the PC hardware. This separation also allows the user information to be located in a physically different location than that of the system configuration. It also allows the user profiles to be updated separately from the rest of the Registry. All settings contained within a user profile can be administered locally or remotely from another Windows 98 PC. Windows 98 enables centralized user management, and the network manager can use the Registry Editor provided with Windows 98 or a variety of third-party tools to automate management of user profiles.

The settings contained in user profiles include the following:

- Windows 98 user interface settings, including desktop layout, background, font selection, colors, shortcuts, display resolution, and so on
- Network settings, including network connections, workgroup, preferred server, shared resources, and so on
- Application settings, including menu and toolbar configurations, fonts, window configuration preferences, and so on

User profiles can effectively be disabled for Windows 98 PCs that have only one user by disabling the option on the Passwords Properties property sheet, shown in Figure 22-3, that gives each user a separate desktop.

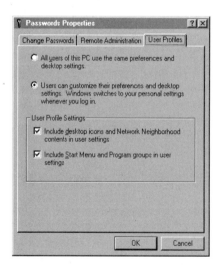

Figure 22-3   *The property sheet for user profiles, enabling and specifying unique desktops, taskbar options, and program groups for each user*

System Policies

System policies are designed to give network managers the ability to customize control over Windows 98 for users of differing capabilities or network privilege levels, including control of the user interface, network capabilities, desktop configuration, sharing capabilities, and so on. Like the other two Registry components, system policies consist of pairs of keys and values. Unlike the other two Registry components, system policies are designed to override any settings that might exist in user profiles or hardware profile. System policies are not necessary to enable a Windows 98 system to boot. They are loaded last and are typically downloaded from a location on the network server defined by the network manager.

System policies can be used to define a "default" setting for the user profile or the hardware profile. Default settings for both a default user and a default computer might solve the problem of preconfigured PCs for network managers. New PC hardware comes preinstalled with Windows and in some cases with the network hardware and software necessary to connect to the corporate network. Many network managers have a networkwide standard Windows configuration that they implement on each PC before the PC is allowed on the corporate network. However, if a PC is delivered directly to a user, as is often the case, the network manager doesn't have the opportunity to install the networkwide standard configuration on that PC. Default system policies can solve this problem. For example, if the networkwide standard Windows configuration consists of a standard set of applications and a standard set of network privileges, such as servers to which connection is allowed, the network manager can preconfigure a default user-based set of system policies to enforce these standards the first time the PC is connected to a network server. Assuming that the user logs on with a valid network logon user name, the network privileges made available will be exactly those that the user is entitled to.

The range of desktop control offered by system policies is comprehensive and includes standard network connections and the enabling and disabling of peer sharing capabilities as well as such controls as password aging. For example, the network manager can define a desktop for a user and then lock down this desktop configuration by turning on the attribute that makes the desktop unmodifiable by the user. The network manager can also ensure that the user has access only to approved applications by not allowing the user to run any other programs. This restriction prevents the user from running programs from the command line or from the user interface browsers and thus prevents installation of additional software. Another example of the way system policies can be used is to disable elements of the Control Panel for users who have the habit of reconfiguring their PCs and as a result require too much attention from the Help desk.

System policies for users

Windows 98 supports a set of system policies integrated with various system components for controlling the Windows 98 environment on a per-user basis. The following areas and system policies can be controlled for users:

- **Control Panel** Within this category of options, network managers can set policies to prevent the user from accessing Control Panel features. Policies include restricting access to the Control Panel's Display settings, Network settings, Printers settings, System settings, and Security settings.

- **Desktop** Policies can prevent users from modifying desktop features. Policies include specifying a wallpaper and color scheme to be used.
- **Network** The network policies provide restrictions to file and printer sharing. Policies include disabling file sharing and printer sharing controls.
- **Shell** The shell (user interface) policies can be used to customize folders and other elements of the desktop and to restrict changes to the user interface. Policies include customizing the user's Programs folder, desktop items, Startup folder, Network Neighborhood, and Start menu. Restrictions include:
  - Removing the Run and Find commands from the Start menu
  - Removing folders and the taskbar from Settings on the Start menu
  - Hiding drives in My Computer and hiding the Network Neighborhood
  - Removing Entire Network from the Network Neighborhood
  - Hiding all items on the desktop
  - Disabling the Shut Down command, which prevents changed settings from being saved at exit
- **System** These policies restrict the use of Registry editing tools, applications, and MS-DOS–based applications. Policies include:
  - Restricting the use of Registry editing tools
  - Running only selected Windows-based applications
  - Disabling the ability to run an MS-DOS command prompt and single MS-DOS application mode

System policies for computers

Windows 98 supports a set of system policies integrated with various system components for controlling the Windows 98 environment on a per-computer basis. The following areas and system policies can be controlled for computers.

System policy settings

These policy settings, which include the following, relate to the computer configuration:

- Identifying the network path for Windows Setup
- Enabling user profile support
- Identifying items to be run each time the computer starts or to be run only once when the computer first starts

Network policy settings

These policy settings, which include the following, relate to the network configuration of the computer:

- Controlling logon settings
- Disabling file and printer sharing

- Activating user-level security
- Controlling password settings
- Disabling remote dial-up access
- Controlling remote access to the Registry
- Defining properties for remote policy updates
- Defining settings for the Client for Microsoft Networks and the Microsoft Client for NetWare Networks
- Setting attributes for the SNMP service

The Role of the Server in Systems Management

In user management, the server plays a central role. All user namespace management is performed on the network server, so Windows 98 uses the native user-level security mechanism built into the network server for user logon authentication and pass-through security. Windows 98 has no built-in user-level security mechanism of its own. As a consequence, network managers can use the familiar server administration tools to manage user accounts for Windows 98.

The second role of the server in user management in Windows 98 is to contain copies of user profiles and system policies. Typically, user profiles are stored in user directories that are read/write enabled for the user. As changes are made to the local copy of user profiles, the copy that resides on the server is updated. Windows 98 keeps the local and network image synchronized. System policies should be stored in a directory that is accessible to all user logons and should be made read-only for users to ensure that only network managers can modify the networkwide policies that the system policies file might define.

23

TV Viewer

IF YOU HAVE A NATIONAL TELEVISION System Committee (NTSC) or Phase Alternation Line (PAL) card installed in your computer, you can watch TV programs in a window on your desktop. Microsoft Windows 98 includes the program TV Viewer, which provides the software you need to receive TV signals on your computer screen. The signals can come from broadcast TV (aerial), a cable TV service, or from the DIRECTV direct broadcast satellite (DBS) service. For all the features of TV Viewer to work, you must be connected to DIRECTV.

Using the TV Toolbar

The TV toolbar, shown in Figure 23-1, slides onto the screen from the right when you press F10, move the mouse pointer to the right edge of the screen, or press the Menu button on the remote control.

Figure 23-1 *The TV Toolbar*

You can use the TV menu to:

- Tune to the Program Guide
- Sign on to watch TV
- Create viewer restrictions
- Create a personal channel list
- Quickly tune to a favorite channel
- Add and remove favorite channels
- Get help

Getting Help

Although mentioned last in the list above, Help is worth covering first—just in case you get stuck anywhere in the process of bringing TV to your desktop. To get Help, take these steps:

1. Press F10 to display the TV toolbar. (Or press the Menu button on the remote control.)

2. On the TV toolbar, click Help. (Move the pointer to Help, and then press the remote-control button used for selecting.) You'll see the first Help screen, as shown here:

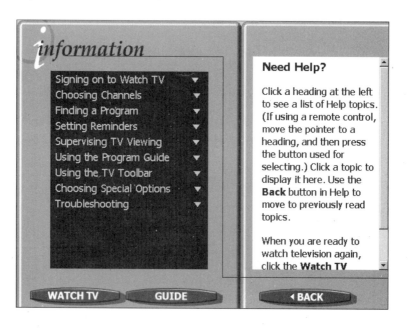

3. Click one of the headings at the left to see the menu for that heading. For example, clicking Finding A Program brings down a Help topic list, as shown here:

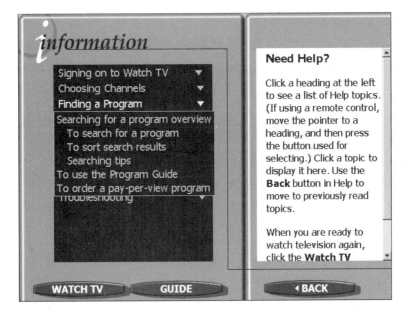

4. Then just click a topic on the menu to see the Help message.
5. When you're ready to return to watching television, click the Watch TV button, or click the Guide button to return to the Program Guide.

Signing On

Signing on to watch TV is important if viewer restrictions have been set for any household members. When restrictions have been set and someone watches TV without signing on, he or she watches as a guest viewer. A guest viewer has the most restrictive viewing privileges and can watch only programs that *any* viewer can watch.

To sign on to watch TV, take these steps:

1. Press F10 to display the TV toolbar. (Or press the Menu button on the remote control.) On the TV toolbar, click Sign On. (Move the pointer to Sign On, and then press the remote-control button used for selecting.) The Sign On dialog box shown on the following page will appear.

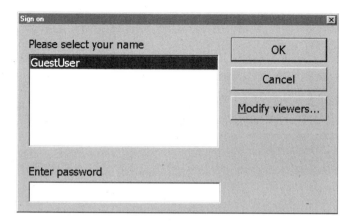

2. In the Sign On dialog box, click your name in the list.

3. Click anywhere in the Password box, type your password, and click OK.

To watch TV without signing on, do one of the following:

- On the Start menu, click TV Viewer.

- Press the TV button on your remote control.

Using the Program Guide

The Program Guide is a TV guide on your television. To use it, press F10 on the keyboard to display the TV toolbar and then click Guide. (Or press the Guide button on your remote control.)

In the Program Guide, TV programming is presented in a grid that displays each channel down the left side and the time of day across the top. You can look through the guide to see what's on, or you can search for a specific program by clicking Search. You can also find other times that a program is on and set reminders for future programs.

Getting the Program Guide

After you start TV viewing, you're given an opportunity to download your local Program Guide. You can download the program guide or change the channel configuration at any time using the TV Config channel. Simply follow these steps:

1. From the Program Guide, click TV Config and select Watch. You'll see the initial screen, shown at the top of the facing page, for setting up your TV Viewer.

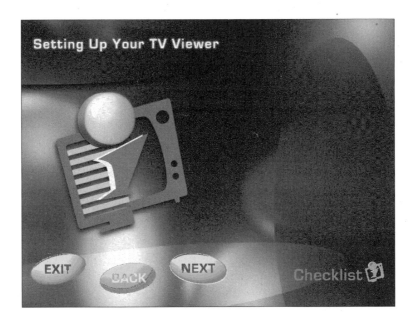

2. Click the Next button, and follow the instructions until you reach the StarSight Web Site Data Download page, shown here:

3. On the Data Download Page, type your zip code with the keypad (making sure you turn on NumLock) and then click Submit. The Select Broadcast Area page will appear.

4. Select the cable provider in your area, and then click Next.

5. Click the Download button to receive the Program Guide. The Data Down-loader connects to the Web, collects the TV listings, and downloads them to your computer.

After you download the TV listings the first time, the StarSight Loader is set up in the Windows Task Scheduler and runs once a day to automatically download the Program Guide. The DTVLoader performs the same automatic download for DIRECTV customers.

Choosing a Program to Watch

To choose a program to watch, take these steps:

1. Display the TV Toolbar, and then select Guide. You'll see a list of channels and programs in the Time page of the Program Guide, as shown here:

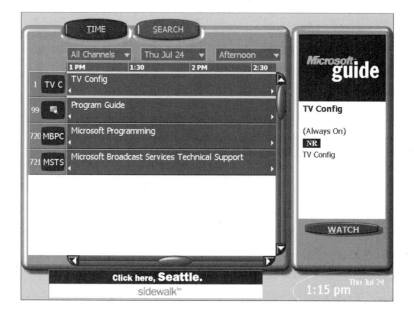

2. Click the program in the Program Guide. (Move the pointer to the program tile, and then press the remote-control button used for selecting.)

3. Click the Watch button.

Keep in mind the following notes:

- Programs that are showing currently are displayed in dark gray tiles.
- You can double-click a dark gray program tile to begin watching the program. (Press the remote-control button used for selecting twice, quickly.)

Finding Other Program Times

To find other program times, take these steps:

1. In the Program Guide, click the program for which you want to find other viewing times. (Move the pointer to the program tile, and then press the remote-control button used for selecting.)

2. Click Search to see the other viewing times in the Search list.

For more details about finding programs to watch, see the "Searching for a Program" section later in the chapter.

Scrolling Through Times

To scroll through times, use the buttons in the Program Guide shown in Figure 23-2.

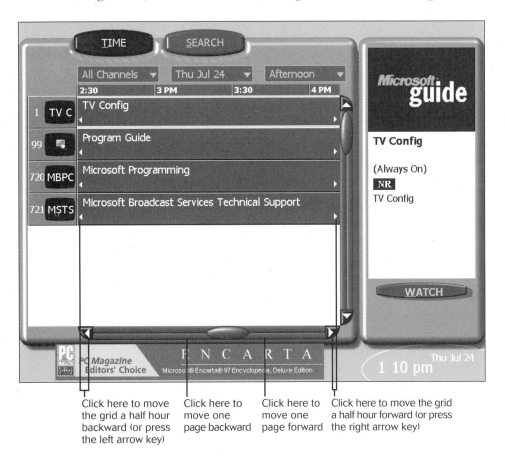

Figure 23-2   *Buttons for scrolling through times in the Program Guide*

Looking at a Different Time of Day

When you display the Program Guide, you see the programs for the current time of day. You might be consulting the Program Guide for shows later in the day. To look at a different time of day, take these steps:

1. In the Program Guide, click the tab displaying the current time period (morning, afternoon, and so on), as shown below. (Move the pointer to the tab, and then press the remote-control button used for selecting.)

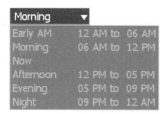

2. Click the time period in which you want to see TV programming.

Looking at a Different Day

Just as you sometimes look ahead in time in the Program Guide, you might want to look ahead to tomorrow's programming or to some day later in the week. To look at a different day, take these steps:

1. In the Program Guide, click the tab displaying the current day and date, as shown below. (Move the pointer to the tab, and then press the remote-control button used for selecting.)

2. Click the day on which you want to see the TV programming.

Returning to the Current Day and Time

After you look ahead to a time later in the day or later in the week, you might want to return to the current time to check TV listings. To return to the current day and time, click the current time at the bottom of the page in the Program Guide.

NOTE

When you click the current time, a program currently showing on a channel that is visible on the grid becomes the selected program.

Understanding On-Screen Icons

TV Viewer can display a number of icons, which are a graphical way to give you information quickly but unobtrusively. To find out what an on-screen icon means, consult the following table.

On-Screen Icons

Icon	What It Means
⏰	A reminder is set for a program.
↻	A program is a rerun.
💬	Closed captioning is available.
🎧	Stereo audio is available.
🔊	Alternate audio tracks are available.
$	There is a charge for watching this program.
G	This program is rated suitable for all ages.
PG	This program contains content not suitable for children.
PG-13	This program contains content not suitable for children under the age of 13.
R	This program contains content suitable only for adults.
NR	This program is not rated.
NR-M	This program is rated for mature audiences.
NR-C	This program is rated as an adult situation comedy.
NC-17	This program contains nudity, adult language, and/or violence.

Controlling TV Viewer

TV Viewer provides a number of controls you can use to manage your viewing. The following sections describe the various ways in which you can control TV Viewer so that you can be sure to get the programs you want.

Changing Channels

To change channels, do one of the following:

- Display the Program Guide, and then click the program you want to watch.
- Click a favorite channel on the TV toolbar, or click the up and down arrow buttons on the toolbar.
- Click the Channels button at the top of the screen, select Favorites from the menu, and then click the channel you want to see.
- Use the Channel button on the remote control.
- Use the number pad on the remote control to enter the channel number, and press the Enter button.

Here's how to find out what's on:

- To find out what's showing on the current channel, press F10, move the mouse over the right edge of the screen, or press the Menu button on the remote control.
- To find out what's showing on another channel, use the Program Guide.

Scrolling Through Channels

To scroll through channels in the Program Guide, use the buttons shown in Figure 23-3.

Changing the Audio Track

To change the audio track, take these steps:

1. Click the speaker icon on the Channel bar. This icon is visible only when alternate audio tracks are available.
2. Select an option from the audio menu.

Click here to move up
one page (or press the
Page Up key)

Click here to move up
one channel (or press
the up arrow key)

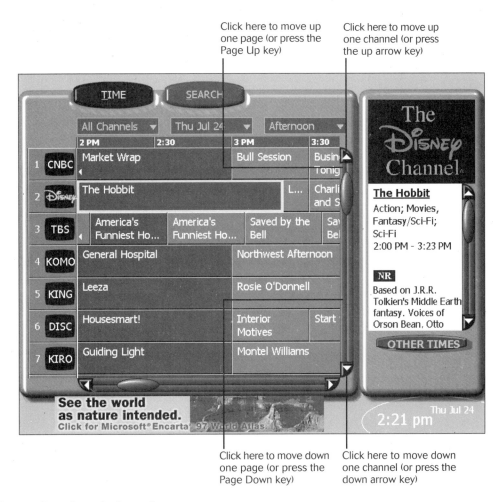

Click here to move down
one page (or press the
Page Down key)

Click here to move down
one channel (or press the
down arrow key)

Figure 23-3   *Scrolling through channels*

Displaying Closed Captions

Just as you can receive closed captioning on a regular television, you can display
closed captions through TV Viewer. Just take these steps:

1. Press F10 to display the TV toolbar. (Or press the Menu button on the remote
   control.)

2. On the TV toolbar, click Settings.

3. In the Settings dialog box, click the Show Closed Captioning check box and
   then click OK.

Searching for a Program

The Program Guide provides a way for you to find a program quickly without having to search through all the programs listed in the guide. You can search for a specific program, search for a program category, or search for a specific channel.

To search for a program, take these steps:

1. Press F10 to display the TV toolbar, and click Guide on the toolbar. (Or press the Guide button on the remote control.)

2. In the Program Guide, click Search. Your screen will look similar to Figure 23-4.

3. If you want to search for a program that is on currently or on a specific day, click All Days and then click the menu choice you want to use.

4. In the Categories list, click a category. Some categories also have subcategories. To view the subcategories, click All <category> and select the subcategory from the menu. You can also search for a specific program or station by typing the name of the station into the Search For box and then clicking the Search button at the bottom of the screen.

Figure 23-4   *Search for a channel*

TIP

If you're watching a show when you click Search, the Search page initially displays all the other times this show appears in the current program listing.

Sorting Search Results

After TV Viewer displays the results of a search, you can sort the Search results either alphabetically by program title or chronologically by time and date.

- To sort search results alphabetically, on the Search page, click Sort By Title.
- To sort search results chronologically, on the Search page, click Sort By Time.

Creating a Personal Channel List

A personal channel list is a list of channels available to each viewer. Before any changes are made, the list contains all channels from all available video sources (network, cable, or satellite). If viewer restrictions have been set, a supervised viewer's channel list contains only those channels allowed by the restrictions. Any viewer can make changes to eliminate unwanted channels.

To create a personal channel list, take these steps:

1. Press F10 to display the TV toolbar. (Or press the Menu button on the remote control.)

2. On the TV toolbar, click Settings. (Move the pointer to Settings, and then press the remote-control button used for selecting.) The following Settings dialog box will appear:

3. In the Settings dialog box, make sure Show Only is selected.

4. To remove a channel from your list, click the check box to the left of the channel name to remove the check mark. (If you want a channel in your list, the check box should have a check mark in it.)

5. Click OK.

The following tips will help you customize your personal channel list:

● Use the Clear All button to remove all channels from the channel list and the Check All button to add all channels to the list.

● If viewer restrictions have been set, you should sign on to watch TV before creating a personal channel list. If you don't sign on, you don't change your personal channel list; instead, you create a channel list for a guest viewer.

● When you surf through TV channels, you see only the channels in your personal channel list. You also see only these channels in the Program Guide.

● If you add your five favorite channels to the TV toolbar, you can get to them quickly by displaying the menu and clicking the one you want. (See the section immediately following for more details.)

Choosing Favorite Channels

You can place five of your favorite channels on the TV menu, from where you can easily tune to them. You can change your favorites as often as you like.

Adding a Favorite Channel to the TV Toolbar

To add a favorite channel to the TV toolbar, take these steps:

1. Tune to the channel you want to add.

2. Press F10 to display the TV toolbar. (Or press the Menu button on the remote control.)

3. On the TV toolbar, click Add.

Here are some additional notes about adding your favorite shows to the TV toolbar:

● You can add up to five of your favorite channels to the TV toolbar.

● If you add a favorite channel when you already have five channels on the TV toolbar, the oldest favorite is removed to make room for the addition.

Removing a Favorite Channel from the TV Toolbar

To remove a favorite channel from the TV toolbar, take these steps:

1. Press F10 to display the TV toolbar. (Or press the Menu button on the remote control.)

2. On the TV toolbar, click the channel you want to remove.

3. Click Remove.

Setting Reminders

In the Program Guide, you can set a reminder for the following programs:

- A special program
- A daily program
- A weekday program
- A weekly program

You can have the reminder appear on the screen 5 or 10 minutes before viewing time.

To set a reminder, take these steps:

1. In the Program Guide or on the Search page, click the program for which you want to set a reminder.

2. Click the Remind button. The Remind dialog box shown here will appear:

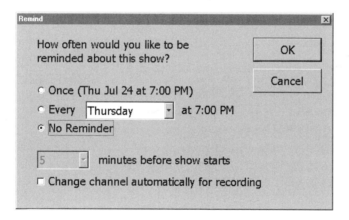

3. Follow the directions in the Remind dialog box, and click OK.

Checking Reminders

To check reminders, take these steps:

1. In the Program Guide, click Search.

2. On the Search page, scroll down the Categories list until you see My Reminders and then click My Reminders. Your screen will look similar to the one shown on the following page.

3. Look through your list of reminders in the right column.

Canceling a Reminder

To cancel a reminder, take these steps:

1. In the Program Guide, click Search.

2. On the Search page, scroll down the Categories list until you see My Reminders and then click My Reminders.

3. Look through your list of reminders in the right column, click the reminder you want to cancel, and then click the Remind button.

4. In the Remind dialog box, click No Reminder and then click OK.

Supervising TV Viewing

If you want to supervise the TV viewing of certain family members, you can designate one or more supervisors in your household. A supervisor can determine:

- Channels available to a supervised viewer
- Program ratings available to a supervised viewer
- A supervised viewer's spending limits for paid programming

To create viewer restrictions, take these steps:

1. Press F10 to display the TV toolbar. (Or press the Menu button on the remote control.)

2. On the TV toolbar, click Sign On. (Move the pointer to Sign On, and then press the remote-control button used for selecting.)

3. In the Sign On dialog box, click Modify Viewers. The following dialog box will appear:

4. In the Modify Viewers dialog box, click Add.

5. In the New Viewer dialog box, type the name of the viewer you want to add, as shown here:

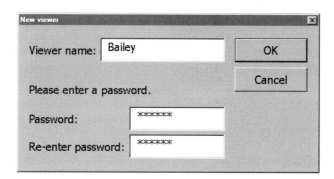

6. Click anywhere in the Password box, and type a password for the new viewer.

7. Type the password again in the Re-Enter Password box, and click OK.

8. Edit this new viewer's restrictions. (See the next section.)

NOTE

If you're not signed on as a supervisor, you can't create or edit viewer restrictions.

Editing Viewer Restrictions

After you set up a new viewer, you need to edit that viewer's restrictions. You can also change the restrictions for a viewer who's already on the list.

To edit viewer restrictions, take these steps:

1. Press F10 to display the TV toolbar. (Or press the Menu button on the remote control.)

2. On the TV toolbar, click Sign On. (Move the pointer to Sign On, and then press the remote-control button used for selecting.)

3. In the Sign On dialog box, click Modify Viewers.

4. In the Modify Viewers dialog box, click the name of the viewer whose restrictions you want to change and then click Edit to open the Permissions dialog box, which is shown here:

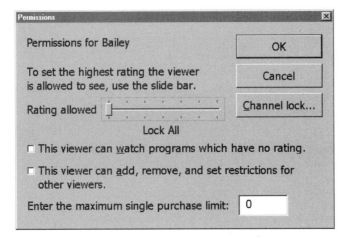

5. Move the slider to set the highest rating allowed for this viewer.

6. Select the first check box to permit this viewer to see programs with no rating (NR).

7. Select the second check box to permit this viewer to administer TV Viewer settings.

8. Click Channel Lock to select and deselect channels for this viewer. The Channel Lock button displays the Settings dialog box.

9. Set the pay-per-view purchase limit for a single program. Many pay-per-view movies are a standard price; for example, $3.99 U.S. Special attraction pay-per-view programs might be priced as high as $49.99 U.S. To permit viewers to order pay-per-view movies, you can set the purchase limit at $5.00 to prevent ordering events with a higher price.

10. Click OK.

Getting Permission to Watch a Program

To get permission to watch a program, take these steps:

1. Tune to the program you want to watch.

2. When you see the "Permission denied" message, click the Please button and ask your parent (or a restrictions supervisor) to fill in the dialog box.

The parent or restriction supervisor takes the steps outlined in the next section.

Overriding Viewer Restrictions

When a viewer with restrictions requests you (as a restrictions supervisor) for permission to watch a program that the restrictions block, you can override that viewer's restrictions on a program-by-program basis. To override viewer restrictions, take these steps:

1. In the Permissions dialog box that appears for restricted programs, click Please.

2. Follow the directions in the Parental Permission dialog box, and click OK.

> **NOTE**
> You use this procedure to make a special exception to a viewer's restrictions. To change the viewer's restrictions permanently, edit the viewer's restrictions.

Removing a Viewer

If the list of viewers includes someone you no longer want to have a viewer account, you can remove that viewer by removing the set of viewer restrictions. To remove a viewer, take these steps:

1. Press F10 to display the TV toolbar. (Or press the Menu button on the remote control.)

2. On the TV toolbar, click Sign On. (Move the pointer to Sign On, and then press the remote-control button used for selecting.)

3. In the Sign On dialog box, click Modify Viewers.

4. In the Modify Viewers dialog box, click the name of the viewer you want to remove and then click Remove.

5. Click Yes to confirm the deletion, and then click OK.

Keep in mind these two points:

- If you're not signed on as a supervisor, you can't remove a viewer.
- GuestUser cannot be removed; it's a permanent viewer designation.

Troubleshooting

If you have trouble with TV Viewer, consult the Troubleshooting section in the online Help. (Select Help from the TV toolbar.) This section in Help covers a variety of problems that can occur when you're installing and using the TV Viewer, including the following:

- Difficulties using the Program Guide
- Blackouts
- DIRECTV issues
- Satellite dish reception
- Pay-per-view programming

Another source of information for troubleshooting is channel 721, Microsoft Broadcast Services Technical Support (MSTS). Select this channel in your Program Guide to find helpful information on downloading, updates, and feedback.

Index

Symbols and Numbers

2-D Positioning, Dynamic HTML, 74, 75
3.3 volt PC Cards, 19
3-D graphics development support, 283–284
16-bit vs. 32-bit components in Windows 98, 318–325
32-bit DLC (Data Link Control) protocol, 20, 217–218
32-bit file system. *See* FAT32
32-bit file system architecture. *See* file system
    architecture, 32-bit
32-bit print subsystem, 234–235
32-bit protected-mode cache (VCACHE), 341–342
32-bit protected-mode FAT file system (VFAT), 341
32-bit vs. 16-bit components in Windows 98, 318–325
32-bit VxDs (virtual device drivers), 200–201
    for MS-DOS–based applications, 329
16550A UART FIFO buffer, 253

A

Abstract Windowing Toolkit (AWT), 64
Accelerated Graphics Port (AGP), 16
AccessDOS, 291
accessibility features, 291–299
    Accessibility TimeOut, 294
    alternative input devices, 298–299
    controlling, 293
    for hearing impaired users, 298
    keyboard and mouse input, 296–298
    limited vision, 295
    software developers and, 299
    status indicator for, 294
Accessibility Properties dialog box, 31
Accessibility status indicator, 294
Accessibility TimeOut feature, 294
Access Pack for Microsoft Windows, 291
Access Pack for Microsoft Windows NT, 291
ACM (Audio Compression Module) codecs, 151
ACPI (Advanced Configuration and Power
    Interface), 16, 381

Active Desktop, 27, 42–45, 91
    adding items to, 43
    Channel bar on, 91, 92
    deactivating or removing items from, 45
    showing/hiding desktop icons, 45
    switching between standard desktop and, 43
Active Desktop Gallery, 43
ActiveMovie, 20, 79, 81. *See also* DirectShow
Active Server Pages, 77, 99
Active Setup, 103–104
Active Setup Log.txt, 103
Active Streaming Format (ASF), 154
ActiveX
    FrontPad support for, 181
    Internet Explorer 4.0 support for, 76–77
    Java Beans and, 64
    scripting engines, 17
ActiveX controls, NetShow, 153
ActiveX Control Viewer, 104–105
ActiveX Scripting, 77, 188
ActiveX technology, 188
Adaptec 8940 200 MBPS host controllers, 322
Add A Printer command, 31
Add New Hardware command, 31
Add New Hardware Wizard, 31, 367
Add Or Remove Programs command, 31
Add Printer Wizard, 31, 238
Add/Remove Programs Properties dialog box, 31
Address Bar, 52, 66
address books, 165. *See also* Personal Address Book
    finding people on, 33
    Outlook Express, 165
addresses
    e-mail, finding, 161–162
    Web, on taskbar, 37
Address toolbar, on taskbar, 37

Add To Favorites dialog box, 84
Advanced Configuration and Power Interface
      (ACPI), 16, 381
Advanced Display property sheet, 372, 373
Advanced Power Management (APM), 16,
      261–262, 382
Advanced Properties button, 372
advertising, NetShow used for, 156
AFC (Application Foundation Classes), 64, 188
AGP (Accelerated Graphics Port), 16
AirMedia, 98, 99
Alt+Tab, switching applications with, 36
America Online (AOL), 19
animation, WinToon playback, 287
anti-virus software, FAT32 and, 343
APM (Advanced Power Management), 261–262, 382
APM (Advanced Power Management) 1.2
      extensions, 16
Appearance tab, Display Properties property
      sheet, 59
Apple QuickTime, 20
Application Foundation Classes (AFC), 64, 188
applications
      sharing, with NetMeeting, 120–124
      shortcuts embedded in, 47
      switching, 35, 36
APPS.INF, 330–331
architecture of Windows 98, See base system
      architecture of Windows 98
ASF (Active Streaming Format), 154
ASPI (Advanced SCSI Programming Interface), 386
asynchronous downloading of data, 77
ATAPI CD-ROM driver, generic real mode, 9
ATI Rage and Rage II chips, driver for, 383
ATM network cards, 205, 214
AT&T WorldNet, 19
AT+V standard (TIA IS-101), 254
audio (sound), 282, 286–287
      WDM, over USB speakers, 322
Audio Compression Module (ACM) codecs, 151
audio (voice) conferencing, 118, 131
      H.323 standard, 119, 130, 136–139
audio stream, intelligent control of, 131
authentication. See also certificates, authentication
      Remote Access subsystem, 272
authentication certificates, 110, 111–112, 164
Authenticode, 107, 108, 110–111
      Java applications and, 64
AutoComplete, 68–69
AUTOEXEC.BAT, 317–318
      MS-DOS mode and, 331
Automatic Proxy Configuration, 105–106

Automatic ScanDisk, 311
AutoPlay, 281
AUTORUN.INF, 281
AVI files, 20, 282
AWT (Abstract Windowing Toolkit), 64

B

Back and Forward buttons, Internet Explorer 4.0, 71
Background tab, Display Properties property
      sheet, 59
backing up Windows 95 system files, for future
      uninstall of Windows 98, 8
Backup utility, 22, 307–309
BackWeb, 99
Banyan VINES, 214
base system architecture of Windows 98, 315–360
      32-bit vs. 16-bit components, 318–325
            VxDs (virtual device drivers), 319–321
            WDM (Win32 Driver Model), 321–325
      components of, 316
      CONFIG.SYS or AUTOEXEC.BAT not
            needed, 317–318
      DriveSpace disk compression, 353–354
      file system, 32-bit (see FAT32)
      font support, 360
      fully integrated operating system, 316–318
      layout of, 325
      memory management, 356–357
      MS-DOS and, 318
      MS-DOS–based applications, support for
            (see MS-DOS–based applications, support
            for running)
      overview, 315–316
      Registry, 357–360
      system resources, 354–355
      Win16-based (16-bit) application support, 325–328
      Win32-based application support, 336–338
      Win32 Driver Model (WDM), 321–325
Basic Webcasting, 94–95
battery life, Advanced Power Management (APM)
      and, 261–262
BFT (Binary File Transfer), 171, 172, 174, 176, 177
Bigfoot, 33
Binary File Transfer (BFT), 171, 172, 174, 176, 177
block I/O subsystem, 347–349
      IDE, ESDI, and SCSI controllers supported by, 349
      IDE drive spin down supported by, 349
      I/O Supervisor (IOS), 348
      mini-port driver, 349
      port driver, 348
      real-mode mapper, 349
      SCSI layer, 349

BMP files, 305
boot sequence, 318
BounceKeys, 296–297
Briefcase, 276–278
Broadcast Architecture for Windows, 98, 99–100
broadcasting. *See* NetShow 2.0
Browse For Folder dialog box, 39
browser. *See* Internet Explorer 4.0
browsing networks, 53
Bug Reporting Tool, 57
bus enumerators, 366
bus mastering, 384
buttons
    task, 36
    taskbar toolbar, adjusting your view of, 39–40

C

cache, 32-bit protected-mode (VCACHE), 341–342
CAM (Common Access Method), 386
Caps Lock key, audio cues for, 298
CardBus (PC Card32), 19, 260
cascading style sheet extensions for printing,
        Internet Explorer 4.0, 71
CD audio, 323
CD disk driver, 385
CDF (Channel Definition Format) files, 89, 91, 93
    Managed Webcasting using, 95–98
    sample, 97
    third-party support for, 99
CDFS (CD-ROM file system), 283, 347
    read-ahead behavior, 385
CDFS.VXD, 385
CDI disks, 385
CD jukeboxes, 385
CD Player, 282
CD Plus (Enhanced Music CD) format, 284–285, 385
CD-quality sound, sound compression for, 287–288
CD-ROM changers, 385
CD-ROM drives
    fast, 283
    generic real mode ATAPI driver, 9
    IDE-based, 386
    MPEG and, 285
CD-ROMs, AutoPlay, 281
CDs
    PhotoCD, 283
    video, 283
CDVSD.VXD, 385
certificate management, 108, 111–112
certificates, authentication, 110, 111–112, 114–115,
        164
CGI (Common Gateway Interface), 185

Change Accessibility Settings command, 31
Change How Your Computer Looks command, 31
Change The Start Menu command, 31
Channel bar, 90–92
Channel delivery architecture, 90
Channel Description File, 43
Channel pane, 91, 93
channels
    premium (*see* premium channels)
    subscriptions to, 91–93
Channels button, Internet Explorer toolbar, 38
Channels Explorer Bar, 52
Channels folder, 29, 90
Channel Subscriptions dialog box, 92
Channel Subscription Wizard, 91
Chat, NetMeeting, 123, 126–128
Chat control, 128
CHIPS tab, Display Properties property sheet, 59
Class 1 fax modems, 171, 177
Class 2 fax modems, 177
clicking, with keyboard, 297
Client for Microsoft Networks, 195, 196, 212–213
Clipboard
    language-specific attributes and, 393
    multilingual support for exchanging information
        via, 399
    shared, with NetMeeting, 122, 124
    video images in, 130
Close All command, Help system, 56
Close All Programs And Log On As A Different User
        option (Windows 95), 34
cluster sizes, FAT32, 342–343
CMM (Color Management Modules), 238
collaboration
    with Internet Explorer, 62, 78
    with NetMeeting, 123, 124
        document collaboration, 121
        via graphics, 125
color depth, changing, 372
Color Management Modules (CMM), 238, 378
Color Management tab, Display Properties property
        sheet, 59
color schemes, high-contrast, 295
Comic Chat. *See* Chat, NetMeeting
comic mode, Microsoft Chat's, 126–127
common dialog boxes, 54
communications, 243–255. *See also* TAPI (Telephony
        API); Windows Messaging
    architecture of 32-bit communications
        subsystem, 244–247
        driver architecture, 246–247
        kernel architecture, 245–246

communications, *continued*
    corporate, NetShow used for, 156
    device and hardware support, 252–254
    goals of Windows 98, 244–245
    HyperTerminal, 254
    modem setup and configuration, 250–252
    Phone Dialer, 254–255
    Plug and Play support for, 245
Compact option, Windows 98 Setup, 9
Component Object Model (COM), 20
Compose New Fax command, 172
Compose New Fax wizard, 173
Compress A Drive dialog box, 353, 354
compressed HTML, 82
compression
    disk, 265–266 (*see also* DriveSpace)
    sound, 151–152
        for CD-quality, 287–288
    video, 151–152
CompuServe 3.0, 19
CompuServe Mail
    MAPI driver for, 275
conferencing. *See also* NetMeeting 2.0
    video, 118, 129–130
        H.323 standard, 119, 130, 136–139
CONFIG.SYS, 317–318
    MS-DOS mode and, 331
configuration
    online registration and information about
        your, 12–13
    questions about, as phase of Windows 98
        Setup, 10
configuration-change message support, 262–263
Configuration Manager, Plug and Play, 366
Connect To The Internet command, 31
Content Advisor, 107
Contents tab, Help system, 56
controllers
    ESDI, 386
    floppy disk, 387
    IDE, 385–386
    SCSI, 386
Control Panel, 30, 31, 57–59
    hyperlinks to Microsoft, 57
    large icon Web view of, 58
    remotely sharing, with help desk technician, 121
Control Panel command, 30
cookies, 113
    HTTP, 96
coordinated universal time (UTC) format, 352
copy command, long filenames and, 336

copying
    files, as phase of Windows 98 Setup, 9
    Help text, 57
corrupted files, reinstallation of, 7
cover page designer, Microsoft Fax, 171
Cover Page Editor, Microsoft Fax, 172, 175
Create Shortcut option, 46
CryptoAPI 2.0, 114
cryptographic service providers (CSPs), 107
CSCRIPT.EXE, 77, 226
CSPs (cryptographic service providers), 107
customer service, NetMeeting and, 121
Customize button, New Active Desktop Item
        wizard, 44
Customize This Folder Wizard, 42
Custom option, Windows 98 Setup, 9
CVT.EXE, 343, 345, 346

D
DAC (digital-to-analog converter), 323
data binding, in Dynamic HTML, 75–76
DataChannel, 99
Data Link Control (DLC), 32-bit, 20, 217–218
date and time formats, international language
        support and, 395
DCOM (Distributed COM), 20, 227
DEC Pathworks, 214
deferred printing, 227, 236, 278
defragmentation, disk, 18, 309–310. *See also* Disk
        Defragmenter
deleting shortcuts, 46
"Designed for Microsoft Windows 98" logo, 368–369
desktop
    Active. *See* Active Desktop
    shortcuts on, 47
    standard, 27
Desktop button, 36
desktop icons, showing/hiding, 45
Desktop Management Interface (DMI), 198, 199
Desktop toolbar, on taskbar, 38
Details view, 50
device drivers
    Internet System Update and, 21
    new or updated, 383–385
    philosophy of Windows 98, 379–380
    virtual (VxDs). *See* VxDs
    WDM (Win32 Driver Model). *See* WDM
DHCP (Dynamic Host Configuration Protocol), 216
Dialing Properties for configuring location calling
        information, 252
dialog boxes. *See also* names of specific dialog boxes
    common, 54

Dialog Box Help Editor, 81
Dial-Up Networking, 197–198
    improvements in Windows 98, 18
    on portable PCs, 266–271
        establishing a remote connection, 267–268
        multilink channel aggregation, 271
        protocols supported, 268–269
        scripting support, 270
        user interface enhancements, 270
    PPTP and, 19, 218–219
    remote e-mail and, 168
Dial-Up Networking Multilink, 271
dial-up protocol support, 196
Dial-Up server, 19, 230, 269
digital audio, WDM, 322–323
digital signatures, Microsoft Fax, 171, 176
digital video, 281–282
    capture and compression of bigger, 289
Digital Video Disc (or Digital Versatile Disc) devices.
        See DVD devices
dir command, long filenames and, 336
Direct Cable Connection, 278
DirectDraw, 285
direction keys, 297
Direct Memory Access (DMA), 384
DirectMusic, 323
directory, Web-based, 133
directory filtering, with NetMeeting, 119, 132
DirectShow, 285–286, 323
DirectSound, 323
DIRECTV, 421. See also TV Viewer
DirectX 5, 64, 283–284, 383
disabilities, features for people with. See accessibility
        features
Disable All Web-Related Content In My Desktop
        option, 43
disk access
    32-bit, 341
    Disk Defragmenter and, 310
disk compression. See also DriveSpace
    on portable PCs, 265–266
Disk Defragmenter, 309–310, 353
    FAT32 conversion utility and, 344
Disk Defragmenter Optimization Wizard, 18, 310
disk drives, 383–384. See also controllers; floppy
        drives
    IDE, 385
    support for, 382–387
disk management utilities, third-party
    exclusive access for, 352
    long filenames and, 351
disk utilities, Windows 98, 307–312

Display Adapter Performance slider, 373
display adapters, chip sets supported as additional
        displays, 376
display drivers
    chaining, 299
    new, 383
    support in Windows 98, 376–378
Display Power Management Signaling (DPMS), 374
Display Properties dialog box, 31
    Web tab, 42–45
Display Properties property sheet, 59, 372–373
Display Properties Settings tab, 58
displays
    Energy Star monitor support, 374
    ICM (image color matching) support, 378
    multiple display support, 16, 371, 373, 374–376
    setting enhancements, 17
Display tool, Control Panel, 57
Distributed COM (DCOM), 20, 227
DLC (Data Link Control) protocol, 20, 217–218
DMA (Direct Memory Access), 384
DMI (Desktop Management Interface), 198, 199
DNS (Domain Naming Service), 216
docking stations, 262
document-centricity, concept of, 47–48
document collaboration, with NetMeeting, 121
Documents menu, Start button's, 30
Do Not Disturb option, NetMeeting, 132–133
double-clicking with keyboard, 297
DoubleSpace, 353
Downloaded ActiveX Controls folder, 104
downloading
    HTML-only (without images) for offline use, 89
    progressive, 81
    selected messages, 168
    subscriptions to Web sites and, 83
DPMS (Display Power Management Signaling), 374
Dr. Watson utility, 21–22
Draft folder, Outlook Express, 165
dragging and dropping
    files, into a Quick View window, 302
    with keyboard, 297
    messages, into mailbox folders, 166
    Whiteboard collaboration and, 125
drivers. See device drivers
drives. See also CD-ROM drives; disk drives; DVD
        devices; floppy drives
    mapping, 53
DriveSpace, FAT32 drives not supported, 353–354
    on portable PCs, 265
dual boot, FAT32 drives and, 345, 346
DVD devices (DVD-ROM drives), 16
    support for, 290

DVD movie playback, 324
DVD-ROM drives, as storage media, 324
Dynamic HTML, 62, 63, 73–76, 90, 188
    2-D Positioning, 74, 75
    data binding in, 75–76
    multimedia controls, 79–81
    Object Model of, 73–75, 77
dynamic keys, Registry, 199, 412

E

EBD (Emergency Boot Disk), 9
ECM (Error-Correction Mode), 171, 177
ECPs (Enhanced Capabilities Ports), 253
EDIT.COM, 306–307
educational presentations, distributing with
        NetMeeting, 121
Eject PC command, 34, 262
e-mail. *See also* Outlook, NetMeeting calls from;
        Outlook Express; Windows Messaging
    NetMeeting 2.0, 120
    notification of site changes via, 86–87
    remote, with Outlook Express, 168–169
    rich-text, with Outlook Express, 165–166
e-mail addresses, finding, 161–162
Emergency Boot Disk (EBD), 9
emergency hotkeys, 294–298
Emergency Recovery Disks, 309
EMF (enhanced metafile) spooling, 233–236
encryption
    Microsoft Fax, 171, 176
    public key, 163
Energy Star monitor support, 374
Enhanced Capabilities Ports (ECPs), 253
Enhanced Music CD (CD Plus) format, 284–285, 385
Entire Network, in Network Neighborhood, 53
environment variables, MS-DOS, 334
Error-Correction Mode (ECM), 171, 177
ESDI controllers, 386
    block I/O subsystem support for, 349
exception handling, structured, 408
Explorer. *See* Internet Explorer 4.0; Windows
        Explorer
Explorer bars, 52

F

fail-over, NetShow, 145, 152
Fast Infrared (FIR) devices, 214, 264
FAT16, converting back from FAT32 to, 344
FAT32, 16, 342–347
    anti-virus software and, 343
    cluster sizes used by, 342–343
    conversion utility, 16, 344–346

FAT32, *continued*
    display of disk free space and, 346
    DriveSpace disk compression not supported, 265,
        343, 345
    dual boot and, 345, 346
    enabling, 344
    Ontrack Systems' Disk Manager and, 346
    performance of, 344–345
    SyQuest SQATDRV.SYS and SQDRIVER.SYS
        drivers and, 346
    Windows NT and, 345
FAT32.BAT, 344
FAT file system, MS-DOS, 16
    long filename support and, 350
Favorites (Favorites folder)
    global, 41
    Thumbnail views of, 66–67
Favorites Explorer Bar, 52
Favorites menu, 28, 29
    notification of changes, 87
Faxback fax information services, 171, 172
faxes. *See* Microsoft Fax
fax machines, Group 3, 171, 172, 174
    poll-retrieve feature, 175
    T.30 standard for, 176
Fax menu item, in Microsoft Fax's Accessories
        menu, 172
fax-on-demand systems, 175
fax viewer, Microsoft Fax, 171
FDISK, 343
FDISK.EXE, 4–5
file extensions, hidden, 48, 351
file management, 50. *See also* file transfer
    from search results pane, 33
filenames
    8.3, 350
    long (*see* long filenames; long filename support)
files
    copying, as phase of Windows 98 Setup, 9
    date/time attributes, additional, 351
    finding, 32–33
    renaming, 48
file sharing
    NetWare network services, 208–211
    user-level security and, 229
Files Of Type box, Browse dialog box, 43
Files Or Folders command, Find menu, 31–33
file system architecture, 32-bit, 339–353
    additional date/time attributes for files, 351
    benefits to users, 339
    block I/O subsystem, 347–349
    CDFS (CD-ROM file system), 347
    coordinated universal time (UTC) format, 352

file system architecture, 32-bit, *continued*
  exclusive access for disk management utilities, 352
  FAT32, 342–347
  file system drivers supported, 340–342
  hidden file extensions, 351
  IFS (Installable File System) Manager, 340
  long filename support, 350
  overview of, 339
file system drivers (FSDs), 204, 205
file transfer
  multicast, with NetShow, 143
  with NetMeeting, 122
FilterKeys, 296–297
final system configuration phase of Windows 98
    Setup, 10
Find dialog box, 32–33
Find Files Or Folders command, 31–33
Find On The Internet command, 33
Find People command, 33
Find utility, 31–33
FIR (Fast Infrared) devices, 214, 264
firewall products, NetShow support for, 152
FirstFloor, 99
floating taskbar toolbars, 41
floppy drives
  controllers, 387
  driver, 383
  LS-120 (120 MB), 384
folders. *See also names of specific folders*
  Customize This Folder Wizard, 42, 182
  in Details view, 50
  document creation from within, 48
  finding, 32–33
  selecting more than one item in, 52
  sharing, with NetMeeting, 124
  on taskbar, 39
  Thumbnail views of, 67–68
Font common dialog box, multilingual extensions
    to, 398–399
fonts, 360
  international language support and, 392, 393
Fonts folder, 60
FORMAT.COM, 4
formatting rules, international language support
    and, 392
forms, on Web pages, 180
Forward button, Internet Explorer 4.0, 71
Four11, 33
Fraunhofer MPEG Layer-3 audio codec, 152
free system resources, 354–355
FrontPad, 23, 78, 179–182
FrontPage, 78
  Webcasting and, 99

FSDs (file system drivers), 204, 205
FTP (File Transfer Protocol), 196
  sharing a folder through, 185
FTP Software Inc. NFS Client, 214
Full HTML Object Model, 73–75
Full-screen mode, Internet Explorer 4.0, 71

G

G.711 standard, 139
G.723.1 audio standard, 139, 151
gamepads, Human Interface Device (HID) firmware
    specification, 322
games, MS-DOS–based
  Sound Blaster emulation for, 322–323
  support for running, 330
GDI heap, 354–355
General MIDI specification, 289
general protection faults (GPFs), hangs, and other
    stoppages, 327
  Dr. Watson utility and, 21–22
  during hardware detection, smart recovery
      mechanism and, 6–7
  Win16-based applications and, 327
Go menu, NetMeeting, 119
GPFs. *See* general protection faults (GPFs), hangs,
    and other stoppages
graphics
  3-D, 283–284
  collaboration with NetMeeting via, 125
graphics adapters
  multiple, 16
  refresh rate of, 17
GREv2 (Generic Routing Encapsulation), 219
Group 3 fax machines, 171, 172, 174
  poll-retrieve feature, 175
  T.30 standard for, 176
GUI-based setup process, 5–6

H

H.225.0 standard, 139
H.245 standard, 139
H.261 standard, 139
H.263 video standard, 139, 151
H.323 standard, 119, 130, 136–139
hangs. *See* general protection faults (GPFs), hangs,
    and other stoppages
hard drives. *See also* disk drives
  bus mastering, 384
hardware detection. *See also Plug and Play devices
    and peripherals*
  hang during, smart recovery mechanism and, 6
  legacy hardware, 8

hardware detection, *continued*
  as phase of Windows 98 Setup, 9–10
  in setup process, 6
hardware panning, 373
Hardware Profile manager, 264
hardware standards, support for new, 16
hardware tree, Plug and Play, 366
hearing impaired users, accessibility features for, 298
Help, 33, 55–57
  Accessibility section in, 293
  HTML, 81–82
  for TV Viewer, 422–423
HelpDesk, 57
Help files, as HTML pages, 55
HID (Human Input Devices), 322
hiding/showing
  Contents and Index tabs for Help information, 56
  desktop icons, 45
high-contrast mode, 295
History Explorer Bar, 52, 66
home page. *See* Internet Start page
hotkeys, emergency, 294–298
HSFLOP.PDR floppy disk driver, 383
HTML (Hypertext Markup Language)
  compressed, 82
  Dynamic, 62, 63, 73–76, 90, 188
    2-D Positioning, 74, 75
    data binding in, 75–76
    multimedia controls, 79–81
    Object Model of, 73–75, 77
  MIME (MHTML), 86, 87, 162, 163
  Outlook Express support for, 162–163
  sharing a folder through, 185
HTML documents
  adding to Active Desktop, 43
  Help files as, 55–56
HTML editor. *See* FrontPad
HTML Help, 81–82
HTML Help ActiveX control, 82
HTML Help Authoring DLL, 82
HTML Help window, 82
HTML Help Workshop, 82
HTTP cookies, 96
Human Input Devices (HID), 322
Hummingbird Communications, 113
HyperTerminal, 254, 305–306

I

IBM AS/400 computers, 20
IBM mainframe computers, 20
ICC (International Color Consortium) profiles, 237
ICM (Image Color Matching), 236–238, 378

icons
  desktop, showing/hiding, 45
  enhancements in Windows 98, 17
  in Web view, 52
ICW. *See* Internet Connection Wizard (ICW)
IDE-based CD-ROM drives, 386
IDE controllers
  alternate, 386
  block I/O subsystem support for, 349
IDE disk driver, 384
IDE disk drives, 385
IDE drive spin down, block I/O subsystem support
    for, 349
IEAK (Internet Explorer Administration Kit), 104,
    105, 111
IEEE 1394 bus, 16, 322
IETF (Internet Engineering Task Force), 140
IFS (Installable File System), 201, 204–205
IFS (Installable File System) Manager, 340
ILS (Internet Locator Server), 132, 134
  setting up your own, 135
IMADPCM, 288
Image Color Matching (ICM), 236–238, 378
implicit connections, 267
IMTC (International Multimedia Teleconferencing
    Consortium), 140
Inbox
  MAPI drivers and, 274
  Universal, 158, 174
Inbox Assistant, 165
Index tab, Help system, 56
information, system
  Microsoft System Information utility, 21
  online registration and, 12–13
information stores, 167–168
InfoSpace, 33
infrared device drivers and utilities. *See* IrDA (Infrared
    Data Association) device drivers and utilities
Infrared Transfer applet, 264
INI (initialization) files
  problems with, 358–359
  role of, 359–360
  Setup program and, 8
input devices. *See also* keyboards; mouse
  alternative, 298–299
INS Editor, 104
Insert WebBot Component command, 182
Installable File System (IFS), 201, 204–205, 340
installed components. *See also* hardware detection
  verification of, 7
installing Internet Explorer 4.0, 103–104
installing Windows 98, 3–13. *See also* Setup,
    Windows 98 (Setup program)

installing Windows 98, *continued*
  batch installation support, 8
  on a freshly formatted hard disk, 4–5
  on a network, 7–8
  system requirements, 3
  uninstalling Windows 98, 8, 10
  from within Windows 95, 4
INT 21H interrupt, 340
integrity check, Setup program's, 7
Intel Internet Video Phone, 130
intelligent control of audio and video streams, 131
IntelliMouse, 18, 388–389
Intel MMX technology
  NetMeeting and, 130
  support for, 20, 287
Interactive Music Bonus Pack, 80–81
Interactive Music control, 79, 80–81
Interactive Music site, Microsoft's, 81
InterColor 3.0, 237
InterLnk, FAT32 and, 346
international language support, 391–399
  benefits for developers, 392–393
  date and time formats, 395
  font substitution, 392
  formatting rules, 392, 395
  localization of Windows 98, 393
  multilingual content support, 396–399
  sorting and searching, 392, 395–396
  switching among languages, 392, 393, 396, 397
  Win32 NLS (National Language Support) APIs, 399
International Multimedia Teleconferencing Consortium (IMTC), 140
International Telecommunication Union (ITU), 139
Internet. *See also* Internet Explorer 4.0
  personalized information delivery on, 23
  private networks on, 19
Internet Client Software Development Kit (SDK), 189
Internet Connection Wizard (ICW), 18, 31, 115
Internet Engineering Task Force (IETF), 140
Internet Explorer 3.0, 102
Internet Explorer 4.0, 61–115
  ActiveX Control Viewer, 104–105
  ActiveX support in, 76–77
  administration tools in, 102–106
    Active Setup, 103–104
  advantages for different types of users, 62–63
  author and developer tools, 188–189
  Automatic Proxy Configuration, 105–106
  browsing capabilities, 22
  communication and collaboration with, 78–82
    (*see also* NetMeeting 2.0; NetShow 2.0;
    Outlook Express)
  multimedia capabilities, 79–81

Internet Explorer 4.0, *continued*
  complaints of users addressed by, 61–62
  Dynamic HTML (*see* Dynamic HTML)
  Integrated Shell option, 17, 63
  languages supported by, 62
  NetMeeting and, 119
  NetMeeting calls from, 133–134
  NetShow and, 148
  new features in, 22–23, 63–73
    AutoComplete, 68–69
    Back and Forward buttons, 71
    complete set of tools, 63
    drag and drop Quick Links, 70–71
    ease of use, 63
    Full-screen mode, 71
    History bar, 66
    Java innovations, 64
    personalized approach, 63
    printing improvements, 71
    ratings system (RSACi), 72–73
    Search bar, 65
    Smart Favorites, 69–70
    Smart Toolbar, 66
    Thumbnail View, 66–68
  Outlook Express integration with, 164
  security features of, 106–115
    Authenticode, 110–111
    benefits, 106–108
    certificate management, 111–112
    Custom security setting, 110
    Java security (sandboxing), 112–113
    privacy protection, 108, 113–115
    security zones, 108–110
  as single Explorer, 41–42, 100–102
  true Web integration, 62, 100–102
  types of innovations in, 62
  Webcasting (*see* Webcasting)
  Web PC and, 102
Internet Explorer Administration Kit (IEAK), 104, 105
Internet Explorer button, on taskbar, 38
Internet Explorer toolbar, on taskbar, 38
Internet Information Server (IIS), 78, 99
  NetShow and, 148
Internet phone, 131
Internet Properties dialog box, Security tab, 109, 110
Internet security zone, 110
Internet Service Providers (ISPs), 18
  Internet Connection Wizard and, 115
  Online Services Folder with links to, 19
Internet shell, integrated, 17, 63
Internet Start page, 182, 183
Internet Start Properties page, 86

Internet System Update, 21
Internet Video Phone, Intel, 130
invitation, NetMeeting, 132
I/O Supervisor (IOS), 348
ipconfig utility, 216
IPX/SPX protocol, 215
IrDA (Infrared Data Association) device drivers and
    utilities, 214
    3.0 standard, 19, 387
    driver, 264, 387
    mobile computing and, 264
IrLan Access Point Mode, 264, 387
IS-101 standard (AT+V), 254
IS-131 standard, 253
ISAPI (Internet Server API), 185
ISDN, 18
ISDN Accelerator Pack, 264–265
ISPs. *See* Internet Service Providers
Items On The Active Desktop pane, on Web tab of
    Display Properties dialog box, 43
ITU (International Telecommunication Union), 139
ITU G.711 standard, 139
ITU G.723.1 standard, 139, 151
ITU H.245 standard, 139
ITU H.261 standard, 139
ITU H.263 standard, 139, 151
ITU H.323 standard, 119, 130, 136–139
ITU T.30 standard, 176
ITU T.120 standard, 119, 122, 136–139
ITU T.127 standard, 122
ITU V.17, V.29, and V.27ter standards, 177

J

Java applets
    FrontPad support for, 181
    security (sandboxing), 108, 112–113
Java applications, Internet Explorer 4.0 and, 64
Java Beans, 64
Java class libraries, 64
Java Development Kit (JDK) 1.1, 64
Java programming language, 64
    AFC and, 188
JavaScript, FrontPad support for, 181
JDK (Java Development Kit) 1.1, 64
joysticks, Human Interface Device (HID) firmware
    specification, 322
JScript, 64, 77
    Automatic Proxy Configuration and, 105, 106
Just-in-Time Java compiler, 64

K

keyboard layouts, international language support
    and, 393, 396–397
keyboards
    accessibility features, 296–298
    Human Interface Device (HID) firmware specifi-
        cation, 322
Kodak PhotoCD, 283

L

languages, international. *See* international language
    support
LANs (local area networks). *See* networking with
    Windows 98
LDAP (Lightweight Directory Access Protocol), 33,
    136, 161–162
Lightweight Directory Access Protocol (LDAP), 33,
    136, 161–162
linear memory addressing, 356
Links folder, 29
Links option, Toolbars submenu, 37
Links toolbar, 37–38, 52, 70
local area networks (LANs). *See* networking with
    Windows 98
localization of Windows 98, 393
local reboot, 402
    Win32-based applications and, 408
log, setup, 7
Login button, 44
Login dialog box, 44
Log Off command, on Start button, 34
long filenames, 48
    corresponding 8.3 filename mappings, 350
    MS-DOS support for, 336
    network clients and, 226
long filename support, 350–351
    Win32-based applications, 338
LS-120 (120 MB) floppy drives, 384

M

MAC (Media Access Control) layer, 205
Managed Webcasting using the CDF, 95–98
MAPI (Messaging Application Programming Inter-
    face), 159. *See also* Windows Messaging
    information stores and, 168
    mobile computing and, 274–275
    open architecture of, 159–160
MAPI drivers
    mobile computing and, 274–275
    Outlook Express and, 158–160

Map Network Drive option, 53
Media Access Control (MAC) layer, 205
Mediamatics MPEG Arcade Player, 286
media-streaming technology, NetShow, 141, 143, 144, 147, 154
memory management, 356–357
memory protection
    MS-DOS–based applications, 332
    Win32-based applications, 338
menus
    context-sensitive, 41
    scrolling, 49
message queues, separate, 328, 337
Messaging Application Programming Interface. See MAPI (Messaging Application Programming Interface)
MFTP (Multicast File Transfer Protocol), 98
MHTML (MIME HTML), 86, 87, 162, 163
MIB (Management Information Base) and MIB-II, SNMP, 198
microphone
    muting, 131
    sensitivity-level setting, automatic, 131
Microsoft At Work, Microsoft Fax and, 171–172, 174, 176, 177
Microsoft Chat. See Chat, NetMeeting
Microsoft Client for Novell NetWare Networks, 195–197, 206–208
Microsoft Exchange
    faxes and, 174
    NetMeeting calls from, 133
Microsoft Exchange Server, Microsoft Mail Post Office and, 170
Microsoft Fax, 159, 170–177
    attaching a document to an e-mail message, 172
    compatibility with fax modems and fax machines, 176–177
    Cover Page Editor, 172, 175
    different types of recipients, sending messages to, 172
    encryption and digital signature capabilities, 176
    fax-on-demand systems and, 175
    integration of applications and, 177
    key features of, 171
    mobile computing and, 275
    "print to fax" interface, 173
    rich-text messaging capabilities, 174
    TAPI support for, 177
    workgroup fax features, 174
Microsoft Flash, 82
Microsoft FrontPad. See FrontPad
Microsoft FrontPage. See FrontPage
Microsoft Home link, 57

Microsoft HTML Help Workshop, 82
Microsoft Infrared Transfer, 214, 264
Microsoft IntelliMouse, 18, 388–389
Microsoft Internet Explorer 4.0. See Internet Explorer 4.0
Microsoft Internet Information Server. See Internet Information Server (IIS)
Microsoft Internet Mail drivers, 159
Microsoft Knowledge Base, 57
Microsoft Mail, Outlook Express and, 168
Microsoft Mail Post Office, 159, 170
Microsoft NetMeeting. See NetMeeting 2.0
Microsoft NetMeeting 2.0 Resource Kit, 140
Microsoft NetShow. See NetShow 2.0
Microsoft Network (MSN), 19, 29
Microsoft Network Peer Services, 208, 213–214
Microsoft Outlook Express. See Outlook Express
Microsoft Paint, 304–305
Microsoft Plus!, 17
    DriveSpace, 265–266
Microsoft Print Server for NetWare networks, 226
Microsoft Protected Store, 107
Microsoft Synthesizer, 81
Microsoft System Information utility, 21
Microsoft Video for Windows, 281–282
Microsoft Visual Basic. See Visual Basic
Microsoft Wallet, 114
Microsoft WordPad, 304
MIDI (Musical Instrument Digital Interface)
    built-in support for, 282, 286–287
    General MIDI specification, 289
    polymessage MIDI support, 288
    USB audio and, 323
MIME (Multi-purpose Internet Mail Extensions), 161
MIME HTML (MHTML), 86, 87, 162, 163
mini-drivers
    architecture, 377, 379
    NDIS, 205
mini-port drivers, 386
missing files, reinstallation of, 7
MMX technology, Intel
    NetMeeting and, 130
    support for, 20, 287
mobile computing, 257–278
    Advanced Power Management (APM) support, 261–262
    Briefcase, 276–278
    challenges of, 258–259
    communications capabilities, 266–275
        Dial-Up Networking, 266–271
        Direct Cable Connection, 278
        dynamic network architecture, 272

mobile computing, communications capabilities, *continued*
    MAPI (Messaging API), 274–275
    Microsoft Fax, 275
    Remote Access subsystem, 271–272
    remote mail, 274
    TAPI (Telephony API), 272–273
    Unimodem, 273–274
  configuration-change message support, 262–263
  data-management challenges, 275–276
  deferred printing, 278
  document viewers, 266
  DriveSpace disk compression, 265–266
  hot-docking and port replicator support, 262
  IrDA (Infrared Data Association) support, 264
  ISDN 1.1 Accelerator Pack support, 264–265
  network support, 197–198
  observations about, 257–258
  PC Cards (PCMCIA), 259–260
  Plug and Play and, 365
  "power aware" applications, 261
  Registry integration, 263–264
modems, 253–254
  centralized setup and configuration of, 250–252
  multilink channel aggregation and, 18, 271
  parallel port, 253
  PC Card, 261
    powering down inactive, 382
  Plug and Play, 253–254
  supported, 383
Modem Wizard, 251
modification date
  file searches on last, 33
monitors, 385. *See also* displays
  loss of sync, 374
  multiple, 16
  multiple display support, 374–375
Monitors tab, Display property sheet, 373, 375
mouse, 387–389
  accessibility features, 296–298
  configuration and customization support, 388
  Human Interface Device (HID) firmware specification, 322
  protected-mode virtual device driver, 388
MouseKeys, 297–298
mouse pointer
  customizable, 295
  keyboard control of, 297–298
movies, DVD, 324
MPEG (Moving Pictures Experts Group), 81
  software-based support for, 285–286
MPEG-4 video standard, 152

MPEG audio, 20
MPEG Layer-3 codec, 152
MPEG video, 20
MPU-401 music synthesis hardware interface, 323
MSCDEX.DLL, 283
MSCDEX driver, 347
MS-DOS, Windows 98 architecture and, 318
MS-DOS–based applications
  ASPI/CAM compatibility for, 386
  printing from, 236
  robustness for running, 404–405
  support for running, 328–336
    accessing network resources with UNC pathnames, 335
    APPS.INF, 330–331
    benefits of, 328
    commands, MS-DOS prompt, 336
    compatibility, 330–331
    consolidated customization of MS-DOS–based application properties, 332
    defaults for, 332
    ending applications gracefully, 334
    graphic-intensive MS-DOS–based applications, 331
    local virtual machine environment settings, 334
    long filename support, 336
    memory protection, 332
    MS-DOS mode, 331
    scalable MS-DOS windows, 334
    toolbars in MS-DOS windows, 333–334
    zero conventional memory footprint components, 329
MS-DOS Editor, 306–307
MS-DOS mode, 331
  FAT32 and, 345, 346
MS-DOS windows
  scalable, 334
  toolbars in, 333–334
MSN. *See* Microsoft Network (MSN)
MSN channels, 43, 52
Mt. Fuji specification (SFF8090), 324
MTS Windows Support Home Page, 57
multicast(ing), 98–100
  with NetShow, 142–143
Multicast File Transfer Protocol (MFTP), 98
multifunction PC Cards, 20, 260
multilingual content support, 396–399
multilingual support. *See* international language support
multilink channel aggregation, 18, 271
Multilink PPP, 271

multimedia, 279–290
    3-D graphics development support, 283–284
    authoring devices, built-in support for, 289
    AutoPlay support, 281
    CD Player, 282
    CD Plus support, 284–285
    development environment for, 287–288
    digital video support, 281–282
    DVD support, 290
    General MIDI specification, 289
    home entertainment, 283–285
    multitasking and, 288
    Plug and Play support, 280–281
    sound and MIDI support, 282, 286–288
    sound compression for CD-quality sound, 287–288
    Surround Video, 286
multimedia applications and tools. *See also*
        NetShow 2.0
    ActiveMovie, 20
multimedia controls, Dynamic HTML, 79–81
multiple display support, 16, 371, 373, 374–376
    display adapter chip sets supported, 376
    enabling, 375–376
multipoint data conferencing with NetMeeting, 118,
        119, 122–126, 132
    application sharing, 120–124
    file transfer, 122
    ITU T.120 standard, 119, 122, 136–139
    shared clipboard, 122
multitasking
    multimedia and, 288
    preemptive, 316–317, 337
multithreading, 317
music control, Internet Explorer 4.0, 80
My Computer, 51–52
    hyperlinks to Microsoft, 57
My Intranet security zone, 110

N

NBF (NetBEUI Frame), 221
NDIS (Network Driver Interface Specification), 201,
        205–206
NDS (NetWare Directory Services), 20
NetBEUI protocol, 215, 217
NetMeeting 2.0, 22, 78, 117
    calling someone with, 131–135
        choosing an ILS to reside on, 135
        directory filtering, 132
        Do Not Disturb option, 132–133
        from Exchange and Outlook, 133
        finding other NetMeeting users to call, 134

NetMeeting 2.0, calling someone with, *continued*
        from Internet Explorer or Windows Explorer,
        133
        multipoint data conferencing, 132
        NetMeeting invitation, 132
        SpeedDial, 132
        Web-based directory, 133
    Chat, 126–128
    conferencing options of, 118–119
    customer service, 121
    distance learning with, 121
    document collaboration, 121
    e-mail, 120
    home users and, 122
    intelligent control of audio and video streams, 131
    Internet phone and audio conferencing, 131
    multipoint data conferencing with (*see* multipoint
        data conferencing with NetMeeting)
    standards, 136–140
    system policies, 135, 137
    technical support with, 121
    telecommuting with, 121
    user interface enhancements in, 119–120
    video conferencing and videophone, 129–130
    virtual meetings, 120
    whiteboard feature, 123, 124–126
NetMeeting 2.0 Resource Kit, 140
NetMeeting SDK, 137
Netscape Netcaster, 99
NetShow 2.0, 23, 78, 79, 99, 141–156
    architecture, 153–154
        Active Streaming Format (ASF), 154
        content authoring and production, 154
        NetShow client, 154
        NetShow server, 153–154
    benefits of, 143–144
    features of, 142–143
        new features in Version 2.0, 145–146
    Internet Information Server (IIS) 3.0 integration,
        142
    key technologies of, 147–153
        audio and video compression tools, 151–152
        content delivery and scheduling, 151
        cross-platform client support, 153
        fail-over, 145, 152
        firewall support, 152
        media streaming, 147
        network bandwidth support, 149–150
        open, standards-based system, 148–149
        partitioning for distribution, 150
        rich-client programmability, 153
        robust and efficient server for heavy-duty
            broadcast, 149

NetShow 2.0, key technologies of, *continued*
    scalability, 149
    tight integration with Internet Explorer, 148
    tight integration with Windows NT Server
       and IIS, 148
    unicast and multicast, 147
    Web-based administration, 150–151
  using, 155–156
NetShow ActiveX control, 153
NetWare Compatible Peer Services, 208–209
NetWare Directory Services (NDS), 20, 211–212
NetWare networks, 195
  Microsoft Print Server for, 226
  Windows 98 integration with, 206–212
    file and printer sharing services, 208–211
    Microsoft Client for NetWare Networks for
      Windows, 206–208
NetWatcher, 200, 210
network administrator, configuration of Network
    Neighborhood by, 53
Network Control Panel tool, 53
Network Driver Interface Specification (NDIS), 201,
    205–206
network fax server, 174
networking with Windows 98, 193–231
  architecture, 200–201
    dynamic nature of, 272
  ATM network card support, 214
  Dial-Up Networking and (*see* Dial-Up Networking)
  Distributed COM (DCOM), 227
  ease of setup and installation, 200
  IFS (Installable File System), 204–205
  installing Windows 98 on a network, 7–8
  Internet access, 195–196
  interprocess communications interfaces, 225
  IrDA device support, 214
  key components of, 198–200
  key features, 194
  long filename support, 226
  management tools, 199–200
  Microsoft network integration, 212–214
  mobile network support, 197–198
  multiple network support, 195
  NDIS 4.1 for multiple protocol support, 205
  NetWare networks (*see* NetWare networks)
  Novell NetWare integration, 195
  Plug and Play support, 197
  printing, 226–227
  protocols supported, 214–225
    DLC (Data Link Control) protocol, 217–218
    IPX/SPX, 215
    PPTP, 218–225
    TCP/IP, 215–217

networking with Windows 98, *continued*
  Remote Access Server, 230–231
  security issues, 227–230
  Windows Scripting Host (WSH), 226
Network Neighborhood, 53–54, 196–197
Network OLE, 20. *See also* Distributed COM (DCOM)
Network Provider, 212–213
Network Provider Interface (NPI), 201, 202–204
network redirectors, 341
  support for multiple, 204
network resources, accessing, from the MS-DOS
    command prompt, 335
network servers. *See also specific servers*
  concurrent support for multiple, 202–204
  installation of Windows 98 on, 200
  installing and running Windows 98 from, 7, 8
New Active Desktop Item Wizard, 43–44
new features in Microsoft Windows 98, 15
  FAT32, 16
  FAT32 conversion utility, 16
  Internet Explorer 4.0, 22–23
  multiple display support, 16
  power management improvements, 16
  reliability and manageability improvements, 21–22
  support for hardware standards, 16
  user interface, 16–20
    32-bit Data Link Control (DLC), 20
    ActiveMovie, 20
    Dial-Up Networking improvements, 18
    Disk Defragmenter Optimization Wizard, 18
    display setting enhancements, 17
    Distributed COM (DCOM), 20
    Infrared Data Association (IrDA) 3.0, 19
    integrated Internet shell, 17, 63
    Intellimouse suport, 18
    Intel MMX processors, 20
    Internet Connection Wizard (ICW), 18
    NetWare Directory Services (NDS), 20
    Online Services Folder, 19
    PCMCIA enhancements, 19–20
    Point-to-Point Tunneling Protocol (PPTP), 19
    remote access server, 19
    Setup enhancements, 17
    Start Menu Organizer Wizard, 17
    Windows Scripting Host (WSH), 17
    Windows Tune Up Wizard, 18
  WDM (Win32 Driver Model), 15
New Toolbar command, 39
notebook computers. *See* mobile computing
notification of new content in Web sites, 83, 86–87
Novell NetWare 3.*x* or 4.*x* server, network logon
    dialog box for, 203

Novell NetWare Directory Services (NDS), 20
Novell NetWare networks. *See* NetWare networks
NPI (Network Provider Interface), 201, 202–204
NRN protocol, 268
NTFS, 345
NTKERN.VXD, 15, 321
NTLM (NT LanMan), 110
numeric keypad, direction keys on, 297
Num Lock key, audio cues for, 298
NWLink, 221

O

Object Model. *See also* Component Object Model
    (COM); Distributed COM (DCOM)
    Dynamic HTML's, 73–75, 77
objects, windows as views of, 48
OLE compound documents, in information stores,
    168
OLE Management Services (OLE MS), 199
Online Help. *See* Help
Online Services Folder, 19
OnNow design initiative, 381–382
OnNow feature, 34
On The Internet command, Find menu, 33
Ontrack Systems' Disk Manager, FAT32 and, 346
Open All command, Help system, 56
Open Control Panel command, 31
Open With dialog box, 302
OPL-2 or OPL-3 music synthesis, 323
Outlook, NetMeeting calls from, 133
Outlook Express, 22, 78, 108, 158, 161–170
    Auto-add feature, 165
    Draft folder, 165
    Find Message feature, 165
    global address books, 165
    HTML support, 162–163
    Inbox Assistant, 165
    integration with Internet Explorer, 164
    LDAP support, 161–162
    messaging independence, 162
    Microsoft Fax and, 170–172, 174, 177
    multiple mailboxes, 165
    notification of site changes through, 86
    offline reading and composing, 164
    Personal Address Book, 165, 166–167
    Personal Information Store, 167–168
    remote e-mail, 168–169
    rich-text mail messages, 165–166
    separate Send and Receive commands, 165
    S/MIME support and security, 163–164
    starting, 169–170

P

Paint, 304–305
panning, hardware, 373
parallel port modems, 253
parameter validation
    of virtual device drivers, 404
    for Win16 APIs, 405
    for Win32 APIs, 406
pass-through security, 229
Password Control, 228–229
passwords, 88
    Internet Explorer 4.0 and, 110
    networking and, 228–229
PC Card32 (CardBus), 19, 260
PC Cards (PCMCIA), 259–260
    3.3 volt, 19, 260
    configuration-change message support, 263
    enhancements in Windows 98, 19–20, 260
    modems, 261
        powering down inactive, 382
    multifunction, 20, 260
    PC Card32 (CardBus) support, 260
PC Card Wizard, 260
PCMCIA. *See* PC Cards (PCMCIA)
PCT (Personal Communications Technology 1.0), 113
PCX files, 305
peer services
    for Microsoft networks, 213–214
    NetWare Compatible, 208–209
Peer Web Services, Windows NT Workstation ver-
        sion 4.0, 185
people, finding, 33
People command, Find menu, 33
Personal Address Book, 158, 165, 166–167
personal certificates, 111, 114
    obtaining and using, 112
Personal Communications Technology 1.0 (PCT), 113
Personal Home Page Wizard, 180, 182–183
Personal Information Exchange (PFX), 113
Personal Information Store, 159, 167–168
Personal Web Server, 23, 184–187
PFX (Personal Information Exchange), 113
Phone Dialer, 254–255
PhotoCD, 283
PICS (Platform for Internet Content Selection), 72,
        73, 114
pictures, adding to Active Desktop, 43
Platform for Internet Content Selection (PICS), 72, 73
Plug and Play, 361–369
    Advanced Power Management (APM), 261
    architecture of, 365, 366–367
    benefits of, 362–363

Plug and Play, *continued*
  BIOS, 362
  bus and port enumerators, 366
  communications support, 245, 253
  compatibility with legacy hardware, 364
  components of, 362
  configuration-change message support, 262–263
  Configuration Manager, 366
  configuration process, 363–364
  detection of devices during Windows 98 setup, 6, 10
  enhancements to the Protocol Manager and Media Access Control layer, 205
  hardware design, 368–369
  hardware specifications, 363
  hardware tree and Registry, 366
  levels of support, 362
  mobile computing and, 365
  mobile network support, 197
  modems, 253–254
  multimedia support, 280–281
  networking components, 201
  PC Cards, 259–260
  pointing devices, 299
  printers, 238, 241–242
  Registry and, 360
  resource arbitrators, 367
  Setup and device installer, 367
  universal driver model, 365
  widespread acceptance of, 363
  Windows 98 support for, 364
plug-ins, FrontPad support for, 181
PLUGPLAY forum (CompuServe), 363, 369
Plus!. *See* Microsoft Plus!
Plus! tab, Display Properties property sheet, 59
Point and Print printing, 226, 239, 241
PointCast, 99
pointer, mouse. *See* mouse pointer
pointing devices. *See also* mouse
  Human Interface Device (HID) firmware specification for, 322
Point-to-Point Tunneling Protocol. *See* PPTP (Point-to-Point Tunneling Protocol)
POLICY.POL, 199, 411, 412, 415
polymessage MIDI support, 288
Portable option, Windows 98 Setup, 9
portable PCs. *See* mobile computing
port drivers, 247
port enumerators, 366
port replicators, 262
ports. *See also* serial ports
  support for more, 253
positioning taskbar toolbars, 40
Post Office, Microsoft Mail, 170

power management, 261–263
  improvements in, 16, 380–382
PPP (Point-to-Point Protocol)
  Dial-Up Networking and, 268
  Multilink, 271
PPTP (Point-to-Point Tunneling Protocol), 19, 218–225
  Dial-Up Networking and, 268
  technical details of, 219–225
    network protocol issues, 221–223
    Windows 98 support, 220–221
preemptive multitasking, 316–317, 337
premium channels, 89–93
  benefits of, 89–90
presentations, with NetMeeting, 120, 121
Print button, Help system, 57
printer drivers, 226
printers
  installing and configuring, 238–239
  Plug and Play, 241–242
  sharing
    NetWare network services, 208–211
    user-level security and, 229
Printers folder, 59, 240
printing, 233–242
  32-bit print subsystem, 234–235
  deferred, 227, 236, 278
  ICM (Image Color Matching) support, 236–238, 378
  improvements in Windows 95, 233–234
  Internet Explorer 4.0 improvements, 71
  managing print jobs, 240–241
  to Microsoft Fax printer driver, 173
  from MS-DOS–based applications, 236
  on networks, 226, 241
  Point and Print, 226, 239, 241
  remote administration of print jobs, 241
  spooler, 234–236
print spooler, 234–235
privacy protection, Internet Explorer 4.0, 108, 113–115. *See also* security
private networks, PPTP (Point-to-Point Tunneling Protocol) and, 19
processes, 317
Prodigy, 19
Program Guide, TV Viewer, 424–429, 432
  setting reminders in, 435–436
Programs folder, shortcuts in, 47
Programs menu, Start button's, 28, 29
  shortcuts in, 47
progressive downloading, 81
property sheets, 47
Protocol Manager, 205–206

Proxy Configuration, Automatic, 105–106
PSTN (public switched telephone network), 119
public key encryption, 163–164
publishing, with Personal Web Server, 184–187

Q

Quick Launch option, on Toolbars submenu, 38
Quick Launch toolbar, 36
Quick Links, 63, 70–71
QuickTime, 20
Quick View, for portable PCs, 266
Quick Viewers, 301–303

R

RAS Multilink, 271
RAS protocol, 268–269
ratings system (RSACi), Internet Explorer 4.0, 72, 114
real-mode drivers, 318
real-mode mapper (RMM), block I/O subsystem, 349
real-mode MS-DOS, 331
    block I/O subsystem and, 349
    FAT32 and, 345
Real-time Transport Control Protocol (RTCP), 138
Real-time Transport Protocol (RTP), 138
reboot, local, 402
    Win32-based applications and, 408
reconciliation handlers, 277–278
recovery mechanism
    Setup's, 6–7
Recreational Software Advisory Council, 73
Recycle Bin, 54
REGEDIT (Registry Editor), 413, 414
REGINFO.TXT, 13
registration of Windows 98, 11–13
Registration Wizard, 11–13
Registry, 357–360
    improvements in Windows 98, 357, 414
    INI problems and, 358
    mobile computing and, 263–264
    networking and, 199, 200
    Plug and Play and, 360, 366
    remote access to, 360
    systems management and, 411–415
    Windows Management Infrastructure (WMI)
        and, 358
Registry Editor (REGEDIT), 199, 413, 414
remote access, 19
    to Registry, 360
Remote Access API, 268
Remote Access Server, 19, 230–231
Remote Access subsystem, 271–272
Remote Administration function, 229–230

remote mail, 168–169, 274
Remote Pointer in NetMeeting whiteboard, 125
removable media devices, 382
renaming
    files, 48
    shortcuts, 46
RepeatKeys, 296
Request A Fax command, Microsoft Fax, 172
Request A Fax wizard, 175
resizing
    taskbar toolbars, 40
    user interface elements, 295
resolution, switching, without rebooting, 372
resource arbitrators, 367
Restart command, 34
Restart In MS-DOS Mode command, 34
retailing, NetShow used for, 156
rich-text mail messages, with Outlook Express,
        165–166
right-clicking
    for context-sensitive properties, 47
    for performing actions on objects, 47
Ring 0 and Ring 3 code, 325
RIPL (remote initial program load), 7
RMM (real-mode mapper), block I/O subsystem, 349
robustness and stability of Windows 98, 401–408
    local reboot, 402
    for MS-DOS–based applications, 404–405
    parameter validation of virtual device drivers, 404
    per-thread state tracking, 403–404
    virtual device driver thread cleanup, 403
    for Win16-based applications, 405
    for Win32-based applications, 406–408
RTCP (Real-time Transport Control Protocol), 138,
        139
RTF (Rich Text Format), international language
        information in, 393
RTP (Real-time Transport Protocol), 138, 139
RTP (Reliable Transport Protocol), 143
Run command, 34
RunOnceEx Log.txt, 103

S

sandboxing, 112–113
saving
    search results, 33
    whiteboard contents, 126
ScanDisk, 310–311
    after improper shutdown, 22, 311
    Automatic, 311
scheduling
    connections to retrieve mail remotely, 169
    Managed Webcasting and, 95–97

scheduling, *continued*
    site downloads, 83, 86
screen capture, NetMeeting Whiteboard and, 125
screen color schemes, high-contrast, 295
screen elements, scalable, 295
Screen Saver tab, Display Properties property sheet,
    59
scripting
    ActiveX, 77
    dial-up, 270
    support for, 17 (*see also* Windows Scripting
        Host (WSH))
scrolling menus, 49
Scroll Lock key, audio cues for, 298
SCSI controllers, block I/O subsystem support for,
    349
SCSI disk devices and controllers, 386
SCSI layer, block I/O subsystem, 349
SCSI Manager, 349
SCSI tape devices, 22
Search Explorer Bar, 52, 65
searching algorithms, international language support
    and, 395
Secure Sockets Layer 2.0/3.0 (SSL), 113
security, 108. *See also* authentication; Authenticode;
        encryption; passwords
    Internet Explorer 4.0, 106–115
        Authenticode, 110–111
        benefits, 106–108
        certificate management, 111–112
        Custom security setting, 110
        Java security (sandboxing), 112–113
        privacy protection, 108, 113–115
        security zones, 108–110
    network, 227–230
    Outlook Express, 163–164
    share-level, 213
    user-level, 213, 229–230
Security tab, Internet Properties dialog box, 109, 110
security zones, 108–110
selecting more than one item in folders, 52
Select Window or Select Area tools, NetMeeting
        Whiteboard, 125
Serial Infrared (SIR) devices, 214, 264
SerialKeys, 298
serial ports
    16550A UART, 253
    support for more, 253
Service Provider Interface (SPI), MAPI, 159, 160
Settings icon on the taskbar, 372
Settings menu, Start button's, 30–31
Settings tab, Display Properties property sheet, 59
Settings Wizard, 30–31

Settings Wizards command, 30–31
setup, Internet Explorer 4.0, 103–104
Setup, Windows 98 (Setup program), 4, 8, 9. *See
        also* installing Windows 98
    better control over installed components, 6
    enhancements to, 8–9, 17
    as GUI-based, 5–6
    hardware detection, 6
    networking and, 200
    network installation location remembered by, 8
    network setup, 7–8
    networks supported, 214
    phases of, 9–10
    scenarios for, 9
    smart recovery feature, 6–7
    verification of installed components, 7
SFF8090 (Mt. Fuji specification), 324
share-level security, 213, 269
shortcut buttons, Help system, 57
shortcut menus, displaying, 35
shortcuts, 46–47
Show Icons option, Active Desktop, 45
showing/hiding. *See* hiding/showing
ShowSounds, 298
Show Text option, Taskbar shortcut menu, 36, 38
Show Title option, Taskbar shortcut menu, 36, 38
shutdown, automatic ScanDisk after improper, 22,
    311
Shut Down command, 34
Shut Down item, Start menu, 34
SIMD (single instruction, multiple data) technique,
    287
single-click feature, 51
SIR (Serial Infrared) devices, 214, 264
Site Builder Network, 189
Site Builder Workshop, 189
site certificates, 112, 115
SiteServer 2.0, 99
SLIP (Serial Line Internet Protocol), 269
SlowKeys, 296
SmartDrive, VCACHE as replacement for, 341
Smart Favorites, 69–70, 84
smart recovery feature, 6–7
Smart Toolbar, Internet Explorer 4.0, 66
S/MIME support and security, Outlook Express,
    163–164
SMP (symmetric multiprocessing), 317
SNMP (Simple Network Management Protocol), 198
SNMP MIB (Management Information Base) and
        MIB-II, 198
SOCKS firewall support, 113
Sony desktop camera (CCM-DS250), 322

sorting, international language support and, 392, 395–396
sound (audio), 282, 286–287
Sound Blaster emulation, for WDM audio, 322–323
sound compression for CD-quality sound, 287–288
SoundSentry, 298
speakers, USB, 322
SpeedDial, 132
SPI (Service Provider Interface), MAPI, 159, 160
spooler, print, 234–235
SSL (Secure Sockets Layer 2.0/3.0), 113
stability of Windows 98. *See* robustness and stability of Windows 98
Standard Buttons toolbar, 52
standards, international communications and conferencing, 137–140
Start menu (Start button), 27, 28–35
    Documents menu, 30
    Eject command, 34
    Favorites submenu, 29
    Help, 33
    Log Off command, 34
    Programs menu, 29
    removing items from, 35
    Run command, 34
    Settings menu, 5, 30–31
    Shut Down item, 34
    Suspend command, 34
Start Menu Organizer Wizard, 17, 34–35
step capture, 289
StickyKeys, 296
still image capture, 324, 385
streaming technology, NetShow, 141, 143, 144, 147, 154
Subscribe dialog box, 44
Subscriptions folder, 85
subscriptions to channels, 91–93
subscriptions to Web sites, 82–89
    benefits of, 83–84
    key features of, 83
    payment not involved in, 83
    underlying technology of, 87–88
Subscription Wizard, 84
SunSoft PC-NFS, 214
Surround Video, 286
Suspend command, 34
Suspend mode, 261, 262
swap file, 356–357
Swedish, sorting in, 395–396
Switch Audio And Video option, NetMeeting, 129
switching applications, 35, 36
symmetric multiprocessing (SMP), 317

SyQuest SQATDRV.SYS and SQDRIVER.SYS drivers, FAT32 and, 346
SYSTEM.DAT, 199, 411
System File Checker, 21, 311–312
system files
    Windows 95, backing up, for future uninstall of Windows 98, 8
    Windows 98
        checking and restoring, 311–312
        System File Checker utility, 21, 311–312
system information
    Microsoft System Information utility, 21
    online registration and, 12–13
System Monitor, 199–200
system policies, 416–419
    for computers, 418–419
    for users, 417–418
System Policy Editor, 199, 415
system policy support, integration of NetMeeting with, 130
system requirements, for installing Windows 98, 3
system resources, 354–355
    per-thread tracking of, 403–404
        Win16-based applications, 405
        Win32-based applications, 406–407
    when a virtual machine ends, 405
Systems Compatibility Corporation (SCC), 302
systems management, 409–419
    Registry, 411–415
    server's role in, 419
    user management, 415–419
system switches, 359

T

T.30 standard, ITU, 176
T.120 standard, ITU, 119, 122, 136–139
T.127 standard, ITU, 122
tables, on Web pages, 180
tape backup utility, 22
TAPI (Telephony API), 245, 248–250, 273
    Microsoft Fax and, 177
    mobile computing and, 272–273
    Outlook Express and, 167, 169
    sharing communications devices and, 250
taskbar, 27, 28, 35–41
    Desktop button, 36
    hiding, 36
    notification icon on, 86
    repositioning, 36
    resizing, 36
    toolbars on, 36–41
        buttons, adjusting your view of, 39–40

taskbar, toolbars on, *continued*
    creating a new toolbar, 39
    floating toolbars, 41
    manipulating, 38–41
    positioning toolbars, 40
    resizing toolbars, 40
  Toolbars submenu, 37–38
Taskbar Properties dialog box, 31
Taskbar & Start Menu command, 30
task buttons, 36
TCP/IP protocol, 19, 196, 215–217, 221
technical support, 57
  with NetMeeting, 121
Technical Support link, 57
telecommuting, with NetMeeting, 121
telephone numbers, auto-dialing, 167
telephony, G.723.1 standard, 151
Telephony API. *See* TAPI (Telephony API)
Telnet, 196
Terminal, 305
Texas Instruments PCI-LYNX, 322
text editor, MS-DOS–based, 306–307
Thumbnail View, 66–68
time
  additional file date/time attributes, 351
  coordinated universal time (UTC) format, 352
TLS (Transport Layer Security), 113
ToggleKeys, 298
toolbars
  context-sensitive, 41
  custom, 28
  in MS-DOS windows, 333–334
  on taskbar, 36–41
    buttons, adjusting your view of, 39–40
    creating a new toolbar, 39
    floating toolbars, 41
    manipulating, 38–41
    positioning toolbars, 40
    resizing toolbars, 40
  Toolbars submenu, taskbar, 37–38
ToolTips, 38
  Smart Favorites, 69, 70
  for window controls, 49
Torso, 99
tracking resources on a per-thread basis, 403–404
training, NetShow used for, 155–156
Transport Layer Security (TLS), 113
Troubleshooting Wizards, 57
TrueSpeech, 288
TrueType rasterizer, 32-bit, 360
true Web integration, 62, 100–102
Trusted Web Sites security zone, 110
TSRs (terminate-and-stay-resident programs), 318

Tune Up Wizard, 18
tunneling, 218
TV Toolbar, 421–422
TV Viewer, 421–440
  choosing favorite channels, 434–435
  controlling, 430–431
  Help for, 422–423
  icons, 429
  Program Guide for, 424–429, 432
  searching for a program, 432–434
  setting reminders, 435–436
  signing on, 423–424
  supervising TV viewing, 436–440
  troubleshooting, 440
Typical option, Windows 98 Setup, 9

U

UDF (Universal Disk Filesystem), 324
ULS (User Location Server), 117. *See also* ILS
    (Internet Locator Server)
UNC pathnames, 53
Undo command, 54
undoing file operations, 54–55
Unimodem (universal modem driver), 245, 246,
    273–274
uninstalling Windows 98, 8, 10
Universal Inbox, 158
  Microsoft Fax and, 174
Universal Serial Bus (USB), 16
Up button, in Standard Buttons toolbar, 52
upgrading from Windows 95. *See* installing
    Windows 98; Setup, Windows 98 (Setup
    program)
URLs (Uniform Resource Locators)
  AutoComplete feature and, 68–69
USB (Universal Serial Bus), 16
USB (Universal Serial Bus) speakers, 322–323
USER.DAT, 199, 411
USER heap, 354–355
user interface improvements in Windows 98. *See*
    new features in Microsoft Windows 98, user
    interface
UserLand Software, 99
user-level security, 213, 229–230, 269
User Location Server (ULS), 117
user management, 415–419
user profiles, 415–416
UTC (coordinated universal time) format, 352

V

V.17, V.29, and V.27ter standards, 177
VCACHE (32-bit protected-mode cache), 341–342
vCards, 162

VCM (Video Compression Module) codecs, 151
VCOMM communications device drivers, 246, 247
VCRs (videocassette recorders), 289
verification of installed components, 7
VeriSign, 111, 112
VFAT file system (32-bit protected-mode FAT file
 system), 341
video
 compression tools, 151–152
 digital, 281–282
  capture and compression of bigger, 289
 Surround Video, 286
video capture, 385
video capture, WDM, 325
video CDs, 283
Video Compression Module (VCM) codecs, 151
video conferencing, 118, 129–130. *See also*
 NetMeeting 2.0
 H.323 standard, 119, 130, 136–139
video drivers. *See* display drivers
Video for Windows, 281–282
Video Quality slider bar, 130
video stream, intelligent control of, 131
video windows, detachable, 130
View As Web Page option, 42, 43. *See also* Web View
Views button
 in Standard Buttons toolbar, 52
virtual 8086 mode, 318
virtual device drivers. *See* VxDs (virtual device
 drivers)
virtual meetings, NetMeeting, 120
virtual memory, 356–357
Visual Basic
 scripting support, 17
Visual Basic, Scripting Edition (VBScript), 64, 77
visual cues for hearing impaired users, 298
visual impairments, accessibility features for users
 with, 295
voice-input systems, 299
VRML (Virtual Reality Modeling Language) 2.0, 79
VxDs (virtual device drivers), 200–201, 319–321
 parameter validation, 404
 thread cleanup, 403

W

Wallet, 114
wavetable music synthesis, 323
WAV files, 20
 NetShow and, 154
WDM (Win32 Driver Model), 15, 321–325, 383
 digital audio (USB speakers), 322–323
 DVD movie playback, 324
 DVD storage and UDF file system, 324

WDM (Win32 Driver Model), *continued*
 Human Input Devices (HID) support, 322
 IEEE 1394 support, 322
 still image capture, 324
 USB support, 322
 video capture, 325
Web addresses, on taskbar, 37
Web authoring, 181–182. *See also* FrontPad
Web-based directory, 133
WebBot components, 182
Web browser. *See* Internet Explorer 4.0
Webcasting, 62, 82–100
 Basic, 94–95
 extensible architecture and multicast support, 98
 Managed, using the CDF, 95–98
 Microsoft software and, 99–100
 premium channels, 89–93
 scalable tiers of, 94
 subscriptions, 82–89
  benefits of, 83–84
  key features of, 83
  payment not involved in, 83
  underlying technology of, 87–88
 third-party support for CDF, 99
Webcrawl, 82, 84, 88, 89
 Managed Webcasting and, 95
Web pages, creating, with FrontPad, 179–182
Web PC, 102
Web Publishing Wizard, 23, 180, 186, 187–188
Web Server, Personal, 184–187
Web Sharing button, 185
Web Sharing Folder Properties dialog box, 185, 186
Web Site addresses
 adding to Active Desktop, 43–44
Web sites
 adding to Active Desktop, 43–44
 posting, with Web Publishing Wizard, 187–188
Website Subscription Wizard, 44
Web tab
 Display Properties dialog box, 42–45
 Display Properties property sheet, 59
Web View, 42, 51–52. *See also* View As Web Page
 option
What's This? button, Help system, 57
whiteboard feature of NetMeeting 2.0, 123, 124–126
WhoWhere, 33
Win16-based (16-bit) applications, 325–328
 robustness for running, 405
Win32-based applications, 336–338
 flat address space, 337–338
 linear memory addressing for, 356
 long filename support, 338
 memory protection, 338

Win32-based applications, *continued*
    preemptive multitasking, 337
    private address space for, 406
    robustness for running, 406–408
    separate message queues, 337
    separate message queues for, 407–408
    structured exception handling for, 408
    Windows NT compatibility, 338
Win32 communications APIs, 246
Win32 Driver Model. *See* WDM (Win32 Driver
      Model)
Win32 NLS (National Language Support) APIs, 399
WinASF, 154
windows
    MS-DOS
        scalable, 334
        toolbars in, 333–334
    as views of objects, 48
Windows 95
    configuration preserved by Windows 98 Setup
        program, 8, 10
    taskbar, 27
Windows 95 Boot Floppy, 4, 5
Windows 98
    applications and utilities in, 301–312
        Backup, 307–309
        Disk Defragmenter, 309–310
        disk utilities, 307–312
        HyperTerminal, 305–306
        MS-DOS Editor, 306–307
        Paint, 304–305
        Quick Viewers, 301–303
        ScanDisk, 310–311
        System File Checker, 311–312
        WordPad, 304
    base system architecture of (*see* base system ar-
        chitecture of Windows 98)
    installing. *See* installing Windows 98
    logo program, 368–369
    new features in. *See* new features in Windows 98
    uninstalling, 8, 10
Windows Explorer, 49–50
    document creation in, 48
    NetMeeting calls from, 133–134
Windows Management Infrastructure (WMI), 199, 358
Windows Messaging, 157–177
    components of, 158–159
    Microsoft Fax, 170–177
    Microsoft Mail Post Office, 170
    Outlook Express. *See* Outlook Express
Windows NT
    Distributed COM (DCOM) in, 20

    FAT32 drives and, 345
    memory model architecture, 356
    Win32-based applications' compatibility with, 338
Windows NT Server 4.0
    challenge/response (NTLM) authentication, 114
    NetShow and, 148–150
        NetShow server, 153–154
    network logon dialog box for, 203
Windows Open Services Architecture (WOSA), 248
Windows Scripting Host (WSH), 17, 77, 226
Windows Socket services, 196
Windows Telephony API. *See* TAPI (Windows Tele-
      phony API)
Windows Update Manager, 57
WinHelp 4.0, 81
WINIPCFG.EXE, 131
WINS (Windows Internet Naming Service), 216
WinToon, 287
wizards
    Add New Hardware Wizard, 31, 367
    Add Printer Wizard, 31, 238
    Channel Subscription Wizard, 91
    Compose New Fax Wizard, 173
    Customize This Folder Wizard, 42, 182
    Disk Defragmenter Optimization Wizard, 18, 310
    FrontPad, 181
    Internet Connection Wizard (ICW), 18, 31, 115
    Modem Wizard, 251
    New Active Desktop Item Wizard, 43–44
    PC Card Wizard, 260
    Personal Home Page Wizard, 180, 182–183
    Registration Wizard, 11–13
    Request A Fax wizard, 175
    Settings Wizard, 30–31
    Start Menu Organizer Wizard, 17, 34–35
    Subscription Wizard, 84
    uses of, 55
    Web Publishing Wizard, 180, 186, 187–188
    Website Subscription Wizard, 44
    Windows Tune Up Wizard, 18
WMI (Windows Management Infrastructure), 199, 358
WordPad, 304
Workgroup Postoffice Admin applet, 170
WOSA (Windows Open Services Architecture), 248
WSCRIPT.EXE, 77, 226
WSH (Windows Scripting Host), 17, 77, 226

X

XML (Extensible Markup Language) standard, 95

About the Author

Russell Borland started as a technical writer for Microsoft® Corporation in 1980, and he quickly rose to Manager of Technical Publications. In 1984, Bill Gates asked him to join a team to help design and develop a new product, code-named Cashmere. This project evolved into Opus, the code name for Microsoft® Word for Windows version 1. Borland helped develop the product specification, the interface design, and the messages in version 1, and he also wrote the printed documentation.

Borland transferred to Microsoft® Press in 1988 to write a book about Word for Windows version 1, called *Working with Word for Windows*. He has since revised this book several times under the title *Running Microsoft Word for Windows*. Borland, now a Master Writer, is also the author of *Microsoft WordBasic Primer, Microsoft Word for Windows 2.0 Macros, Getting Started with Microsoft Windows 3.1, Running Microsoft Mail for Windows 3, Microsoft Exchange in Business,* and *Running Microsoft Outlook 97.* He is coauthor of *Windows 3.1 Companion* and *Windows for Workgroups Companion.* Microsoft Press publishes all these books.

Borland earned a bachelor of arts degree from Whitworth College, a master of arts from Portland State University, and a Ph.D. from the University of Washington.

In 1992, at the age of 46, Borland took up motorcycle riding. His first bike was a 1992 Harley-Davidson FXRS-Con Low-Rider Convertible. He named this bike "Gloria" and its engine "Lore, the Evo Twin." In 1993, Borland traded Gloria for a blue 1993 Harley-Davidson FLHS Electra Glide Sport, which he named "Blake." Whenever possible, Borland rides Blake back and forth the 90 miles from his home at the base of Sauk Mountain to Microsoft.

THE MANUSCRIPT FOR this book was prepared using Microsoft Word 97. Pages were composed by Microsoft Press, with text in Garamond and display type in Cosmos Medium. Composed pages were delivered to the printer as electronic prepress files.

Cover Designer
Greg Hickman

Cover Illustrator
Henk Dawson

Interior Graphic Designer
Kim Eggleston

Principal Compositor
Sandra Haynes

Indexer
Maro Riofrancos

Take the whole family *sightseeing!*

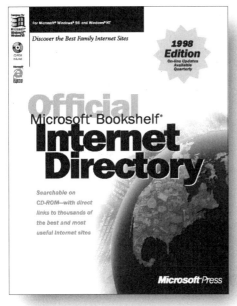

For Microsoft® Windows® 95 and Windows® NT

Discover the Best Family Internet Sites

1998 Edition
On-line Updates Available Quarterly

Official
Microsoft® Bookshelf®
Internet Directory

Searchable on
CD-ROM—with direct
links to thousands of
the best and most
useful Internet sites

Microsoft Press

U.S.A.	**$39.99**
U.K.	£37.49 [V.A.T. included]
Canada	$55.99
ISBN 1-57231-617-9	

Want to: Raise ferrets? Explore space? Recognize consumer fraud? Find a better job? Trace your family tree? Visit the world's great castles? Make bagels? Pursue the paranormal? Well, go for it! The OFFICIAL MICROSOFT® BOOKSHELF® INTERNET DIRECTORY, 1998 EDITION, gives you reliable, carefully selected, up-to-date reviews of more than 6000 of the Internet's most useful, entertaining, and assured-to-be-functional Web sites. The searchable companion CD-ROM gives you direct, instant links to all the sites listed—a simple click of the mouse takes you wherever you want to go!

Developed jointly by Microsoft Press and the Microsoft Bookshelf product team, the OFFICIAL MICROSOFT BOOK-SHELF INTERNET DIRECTORY, 1998 EDITION, is updated regularly on the World Wide Web to keep you informed of our most current list of recommended sites. The latest version of Microsoft Internet Explorer is also included on the CD-ROM.

Microsoft Press

Discover *in a* **flash** how to publish on your **intranet** or the **World Wide Web!**

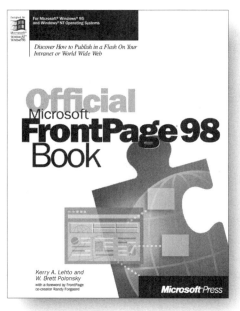

U.S.A. **$24.99**
U.K.   £22.99 [V.A.T. included]
Canada $34.99
ISBN 1-57231-629-2

The OFFICIAL MICROSOFT® FRONTPAGE® 98 BOOK gives you all the information you need to use Microsoft FrontPage 98 quickly and effectively. Packed with creative insights, this book is the ideal guide to follow as you build great Web pages.

The OFFICIAL MICROSOFT FRONTPAGE 98 BOOK shows you how to:

- Employ wizards, templates, page editing, graphics, themes, forms, and FrontPage components to create awesome-looking Web pages

- Populate Web sites with Microsoft Office–based documents and files

- Create and edit frames-based sites using WYSIWYG in the FrontPage Editor

- Take advantage of FrontPage's advanced features to use ActiveX™ controls, Java™ applets, plug-ins, PowerPoint® animations, VBScript, JavaScript, your own HTML code, and more

- Manage your Web site

- Use Personal Web Server and the server administrator

Microsoft®*Press*

Register Today!

Return this
Introducing Microsoft® Windows® 98
registration card for
a Microsoft Press® catalog

U.S. and Canada addresses only. Fill in information below and mail postage-free. Please mail only the bottom half of this page.

1-57231-630-6A   *INTRODUCING MICROSOFT® WINDOWS® 98*   *Owner Registration Card*

_____

NAME

_____

INSTITUTION OR COMPANY NAME

_____

ADDRESS

_____

CITY   STATE   ZIP

Microsoft®*Press*
Quality Computer Books

**For a free catalog of
Microsoft Press® products, call
1-800-MSPRESS**

BUSINESS REPLY MAIL
FIRST-CLASS MAIL   PERMIT NO. 53   BOTHELL, WA

POSTAGE WILL BE PAID BY ADDRESSEE

MICROSOFT PRESS REGISTRATION
INTRODUCING MICROSOFT® WINDOWS® 98
PO BOX 3019
BOTHELL   WA   98041-9946